Data Processing for Educators

MODERN METHODS IN EDUCATION

a series under the editorship of

MURRAY TONDOW

Data Processing for Educators

BY ALVIN GROSSMAN

AND ROBERT L. HOWE

EDUCATIONAL METHODS INC. / *Chicago*

Library of Congress Catalog Card Number 64-21377

First Published 1965 by Educational Methods, Inc.
A subsidiary of Aldine Publishing Company
64 East Van Buren Street, Chicago, Illinois 60605

Printed in the United States of America

To our wives—
Marjorie and Norma—
whose skepticism prompted us to write this volume.

FOREWORD

The impact of computers and computer sciences upon our society is growing daily; education is no exception to this phenomenon. No one can foresee the ultimate contribution of these amazing instruments, but most knowledgeable scientists and scholars are convinced it will be immense; here, too, education is not exempt. The educator who sees the computer only as an oversized calculator has missed the essence of the computer revolution. In our time we can expect the structure, form, and process of education to become as different from today's education as night is from day. The computer sciences are playing an increasingly important role in these dramatic and far-reaching changes.

This book makes a major contribution to education by assisting educators to better understand the mysteries and pleasures, the nature and applications of electronic data processing. In clear and simple language, it pushes aside the shrouds of mysticism that have surrounded electronic data processing in education and presents for the educator a straightforward and understandable view of this field.

MAX RAFFERTY
State Superintendent of
Public Instruction
California

PREFACE

This is the age of information. The United States, indeed, the entire world, is demanding more and more information in order to make intelligent decisions on what should be done, when, and by whom. These informational demands come not only from big business, industry, or government; they are being made by all who are caught up in the complexities of modern decision-making.

Educators too have been enthralled by the dramatic aspects of the emerging technology that makes possible more efficient information systems. All too often, however, it is the technology that is in the limelight, while the information systems upon which the technology is based are relegated to a dark corner. This unfortunate, but painfully accurate picture of the development of information processing systems in education underlines the need to understand that data processing technology is only incidental to the basic information system. Systems must come first; technological implementation follows.

Some over-enthusiastic proponents of automation have glibly described the wonderful accomplishments of machines, but have overlooked the time-consuming, tedious, and painstaking systems work without which the machines would be virtually useless. Many educators have been seduced by the glamour of this new product of man's imagination and have awakened too late to find that the path through the garden of golden promises is strewn with thorns.

Data Processing for Educators has been written to strip the tinsel and window dressing, the mystery and misconceptions from this new field, and to examine in the cold light of reality just what these machines and their automated systems can do for education.

It is written for educators, in terms we believe educators will understand. They are said to have a language of their own, one that generally excludes most non-educators. The field of data processing also has developed its own highly technical language, one that generally is understood readily by technicians, but rarely by others.

This book has been written to present the concept of school information systems in a clear, concise, and logical manner. It is designed specifically for educators, but it should be of interest to all readers who have a special interest in educational processes. This includes parents, school board members, data processing technicians, guidance counselors, educational personnel and other specialists.

The primary concern of the book is the presentation of a totally integrated information system that ties together the many diverse aspects of the instructional and administrative program. Such a system must ultimately be of considerable benefit to the pupil.

The plan is to provide an overview of the relationship of information systems and technology to education. Then comes the historical development of the technology itself, followed by a description of machines and machine functions. A detailed look at systems in the study, design, and implementation phases will show the educator what steps to follow to get started in the field. Typical educational applications are discussed as foundations for a total system.

In discussing the potential of Electronic Data Processing (EDP) for education, various areas of impact are discussed, significant projects are reviewed, and organizational implications are studied. Finally, a look is taken at what the future may hold, and some thoughts are advanced on the overall implications of automated systems. A comprehensive glossary is included for reference purposes. Numerous descriptions of operating programs are used throughout.

No attempt has been made to present the history of education, its basic foundations and specialties, a technical treatise on computers, or a comprehensive report on every possible educational use to which automation can be put. The overriding goal of this book is to present an understandable picture of the importance of information systems in education. and how automation may be of great assistance in developing and using these systems.

The authors wish to acknowledge with a sense of gratitude the contribution of the many people who assisted in the development of the manuscript, especially to William Behnk who is responsible for the chapter on Registration and Scheduling; Don Crisler who served as Project Director of the California State Pilot Project in Data Processing and who made innumerable contributions to the development of the book; to Charles F. Wilkes for his contribution in many sections of the book and his consulting help in the development of the state venture; to Tom Wogaman who served as Assistant Director of the State Pilot Project and whose doctoral dissertation contained the first comprehensive evaluation of teacher and administrative satisfaction with data processing services; to Mrs. Nellie Moos for her many hours of typing and proofreading of the manuscript; to the California Association of Public School Business Officials for permission to use material from their data processing handbook; and to the California State Advisory Committee on Integrated Data Processing for the guidance and direction furnished over the past five years.

We would also like to thank the Educational Testing Service, Princeton, New Jersey, for permission to reproduce their test scoring form; the computer manufacturers for permission to use photographs of their equipment; and last, to the several school districts which allowed us to reproduce the forms used in their data processing systems.

A. GROSSMAN
R. HOWE
Sacramento, California

CONTENTS

Foreword vii

Preface ix

PART I: *Setting the Stage*

Chapter 1. An Introduction to Automated Information Systems 3
Chapter 2. Historical Development 10
Chapter 3. The Anatomy of Data Processing 17

PART II: *Developing An Educational Data Processing System*

Chapter 4. Organizing the Systems Study 39
Chapter 5. Systems Design 59
Chapter 6. Moving to the Automated System: Personnel Requirements 72
Chapter 7. Moving to the Automated System: Equipment and Implementation 84
Chapter 8. The Economics of the Program 104

PART III: *Typical Educational Applications*

Chapter 9. Mark Reporting 125
Chapter 10. Test Scoring and Reporting 152
Chapter 11. Attendance Accounting 170
Chapter 12. Registration and Scheduling 186
Chapter 13. Cumulative Records 213

PART IV: *Potential for Education*

Chapter 14. Impact of Educational Data Processing on Schools 231
Chapter 15. Organizational Implications 242
Chapter 16. Significant Projects in EDP 260
Chapter 17. The Future of EDP in Education 272
Chapter 18. Some Educational Implications of Automation 283

Appendix I. Definition and Specifications for Positions in Educational Data Processing 293
Appendix II. Example of Mark Section of a Procedural Handbook 304
Appendix III. Tentative Proposal for Content of Master Files 307
Appendix IV. Entry, Withdrawal, and Dropout Definition and Code 316

Glossary 321

Index 355

ILLUSTRATIONS

Figure

1. Diagram of an Educational Information System 7
2. Abacus 10
3. 80 Column Card 20
4. 90 Column Card 21
5. IBM 083 Sorter 24
6. IBM 407 Tabulating Machine 24
7. UNIVAC 120 Calculator 26
8. UNIVAC 1004 Processor 26
9. Honeywell 200 Magnetic Tape Unit 28
10. IBM 1301 Disk File 29
11. Core Memory Plane 29
12. Schematic Diagram of a Computer 31
13. Monrobot XI Computer 32
14. Radio Corporation of America 301 Computer 32
15. IBM 1401 Computer 33
16. Honeywell 200 Computer 33
17. UNIVAC 1107 Computer 34
18. Control Data Corporation 1604 Computer 34
19. Radio Corporation of America 601 Computer 35
20. Control Data Corporation 6600 Computer 35
21. Narrative Detail Form 48
22. Flow Chart Symbols 50
23. Industry Compatible Flow Chart Symbols 51
24. Grid Chart 54
25. Data Sheet 57
26. Test Score to Performance Analysis 67
27. Superintendent's Educational Planning Report 69
28. Planning the Equipment Delivery Schedule 96-97
29. Manpower Loading Chart 100
30. Procedural Steps for Mark Reporting—Card Oriented . . . 127
31. Procedural Steps for Mark Reporting—Document Oriented . 128
32. Teachers' Mark-Sense Marking Card Used in California State Pilot Project 130
33. Teachers' Mark-Sense Marking Card Used in Indianapolis Schools 130

Figure

34. Report Card Used in California State Pilot Project 131
35. Report Card Used in Williamsville Central School District . . 132
36. Pressure-Sensitive Labels Used for Recording Student Marks . 134
37. Student Mark-Analysis Report 136-37
38. Teacher Mark-Analysis Report 138-39
39. Course Mark-Analysis Report 140-41
40. District Mark-Analysis Report 144-45
41. Class-Size Analysis Report—School 146-47
42. Class-Size Analysis Report—District 148-49
43. Test Score to Performance Analysis Report 150
44. Typical 805 Test Answer Sheet 154
45. Samples of FAST Answer Cards 156
46. IBM 1230 Test Scoring Machine 157
47. Digitek 100 Test Scoring Machine 157
48. Class Roster of Test Scores 160-61
49. Class Roster of Differential Aptitude Test 162-63
50. Procedural Steps for Test Scoring 164-65
51. Student Test Profile Card 167
52. Roster of Test Results 168
53. Attendance Accounting Apportionment Report 172-73
54. Cards Used for Recording Student Absences 174
55. Attendance Register 176-77
56. Procedural Steps for Attendance Accounting 179
57. Computer-Prepared Attendance Accounting Document . 182-83
58. Irregular Attendance Report 184
59. Card Used to Record Course and Code Number . . . 190
60. Card Used to Mark-Sense Selected Courses 190
61. Procedural Steps for Secondary Scheduling . . . 192-93
62. Course Selection Form 195
63. Mark-Sense Card Used for Data Collection 196
64. Course Request Verification 199
65. Course Conflict Matrix 200-01
66. Master Schedule Coding Form 202
67. Simulation Scheduling Run Output 204-05
68. Student Scheduling Production Run 206-07
69. Master Schedule List 208-09
70. Sequence of Events in Pupil Scheduling Process 211
71. Academic Record Form Used in Vallejo, California . . . 219
72. Academic Record Form Used in Napa, California . . 220-21
73. Comprehensive Student Report 222-23
74. Student Profile Record 224
75. California Guidance Report 226

Figure
76. Undesirable Placement of Data Processing Center —Business Division 246
77. Undesirable Placement of Data Processing Center —Instructional Division 246
78. Undesirable Placement of Data Processing Center —Research Division 248
79. Desirable Structure for Information Services 249
80. Desirable Structure for Information Services 250
81. Desirable Structure for Information Services 251
82. Radio Corporation of America Video Data Terminal 280

TABLES

I. Growth in Use of Computers 1960-65 36
II. Advance Preparation for Design Sessions 62
III. Suggested Contents of the Agenda 63
IV. Per Pupil Costs—Machine Rental and Miscellaneous Expenses . 112
V. Personnel Costs—Number of Machines and Applications . . 112

PART 1

Setting the Stage

1

AN INTRODUCTION TO AUTOMATED INFORMATION SYSTEMS

Information systems have been thought to be a traditional part of most educational institutions. When closely scrutinized, however, the information from these systems turns out to be the result of "guesstimations" based on long years of experience and intuition. The masses of raw data fed into such systems have usually overwhelmed them, and, consequently, the data rarely have been processed adequately. Illustrating this are the large boxes of data from testing programs that are stored in dark corners and the overburdened files of cumulative folders. These mountains of paper could be converted into something quite meaningful and useful if an operational system were installed.

An information system is nothing more than a planned method of collecting necessary data and converting it to summaries and other reports that serve some vital purpose in the educational program. All of these systems are powered either by hand (manual systems) or by machine (automated systems).

ORIENTATION TO EDUCATION

Some background is needed to place in perspective the specific subject matter covered by this book, since it is neither an encyclopedia of education nor of automation. Rather, the book is an introduction to the marriage of both these fields of specialization, a marriage which has produced a field which in itself is becoming a specialty. Norbert Wiener coined the word "cybernation" many years ago; John Diebold has become famous for "automation." *Data Processing for Educators,* then, is intended to be a first book on "edumation," the subject of automation in education, or, more specifically, the automation of educational intelligence systems. This is a primer designed to give a picture of what these systems and machines may hold in store for education in this third quarter of the twentieth century.

Professional educators at all levels, from kindergarten to university, classroom to administration, have always considered information to be the foundation of their work. In one sense this is true, but information in its raw form is data; in its refined form it is intelligence.

Educators are charged with a primary goal that has been stated as "the achievement and dissemination of knowledge, the cultivation of the intellect, and induction into the uses of reason." Converted to automation's language, this goal can be interpreted as charging educators with the development of effective information processing systems in each of their students. Such systems enable the student to recognize items of data, to relate these items to his value system of social-ethics, to analyze the meaning of these data and to convert them to some acceptable course of action.

Educators also are charged with many other tasks, some of great importance, such as imparting specific types of data, i.e., multiplication tables and rules of grammar; others more trivial such as handling lunch money, sharing funds, bus tickets and such clerical activities; performing non-instructional chores—marking papers, scoring tests and recording data on cumulative folders; and supervising student groups in various extra-curricular activities.

Many persons have selected education as their life's work because of its altruistic and worthy goal and the possibilities of living a richly rewarding life on a high philosophical plane. Others have selected teaching as a combination of this main goal and some of the earlier-mentioned tasks, feeling that their role is one of leading the nation's youth down the "right" path. Still others have selected education for the routine and security of the other tasks listed.

Many who started with high hopes and great expectations toward the golden goal have been led to disillusionment by the tremendous tasks. In those instances where this has been coupled with either antiquated or too rapidly changing curricula, unrealistic class size, autocratic administration, or unruly pupils, they have subsequently changed to some less frustrating as well as more lucrative field.

Functional information systems can do much to make teaching the attractive and rewarding profession that it should be, and may provide the stimulus needed to retain those who are teaching now, and even bring back into the fold those who have become disenchanted.

Our supply of teachers today probably is adequate to meet the demands of growing enrollments if all who have qualified for teaching certificates were in fact employed as teachers.

How do information systems relate to the goals of teaching? In many ways, for the basic questions must be asked: What is education to accomplish? Why should education do this? How? When? And by whom?

These are both philosophical and practical questions; but they form the foundation for all that transpires in education. How do our avowed goals—our philosophy of education, if you will—differ from what we actually are doing in our school each day? Is our goal individualized instruction? Is our goal the development of straight-thinking, young Americans? Is our goal the production of persons who are understanding and appreciative of their native heritage and culture, as well as those of others? Or is it all of these and more?

Some of these matters will best be left to educational psychologists, philosophers, and all of those who have considered these problems more deeply. Our concern here is to relate all of these areas to a central point, that of the implications this modern technological revolution may have for the entire field of education. Such questions are best considered from this total central standpoint rather than from the disparate viewpoints of the various subparts of education: instruction, curriculum, guidance, research, and administration.

Does an information system, especially one using data processing equipment, fit into the total picture? Indeed it does, for it offers more to the field of education than anything since the days of Gutenberg and his printing press.

Data processing equipment is playing an increasingly important role in the operation of today's schools. It has had very significant applications in curriculum, through the teaching of electronic data processing principles and concepts; in instruction, through the use of various automated devices used to improve and supplement the skills of the teacher; in the business office, through the use of electronic record-keeping devices; and in administration, through the use of electronic data processing equipment for improved management information systems.

Unfortunately, school districts have developed and implemented very few of these applications on an integrated basis. A typical school district with any automated processes usually will have some business records automated and perhaps one other application. These ordinarily have been developed by different staff members who usually have not exchanged information on the uses and purposes of their systems.

School administrators are becoming increasingly conversant with data processing methods and applications. The demand for additional information by school boards, state departments of education, and the public has caused these educators to investigate more efficient and effective ways of handling information. Noting that their brothers in business have made astonishing gains in processing information, and also noting that some progressive schools have made great advances in certain areas of data processing, many school administrators have come to accept—perhaps grudgingly—the fact that modern computers may hold the answer to many of their problems.

Schools generally have made little effective use of data processing because (1) school budgets are restricted by law to the extent that it is difficult to finance the machines needed to do a complete job and (2) school operations are fixed by tradition to a greater extent than those of business and industry.

Schools traditionally have been faced with the problem of maintaining adequate and modern programs with financial resources that remain fairly constant in relation to the number of pupils served. They must stay alert to opportunities that make it possible to secure maximum purchasing power from each budget dollar. The use of automated equipment to handle certain limited phases of the educational program appears to be one means by which the purchasing power of the education dollar can be increased.

The more dramatic and significant way of increasing the purchasing power of the school's dollar, however, is the establishment of a total, integrated system for processing the data of an entire school district. This system should be designed to relate the information collected in the business office with the information collected in relation to the instructional program—and all of this with the information collected for the administrative application. (See Fig. 1, p. 7.) In short, all information collected for any of the specific data processing systems would be usable for the generation of appropriate reports for specific staff members. In the past it has often been necessary for the instructional staff to collect data that was already available in a different form and for a different purpose in the central office. A properly constructed integrated data processing system would eliminate this fragmented approach; it would have all data available to meet the needs of most persons in the school district.

This total system would result in at least three major gains: (1) essential financial, instructional, and pupil personnel records would be secured with a minimum expenditure of staff time; (2) maximum use of professional staff members' time for professional purposes would be obtained by reducing to a bare minimum the amount of clerical work required of them; and (3) data would be available at a time when it could be used most advantageously in helping students to attain their full potential—that is, as a basis for both guidance and instruction.

A limited number of school districts across the country are utilizing automated data processing machines both for handling business operations and for collecting and maintaining pupil personnel data. The kind and quantity of equipment used and the practices employed in using the equipment vary widely. Most educational practices require the use of a large volume of pupil personnel data. These data include test scores, school attendance figures, marks, and grade point averages, and other types. All of these data are used as a basis for guidance, instruction, curriculum planning, and many other phases of education.

The business branches of educational institutions generally are organized so that non-teaching personnel process most of the business data. Figure 1 illustrates how data processing can be utilized in a total information system to serve a school district. Most of the work involved in the processing of pupil personnel data also is clerical in nature and should be performed by non-teaching personnel. In practice, however, much of the

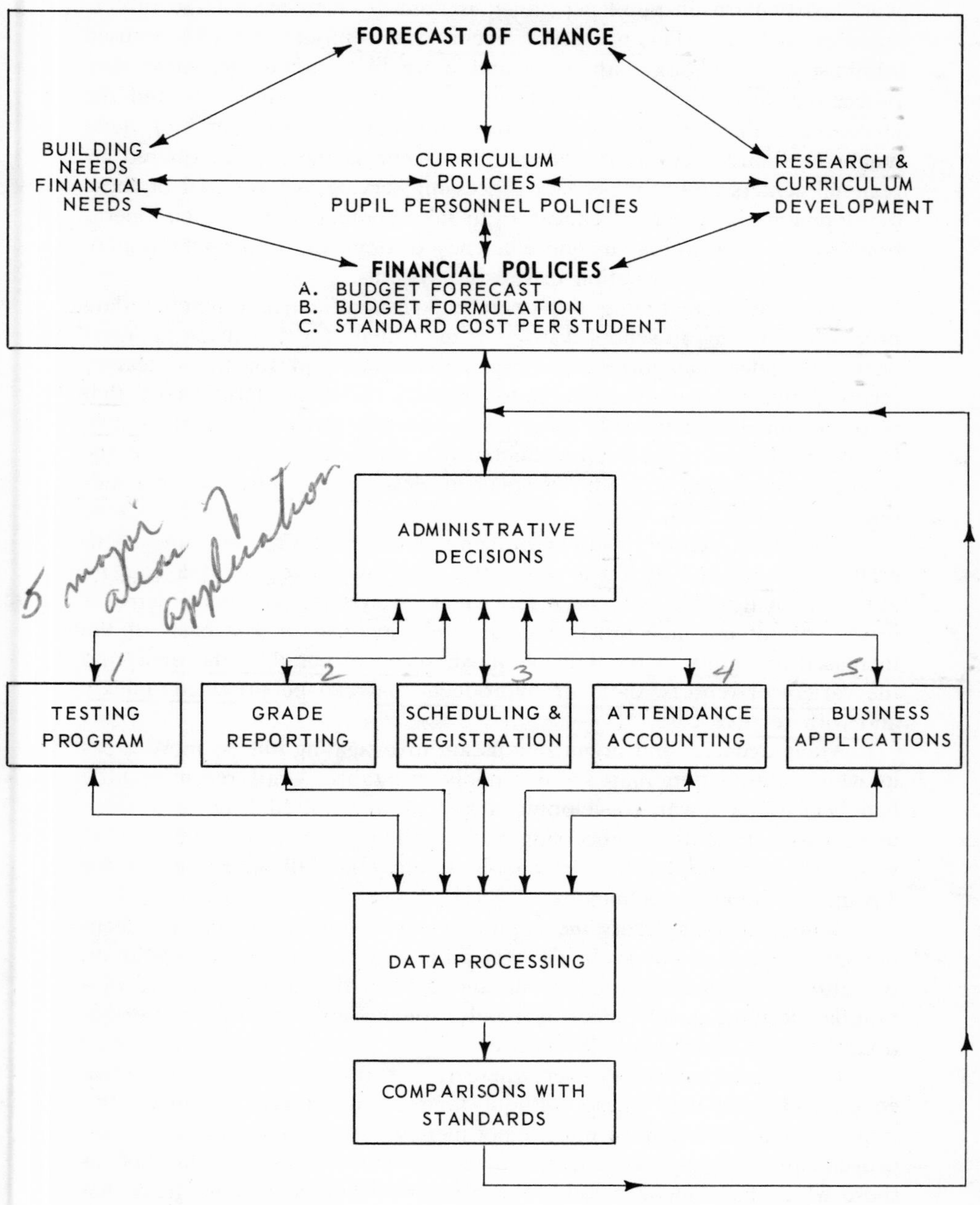

FIG. 1. *Diagram of an Educational Information System*

work, particularly in pupil personnel, is done by members of the professional school staff. This misuse of teacher and counselor time has caused administrators to look with more and more favor upon electronic data processing devices including small and medium sized computers and the attractive dollar savings resulting from the purchase or rental of these machines. Fairly new to the educational scene is the service offered by regional centers and reliable data processing service bureaus. All of these developments have caused educators to take another look at their operations with a view to maximizing efficiency through the implementation of more appropriate information processing systems.

Information regarding the operating costs of current manual data processing systems in school districts is inadequate for a realistic financial analysis. Budget categories for clerical assistance and for the necessary record forms are usually available for inspection, but the largest cost, that of professional staff time, is concealed under the general account of professional salaries. It has been estimated that upwards of one-fourth of the teachers' and counselors' time is spent in clerical tasks involved in handling educational data.

Therefore, school districts utilizing data processing machines generally have justified their use when the data are processed at a cost no greater than it would have been for a manual system. Apparent increases in the cost of machine processing are often justified on the basis of the increased reliability of the data obtained, speed of handling the data, and the variety of reports, data, or byproducts that can be provided quickly and with relative ease.

Many agencies and organizations are investigating one or more areas in which automation may serve schools profitably. Until recently, little had been done toward developing a system that would lead to a total, integrated information processing system. This system will be needed within the very near future if schools are to take full advantage of the advances in modern technology.

School districts across the country need to appreciate that the technology of our time has given rise not only to a new industrial revolution but also to an organizational revolution. And at the heart of this revolution has been the development of the electronic computer and the informational systems which underlie its use.

Enlightened educators everywhere realize that they cannot meet the educational challenge ahead without far-reaching internal changes and improvements. These must include not merely refinements and modest improvements of existing practices, but revolutionary breakthroughs such as those which have made possible the dramatic technological progress that marks this new space age. It is urgent that all educators study and prepare for the impact of computer technology on education.

For the first time in the history of education it is feasible and practical to develop a system that (1) allows the development of a historical file on all pupils, starting at kindergarten and extending until they leave school; (2) makes available the data for prediction studies, validation of curricula, correlation of test scores, marks, attendance, and other factors; (3) prepares reports and needed statistics when required, and while usable rather than after they have become obsolete; (4) presents the opportunity to relate student performance data to curricular data that then can be programmed for individualized units of instruction, taking advantage of all the best instructional aids and audio-visual devices, and that will permit the development of the most effective program for each pupil.

This does not lead us to the vision of 1984 any more than did the discovery of atomic fission necessarily lead us to the destruction of the world. Such developments must be viewed in proper perspective. *Data Processing for Educators* was written to give this perspective.

2

HISTORICAL DEVELOPMENT

The history of the development of computational instruments, like that of all of technology, may be represented by a J-type curve, one showing little progress during its long prehistory and early history. From all evidence, the only tallying devices used in the early history of mankind were fingers, sticks, knots and beads or some simple graphic equivalent. The curve then begins to rise slightly indicating an occasional early breakthrough to more sophisticated computational means. And finally, in very recent times, the curve rises sharply to portray an unusual proliferation of new instruments of computation.

An early and significant milestone in the history of computer development was the abacus which came into social use in the Middle East about 3000 B.C. and later diffused into Asia. An abacus consists of several rows of beads which slide on rods in a rectangular frame. A cross-member divides the frame so that each row of beads has a sector with one, or on some abacuses, two beads, and another sector with four or sometimes five beads. Figure 2 shows the special features of the abacus. The significance of the abacus lies less in its simple mechanical basis than in the number concept which it embraces. It confirmed and took advantage of a system of positional numbers, most commonly based on decimals, which turned out to be a highly civilizing number system. The abacus, in skilled hands, is generally an efficient and fast computer.

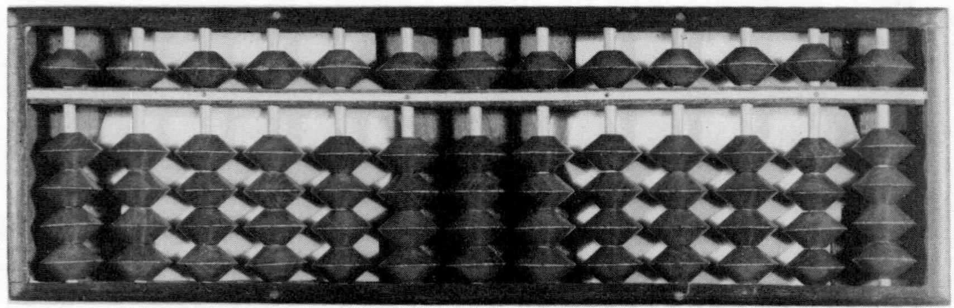

FIG. 2. *Abacus*

Only at the beginning of modern times, following 1600 A.D., were new computational devices of much merit invented. A significant innovation and perhaps the first analog computer was the slide rule. Again, the mechanical aspect of the slide rule was secondary to a new concept of how numbers might be used. The slide rule, invented by Oughtred in 1630, took advantage of logarithms and of a logarithmic scale which had been made available earlier through the efforts of Napier. The slide rule performs multiplication and division by adding and subtracting logarithms. This is accomplished by putting logarithmic scales on two parallel rulers which when moved in relation to each other show always a proportional relationship between the scale positions. Instead of using numbers alone, the slide rule makes the actual distances on the rulers analogous to designated number values. Therefore, it is an analog rather than a digital computer such as the abacus. Unlike the abacus which, unless an error is made, will always be accurate down to the last digit, a slide rule is only as accurate as the precision of its physical parts. But the slide rule's usefulness is noteworthy in making fast relational computations, some of which would be laborious if made by digital means.

FIRST STEP TOWARD AUTOMATION

At about the same time, thought was being given to mechanizing the principles long represented in the abacus. Blaise Pascal built the first mechanical adding machine by developing a system in which, instead of sliding beads on a stick, numbers—specifically the ten digits—were put on the periphery of a wheel. This resulted in a number wheel which could be rotated to effect counting. Instead of a different stick for each power of ten, a different number wheel was used to indicate each positional number. It was then simple enough mechanically to orient the wheels so that a complete revolution of one of them would bring a cleat against the wheel in the next greater positional category to advance it one digit in order to effect a carry, thus doing automatically what on the abacus would have required several movements to accomplish.

In direct lineage with today's digital computers was a machine broadly conceived by Charles Babbage in the 1830's. Babbage's work may have been influenced by Jacquard's mechanical programming of a loom about a generation before. Babbage obtained a grant from the British government to produce what might be called an externally programmed general-purpose computer. His invention was largely a failure because steam, unreliable and unwieldy, was the only power then available.

Babbage's system was strikingly similar to systems now in use, and his ideas did, in fact, influence the builders of the first fully automatic large-scale computer a century after him, the Harvard Mark I. In the half-century following Babbage, his efforts at computer systems building were largely forgotten except as an historical incident. Desk calculators were developed, but not automatically controlled computers. The development of modern calculating devices in the 17th century and of the typewriter in the 19th century provided aids for calculating and recording.

Calculating machines were developed which could perform simple arithmetical operations quickly and accurately, and some of them were able to print results on paper. Since people are slow and inaccurate at arithmetical operations, invention and improvement of calculating devices which would add, subtract, multiply, and divide was an important step forward.

Manual writing speeds, sometimes as slow as ten words a minute, were increased to 60 words a minute by the typewriter. More important, legibility was improved and the preparation of multiple copies with carbon paper and duplicating devices became possible.

The functions of the typewriter and the calculator were combined to create bookkeeping and accounting machines which have control bars to aid the operator in performing such multiple operations as preparing statements, ledgers, and journals.

PUNCHED CARD BEGINNINGS

The punched card technique for providing a flexible storage of information which began with the Jacquard card and was used by Babbage, provided, after 1890, the basis for new developments in punched card usage. Herman Hollerith, who was working for the United States Bureau of Census, used punched cards to process census data. For these he built a sorting and counting machine with which he was able actually to speed up the processing of the 1910 census.

The principle of the punched card equipment was simple. Holes representing data were positionally punched in the cards. These were detected as a card went past a sensing device. In the method adopted by International Business Machines Corporation (IBM), the card is an insulator separating two sets of electrical conductors. A particular hole (or holes) in the card signifying, by its vertical position, a number or some alphabetical character breaks the insulation at that point and permits contact of a brush, completing a particular circuit which then tabulates the information indicated or directs the card to the proper sort area, or both. The early versions of punched card equipment developed for the census enumeration had space for punching 240 holes, each hole representing the presence or absence of a single fact in "yes-no" form. A person's age could be represented by punching one of 85 holes.

Punched cards were important because data stored on them could be processed electromechanically. This requires that people follow instructions for handling cards and employ suitable programs in the form of wired plugboards inserted in the machines.

The basic operations of punched card machines are punching, sorting, calculating, and printing. Early versions of punched card machines required manual effort in punching data in cards, handling cards individually during the sorting operations, and counting the sorted cards. Since Hollerith's work in 1890 machines have become more automatic so that less manual effort is required to originate data, sort cards, make calculations, and copy results from tabulators. Present-day punch card machines and electronic calculators, with people handling cards only between machine stages, can receive punched input data, perform about a dozen different arithmetical and logical operations at rapid speeds, and produce either printed reports or punched cards for further processing. The substitution of punch cards for manual processing has led to important changes in procedures.

EARLY ELECTRONIC COMPUTERS

The first commercial electronic data processing system dates back only about fifteen years. This is a remarkable fact when one considers that the proliferation of increasingly efficient large-scale computers since then has set a record in the history of technology. The impact of data processing systems upon civilization, while not yet fully appreciated or understood, seems destined to make them one of the most significant developments of our times.

An early contribution to electronic data processing development came in 1919 when a paper describing an electronic "trigger circuit" was published by W. H. Eccles and F. W. Jordan in the first volume of "Radio Review." The trigger circuit could be used for counting and was at the time regarded, like Babbage's engine, as a mere curiosity, but it was a hint that the new science of electronics could be used as a computational aid.

Strictly speaking, the history of *electronic* data processing begins in the 1930's. Earlier developments like punched cards and punched tape belong to the history of mechanical data processing. Electronic data processing using magnetic tape as input, began with machines made by Dr. Howard H. Aiken of Harvard University and the inventors of ENIAC, Dr. John W. Mauchly and Professor J. Presper Eckert of the University of Pennsylvania.

Dr. Aiken and Dr. Mauchly advanced their first suggestions and ideas for electronic computation during the 1930's, but it wasn't until the pressure of World War II that they were able to put these ideas into action. These projects fulfilled the plans originated by Babbage and others, using some of the techniques devised by Hollerith and his successor at the Census Bureau, and developing further a technology directly traceable to Eccles and Jordan.

In the spring of 1943, Dr. Mauchly, then Associate Professor of

Electronics at the Moore School of Electrical Engineering, University of Pennsylvania, submitted a memorandum to the Army Ordinance Department outlining a plan for a general-purpose computer using electronic counting circuits. The ultimate result of this was ENIAC, the first all-electric digital computer, completed in the fall of 1945.

Dr. Aiken, working with the United States Navy Ordinance Department and IBM, in 1944, after five years of work completed Mark I, the first large-scale general-purpose digital computer. However, it was constructed entirely of mechanical parts and, although it was 20 times as fast as a desk calculator and could perform better than three additions a second, it had severe limitations. The Harvard Mark I was retired to the Smithsonian Institute in 1964.

ENIAC represented the first major break with the past since it was entirely electronic except for the punched card input machinery which had been modified to work with the electronic circuitry. Modern computing systems seem to have evolved from a wedding of the techniques of ENIAC and Mark I. Three more computers for the Navy's Bureau of Ordinance followed Mark I. These were the Aiken Relay Calculator, Mark II (completed in 1947); Harvard Mark III (completed in 1949), and the Harvard Magnetic Drum Calculator, Mark IV (completed in 1951).

There is a profusion of "firsts" in the development of electronic computers and everyone of them can be justified on one basis or another. For example, Dr. Vannevar Bush, then Professor of Electrical Engineering at Massachusetts Institute of Technology, developed the first large-scale computing machine in 1925. He developed a more comprehensive analyzer in 1930 and another in 1942.

Many other "firsts" are claimed and substantiated in the various universities which were working on computer projects. The record of commercial "firsts" is much more distinct. In 1946, Eckert and Mauchly formed a business partnership, the Electronic Control Company, to promote the commercial use of electronic computers. This was later incorporated as the Eckert-Mauchly Computer Corporation which, in 1950, completed a BINAC computer for Northrop Aircraft, Inc. Like all its predecessors, BINAC was a scientific computer and the first to use the principle of complete internal self-checking. It was really two computing systems, each operating independently, with the results of each being checked constantly by the other to insure complete agreement.

Before BINAC was completed, the company had completed UNIVAC, the first computer ever to be planned and produced to handle both numbers and descriptive information. It was also the first to separate input and output from the actual computation facility. Both of these characteristics made the commercial use of computers economically attractive.

At about the same time that Eckert and Mauchly formed their first partnership, a group called Engineering Research Associates, Incorporated, was formed in Minneapolis to build computers for government, commerce, and industry. This group produced the ERA 1101 which was put to work in 1950. This was about the time Remington Rand, Incorporated, abruptly entered the computer business by purchasing both the Eckert and Mauchly enterprise and ERA to combine them with their own laboratory operation which had produced the 409 series of punch card electronic calculators.

The ERA 1101 then became UNIVAC 1101 and the Remington Rand punch card calculators became the UNIVAC 60 and 120. In 1951 a UNIVAC went to work for the Bureau of the Census, and in 1952 a UNIVAC I computer in Remington Rand Headquarters in New York went on television to forecast the Eisenhower landslide. Much to the chagrin of public relations personnel and programmers alike, UNIVAC I accurately forecast the results of the election on the first print-out, but the people involved did not have confidence in the new so-called "giant brain" and accordingly reprogrammed it to come up with results which they thought were more realistic. They later found the computer's first forecast was the best, thereby learning a valuable lesson about the capability of the new equipment.

Although IBM had been active in the electronic computer field since 1939 when it began working with Dr. Aiken, the company did not become commercially active until 1953 when the first IBM 650 was planned. This preceded the 700-series of which 701 represented the first clean breakaway from punched card equipment. A previous large-scale computer was completed in 1947 and filled a large room in the IBM World Headquarters Building at Madison Avenue and 57th Street in New York. It was, at the time, a major effort in the field.

EDP EXPANDS RAPIDLY

Since the mid-1950's the growth of the EDP industry had been nothing less than explosive. Old, established business equipment manufacturers swung quickly into line to produce their own computers—Burroughs, National Cash Register, Underwood, Royal-McBee, and others. The Office Equipment Manufacturers Institute became revitalized and reorganized as the Business Equipment Manufacturers Association and staffed its office to handle the problems of standards within the EDP industry.

Electronics firms like RCA, Honeywell, and Collins Radio moved into the computer field. Corporations have reorganized several times in the short span of ten years to move into a stronger sales position with their computers. Engineers have formed innumerable small companies to produce peripheral gear and various types of "black boxes" for computer systems. Telegraph and telephone companies too, were quick to see the potential for their equipment and services in data transmission.

The growth of a great civilization with its highly complex engineering, technology, business and industry has produced an enormous growth in the amount of information to be handled and used for operations. This has provided the push, the energy, the urgency behind the rapid development of the automatic handling of information, which has culminated in computers and data processing systems of enormous complexity and efficiency.

3

THE ANATOMY OF DATA PROCESSING

The typical educator's conception of electronic data processing can be likened to the fable of the blind men and the elephant. Each one in turn touched the animal and then described it to the others. One touched the elephant's leg and described it as resembling a stout tree trunk, another touched its trunk and described it as a mighty serpent, and so on. It can be said that many educators have evaluated data processing technology in much the same way as the blind men did the elephant. They have evaluated the whole animal on the basis of some contact with one part of its anatomy. In this chapter we shall describe its many parts in order to develop the whole picture of the anatomy of data processing.

IMPLICATIONS FOR SCHOOL PERSONNEL

Incorporating electronic data processing methods into a school system has many implications for school personnel. A major advantage lies in the production of more accurate and up-to-date information. Shorter delays in processing can make more frequent reporting practicable. Another advantage is that of overcoming inertia. Almost everyone in a school district knows how the operation of his district can be improved, but so often improvements are inordinately slow in coming. Either no one is available to plan them, or, if changes are made, someone is offended by them. The enthusiasm and the effort that nearly always accompany a study for a proposed automatic data processing system are useful in overcoming inertia. Some observers say that fear of change is a greater obstacle to the adoption of new methods than is inertia. It appears, however, that the introduction of new equipment often facilitates the *immediate* adoption of many changes that are later refined for greater efficiency. This viewpoint reflects the belief that people are more willing to use new equipment than to accept novel ideas.

MEANING OF DATA PROCESSING

It should prove helpful, first, to attempt an explanation in layman's language of what is meant by "data processing." This term encompasses a whole range of operations from the input of data to the output of results.

The word "processing" alone is usually restricted to those operations not included in data collection, rearrangement, or output. As an illustration, processing might involve the following kinds of operations:

1. Updating student and teacher files.
2. Computing test scores and issuing reports.
3. Making decisions based on quantitative criteria, such as allowing a student to register in a certain class if the prerequisites have been met and his schedule will accommodate that class.
4. Estimating enrollment based upon prediction of community mobility and other related projection data.
5. Recognizing and dealing with exceptional cases.
6. Looking up table values, such as converting a raw score to a percentile score, or converting an "A" mark into a mark-point average.

"Input" is closely tied to data collection. This means capturing facts when they are available; they may be processed later, when needed. The original capture of data or the origination of data includes three stages—collection, conversion, and verification—required to get facts into a form suitable for processing. Facts are the raw material of data processing.

The medium that is most efficient for the original collection of data must often be converted to a different medium for further use. Some schools, for example, initially record information on tape recorders; conversion is thus required for further processing. In manual data processing one may work with oral, handwritten, or typed data, but electronic data processing equipment usually requires that data be recorded in a carefully prescribed form. Data from handwritten documents are usually punched into cards manually for input to an electronic processor.

Data are verified to attain a desired degree of accuracy. Some inaccuracies, a slight misspelling of a name, for example, are not too important; but other inaccuracies, such as crediting the wrong student with a variety of marks or test scores, may be intolerable. Verification should include checking data to determine whether they are complete, plausible, and acceptable.

"Output" preparation follows the origination and manipulation of data. Because results are seldom in precisely the form desired, it is often necessary to select what is wanted and to present it in acceptable form. The content, frequency, and format of an output are determined jointly by the people who use the output and by those responsible for processing it.

In summary, data processing involves (1) collecting data for new transactions; (2) manipulating new inputs and data already in files according to a prescribed plan; and (3) producing output documents for various purposes.

DATA PROCESSING MACHINES

Most educational data processing installations fall either into the electro-mechanical punch card type or the computer type. The punch card machines are frequently referred to as Electric Accounting Machines (EAM) or unit record installations. The unit record concept means that each card is acted upon before another is considered. The speed of these electro-mechanical data processors is limited to the speed at which gears can be turned, cards can be moved, relays can be opened and closed, i.e., they are limited to those speeds at which physical objects can be accelerated. An electronic computer, on the other hand, accomplishes most of its functions by controlling the traffic of electrical energy within its circuitry. Electrical energy travels at the speed of light. Electronic computers permit many cards to be considered before action is taken on any or all the data they represent. Electro-mechanical data processors are special purpose machines, i.e., each machine does a specific task. Cards are passed from machine to machine just as forms are passed from desk to desk in a manual system.

The electronic computer is a general purpose machine, i.e., it is capable of performing any data processing task. It does not do a job piecemeal, but accomplishes an entire function automatically with a minimum of manual intervention. Computer based installations frequently are classified as EDP, or those with electronic data processing. The majority of school districts using data processing equipment have punch card installations, and therefore this type of machine will be considered first.

The Punch Card

The basis for the entire punch card system is a piece of paper of standard size, shape, and thickness. A typical punch card is 7⅜ inches long by 3¼ inches wide. It is .007 inches thick. It has 80 vertical columns and 12 horizontal rows. Figure 3 illustrates a typical punch card of the IBM type. Groups of cards are called "decks." It should be noted that the punch card is standard in size and shape and thickness throughout the entire data processing industry. However, Remington Rand has a card format which uses two groups of 45 vertical columns each and which receives round holes instead of the rectangular ones of IBM. An illustration of this card is shown in Figure 4.

Machines process data from the cards by changing the punched holes into electrical impulses. Circuits are completed as wire brushes read the holes by making contact with a roller underneath the card. If there is no hole in a particular column the circuit is not completed and therefore no data is transmitted. When a punched hole is read the datum represented by that hole will:

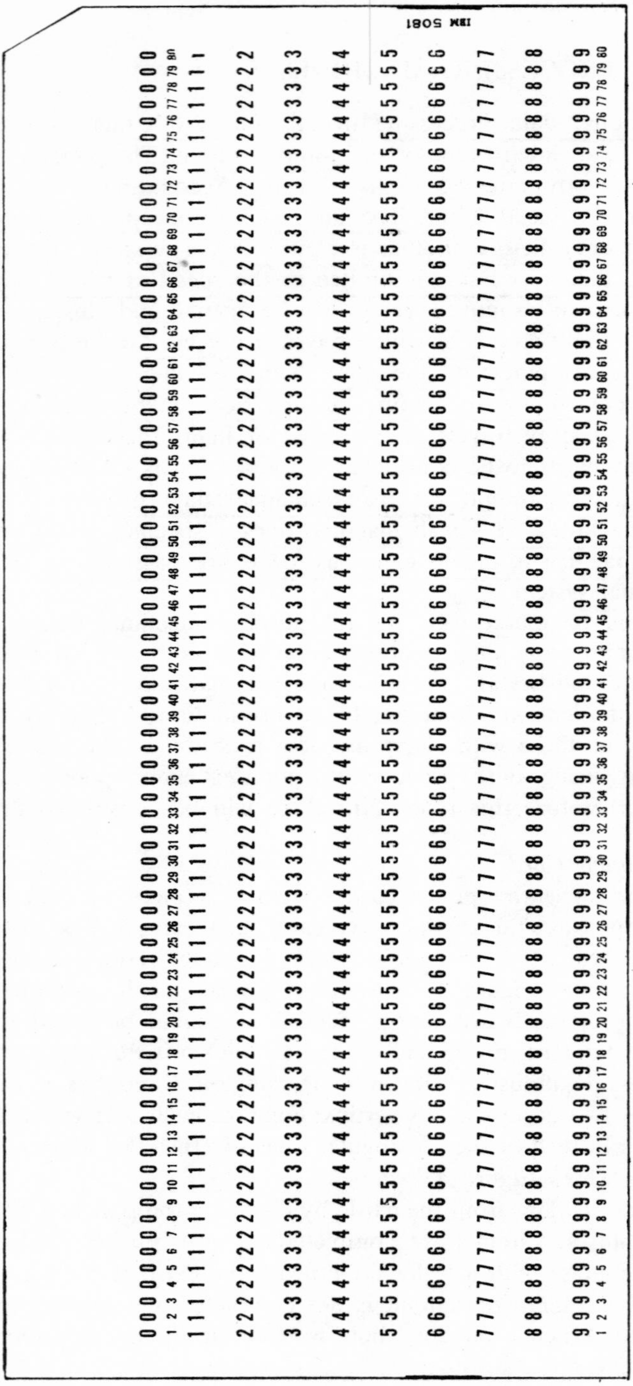

FIG. 3. *80 Column Card*

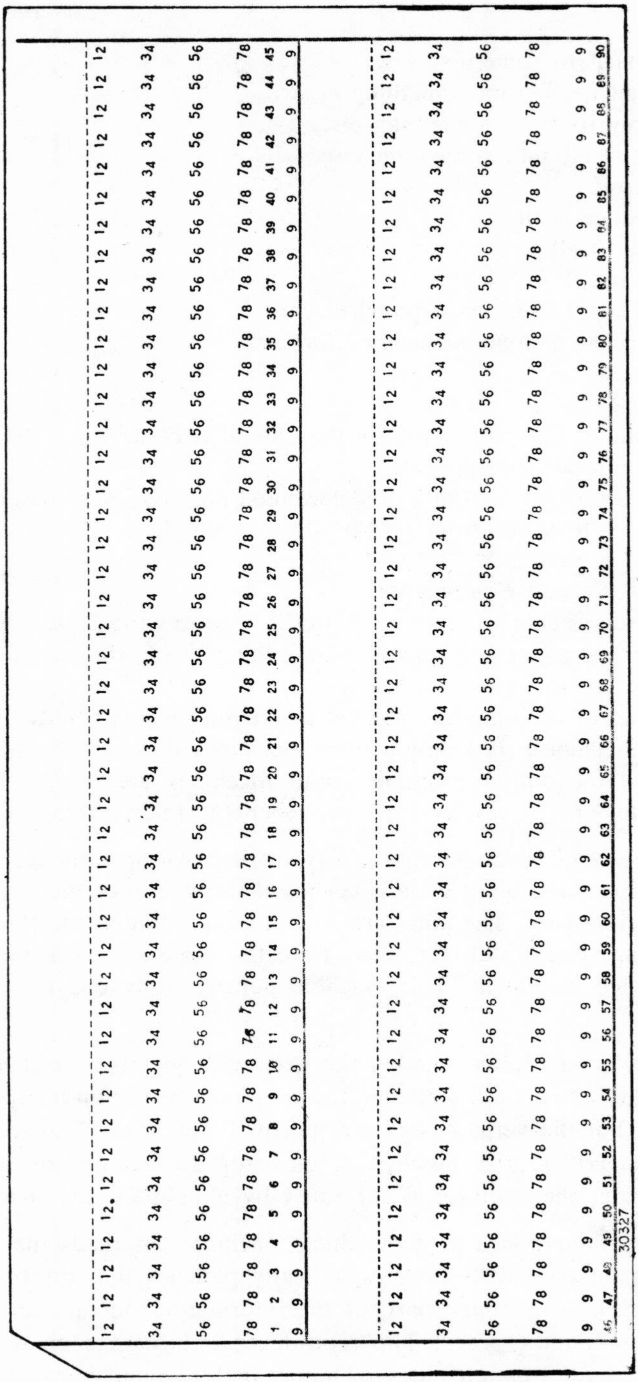

FIG. 4. 90 Column Card

1. Add itself to something else.
2. Subtract itself from something else.
3. Multiply itself by something else.
4. Divide itself into something else.
5. List itself.
6. Reproduce itself.
7. Classify itself.
8. Select itself.
9. It will print itself on a punched card.
10. Produce an automatic balance forward.
11. File itself.
12. Post itself.
13. Reproduce and print itself on the end of a card.
14. Cause a total to be printed.
15. Cause a form to feed to a predetermined position, or to be ejected automatically, or to space from one position to another.

Unit Record Equipment

Punch card systems are extremely useful in processing large volumes of data. They are capable of doing many things with the information punched in the cards.

Three types of machines are needed to provide this capability. These are the input machines, the manipulators (machines that actually process the cards), and the output machine. Input machines are of four main types: (1) keypunch (2) verifier (3) reproducer (4) interpreter.

1. *The keypunch* is comparable to a typewriter. An operator reads the source information and types it on a keyboard which causes the machine to punch holes in a card. The holes are punched according to the standard Hollerith coding system and, therefore, have the same standard meaning as would a typed document. This machine punches only one card at a time.

2. *The verifier* indicates whether the keypunch operator punched the right information into a card. Actually, the keypunch operation is repeated on the verifier but the verifier does not punch. If the card is correct according to the verifier, it is notched. If an error has been made in the original punching, the operator is informed by a light on the machine.

3. *The reproducer* is a card punching machine that reads the holes or information on one card and automatically punches that information into another card. All, or just part, of the information on one card can be punched into another card. The reproducer reduces the chances of error in handling information because the original keypunching operation does not have to be repeated.

4. *The interpreter* translates the coded information from the punched holes in a card into printed characters on the face of the card. It permits persons who may not be familiar with the card's code to read the information contained therein. The interpreter makes these cards meaningful to the teacher, counselor, clerk, and administrator.

Manipulating machines are of three main types: (1) sorter (2) collator (3) summary punch.

1. *The sorter* can sort cards in a desired sequence, such as alphabetical order by sex. It has a conveyer arrangement along which the cards are carried until they drop into an appropriate pocket according to the code punched into the card. Sorters sort only one of the columns at a time; therefore, in order to alphabetize a deck of cards it must be passed through the sorter many times. Figure 5 shows an IBM 083 1000 card/minute sorter.

2. *The collator* merges the punched cards. If there are two decks of cards, one containing the names and addresses of students and the other containing the names and grades for each student, the collator will merge these two decks into one in a sequence matching each student's name and address with his grades.

3. *The summary punch* is linked by a cable to the tabulator described below. Data accumulated from many cards can be punched into one card that then carries the total of these data. The summary card represents many other cards and greatly reduces the card volume for subsequent processing. Summary punch capability generally is incorporated in the reproducer mentioned above.

Output machines are of two major types: (1) accounting machines (2) calculators.

1. *The accounting machine*—also known as a tabulating machine or tab—is also a printer. It can read the punched holes in a card, interpret them, and produce a printed record such as a report card. This machine is capable of addition, subtraction, and simple multiplication. Under certain conditions the machine can read a deck of cards, accumulate information, and then print a summary. Figure 6, shows an IBM 407 tabulator.

2. *The calculator* is simply a high speed multiplier and divider that works with punch cards. The machine will calculate the number of mark points earned and the number of units completed as punched into the students' mark cards and will produce a new punch card from which the accounting machine will print accumulative mark-point average. Figure 7 shows a UNIVAC 120 calculator.

FIG. 5. *IBM 083 Sorter*

FIG. 6. *IBM 407 Tabulating Machine*

In addition to these machines, there are several peripheral devices, including the forms burster and the decollator, a device used to separate the carbon sheets from the printed forms.

All of the above-described machines are known as wired control panel machines. Control is accomplished on each of these machines through a wired control panel or plug board. A specially trained technical person has to wire the control panel in order to make the machine perform as desired. A control panel from a UNIVAC 120 calculator can be seen in Figure 7.

The Twilight Zone

In between unit record equipment and a full-fledged computer is a type of equipment known in the industry as "card processors." Two major manufacturers—Remington Rand Univac and IBM—have only recently opened up this new area. The avowed purpose of this type of equipment is to provide a bridge for growth continuity between present punch card equipment and larger-scale computer systems.

The Univac equipment is known as the 1004 card processor and can be used with both eighty and ninety column cards. It combines the core storage of a computer with the ease of plug board wiring and operates two or three times as fast as conventional punch card equipment. It consolidates, in a single unit, three basic machine functions: card reading, arithmetic processing, and high speed printing. Figure 8, on page 26, shows a 1004 processor.

The IBM 1401-G, is a modified version of the widely used IBM 1401 data processing system. It is described as a high performance card processing system; unlike other 1401 models, it does not use magnetic tape drives or disk file storage. Instructions are given to the machine through the stored program concept.

Both of these machines offer near-computer performance at much less cost than a full-fledged computer system.

The Computer

> Popular imagination is likely to picture the automatic computer as a "black box" into which one casually feeds raw information, and which, after a slight pause, responds by spewing forth reports, statements, schedules, analyses, statistics, and solutions. But in fact an automatic computer usually consists of several items of equipment each performing a definite function. The raw information which the automatic computer processes is, in practice, far from raw. Typically, it is the result of extensive collection, verification, and processing. Again, to get even one small report from an automatic computer much intensive, skilled human labor must first work out directions for how the computer is to produce the report.[1]

1. Ned Chapin. *An Introduction to Automatic Computers* (Princeton: D. Van Nostrand Co., Inc., 1963), p. 6.

FIG. 7. *UNIVAC 120 Calculator*

FIG. 8. *UNIVAC 1004 Processor*

Wired control panel machines and stored program machines, as computers are called, are alike in possessing five major functions: (1) input (2) storage (3) control (4) arithmetic (5) output.

Differences between these two types of machines arise primarily in how the functions are accomplished. For example, on wired control panel machines, control is accomplished with a control panel; on stored program machines it is accomplished with coded instructions stored in the machine.

Another difference arises in reading the input. With wired control panel machines, (1) only the contents of card columns which are wired are usable, (2) of these columns which are wired, only the information going to a storage unit (if there is one on the machine) retains its original identity, and (3) all card information not in storage is lost after the card leaves the reading station. On the other hand, with stored program machines, (1) when a card is read, all columns of card data automatically enter the machine; no control panel wiring is necessary, (2) the columns of data enter storage, so that original identity is retained, and (3) use of the card data is not limited to the time during which the card is passing the reading station of the input device, but can be made at a later time, since it is retained in storage.

The terms, input, storage, control, arithmetic, and output are rather meaningless until we relate them to a well known object—the human body.

Our body possesses the same type of components as does a general purpose computer. First we posit an imaginary situation in order to watch the reaction of the components. Suppose you are standing in front of a stove and you have no idea as to the stove's purpose or method of operation. You reach down and touch one of the red burners. Immediately your sense of touch recognizes a change in temperature. Your senses—seeing, hearing, smelling, tasting, and feeling—are your *input* devices. The delicate nerves in your fingers send the temperature change information through your central nervous system. The system itself decides that this impulse is more important than any of the other thousands of impulses that are traveling along it at this instant; therefore, it routes this priority impulse to the brain. The central nervous system can be compared to the *control* function of a computer. The brain interprets the impulse as one of pain and makes a decision; it sends an order back through the central nervous system to the muscles in the hand. The brain is performing the decision function similar to the *arithmetic* and *logic* unit of the computer. The muscles in this case are serving as *output*. The hand is jerked away almost before you realize that you had touched a hot object. The next time you see a stove you will be more careful about touching it because when the brain was sending information back to the muscles, it stored the impulses of pain and fear in a section of it we call memory. This is similar to the *storage* unit of the computer.

Generally, there are six types of storage: (1) magnetic tape, (2) magnetic disk, (3) magnetic drum, (4) core, (5) mechanical, and (6) vacuum tube. Figure 9 illustrates a magnetic tape used in one of the Honeywell data processing systems. Figure 10 shows a disk file used in an IBM data processing system. Although different from each other in physical makeup, they are alike in their function, which is to store information. These various types of storage exist because of different needs created by the many applications for which computers are used.

Core storage is one of the more commonly used storage devices. Figure 11 shows a core memory plane. For machines utilizing it, operations requiring the reading of information and writing of the information into storage are extremely fast, the time required to read or write a character is expressed in terms of billionths of a second. (A billionth of a second is commonly known as a "nanosecond"; a millionth of a second as a "microsecond"; a thousandth of a second as a "millisecond").

FIG. 9. *Honeywell 200 Magnetic Tape Unit*

FIG. 10. *IBM 1301 Disk File*

FIG. 11. *Core Memory Plane*

"An automatic computer is a machine that manipulates symbols in accordance with given rules in a predetermined and self-directed manner."[2]

It is composed of a number of devices which are electronically linked into one operational system. In computer parlance, the components and the devices from which a computer is constructed are known as "hardware."[3] The coded programs fed into internal storage to make the computer operate on data are called "software." The system functions in the following manner:

1. The input device reads coded data and makes this information available to the computer for processing. Sources of these items of data are generally punch cards or reels of magnetic or punched tape.

2. Once the information is read into the computer it is held in the internal storage unit. All data in the storage unit are indexed and can be referenced instantaneously.

3. The processor or central processing unit (CPU) performs the operations on the stored data. The central processor, in addition to performing various mathematical operations, can shift items of data from one place in any record to another and can make comparisons to test omissions encountered in processing and can take action appropriate to its previous instructions.

4. The control unit co-ordinates the entire computer system and is responsible for the proper functioning of all units. The control console is a device used by an operator to supervise manually the computer operations; it gives him power to maintain positive control over the computer's functioning.

5. The output devices take the process data and record it on punched cards, magnetic tape, or more commonly, on paper forms. Educators undoubtedly are most familiar with the computer printed form which can be prepared on high speed printers at better than one thousand lines per minute.

Data proceed through an electronic computer in a definite pattern of flow. The flow starts at the input where data are received into the machine. Data then proceed through the processing operations. Resulting data, produced by the electronic computer, flow from the computer as output. A schematic diagram is illustrated in Figure 12.

COMPUTER SIZES

Only in the world of purebred dogs do we find more variation in size and adaptability than the computer field. Most experts seem unable to

2. Chapin, *op. cit.*, p. 7.
3. *Ibid.*

agree on size classifications. Some base their judgments on price, others on capability, and still others on various combinations of these. For the purposes of this discussion we will use the terms small, medium, large, and giant.

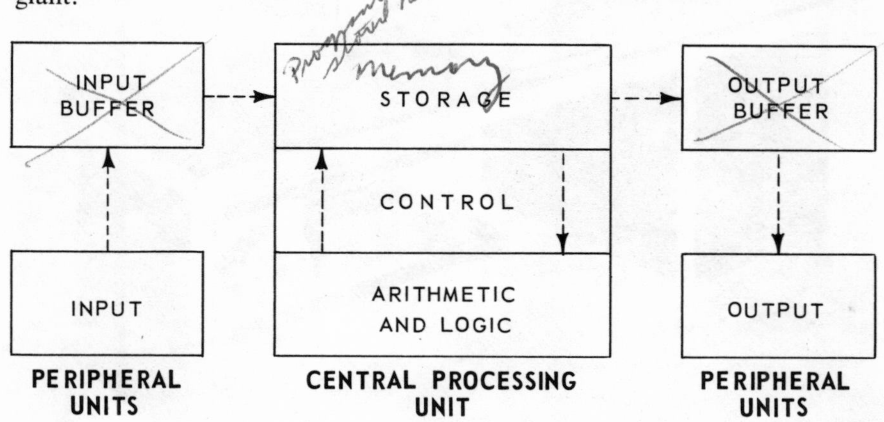

FIG. 12. *Schematic Diagram of a Computer*

Illustrative of the small computers are the Monrobot XI and the General Precision LGP 21. These computers typically rent for about $750 per month. Figure 13 shows the Monrobot XI.

The medium-sized computers are the most plentiful and include such popular machines as the Radio Corporation of America 301, International Business Machines 1401, National Cash Register 315, Burroughs 280, Honeywell 200, UNIVAC SS 80 and 90, and the General Electric 225. All these computers use some form of core storage and have magnetic tape, disk files, or other forms of external storage. They range in rental price from $5000 to $8000 per month depending upon the optional equipment ordered. Figures 14, 15, and 16 illustrate a variety of these machines.

The large category includes such machines as the Philco 2000, International Business Machines 7080 and 7094, UNIVAC 1107, Control Data Corporation 1604 and 3600, Radio Corporation of America 601, and the Honeywell 1800. These range in rental from $32,000 to $76,000 per month again depending on the optional extras. Figures 17, 18, and 19 are illustrative of such equipment.

Very few commercial computers are found in the giant category. To date only the Control Data Corporation 6600 is being offered for commercial lease. However, other computers such as the International Business Machines 7030, commonly known as the "STRETCH," and the UNIVAC LARC have been produced, but they are no longer being marketed. Computers in this category are usually to be found in such places as the Atomic Energy Commission and the National Aeronautics and Space Administra-

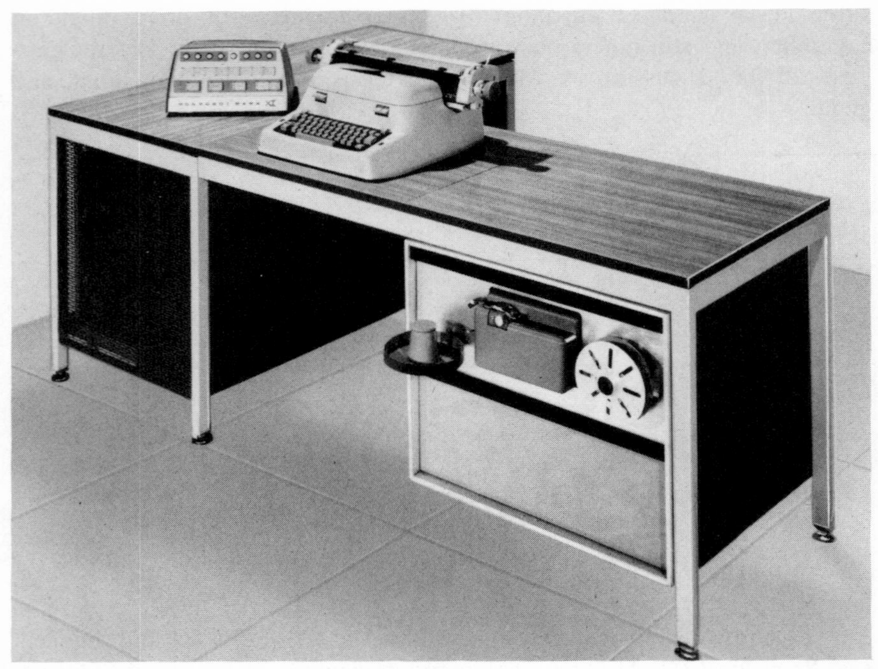

FIG. 13 *Monrobot XI Computer*

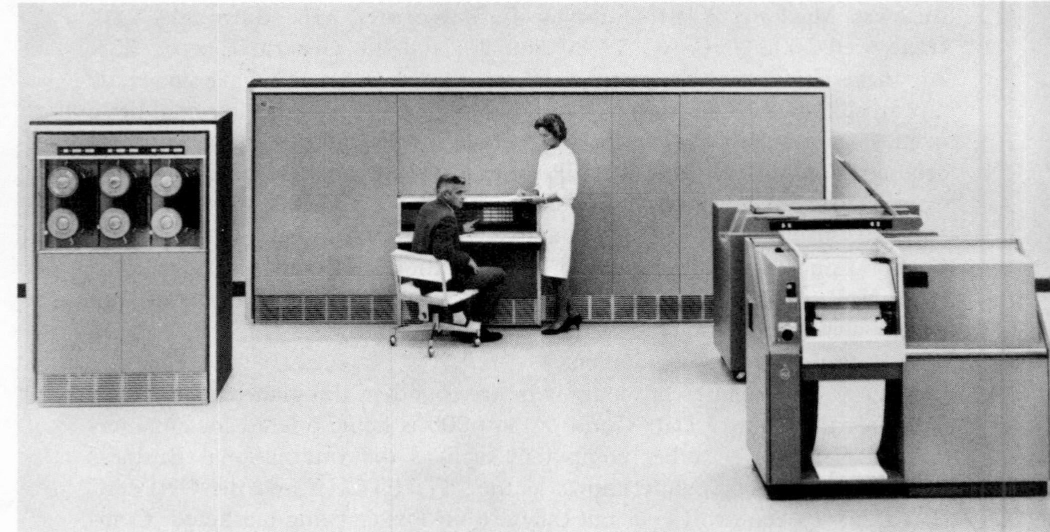

FIG. 14. *Radio Corporation of America 301 Computer*

FIG. 15. *IBM 1401 Computer*

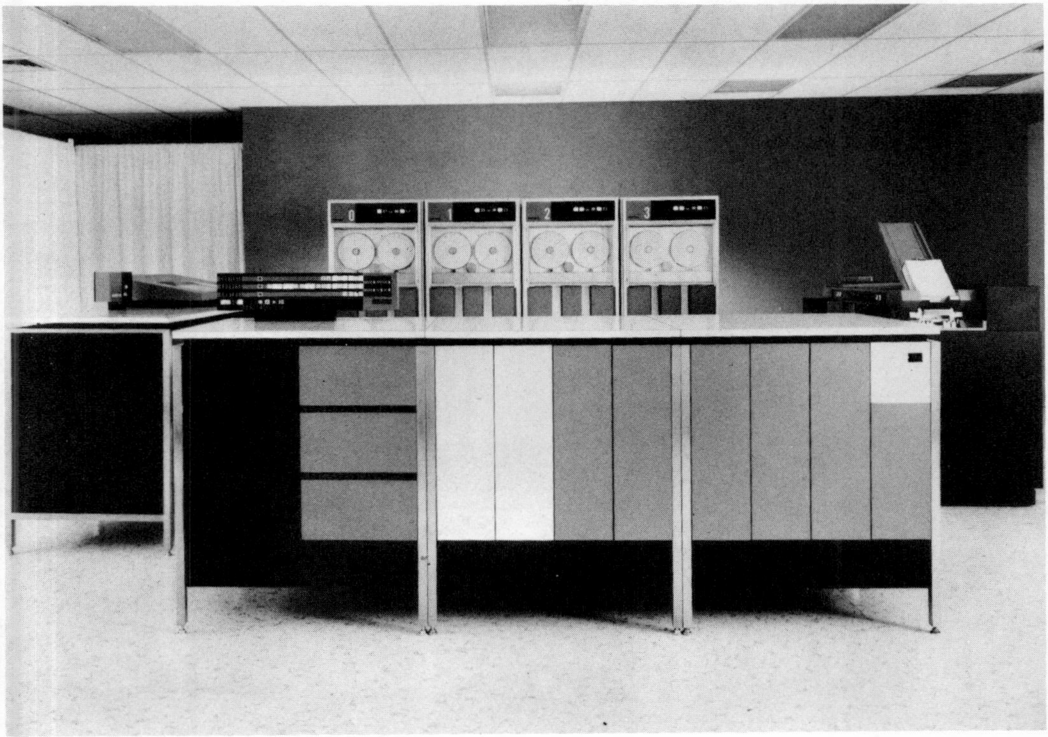

FIG. 16. *Honeywell 200 Computer*

FIG. 17. *UNIVAC 1107 Computer*

FIG. 18. *Control Data Corporation 1604 Computer*

FIG. 19. *Radio Corporation of America 601 Computer*

FIG. 20. *Control Data Corporation 6600 Computer*

tion. Some large research organizations and universities may also find use for such equipment.

While there are comparatively few of these giant size computers around today, many experts predict a phenomenal growth of computers in this category. If you would like to have one, expect to pay in excess of $75,000 a month in rental. Figure 20 illustrates the Control Data Corporation 6600. This computer can process three million instructions per second. It is made up of ten independent computers that feed an ultra-fast central computer. For about $1 worth of its time, the 6600 will simultaneously calculate one million additions, multiplications, subtractions, and divisions.

The growth in use of computers is shown in Table I which summarizes census data prepared by the Diebold Group.[4]

TABLE I

Date	Total Number of Computers (installed)
January 1960	3,612
January 1961	4,528
January 1962	7,305
January 1963	11,078
January 1964	15,867
January 1965	22,496

4. *Automatic Data Processing Service Newsletter,* Volume VIII, Number 18, Feb. 3, 1964.

PART II

Developing an Educational Data Processing System

4

ORGANIZING THE SYSTEMS STUDY

A school district organization can be thought of as a series of interconnecting channels, not always well structured, but interrelating with one another and with the larger community. Students, materials, and other resources flow through these channels to create the conditions necessary for the proper functioning of the district. Educational data processing is the part of the district's operation that is concerned with the attempt to record, measure, and control the flow of information through the channels that make up a district's "circulation system."

Many school districts are suffering from hardening of the arteries of this system. Vital information is not being speeded through the system in time to be used effectively. In some districts, important data is not even collected at a central source (the district office) to be pumped to vital subunits (schools) that need the data for decision-making.

As student enrollments continue to grow, the amount of paperwork necessary for the proper functioning of the school threatens to strangle the circulation system. For each of the millions of pupils in the public schools, hundreds of items of basic data are collected, evaluated, collated, read, copied, indexed, summarized, and filed. These data are subsequently used for various purposes which include better understanding of the individual student, evaluating his educational progress, determining teacher loads and requirements, making budget requests, allocation of budget amounts, apportioning school funds and costs, revising curriculum, and presenting to the taxpayer a current picture of school costs and problems.

Although many of the activities concerned with the processing of such data are primarily clerical in nature, much of the increased burden has fallen to professional staff members, taking time from their primary functions. Already harassed administrators become more harassed, and in their search for assistance to facilitate their administrative duties they often recruit counselors and deans, in turn taking them away from their primary duties. Thus, a vicious and never-ending cycle is set up which in the long run robs the school of its effective operating personnel just to keep from being inundated by paperwork.

There is evidence to show that by using data processing equipment, the schools can develop more efficient processes, and can also relieve administrators, counselors, and teachers from non-professional clerical routines.[1] Figure 1 on page 7 illustrates the ideal flow and use of information in a school district using data processing.

Today, growing numbers of school districts are moving toward the use of data processing equipment.[2] School administrators are becoming more aware that data processing equipment can help them obtain vital information relative to the district's operation and to deal with the increasing complexity and volume of work. The most successful decision-makers will be those who can most efficiently process, interpret, and put facts to use. While no technology can make decisions, it can put tools for decision-making into the hands of the right people at the right time.

The introduction of high-speed data processing systems can make significant changes in the structural interrelationships of school districts and provide more accurate and timely data on which to base critical decisions. Unfortunately, too often, too many people take part in decision-making, with too much reliance on obsolete information that masquerades under the name of experience.

The balance of this chapter will be devoted to describing (1) some possible school applications for data processing equipment and (2) how an administrator can launch a data processing systems study.

Student Records Applications

1. High School Registration
   a. Tabulations of positions by subject
   b. Student schedules
   c. Class list
   d. Counselor's list
   e. Alphabetic list
   f. Cross-tally of course conflicts
   g. Student locator cards
2. Attendance Records
   a. Class list
   b. Absentee list
   c. Daily attendance reports
   d. Monthly attendance reports
   e. Annual attendance reports
   f. Irregular attendance reports (cuts and unexcused absence)
   g. Record of new pupils
   h. Record of dropouts
   i. Statistics on attendance
3. Mark Reporting
   a. Report cards
   b. Permanent records
   c. Honor lists
   d. Failure lists
   e. Correlations with other relevant data
   f. Statistics

1. "Processing Pupil Personnel Data." *Bulletin of the California State Department of Education,* Volume XXXI, No. 2, March, 1962.

2. "A Report of an Experiment." The State Pilot Study in Educational Data Processing. California: Richmond School District, July, 1964.

4. Testing and Test Analysis
   a. Individual student test reports
   b. Progress reports
   c. Counselor's special listings
   d. Correlation of ability and achievement
   e. Correlation of ability, achievement, and marks
   f. Subject mark distribution
   g. Class and school progress reports

5. Cumulative Records
   a. Students' computer printed record
   b. Gum label attachment from testing and mark reporting activities
   c. Cumulative record reports by counselor and teacher

6. School Census
   a. Report to the state
   b. List of children eligible to attend kindergarten
   c. Name and address labels for mailing
   d. Population studies within district
   e. Schedule transportation of children and routing of buses
   f. Identification of children with special handicaps
   g. Separate lists for boys and girls
   h. Special list of non-resident minors

Business Office Applications

1. Budgeting
   a. Budget requests
   b. Budget worksheets
   c. Projected salary increase cost
   d. Cost analyses

2. Purchasing
   a. Purchase order
   b. Purchase order register
   c. Bid specifications
   d. Encumbrance document
   e. Product and vendor statistical information
   f. Follow-up documents

3. Payroll
   a. Payroll register
   b. Salary checks
   c. Earning statements
   d. Earning record
   e. Withholding tax reports
   f. Retirement reports
   g. Reports for salary analysis

4. Supply Requisitions and Inventory
   a. Tabulations of requisitions
   b. Adjustment of inventory records
   c. Distribution of cost to schools and plants

5. Appropriation Accounting
   a. Warrant register
   b. Expense warrants
   c. Appropriation ledger
   d. Financial reports to the board
   e. Financial reports to schools and departments
   f. Financial reports to the state
6. Other Accounting and Record-keeping Applications
   a. Cafeteria accounting
   b. Cost accounting
   c. Equipment records
   d. Bus scheduling
   e. Bus passes
   f. Textbook inventory
   g. Booking of visual and audio aids, research and statistics
7. Personnel
   a. Personnel records
   b. Qualification records
   c. Job evaluation
   d. Retirement status reports
   e. Leave records
   f. Teacher contracts
   g. County notices of employment
   h. Teacher assignments

SYSTEMS STUDY

In the earlier days of data processing, the process of estimating the balance of advantages and disadvantages for using data processing equipment in an organization became known as a "feasibility study." Such a study attempted to determine the technical, operational, and economic justification of doing a given set of applications with the aid of data processing equipment. From industry we have learned that the increasing use of automated equipment has melted away the elaborateness which characterized the early feasibility studies. In the early days, a feasibility study attempted to determine whether automatic equipment could be used for particular applications. It was found that applications were almost always technically feasible as long as information alone was to be handled, as long as a rule of transformation could be stated linking the input and the output. Nowadays, because the immense capability of the electronic computer is widely recognized, technical feasibility is often taken for granted until proven absent. And it is also widely recognized that a feasibility study is really a forecast of the impact of an entire data-handling system, not just a review of the possible uses to which equipment might be put. In this book we will refer to such a study as a "systems study," since it is apparent that most applications are feasible.

As you read on, it will become evident that there is a great deal of work involved in a systems study. It should be noted that this work is not particularly difficult or complex, and does not require the intelligence of a genius. It does require a great deal of effort. And if the work is done properly, a successful data processing system will result. Remember, however, that a data processing system will not solve all of your problems. It has no magic powers; it cannot see into the future; it will never produce results that are better than the men who think of uses and ways for it to work. As you can begin to see, the system itself is most important.

There are two points which should be stressed at the outset. First, every school district has its peculiarities and, therefore, must work out its own methods to implement the study. Second, even experts in this field do not always agree on the best methods. Every idea may be improved upon, and new ideas are being developed every day.

Organizing and Planning the Study

Mr. Leo Kornfeld, Management Consultant, Cresap, McCormick and Paget, states:

> As elementary as it sounds, there is only one way for a school district to decide whether or not it should commit itself to data processing. They should form a committee composed of the superintendent, business manager, and a representative of the school board. Its job should be to decide if automation is really necessary, and if so to decide the type of system.[3]

This plan should reflect the desires of the administration, as well as technical consideration for the systems team.

According to Laden and Gildersleeve:[4]

> Ideally, when the systems designer enters a data processing area scheduled for computerization, the only information he needs is a complete description of the output required from the data processing system in terms of content and timing. The systems designer can then set about constructing the optimum computer data processing system within the strengths imposed by equipment limitations, company policy, availability of required input and so on.
>
> In practice, the situation is seldom this clearly defined. Instead, the systems designer finds himself operating in a situation that manifests considerable sponginess. There is no formal definition of the total output requirement of the system. There is no single line official who is familiar enough with the spectrum of output to create such a definition. The purpose of some of the outputs presently produced is not clear. Recipients of other output are not satisfied with the information they are getting, they are not sure what information they would like to receive.
>
> Assuming that the systems designer gets the output defined, he

3. Leo Kornfeld, "What Every School Man Should Know About Data Processing." *Journal of School Management,* Vol. 6, No. 10.

4. H. N. Laden and T. R. Gildersleeve, *System Design for Computer Applications.* John Wiley and Sons, Inc., New York 1963. p. 228

then gradually discovers that the character of the restraints within which he is to build his system are not the most desirable. Policy that governs a particular course of action is riddled with exception and is so fuzzy as to be subject to several interpretations, all of which have been used at one time or another in the history of the operation. Too much information is available for some processes, not enough is available for others.

In light of the situation in which the systems team finds itself, there are two approaches to the question "How is a systems study undertaken?" In the first approach, the team becomes completely familiar with the current manual system and from there designs a new system. In the second approach, the team first determines the desired end products of the system and then develops a new system that will produce them. Advocates of the second approach point out that by disregarding the present system entirely, costs and time are diminished. Chapin[5] feels that the first approach leads down a blind alley in which the feasibility investigation can easily become lost. Advocates of the first approach point out that although it takes longer, a study of the present system reveals (1) its defects, strengths, and costs and (2) the "office politics" that must be coped with in effecting systems changes. There is, generally speaking, no merit per se in knowing how the present system operates or how it has evolved. The defects and strengths of the present system that are important are those which the administrator feels to be important, since these affect acceptability of the system. To base a study solely upon the input and output observed in the present system is to limit severely the possible benefits to be obtained in converting to the use of an automatic computer.

As Chapin has indicated, many feasibility studies have revealed that most of the advantages gained from the application of an automatic computer come not from the use of the automatic computer itself, but from changes in the basic design of the systems to be used in the organization. For our purposes we will deal with a combination of both approaches trying to utilize the best features of each.

Scope of the Study

The study plan should be amplified as extensively as administration requires. In all cases, the study purpose will have to be stated precisely; areas must be defined for inclusion in or exclusion from the study; depth of the study must be agreed upon, and a cost budget compiled for the estimated span of the work. Out of a general agreement of project scope, more detailed schedules are often prepared to include personnel assignments and the sequence in which work will affect each selected area of the district's operations.

5. Chapin, *op. cit.*, p. 4.

Organizational Charts

The initial task of the study is to learn where data are being processed. To learn this we must obtain a picture of the district. The best way is to obtain an organization chart to help define those units and subunits doing the data processing job. Then we should be able to work directly from the charts rather than studying data processing in a hit or miss fashion. In some districts the team may have to draw their own charts either because none will be prepared or the official ones will not supply a sufficient amount of detail. Often organizational charts do not tell the whole story. The de facto power structure in the district may actually lie outside the superintendent's office. It is important to know where the actual key to power resides even though this information never finds its way into print.

Collection of Documents

The outputs of the district consist of many seemingly unrelated documents. We need to collect these documents for the following reasons:

1. We must have a thorough knowledge of the entire system. We must know what documents come into the system—i.e., are processed in the system but do not leave it—and what documents make up the output of the system. We cannot know the whole system without knowing every document that passes through it.

2. Many of the documents in the present system will have to be processed in the new system. In the majority of cases documents such as reports, source documents, records, etc., will have to be processed whether a manual, mechanical, or automatic system is employed. Therefore, we want to be very careful to have all the documents of the system included in our study.[6]

In addition to the documents, the team should gather information on the following subjects:

1. The objectives of the system being studied.
2. The existing procedures.
3. The administrative unit doing each job.
4. The policies governing the current system.
5. The effectiveness of each procedure.

The following outline was used by the California State Advisory Committee on Data Processing in their systems study of twenty school districts in California.[7]

6. An Approach to the Basic Techniques of System Analysis, *"Handbook of the Processing Division, Radio Corporation of America,* 1961.

7. "A Report of A Study—Processing Pupil Personnel Data," *Bulletin of the California State Department of Education,* Vol. XXXI, No. 2, March, 1962.

PROPOSED OUTLINE OF TOPICS TO BE COVERED DURING TEAM VISITATION

A. *Pre-Registration and Registration*

1. Course planning by individual student
   a. Background of the student
   b. Forms on which planning occurs
      (1) List of school courses
      (2) School curriculum
      (3) Student plan
         (a) For following year
         (b) For 3 or 4 years
2. Course planning by school
   a. Tally of requests
   b. Design of master schedule
3. Assignment of students to classes
   a. Student and teacher notification
   b. Preparation of central file
   c. Teachers' lists
   d. Tally board
   e. Procedure for schedule changes
   f. Late enrollees and withdrawals

B. *Grade Reporting*

1. Origination of form
2. Manner in which teacher reports
3. Types of grades utilized
4. Disposition of the teacher's report
5. Preparation of final distributed report
6. Distribution of report
   a. Provisions for verification by parent
   b. Disposition by parent
   c. Comments
7. Failure or warning notice
8. Recording

C. *Testing*

1. Distribution of materials
2. Administration of tests
3. Collection of answer sheets
4. Scoring
5. Processing and conversion of data
6. Reporting of pupil scores
7. Administrative and school reports

8. Lists of tests and schedule
9. Recording of test scores

D. *Attendance Accounting*

1. File origination forms and sources of information
   a. Ledger—(A.D.A. register)
   b. Census or enrollment cards
   c. Parent signature cards
2. Absence reports—hourly and daily, including notification of future absences
3. Attendance office procedures for reported absences
4. Re-admission procedures and verification
5. Recording (ledger)
6. Preparation of periodic legal reports, federal, state, county, district
7. Enrollment alterations
   a. Late enrollees
   b. Withdrawals

E. *Statistical Reports*

1. Status reports or surveys
   a. Age-grade surveys
   b. Enrollment predictions
   c. Teacher load
   d. Tests
   e. Distribution of marks
   f. Population characteristics
      (1) PL 874
      (2) Projections
      (3) Special education
      (4) Student birthplaces
   g. Lists
      (1) Alphabetical and numerical
      (2) By grade level
      (3) Athletic eligibility
      (4) Honor roll
2. Research

Method of Data Collection

The major concentration of the study should be on output documents. At least two members of the team should interview key personnel in each operation. One team member should record a narrative documentary of the flow of data used in creating the output document, while the other team member should flow-chart the information. Later, both can fill out a narrative detail form. A suggested form often used by the authors is

REFERENCE	WHAT = PROCESSING ELEMENTS	WHO	WHEN	HOW

Where = a brief indication of the person or agency primarily responsible.

When = specific dates, or seasons, or "periods" (e.g., every four weeks, daily, at end of marking period, yearly, etc.).

Where = "address" to or from whom or what (i.e., transmittal address).

How = Instrumentation (manually, student fills it out, IBM, adding machine, key-sort, etc.).

REFERENCE = see document #.

FIG. 21. *Narrative Detail Form*

shown in Figure 21. By doing this, complete and comparable reports are secured for each area under study. It is important that each narrative report be accompanied by a flow-chart. This helps to make clear the clerical operations involved and can be of special value for the following purposes:

1. Checking the accuracy of the team's interpretation of the system being studied.
2. Tracing the information flow. The diagram will inevitably cross departmental lines and portray the functional relationship of administration, teaching, counselling, and the business office. Time lags, duplication of effort and information, and other inefficiencies can be identified easily.
3. Securing information needed in planning new systems or in the modification of existing systems; also in comparing existing procedures with proposed procedures.

Specific Steps to be Taken

The following specific steps should be taken to insure a comprehensive analysis of the system under study:

1. Become familiar with all the interrelated groups involved in the operations being studied.
2. Develop a flow-chart, which indicates the interrelationship of guidance, administration, business, and faculty groups so that the departmental relationships and a general picture of the direction of information flow becomes known—and in turn provides a basis for a more detailed analysis. (Flow chart symbols are shown in Figure 22)
3. Make a detailed survey of functional operations through consultation with personnel who are actually doing the work as well as with the school principal and district superintendent. The narrative information collected during the interviews should be detailed enough to achieve full and accurate recording of the information secured.
4. Develop a "first approximation" flow-chart of the operation—supporting it with enough narrative detail to highlight the uncharted parts of the system.
5. Review the charts with the head counselor, principal, chief accountant, and all other key personnel. Correct any discrepancies (but only after verification of the change by the person actually performing the task), and modify the charts as required; repeat this process until all persons involved are in agreement that the team has a complete and accurate picture of the operation.

When collecting data, it is better to obtain completed source documents and reports rather than blank ones, especially when you are unsure of the contents of the documents themselves.

In making a flowchart a standard system should be used throughout. The following symbols are generally used throughout the data processing industry.

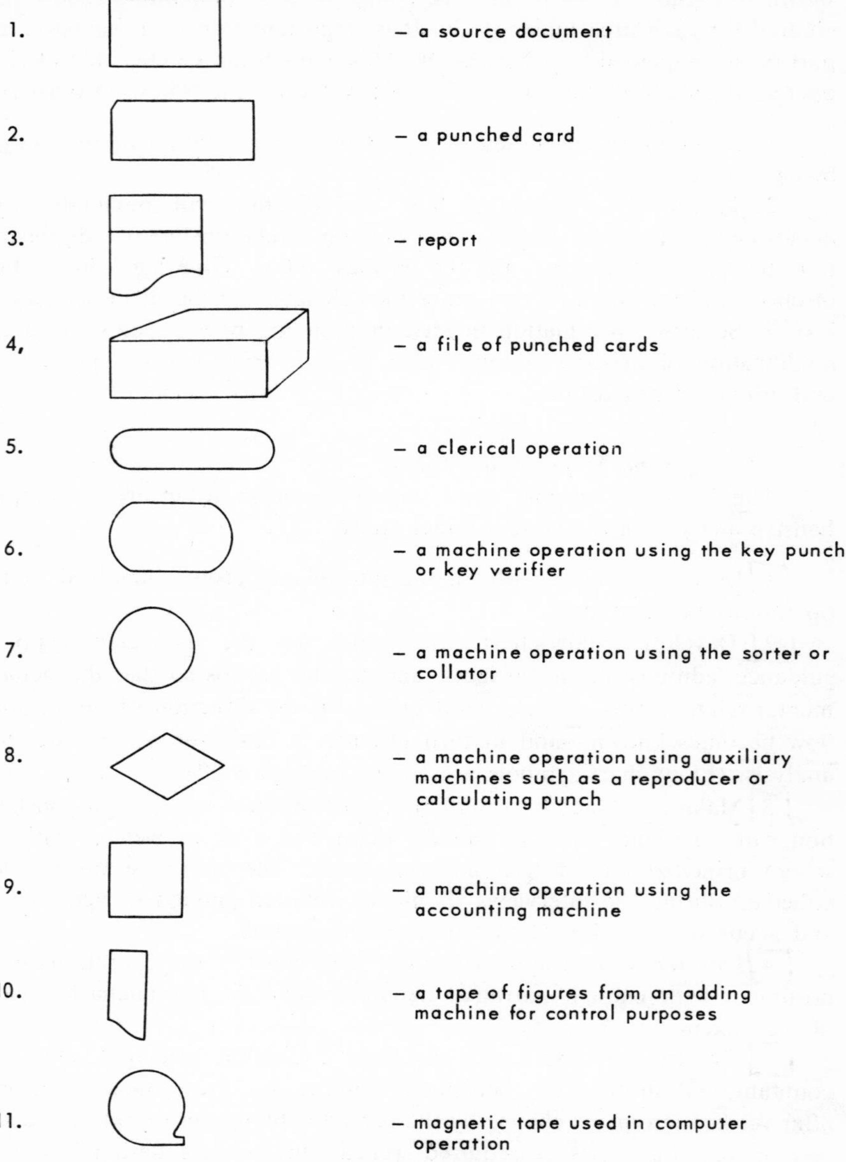

FIG. 22. *Flow Chart Symbols*

In making a flow chart a standard system should be used throughout. These symbols are generally used throughout the data processing industry. Figure 23 illustrates a new set of flow charting symbols which has recently been adopted as standard for the entire data processing industry. However, they are still too new to be in widespread use.

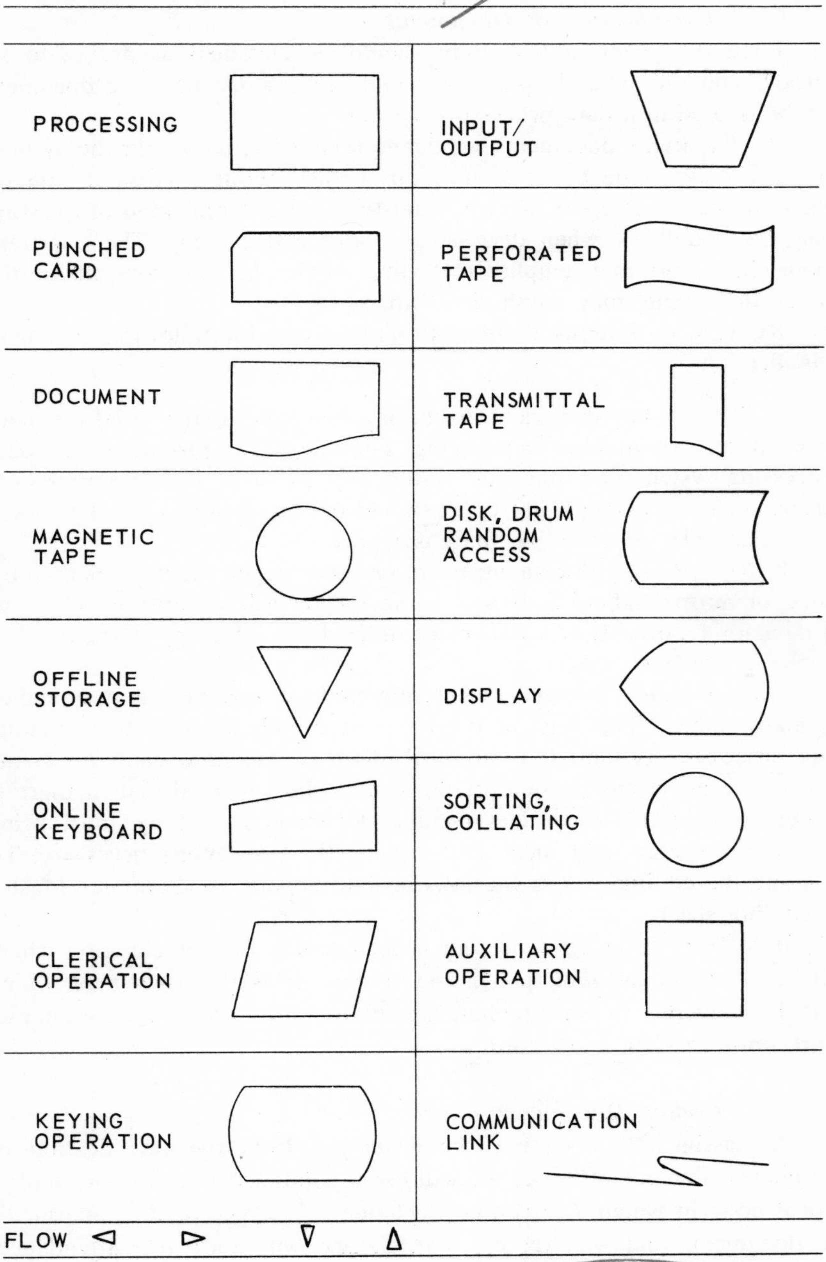

PROCESSING	INPUT/ OUTPUT
PUNCHED CARD	PERFORATED TAPE
DOCUMENT	TRANSMITTAL TAPE
MAGNETIC TAPE	DISK, DRUM RANDOM ACCESS
OFFLINE STORAGE	DISPLAY
ONLINE KEYBOARD	SORTING, COLLATING
CLERICAL OPERATION	AUXILIARY OPERATION
KEYING OPERATION	COMMUNICATION LINK

FLOW ◁ ▷ ▽ △

FIG. 23. *Industry Compatible Flow Chart Symbols*

Classification of Documents

Each document in the study should be classified according to its purpose and use. The classification should reflect just how the document will be treated in a data processing system.

By classifying documents we define their function within the system. This gives us a clue to what questions to ask about a given document. When discussing a report, we will want to ask a different kind of question than we would ask when discussing a source document. The questions about the report may emphasize "why," while the questions about the source documents may emphasize "where."

RCA, in its Systems Training Programs, uses the following document classifications:

a. *Report*—any document, form, or other paper that is used for management decision-making or planning. The report is a product of the data processing system; it is the end result, and as such, should *not* require further data processing. The report should not "back up" any other document. Example: A class size analysis report.

b. *Record*—any document, form, or other paper which is maintained daily for normal school activities. From the record, we abstract elements of data for reports. It is a document utilized for reference purposes. Example: Attendance roster.

c. *Intermediate document*—the intermediate document may be called by many names. This type of document is usually internal to a manual data processing system. It is primarily used to facilitate data processing rather than as an end product of the system. In a manual system there is a great amount of input data (source documents), and we must bring these data together, edit them, and provide the few reports necessary. To facilitate the editing we use the intermediate document. Example: Master scheduling sheet.

d. *Source document*—the source document is the vehicle upon which data first enters the data processing system. It is this document which must be converted to machine language in an automated system. Example: Mark-sense teacher mark card.

Coding Documents

A classification code may be developed from the classification of documents. For our purposes we will use a combined numeric and alphabetical code in which *1* = source document, *2* = record, *3* = intermediate document, and *4* = report. To this we will add: *a* = attendance, *b* = business, *c* = cumulative record, *m* = mark reporting, *t* = testing, and *r* = registration and scheduling. As an illustration, a student's mark card used in mark reporting would be classified as *1m, 1* for a source document and the *m* indicating the mark reporting area.

It is important that each member of the team be consistent and uniform in applying the code. If we do not follow this rule, the classifications become meaningless. Each document should have only one code set. This should hold true in 90 per cent of the cases. In the other 10 per cent, the document may have as many as three codes. The change in code usually reflects the change in the function of the document. In some cases, a document may serve initially as a source document and later re-enter the system as an intermediate document. These cases are rare.

Those documents which have nothing to back them up may be classified as source documents. Those documents which are backed up but do not back up any other document are coded as reports. Those documents which do not fall into either category and are processed on a daily or as required basis may be classified as records. Those documents which are processed on a weekly, monthly, or longer basis may appear to fall into the record category but may actually be intermediate records.

Grid Chart Construction

One of the easiest ways of graphically presenting the data that has been collected is to use the grid chart technique. The grid chart is a systems analysis technique which may be employed to describe a wide variety of relationships. Its use is limited only by the imagination of the user. It is of special value when coupled with document classification, and may be used with elements of data or with complete documents. It may point out redundancies or other unnecessary elements of data. It may show us where we can combine documents, or give us clues about the extent to which integration is possible in the system under study. It also may be used to insure completeness in our collection of documents and correctness in coding.

Figure 24 depicts a typical grid chart form. The heading should reflect (1) the area under study (i.e., mark reporting, attendance accounting, student scheduling, etc.), (2) the subareas, if any are present, and (3) the organization that is doing the data processing. Later we may expand to an area chart or even a chart which depicts the whole scope of the study.

The output section—labeled "End Products"—reflects the various output documents of our system. It will include (a) reports, (b) intermediate documents, and (c) records. For each output document we should record the document title, document classification, and frequency of use.

The input section should reflect every input document which *backs up* a given document. This section may show the source documents, records, and intermediate documents. For each input document, we should record the document's title and classification. We can then demonstrate the relationship between input and output by placing an "X" in the proper square.

MAJOR AREA **Student Scheduling**

SUBAREA **Registration**

ORGANIZATION **Westport High School**

FREQUENCY ▷			SA	M	A	SA	SA	A	SA	SA
▽	DOCUMENT CODE ▷		1 R	1 R	1 R	1 R	3 R	4 R	1 R	1 R
	▽	END PRODUCTS (Data Processing Activities) / INPUT DOCUMENTS	Pupil Schedule Cards	Summary of Enrollment	Final Master Schedule	Summary of Registration by Grade	Schedule Cards	Final Tally Sheet	Freshman Registration List	New Student Registration List
A	3 R	Pre Registration Tally	X					X		
A	4 R	Previous Year Master Schedule	X							
A	2 R	Enrollment by Period		X						
M	2 R	Transfer Student Documents	X							X
A	3 R	Course Tally Sheet				X		X		
SA	2 R	Schedule Cards			X					
SA	2 R	Freshman Registration Forms	X				X			

Frequency
A=Annual
M=Monthly
D=Daily
SA=Semi-Annual

FIG. 24. *Grid Chart*

Rules for Analysis

We are now able to apply certain rules for analyzing the chart. They are:

1. Reports should appear only in the output section. Reports, by definition, should not back up further data processing, hence, they appear only as output.

2. Source documents should appear only in the input section. Source documents, by definition, are not backed up by any other documents, hence they appear only as input.

3. Records may appear in both the input and output sections. Records may or may not back up other records, intermediate documents, or reports, hence, they may appear as either input, output, or both.

4. Intermediate documents *must* appear in both the input and the output sections. Intermediate documents are used in the preparation of reports or records, hence, they serve as input to these documents.

Intermediate documents are derived from source documents and/or records and serve as output from these documents. One exception to this rule is that the intermediate document may not appear both as input and output within a single organization. The document may be developed within one organization (shown as output) and sent for preparation of a report to another organization (shown as input). Therefore a comparison of the charts for all organizations in a given area should be performed to insure that all intermediate documents do serve in both sections.

5. We should be able to trace every report back to one or more source document.

The next step is to develop all document grid charts. When complete, review them for:

Incompleteness—by violation of rule 5.

Miscoding—by violation of rules 1, 2, and 4.

Documents which are outside the scope of the study—by violation of rule 5.

Any time we find a violation of the rules we should resolve it by re-interviewing the relevant personnel.

Analysis of Current Files

A complete analysis of the current files is a very important phase of systems analysis. A written survey of the files should include such information as: (1) identification and statement of the purpose of the file, (2) numerical statements of maximum size, average size, and percentage of occurrence of the elements of data contained in the file, (3) volume of data for average periods, and the possibilities for file expansion, (4) sequence of data in the file and reasons for this sequence, (5) frequency of maintenance of the file. It is suggested that this information be detailed on a data sheet as shown in Figure 25 and summarized on 5″ x 7″ cards for each file maintained. A fuller explanation of the file information needed is given below.

1. *Identification and Purpose.* The file should be identified in a concise and clear manner. The identification, along with the reasons for the maintenance of the file, should be placed at the top of the card prepared for this file.

2. *Elements of Data.* A listing of the data appearing in the file should be placed on the card along with the average and maximum size of the elements of data and their percentages of occurrence.

3. *Volume.* The volume of data affecting the file during average and peak periods should be shown on the summary card. Any possibilities for file data expansion should be noted.

4. *Sequence.* Major, intermediate, and minor sequences used in the file should be noted on the card.

5. *Frequency of Maintenance (Updating).* A statement on the card concerning the updating frequency of the file is important. Is the file updated daily, weekly, bi-weekly, monthly, or how often?

6. *Special Appendages or Characteristics.* Any special appendages or characteristics of the file should be noted and explained.

After analyzing the files, we should draw up a grid chart similar to the one drawn up for reports. Basically, it helps to call attention to the multiplicity of use of those output data maintained in the files, and it may lead to record consolidation.

Analysis of Source Documents

An analysis of all input items is an essential phase of the systems analysis. It is again suggested that a card be prepared for each input item so they can be handled easily. The card should contain such information as: (1) definition of and statement of the purpose of the source document, (2) method of origination, (3) elements of data contained therein, (4) the volume for both average and peak periods, (5) preparation frequency, and (6) the files affected.

1. *Identification and Purpose.* The identifying words should be brief but fully descriptive. This should appear at the top of the card along with a short explanation of the purpose of the source document.

2. *Method of Origination.* The point and the method of origination are important items. This information when assembled, will point out the presence of duplicated input items in any division of the operation, and will lead to combining those documents that are similar in nature.

3. *Elements of Data.* The elements of data appearing on each docu-

IDENTIFICATION	NO. OF MSGS.
Student Master File	6000
SEQUENCE	**USE**
Student Name-Number	Pupil Personnel Services

Item No.	Sub Item	DESCRIPTION	NO. OF CHARACTERS Max	NO. OF CHARACTERS Ave	% USE	WTD Ave
1	A	School District	2	2	100	2
	B	County	2	2	100	2
	C	School	3	2	100	2
	D	Student Number	10	10	100	10
	E	Grade	2	2	100	2
	F	Birth Date	5	5	100	5
2		Student Name	30	24	100	24
3		Grade Point Average	3	3	100	3
4		Rank in Class	4	4	100	4
5	A	Cumulative Absences	3	3	100	3
	B	Current Absences	2	2	100	2
		Total Characters of Information	66			59

FIG. 25. *Data Sheet*

ment should be listed on the card prepared for that document, indicating its fixed or variable nature. Further statements should also be given regarding average and maximum size of the data items and their percentage of occurrence.

4. *Volume*. The volume of data contained on the source documents will vary in accordance with daily, seasonal, cyclic, and long term activities. These variances in the volume of data should be noted on the summary card.

5. *Frequency*. The frequency with which the source document is prepared should be noted on the card. This notation may consist of only a few words such as "Prepared daily," "Prepared weekly," "Prepared as needed," etc.

6. *Files Affected*. A listing of the files affected by a particular source document should be listed on the card prepared for the source document. This information serves as an aid in the later grid chart analysis of source documents and files.

A summary of source documents using grid charts should be made. The procedures for preparing these grid charts are the same as those described in the previous sections.

5

SYSTEMS DESIGN

The purpose of the systems study is to obtain information from which an optimum system can be designed within the resources available. Once having studied the present system, we may begin to design an optimum one. The final degree of optimization will be obtained only after specific equipment is selected and its capabilities are utilized in processing data. We cannot begin to optimize our system without regard to specific equipment.

Canning has stated:

> The design of a good data processing system is a challenge to all who undertake it. The goal should be: an efficient, economical, streamlined system that provides effective integration of both manual and EDP aspects.
>
> The system should exploit the capabilities of the data processing equipment. You do not achieve these goals by transferring to the automated system the present manual system practically unchanged.[1]

To place the subject of design in its proper perspective, let us briefly review the sequence of events in a typical data processing project, after the administration has approved the project.

The first step is to study and analyze the present system in order to help define the true requirements for the new system.

The next step is to formulate the preliminary design of the new system, including both manual and automated aspects.

Then the economics of the new system are evaluated, based on the preliminary design. At this point the broad category of data processing equipment may be selected, again based on the preliminary design.

Now, based on the economic evaluation and other expected benefits, the administration should decide whether or not to go ahead with the project. If the decision is positive, detailed preparation should begin. This stage includes completing the system design, programming or wiring of panels, site preparation, conversion, and so on. Following conversion, operation of the new system commences.

Looking back over this list, one can see what a key role preliminary design plays. This is the stage where the main creative work should occur

1. *EDP Analyzer*, Guidelines for EDP systems design. Canning Publications Inc., Vol. 1 (1963), No. 10, p. 1.

in the whole data processing project. The economics of the project have been based on it. Equipment has been selected on the basis of it. It sets the schedule for installation of the data processing equipment and conversion to the new system.

If preliminary design has been superficial its weakness will become apparent. As a result several changes may take place: often more equipment is ordered because it becomes apparent that the equipment selected initially won't do the job; the installation schedule is lengthened, and more staff is added to compensate for greater workloads.

Since design, particularly preliminary design, is so crucial to the success of a data processing program, we should explore the questions: What is good design? How do you go about designing a system to meet your needs?

The characteristics of an "ideal" design are not always possible to achieve in a particular situation. It is not unusual for a design team to find that they must make some compromises. They should strive, however, for the "ideal" design and compromise only when all possibilities of obtaining it have been exhausted.

DESIGN SESSIONS

The installation of an electronic data processing system involves changes in systems and procedures, and often these changes are sizeable. It is the principal who is usually responsible for the operation of the school organization, and he will be using the outputs from the EDP system. One of the basic problems of installing an EDP system is getting principals deeply involved in the system's design so that they will understand how they will operate after the new system is installed.

It is not uncommon for school principals to give only passing attention to the EDP plans during the systems study, on the assumption that the equipment will never be ordered or that it will not affect them. After it is ordered or after they see that they will be affected, they give more attention to the plans. But since they have not thought through how they can best operate with an EDP system, they often ask that the EDP system give them output comparable to the existing reports and forms, and on a frequent basis. The result, too often, is a significant increase in EDP time and costs over what was estimated in the feasibility study.

"EDP design sessions" are used to obtain the active participation of administrators during the installation of an EDP system, and thus to avoid the problems discussed above.

One of the best statements on data processing design sessions has been published by Canning in the *EDP Analyzer* for May, 1963. With permission of Canning Publications, Inc., this section on design sessions is based mainly on that report.

Design sessions can be used successfully at several points in the EDP program:

1. At the outset of the program (before the detailed requirements study gets underway), to lay out the scope of the EDP study, set some major system objectives, and pinpoint problem areas. The assistant superintendents and principals participate in these sessions.
2. After the preliminary design of the EDP system has been accomplished, to review the operating feasibility of the systems plans and the proposed output reports.
3. After the EDP system has been installed and conversion completed, to see how reports can be simplified and system performance improved.

The success of EDP design sessions hinges upon several requirements:

a. The design sessions must have the support and approval of top administration.
b. They must have careful advance preparation, including an agenda and copies of major reports and operating documents.
c. The participants must be selected with care.
d. The full-time attendance of the participants is mandatory.
e. The sessions should be held on consecutive days at some location where interruptions and distractions are minimized.

Once the agenda has been developed, the length of the design sessions can be determined. In practice, these sessions have lasted from two days to two weeks.

Top Management Support

Design sessions require the full-time participation of selected members of the administration. Only by giving their full-time attention to it will they be able to concentrate effectively on the subject under discussion.

Obviously, to take a number of key administrators away from their jobs from two to ten days is an expensive undertaking. Top administration must understand, support, and approve the reasons for the design sessions. Furthermore, top administration must specifically indicate this support and approval to the selected participants. It is not uncommon to find one or more of the selected staff have slipped back to their offices for a few hours during a session or are "too busy" to attend. Such actions can seriously jeopardize the success of the sessions, and top administration should help to discourage them. If administrative support is lacking, the sessions probably should not be held.

Advance Preparation

The scope and objectives of the design session should be clearly defined in advance. Through discussion with members of administration, the person responsible for organizing the design session should clarify the desired goals and identify the operations to be included in the discussion.

Table II lists the steps to be taken in the preparation of design sessions. One or two months may be required to carry out these steps and to select dates for the design sessions that are most convenient for the participants.

TABLE II
ADVANCE PREPARATION FOR DESIGN SESSIONS

1. Suggest the names of the participants for top administration approval.
2. Select the dates of the design sessions to be held, considering the schedule requirements of the selected participants and making sure that the sessions take place on consecutive days.
3. Arrange for the meeting location and the necessary facilities; note that a location away from the district's premises is most desirable.
4. Develop the agenda (see Table III).
5. Gather supporting material, including copies of all major reports and operating documents from the areas under discussion, and arrange them in sets.

It is important that the design sessions be held on consecutive days. Experience indicates that the sessions need most of the first day to gain momentum. By the second day interest is aroused and participation is lively. Were a significant time lapse to occur between sessions, the momentum would not carry over. It is also important that the sessions be scheduled so that none of the participants have just cause to be absent. If a participant is absent, particularly if he has been active in the discussion, the group has difficulty adjusting.

The design session should be held at some inactive location so that discussions are not jarred by phone calls and other interruptions.

Supporting materials should include copies of actual documents and not just blank forms. One set of these documents should be given to each participant at the design sessions. Supporting material should be as current as possible. In addition, some of the selected material should illustrate one or more problem areas in the present system.

Two other types of supporting materials have proved helpful. One is a breakdown of monthly or annual costs within the areas being discussed, primarily to show clerical and data processing costs within the different organization units. The other is a summary of present major systems timing—the elapsed time between the receipt of a transaction document and the resultant action.

The agenda is usually two or three typewritten pages in length. A draft of the agenda should be prepared by the person organizing the design sessions and submitted to appropriate members of top administration for modification and approval. After approval, copies should be distributed to all participants in advance of the design sessions themselves. Table III lists the information that the agenda should cover.

TABLE III
SUGGESTED CONTENTS OF THE AGENDA

1. A statement of the objectives of the design sessions—what is to be accomplished.
2. A statement of the scope of the discussions—what operations will be pertinent to the discussion and what types of operations should not be discussed.
3. A list of the participants.
4. Designation of the dates, location, and daily schedule of the sessions.
5. An indication that the sessions are to receive the full-time attention of the participants for the designated period.
6. The specific subjects that will be discussed and a tentative time schedule for discussing them; this should remain flexible, in case some subject is found to require more time than originally estimated.
7. Some possible systems approaches for solving certain operating problems may be included, to help initiate thinking among the participants.

Who Should Participate

The size of the group should be kept small to encourage discussion and participation by all attending; six to eight people is a good size. If necessary, other people can be invited at specified times, when subjects are discussed in which they have special competence.

Preferably, the group should consist of the heads of the operations being discussed. As an example, one of the design sessions may concern student scheduling. The participants then should include all head counselors and the person in charge of developing the master schedule. Someone knowledgeable in EDP and punched card systems should be present to indicate abilities and limitations of the computer equipment.[2]

The selected participants should have a positive attitude toward system improvement. Constant critical or non-cooperative attitudes on the part of any of the participants can have a damaging effect on the sessions.

2. In one case it proved helpful to present a one-half day session on the principles of EDP to the participants, prior to the design sessions, just to take some of the mystery out of the subject.

How to Conduct the Sessions

The discussion leader should be the highest level executive of those participating and the one whose operations would be most affected by the new system. He should keep the discussions "on the track" and see that worthwhile results are obtained.

A record should be kept of the significant points raised at the session. It is suggested that a 3′ x 4′ blackboard and a polaroid camera be on hand. As significant points are raised, they may be listed on the blackboard, where all can see them; and when the board is filled, the camera, placed at a suitable distance, can record the information and make it available for immediate reference. This method has proved to be more useful than the conventional and cumbersome methods of note-taking or tape recording.

The participants should be urged to speak frankly, but in a constructive way. The discussion leader should encourage the participants to question the need for present reports, the present timing of reports, the number of copies, etc. In the give and take of the discussion, the participants are inclined to look more critically at some of the "sacred cow" reports and documents of the present system. Requests for new reports should also be subjected to critical analysis, to see if they would really be beneficial.

Thinking of the group should be directed toward the future system. Any discussion of past mistakes must be handled very carefully. Perhaps it is best not to discuss them at all. If they are discussed, no attempt should be made to assign blame; rather, a brief discussion might center on how best to avoid repeating them.

Also, the participants should not leave the sessions thinking that what they have proposed is firm or final. They should allow some flexibility for the study team, which may come up with changes and improvements.

Desirable Results of the Sessions

In general, the design sessions should formulate reasonably firm recommendations on the outputs of the new data processing system. Thus, the design sessions should be concerned mainly with the outputs which the administrators feel are needed in running the schools. In the course of discussing outputs, some attention usually is necessarily directed toward inputs, files, and processing, but this should be minimal.

The participants may discuss subjects or operations about which they do not feel knowledgeable enough to make firm systems recommendations; or the participants may have difficulty in completely defining some desired new output or some modification of the existing output. For both cases more studies are needed, and the design sessions should provide a framework within which the detailed studies can be performed.

If the sessions have been successful, the participants will have seen the difficulty of preparing ledger-type records from EDP and will have settled on adequate substitutes. Also, from the design sessions should emerge a fairly clear picture of which operations should be converted to EDP and which operations should be deferred.

Near the end of the design sessions, all the projects discussed should be listed on the blackboard. By reviewing the entire list, the participants can judge the relative importance of each project and can assign priorities.

An approximate overall schedule should be laid out for accomplishing the desired end results. Within this schedule, intermediate target dates should be assigned. When assigning these intermediate dates, responsibility assignments should be made. As specific people are assigned these projects, and as the existing workloads of these people are considered, it is often found that the intermediate target dates must be set off further into the future.

This time-and-action schedule, with specific responsibilities assigned, is an important product of the design sessions. The discussion leader should make sure that time is allowed for doing it properly, before the sessions end.

Some By-Products of the Design Sessions

Perhaps the most valuable by-product of these sessions will be the education which the participants receive on other parts of the district's operation. Even participants who have been with a district for many years have been surprised at how much they learn in these sessions.

Another important by-product is the enthusiasm and support for the EDP program which these sessions engender in the participants. Moreover, once they become convinced about a desirable course of action, their enthusiasm goes a long way in converting top administration to their point of view.

Also, the design sessions direct the full attention of the administrators to the outputs of the EDP system and to how each department will use these outputs. As the administrators come to grips with these problems, they will begin to concentrate on ways to make an orderly transition from the present system to a new system. Under the proper conditions EDP design sessions can be a very useful and productive step in designing a district's data processing system.

ELIMINATION OF DOCUMENTS

The information contained in the intermediate documents that were used in the manual system, may be handled internally by the data processing equipment because such documents were used to facilitate data processing. Hence the paper forms which were formerly used to hold this information are no longer needed. Most commonly the intermediate document is eliminated. By reviewing such factors as distribution, use of item, etc., from the previously prepared interview data the extraneous reports will be revealed. If a report can be eliminated, a check should be made to determine if any document which backs up this report can also be eliminated. An item check on the grid chart will show where other documents can be eliminated.

COMBINING INFORMATION

Sometimes, by the addition of a few more items, one report can serve the purpose of two or more. Processing may be reduced if reports can be combined. An analysis of the elements of data on the grid chart can point out where combinations are possible.

CHANGE IN FREQUENCY

During the interviews it may have been determined that there is a need to change the frequency of a given report. If this appears to be the case, a careful study must be made of the important file data, as well as the flow process chart, to determine if a frequency change is possible. New procedures for handling input and a change in the sequence of processing probably will be necessary if frequency changes are to be made.

CHANGE IN FORMAT

A change in the format of a report may prove of value in bringing the more important information to the recipient's immediate attention. Those items which require action may be prominently placed on the report, thus saving the recipient from wading through a vast amount of less important but necessary data. Figure 26 shows how, by incorporating a comments column, the essential information is highlighted.

LEVEL REPORTING

With automatic data processing, we can take a basic report and through successive eliminations and summarizations, develop many reports, each applicable to a particular level of administration. Figure 27 shows a report prepared for the district administrator. Similar reports on the same data can be constructed for principals and even department chairmen.

R/D CENTER
CALIFORNIA STATE DEPARTMENT of EDUCATION

TEST SCORE TO PERFORMANCE ANALYSIS

TEST IDENTIFICATION		TEST DATE				SCHOOL NAME		SCHOOL ADDRESS		DATE	COUNSELOR
		TEST SCORES-AREA				MARK AVERAGE BY AREA				AREA INDICATED BELOW NEEDS FURTHER ATTENTION	
INT TEST SCORES XXXX XXXX XXXX	STUDENT NAME	LANG	READ	ARITH	TOTAL	LANG ARTS	MATH	SOCIAL SCI	TOTAL GPA		
	AMOS, JOHN F.	7	6	7	7	2.72	2.61	3.19	2.85		
	CHATTERY, LADY B.	8	8	7	8	2.37	3.52	2.68	2.77	LA SS BELOW EXPECTANCY	
	DEVER, CARL P.	4	4	3	4	3.21	3.31	3.69	3.42	ALL FAR ABOVE EXPECTANCY	
	EVANS, THOMAS R.	4	3	9	6	1.82	3.62	1.59	2.08	TOT GPA BELOW EXPECTANCY	
	PRYZNEWSKI, WENISLAUS O.	7	7	8	7	2.81	2.23	2.97	2.74	M BELOW EXPECTANCY	

EXPLANATION
FAR BELOW EXPECTANCY
BELOW EXPECTANCY
ABOVE EXPECTANCY
FAR ABOVE EXPECTANCY

FIG. 26. *Test Score to Performance Analyses*

ADDITIONAL ITEMS OR REPORTS

Additional items, or even an entirely new report, are sometimes vitally needed by the administration. The need for new information may give rise to the need for an additional source document or a new entry in the file or a new sequence of processing to arrive at the proper output. The sequence of data processing may have to be modified or expanded to handle additional requirements. In the majority of instances, no change can be made in the output document report, especially when the report must go forward to a higher organization.

Once the output documents have been analyzed, the results should be noted on the actual document. Also the interview document should reflect the nature of the change and its effects on such items as workload and routings of the report.

SOURCE DOCUMENT ANALYSIS

All the various changes discussed in regard to output reports are equally applicable to source documents. Through analysis of the grid charts we may find we can eliminate either items or entire documents. Or we may have to add additional items or documents, and these must be reflected on the grid charts. We must also establish new schedules for preparing source documents and develop procedures for the preparation of additional source documents.

Any changes in source documents should also be reflected in the workload statistics. The workload should be broken down into two parts reflecting the number of documents and the number of transactions. This is especially necessary where there are multiple line entries on the source documents. The conversion of source documents, although an important subject, will not be treated here because the media and the devices used depend upon the hardware selected. We should determine, however, where the documents are prepared and where they are processed. These factors are important in determining where, and how much, conversion workload is present in the system.

FILE DESIGN

The final arrangement of the files will not be possible until specific equipment has been selected. We can, however, develop the files along functional lines at this time. In a school district large enough to have undertaken a comprehensive systems design, the files will probably be on some type of magnetic storage and it will be the job of the systems team to develop files within the capabilities of the specific computer selected. Content

R/D CENTER
CALIFORNIA STATE DEPARTMENT of EDUCATION

SUPERINTENDANT'S EDUCATIONAL PLANNING REPORT

DATE
DISTRICT
INTELLIGENCE TEST
ACHIEVEMENT TEST

SCHOOL	INTELLIGENCE			ACHIEVEMENT				MARK AVERAGE BY AREA				REMARKS
	LANG	N LANG	TOTAL	LANG	READ	ARITH	TOTAL	LANG ARTS	MATH	SOCIAL SCI	TOTAL GPA	
HIRSCH JR. HIGH	7	6	7	7	7	8	7	3.35	3.71	3.57	3.51	AS EXPECTED
SOUTH SHORE JR. HIGH	4	6	5	4	4	5	4	1.38	2.19	2.23	1.81	LANG ARTS BELOW AVERAGE
MAYFAIR JR. HIGH	5	5	5	5	5	5	5	2.19	2.31	1.92	2.18	AS EXPECTED
GREGORY JR. HIGH	4	3	4	3	3	3	3	1.51	1.71	1.63	1.61	AS EXPECTED
TIFFANY SR. HIGH	5	5	5	4	5	4	4	2.62	2.81	2.70	2.61	ABOVE AVERAGE
WELLS SR. HIGH	5	7	6	5	5	6	5	2.32	2.41	2.30	2.31	AS EXPECTED

EXPLANATION
STANINE SCORES

FROM 0 TO MID-POINT OF 3 - BELOW AVERAGE
FROM MID-POINT OF 3 TO MID-POINT OF 7 - AVERAGE
FROM MID-POINT OF 7 AND ABOVE - ABOVE AVERAGE

FIG. 27. *Superintendent's Educational Planning Report*

of the files should, by this time, be firmly established by the analysis. Those items which were eliminated from reports should be removed from the files. An accurate picture of the workload left after these eliminations should be presented. In most cases, more than one file will be required.

We may consider the possibility of file consolidation if we find some common elements of data being used to prepare reports. This consolidation is reported on the grid chart. Next we may determine if it is possible to develop an uninterrupted flow of data from the input to the output. Can the files be arranged in such a manner that we process each input completely? We also want to develop a method for pulling out a particular record when it is required. We should arrange our files in terms of the job to be done. We must also decide what identification information will be placed on each file including title, date the file is to be erased, and any other pertinent information. Finally we should edit the content of our new file to determine (1) if we can produce all required reports from the files and manipulate data so that the file will have current information when needed for reporting, and (2) if there are any elements of data being maintained in the file that could otherwise be produced by manipulation. We should also analyze our grid charts for elements of data which, although available to the system on the source documents, have not been used because of the extra effort required in the manual system or because of the limitations of a punch card. It is a relatively simple matter to save these data in the files of an automatic data processing system for future administrative use.

PROCESSING

The last area for consideration is processing. We have looked at the output, input, and files. Each of these areas is related to processing. In order to understand the present system we developed flow charts, and narrative reports, and grid charts. Now we again turn our attention to these reports and charts, this time to aid us in the development of the processing in the new system. We should first remove all charts or documents which will not be present in our new system. Then we may remove from the flow charts those blocks which show processing of items no longer needed in our new system. After we have completed these steps, we must study the remaining processing carefully and determine if:

1. We are doing processing which should be eliminated even without the use of mechanization. For example, repeated examination of the document by several organizations.

2. We are doing processing which can be eliminated by the use of mechanization. Some processing which required administrative authority will require special action if we hope to mechanize it.

3. Some of the processing can be combined. Grid charts will help in making this determination.

4. Perhaps we can rearrange the sequence of processing to lead to reduced reporting time and further combining of documents.

5. The various functions of data processing can be integrated so that we can make the optimum use of the entrance of data into the system.

6. Our processing is edited to include the necessary steps for additional administrative requirements.

We must be sure that all processing is completed before the data are needed for an administrative requirement. This requires the development of a schedule of processing to produce the desired output at the proper time. We are ready now to redraw the flow charts for the new system. We may now describe the new system in detail. A series of flow charts can be prepared according to the various frequency periods. A separate chart may be made which depicts the daily, weekly, monthly processing, etc. Charting in this manner will help determine if all data are available when needed, and when coupled with volume, will show peak workload. A narrative and overall chart may also be prepared at this time.

We have looked at our present data processing system and from it have developed as close to an optimum system as is possible without reference to a specific computer. We now know (1) what input we must have, (2) when it must enter the system, (3) the content, and to a degree the format of the files, (4) the output requirements of the new system, and (5) the processing which must take place to provide these outputs when they are required.

6

MOVING TO THE AUTOMATED SYSTEM: PERSONNEL REQUIREMENTS[1]

The die is cast. You have decided to move ahead and install a data processing system in your district. You're ready to leave the "why" phase and enter the "how" stage.

The time for generalities is past. Now the "nuts-and-bolts" approach takes over. Planning must take on a new dimension, one which is specific, detailed and completely practical.

NEED FOR PERSONNEL POLICIES

Those who have installed data processing systems in both industry and education have learned, often through bitter experience, that many employees accept change and innovation reluctantly. Furthermore, the success of a data processing installation depends heavily upon the data gathering efforts of a large number of employees in the organization.

To insure that the installation will function smoothly and efficiently and will have a minimal disorganizing effect upon the school district, a sound and carefully thought-out set of personnel policies should be developed during the early planning phase of the project. The essential elements of these policies should be included in the initial announcement of the new system to all employees.

Properly developed, publicized and executed, such policies can help to establish accepting and cooperative attitudes on the part of employees toward the new data processing center, to alleviate feelings of uneasiness and job insecurity among employees, and to eliminate negative rumors and other reactions which might have an adverse effect upon employee morale.

The following factors should be important considerations in the development of these policies:

1. A relatively large number of people in an educational organization handle input data and have a hand in preparing it for processing. The failure of anyone to carry out his part of the operation can hinder or destroy the advantages being sought from the system. Thus it becomes of para-

1. Acknowledgement is made to the California Association of Public School Business Officials for permission to use sections of the 1963 *Data Processing Handbook* in this and the following chapter.

mount importance to develop in all employees a willingness to cooperate and a knowledge of what needs to be done.

2. Use of data processing in certain applications (e.g., mark reporting) represents a radical shift in methods that have been used for years, in some cases for decades, by the teachers or other personnel involved. It is not surprising that a certain amount of resistance to this change should develop, particularly if there are accompanying fears about loss of jobs or the machines taking over the teachers' traditional functions.

3. Any loss of morale, even though temporary, on the part of teachers could have a negative effect on the educational program as a whole.

4. For a large proportion of the people involved handling data is a secondary function. Their main interest and training lie in other directions.

5. In some cases the introduction of data processing carries an impact on related functions in other aspects of the school's program. It is not surprising that misunderstandings and even opposition could arise.

6. Fiscal procedures have direct implications for the accounting department, as do educational applications for school secretaries, attendance personnel, and other clerical staff. Any policy statement must consider possible fears of both groups since each will have knowledge of other districts which utilize combinations of both types of applications.

7. Advance planning may indicate a definite displacement of one or more individuals. The possible use of their skills either within the data center or, with appropriate in-service training, in some other position of equal or better status should be given a great deal of consideration. Usually, an intimate "member-of-the-family" type of relationship exists among the staff members of any school district. Failure to consider the feelings of individuals even slightly affected by the anticipated changes, can arouse widespread resentment and distrust which could linger long after the reassigned personnel are engrossed in new duties. While such resentment may be completely masked by compliant outward behavior, there are many ways in which it can hamper or even destroy the effectiveness of the service which a data center can provide.

9. School involvement should receive high priority in the preliminary planning of specific applications. Such involvement of the appropriate individuals who will either supply source documents for the data center or utilize the end-products from the center, will be needed to accomplish a number of valuable services.

COMMUNICATIONS WITH PERSONNEL

Once a clear and workable set of policies has been established, it is necessary to provide for the development within the organization of an atmosphere that is conducive to acceptance of change. Equally important is the need to establish and maintain good relationships between the data processing installation and the non-operating personnel of the district.

This dual goal can be achieved by establishing two vital links in the organizational chain, (1) a workable system of communicating with the personnel involved and (2) an effective in-service training program for non-operating personnel.

PROVIDING FOR AN ATMOSPHERE OF CHANGE

If good communications with personnel are to be established, it is essential that a climate be developed that encourages a free flow of ideas in each direction. In short, there must be a willingness to communicate and the freedom to do so. Personnel should feel free to make suggestions or requests and report errors or shortcomings without fear of "sticking their necks out" in an area in which they are relatively inexpert. Even though this kind of free exchange may produce many trivial or absurd suggestions, it helps the data processing staff to acquire a picture of the district's needs and it could be a source of valuable ideas. Without this kind of climate, the data processing staff may never become aware of certain ways in which the data processing installation could more effectively help the district. It is axiomatic that the data center staff members be receptive and cooperative in the manner in which they receive and discuss suggestions from non-operating personnel.

The attitudes of non-operating personnel can be strongly influenced by their contacts with staff members of the data processing center. In view of the rumors that can get started and the fears which personnel frequently demonstrate when a major change is about to be introduced, it is important that non-operating personnel be taken into confidence as soon as possible. The initial announcement concerning the installation can serve a vital role in creating a desirable climate among the personnel.

Before that initial announcement is made to the general public, however, the chief school officer should announce to the district staff the decision to install a data processing system. One suggested method of handling this announcement is through a letter from the superintendent to each employee. This letter should include the following:

1. Announcement of basic facts (e.g., estimated date of installation).
2. A brief statement of personnel policy to ease fears concerning loss of jobs by clerical employees or undue interference in teaching functions.
3. A brief summary of what the district hopes to gain by conversion to machine processing.
4. Invitation to participate in planning and making suggestions concerning procedures and end-products after conversion to data processing.

MEANS OF COMMUNICATION

In addition to establishing a favorable climate, it is necessary to establish channels of communication in both directions. The chief school administrator, and other members of his staff, must take the lead in this area. Here are some techniques:

1. Establish liaison with a representative from each school and/or department using data processing. These representatives, collectively or individually, could serve as a means of transmitting instructions, announcements, and suggestions in both directions. They could also supervise the use of data processing procedures in their respective units. The representatives selected should have sufficient status to get the job done. They must have initiative, familiarity with the district, ability to get along with others, and flexibility toward new ideas. Collectively they can assist in planning, evaluating, and drawing up new applications.
2. Regular forms should be provided for specific functions, such as the establishment of schedules, requests for special services, suggestions, notation of error, and evaluation of specific services.
3. Memos can be issued, as needed, announcing new applications, explaining procedures, or scheduling projects and work assignments.
4. Communication with personnel should include a conscientious follow-up of new services to determine personnel reaction, evaluation, and suggestions for improvement.
5. All requests regarding new or special services from non-operating personnel should be channeled through the head of the data processing installation. It is important that non-operating personnel be kept from making such requests of operating personnel in the data center, and it is equally important that operating personnel not make commitments, or change schedules or procedures, without the knowledge of the head of the data processing installation.
6. Consideration should be given to the establishment of special committees for major jobs or areas (e.g., attendance, budget, or report cards).
7. After the decisions regarding applications and their sequence have been made and the policy regarding personnel utilization determined, this information should be communicated to the total staff of the district. Meetings called for that purpose should be conducted by an individual who has the respect and trust of the staff. It may also be necessary to utilize, in a liaison function, those members of the district data processing committee who can carry the message with conviction and sincerity. Explanation of the benefits to be gained must be couched in terms which leave no doubt of the direct benefits which will accrue to the school personnel.

IN-SERVICE TRAINING OF NON-OPERATING PERSONNEL

The initial announcement and other preliminary steps, if properly carried out, will help to create the proper atmosphere in the organization and to establish the necessary communications patterns. A great deal more is needed, however, to insure the efficient operation of the new data processing system.

In any change as important as the conversion to machine data processing the initial experience with the new system can have a very strong influence on subsequent attitudes toward the system. Thus it becomes imperative that personnel be given the necessary training to make the initial experience as successful as possible. Further provision should be made for training new employees and for continuous in-service training as needs arise.

The training program cannot be left to chance. It calls for definite planning and, particularly in the initial phase, for a definite schedule. Since scheduling must vary to suit the needs of the district, no effort will be made here to define a schedule that would be applicable to all. The following suggestions represent the basic steps to be covered when developing a schedule to suit a district's needs:

A. Hold general orientation sessions for:

1. *Heads of administrative departments, principals, and counselors*—the first round of orientation sessions should be held for this group. While many of these people will not be dealing directly with input data, their support can be an important asset when it comes to dealing with other personnel.

2. *Faculty or department staff*—these sessions can be held as either large or small group meetings.

3. *Clerical personnel*—at least two people in each department and/or school should be familiar with their respective applications. This training can be handled on an individual basis if desired.

These sessions should include an overview of the entire application being studied as well as closer scrutiny of those aspects with which the personnel in the session are most concerned. Every effort should be made to instill an awareness in each person of his importance in the total data processing operation.

Liberal use of audio-visual aids and/or sample materials can be effective at these sessions. Ample opportunities should be allowed for questions and suggestions concerning the future.

B. Distribute attractively designed brochures which describe the following:

1. Basic philosophy of the district with respect to data processing.
2. Purposes and use of data processing—what the districts hope to gain.
3. General description of the various applications to be handled by machine data processing. These should not be complete technical descriptions. Rather they should be written in terms readily understood by laymen.

SELECTION OF OPERATING PERSONNEL

In recruiting technical personnel for a data processing installation one must never lose sight of the limitations imposed on an installation by the quality of the personnel selected. Most new employees will be unacquainted with school work. This is a severe limitation, and poses a problem in seeking to determine equipment requirements. Machine complexity may actually have to be held down so that the uninitiated personnel will have a chance to learn more about educational applications and procedures. Generally speaking, the most successful installations have begun by tackling one job at a time, and only when that job has become relatively routine does the next begin. Progress under this regime will necessarily be relatively slow at the beginning.

SELECTION OF A DIRECTOR OF INFORMATION SYSTEMS

After the decision has been made to install an automated information processing system, the most important step to be taken is the selection of a staff member who will become the leader of this installation—the director of information systems.

During the feasibility study phase, it was quite appropriate for the superintendent or his assistant to serve as chairman and to take a position of leadership in determining whether or not the district's information system needed modernizing and whether data processing hardware could be of value.

Now, however, a specialist in the field is needed to take over the operational aspects of the information processing system. Depending on the size of the district, he might be an assistant superintendent who is charged with the overall responsibility for seeing that information is where it should be on time, or he might be someone on the director's level who reports directly to the superintendent. In either case, it is vital that the table of organization reflect the uniqueness of the position. It should show that the director reports directly to the individual who oversees all facets of the total educational program—the superintendent. Some may doubt the need for this top level involvement, but it is vital for an efficient operation. Consider the decisions that will have to be made as the information system is activated in the various operational areas of the district. Who decides on a process—and its priority—when the heads of the business, instructional personnel, pupil personnel, research and administrative divisions converge on the processing center? It must be someone who has great skill and ability plus the authority to make decisions.

Also consider the fact that the director, in addition to having the ability to organize, prepare, and make meaningful presentations to administration and school boards, must have the authority to command their respect. With him rests the responsibility for obtaining approval for needed innovations and for overcoming entrenched interests and natural resistance to change. The position should carry with it the administrative authority to speak for the district.

The man to whom such authority is entrusted must be first and foremost, an educator—not a technician—and one with considerable experience in the overall field of education. Rarely have technicians succeeded in this position because they are oriented to the problems of business and industry and have neither an understanding nor an appreciation of the approach that school systems specifically must take to problems.

However, he must also have some training in the technical aspects of data processing, although it need not be extensive "hands on" experience. The technical competence of the director should be sufficient to enable him to understand the technical processes and the mechanical shortcomings of the equipment installation. Without this knowledge he will be at the mercy of his technical staff and will be unable to converse intelligently either with the machine operators or the educators about technical problems.

In an earlier section it was pointed out that a system is composed of the people in a district who generate, use, and collect information, and the ways in which it is generated, used, and collected—including any machines that have a bearing on the process. While it is possible to divorce machines from the system, it is completely impossible to divorce people from it. The automated system represents the interaction of the man and the machine in a logical sequence. The result of these interactions is what is unique. The director must have a fine sense of balance and be able to understand and convey to others the feeling that the system is more than the total of the individual segments. In short, the director of information systems must be an educator. He must know systems; he must know people. He must be able to work with both. He must be creative but prudent. He must be able to stand up under pressure.

Few people have the combination of qualities required of a director. Typically the position is compromised by selecting an existing staff member, exposing him to a limited amount of training, and putting him in charge of the previously established installation. This often leads to chaos.

Remember the Dutch boy who plugged the hole in the dike with his finger? Well imagine that he was commissioned to repair the dike. He knew that something had to be done, but because he had his hands full he was not able to do more than just stand there. The educator who does not have a clear conception of the importance or magnitude of an information system, much less an understanding of the tremendous possibility of machines in the system, may not be able to perform any better than the boy.

The work load of the director will not be as regular as that of a classroom teacher or a regular school administrator; consequently, his assignment should be on an eleven- or twelve-month basis. The job may demand that he work nights, Saturdays, and holidays, and this need be recognized and accepted as part of the director's responsibility.

TECHNICAL PERSONNEL REQUIREMENTS

Staff needs generally follow a typical pattern. There will, of course, be need for a manager of the data processing installation, that is, the man who actually is in charge of running the machines. Depending on the size of the school district, there will be need for machine operators, programmers, keypunch operators, systems analysts, and clerical help.

Data processing personnel should, of course, be people of considerable general intelligence. In addition, however, they should also possess certain specific aptitudes. The measurement of these aptitudes may to some extent be accomplished with the aid of an aptitude test which data processing equipment manufacturers will supply on request. Grades obtained by those taking these tests have proved to be related to subsequent success in the data processing field.

Other equally important qualities also merit consideration. Among these are the experience and past performance of the individual being considered, his educational qualifications, his interest in data processing, and his knowledge of those areas of education being considered for data processing applications.[2]

It must be noted that many persons have entered the data processing field because it is a growing and dynamic one. Some of these are competent; others are not. The competent ones are employed steadily and have no problem in handling their assignments. In order to obtain and retain competent personnel it is necessary to offer adequate compensation. In this case schools are competing with business and industry. Schools generally have salary schedules which do not compare favorably with those in business. Consequently, schools must either raise salaries so that they are competitive, or suffer the burden of a quick turnover, or face the risk of not finding competent staff members. Any of these courses may be expensive,

2. In selecting data processing personnel, the publication *Occupational Outlook Handbook,* prepared by the Bureau of Labor Statistics, 1963-64 edition, describes many occupations in the field of data processing. It is available through the United States Government Printing Office, Washington, D.C.

but in the long run it is less expensive to pay staff members an adequate salary than to train new ones at frequent intervals. It is also quite difficult to maintain the type of production necessary for an on-going system when staff members are constantly leaving and new members are in the process of being trained to work in the system.

Schools are very sensitive about the problem of salaries. Most districts have schedules which are extremely rigid. Few schedules reflect appropriate classifications in this new field of information processing.

The technicians usually are classified on a par with clerical personnel, which is unrealistic in terms of comparable positions in industry. Workers in the field of data processing, who can command relatively high salaries in industry, are unlikely to succumb to the lure of job security which is offered by school employment, often in lieu of a competitive income.

This places school districts in a position to do one of two things—raise salaries and risk criticism from other classified employees, or train existing workers to do the work required. Schools are in business to teach, so lower salaries can be justified in terms of skills learned. This usually is a losing proposition, because once a person is trained to perform these new skills, he is in a position to go elsewhere and earn more money, and he usually does. The districts must then start the training process over, with the same end result. In the long run it is less costly and more productive to pay the technical staff the necessary amount to assure some continuity of production. This also will provide a better operating system that will automatically advance the cause of the district significantly. Schools and automation are new allies, and much will happen in the next few years. Districts with a firm foundation will be able to advance faster and further than those that attempt to put together a makeshift system.

MANAGER OF DATA PROCESSING

Equal in importance to the director of information processing systems is the data processing manager. A description of this job will be found in Appendix I. The manager should be selected early in the conversion process. He should be hired, however, after the director of the information processing system.

Securing a key person for this role can insure the success of this vital installation. The district should secure a manager who is trained and experienced in business applications. The knowledge of educational functions required of a manager can be given on the job by the director during the planning and development stages. The district would be very fortunate but unlikely to find an individual with the unique combination of business and educational applications experience, since the latter is so new to the general field of data processing.

One of the major tasks of the data processing manager will be to see that the machines are operating efficiently and that they are well integrated with the information system that has been developed. He is the technical expert that the educators will call upon to answer the more complex and sticky questions. His experience must be broad and general in the field of data processing, and he must be one who is able to relate this experience so that others may understand and have confidence in what he says. In addition to several years as an operator and supervisor of machine installations, his experience must also include some systems analysis. This is the man that will actually take the information that is generated from the analysis of the information needs of the districts and plan the logical interrelated flow to accomplish the total data processing mission. He will be in a position to offer many valuable suggestions in the collection of the data and the projection of time and cost figures.

Since the responsibility for successful production within the data processing center rests with him, and since such success depends not only on satisfactory equipment and efficient procedures, but also on the ability of the machine operator to understand the procedures and make correct and efficient use of the machines, the manager must be able to evaluate personnel. It will be part of his job to review the available personnel and determine the extent to which employees must be brought in from the outside. Personnel, of course, must be evaluated objectively, but the manager's opinion should be given primary consideration.

ADDITIONAL TECHNICAL STAFF

Depending upon the complexity of the data processing installation, such personnel as programmers, tabulating machine operators, systems analysts, and keypunch operators need to be employed. A programmer is not necessary in a punch card installation, while a systems analyst may or may not have a place in such an installation. Both are necessary in a computer installation.

There are several factors that come into play in determining the availability of such employees. If the equipment is relatively complex, it may be necessary to advertise over a wide area to obtain the necessary skills and experience. If the labor supply does not provide these types of employees, this fact should be determined far enough in advance so that plans may be made for sending personnel already employed to the manufacturer's school for the necessary training in the use of the equipment.

Even though optimum conditions exist which assure an adequate number of trained and experienced machine operators, the manager should not be denied the option of hiring needed personnel before procedures are scheduled for production. Certain large volume procedures may be similar to fiscal operations in the business world, thereby allowing an experienced machine operator to achieve relatively high speed within a short time.

School districts, on the other hand, generally have a variety of small volume fiscal jobs. Also, educational procedures used in student accounting are often sufficiently different to present a marked departure from the machine operator experience elsewhere. These new employees, therefore, should be scheduled for placement on the job well in advance of the critical production stages, so that they obtain the familiarity, proficiency, speed and accuracy required of the procedure when it goes into full operation.

It seems to be characteristic of people generally to remember one failure while forgetting a thousand successes. Failure to provide in the employment schedule for placement of new employees on the job in advance of the time of critical need can cause deadlines to be missed and delivery to be delayed. This can set an undesirable tone among district employees outside the data processing center. They have little opportunity to know the reasons for such failure to deliver as promised. Once successful delivery has taken place and adherence to the promised schedule has been established over a period of time, a point will have been made—namely, that the data processing personnel can do their part. Temporary delays at some future time will have less impact after a favorable impression has been established.

After the installation has been functioning for some time and additional procedures are added, there undoubtedly will be refinements made in the type of equipment to be used for the new workload. Since the new equipment carries with it the implications that additional personnel with a greater degree of competency will be needed, the district will wish to consider two possible paths. First, they may obtain the new employees with these additional skills from the outside and maintain their present personnel at their assigned duties; second, they may consider the possibility of additional training at the manufacturer's school for interested personnel within the present staff. If the capacity to learn the new techniques exists within the present staff, the district might well be advised to choose the second alternative. Promotion from within has obvious morale benefits. It also allows the district to seek less skilled employees to fill positions left vacant by such upgrading.

Job descriptions of the various technical positions will be found in Appendix I.

TRAINING OF OPERATING PERSONNEL

Education in the field of data processing is imperative when considering installation of equipment. In the first place, the administrators responsible for making the decision to install a data processing system must be able to evaluate its effects on the district. Most data processing manufacturers offer courses at the executive level so that such evaluation may be properly made.

A more extensive education program is required after the decision to install a data processing system is made. These classes will consist of detailed training on specific data processing systems for persons who will perform such duties as board wiring, systems analysis, programming, and operations functions.

You can generally count on the manufacturer's representatives to assist you throughout your period of preparation. As your application procedure and wiring or programming efforts move forward, your personnel should become increasingly proficient. Most of your technically trained people will require additional schooling. The equipment manufacturer has a major responsibility to supply the needed training.

Periodic in-service training should be scheduled for all staff members to review procedures being used. This will provide an opportunity for feedback and evaluation, as well as an opportunity to make the staff aware of any new or changed conditions within the appropriate procedures.

7

MOVING TO THE AUTOMATED SYSTEM: EQUIPMENT AND IMPLEMENTATION

At this time we turn our attention to the selection of equipment. Until we have settled upon the configuration needed to serve our needs we can do little more planning.

A few words of caution are in order at this point. Once you have made public your decision to move ahead you will be approached by sales personnel from a variety of hardware manufacturers. Each will have a specific proposal to make and most will tell you their equipment can do whatever task you wish to undertake. Much of what they say is true. However, it is wise to weigh carefully all information and advertising literature. In fact, this would be an excellent time to invest your money wisely and obtain the help of a reputable EDP consulting firm—or even better, a consultant who knows both schools and hardware.

It is important to realize that there are many stumbling blocks in connection with choosing the right equipment for specific data processing applications. Although each application may be different, numerous applications can be made with multipurpose machines if appropriate equipment and proper systems procedures are employed.

It should be a cardinal principle that the progress needs of the educational system should dictate the kind of equipment to be used, rather than equipment availability dictating the kind of system or program that should be developed. In many instances, data processing procedures have been designed to fit the equipment on hand. Better practice dictates that the system be designed according to the needs of a school district and only then the needed equipment be secured.

When the decision to order data processing equipment has been made, a study should be initiated of all the available equipment in the approximate range of the expected installation. Several factors must be considered in making this determination. Immediate machine requirements must never overshadow potential machine requirements. The decision to use one type of equipment, which serves short-term needs, may, in the long run, be expensive and damaging when growing program requirements force the discarding of that equipment and the acquisition of new equipment with greater capacity. This situation may lead to excessive and too frequent changes in clerical tasks supporting the installation, to employee demoralization, and, ultimately, may be damaging to the entire system. This should not serve to restrict normal growth, but merely to point out that growth must be anticipated and planned for well in advance.

During the systems analysis phase of the study, a count was made of the approximate number of items to be processed. Having determined this, it now becomes important to refer to this information to help determine peakloads at various periods of time. Once this determination has been made, the processing speed of each piece of equipment being considered should be evaluated to determine whether they have the basic capacity to handle the anticipated volume. Consideration must be given anticipated growth to a point where no further expansion of equipment is desirable. The installation must not be overloaded before it has a chance to develop efficient operating procedures, and before the investment in wiring or programming for the initial equipment has been recovered, at least to the point where it is possible to justify changing to more advanced equipment requiring rewiring or reprogramming.

In school districts, the character of the work performed plays a large part in determining peakloads to be processed, and hence the requirements for equipment to handle such peakloads. For example, if only financial accounting is to be performed in the early years of installation, work will be at a relatively even pace and deadlines sufficiently flexible to allow a modest installation, with the understanding that work may be somewhat delayed at the few peak periods of the year. If educational data, such as report cards, are to be processed, the relatively large volumes and the urgency of deadlines may indicate that a larger installation with faster machines is required for this one application. It is obvious that all applications would benefit accordingly since additional applications which had been determined during the systems design phase could then be activated to fill otherwise unused capacity.

EQUIPMENT EVALUATION AND SELECTION[1]

We have reached the point now where we wish to solicit equipment proposals. We know full well that the system may ultimately be modified after we select our equipment (to take advantage of individual equipment characteristics), but the system described in a proposal request should be one that would work successfully if installed as stated.

This section is divided into four parts: (1) a request for proposals; (2) analysis of bidders' proposals; (3) comparison of bidders' proposals; and (4) deciding on a particular proposal.

1. From *A Data Processing System for State and Local Governments,* Edward F. R. Hearle and Raymond J. Mason. Prentice-Hall, 1963.

THE REQUEST FOR PROPOSALS

To obtain meaningful proposals from manufacturers, the request for proposals must be meaningfully put. This means that the problems they will be asked to solve will be clearly defined.

A system should be described to prospective bidders in terms of its desired results. The systems study determined that certain inputs and outputs were necessary and that certain items were to be kept in files. A systems description should specify in detail these required inputs, outputs, and files. It should also state precisely how the outputs are obtained from the input and file items so that the bidders can determine the amount of processing and computing involved. Usually, a series of simple flow charts can describe the relationship among inputs, files, and outputs.

In these charts, the system must be divided arbitrarily into equipment processing procedures or runs, only for the purpose of describing the problem and indicating a possible solution. The bidders must understand that they are free to rearrange the runs as they see fit, by combining runs or dividing single runs into several different ones. The only restriction is that their solutions must produce the required outputs from the indicated inputs and file items. Since bidders' personnel usually have considerable systems experience and are often able to contribute new ideas for solving the problems, requests for proposals should try to avoid rigid restrictions on the input and output formats, and especially on the file configuration.

In addition to flow charts, a brief narrative describing each application and what it accomplishes should be included. Such a description gives a useful overall picture of the total problem area.

In describing each input, output, and file in the request for proposals, the following points should be included for each document in file:

Input Documents

1. Purpose of the document: how it is originated and what it accomplishes in the processing.
2. Description of each information item (field) on the document.
3. Maximum length, average length, and percentage of use of each item.
4. Maximum and average number of characters per document.
5. Maximum and average number of such documents per time period.
6. Any special information pertaining to the document.

Output Documents

1. Purpose of the document.

2. Description of each information item on the document.
3. Maximum length, average length, and percentage of use of each information item.
4. Maximum and average number of characters per document.
5. Maximum and average number of records per document (when a document consists of many records, such as a tabulated listing).
6. Maximum and average number of documents per time period.
7. Exact format of the document, whenever no deviation can be accepted. If a specific format must be adhered to, the format must be shown. The exact size of the form, the number of lines of printing, and the number of blank lines must be shown. This information is important for the timing of printing operations.
8. Time requirements.
9. Any special information pertaining to the document, such as time deadlines.

Files

1. Description of each information item in the file.
2. Maximum and average length of each information item in the file.
3. Maximum and average number of records per file.

Bidders must be cautioned to solve the problem given, so that in comparing proposals any differences in equipment, timing, etc., will not be due to dissimilarities in the problems solved. After a particular bidder's equipment has been selected, the problem will no doubt be changed considerably before actual operations begin in order to take advantage of the unique features of the equipment configuration selected. However, these changes should not be seriously considered until the proposals have been compared for the solution to the particular problem as originally specified.

Bidders should be told to inquire immediately if they have any doubts about the system. They can thus avoid submitting unacceptable solutions due to misunderstanding. The bidder, not the customer, is responsible for the acceptability of the bid.

The request for proposals should state whether equipment is to be in use 100 per cent of the time, or whether a certain amount of free time is desired for possible future expansion of applications. If free time is desired, the amount must be specified. Depending on the type of equipment proposed, the desired amount of expansion can sometimes be provided with little idle time at the outset by adding various components as needed in a modular, or building-block, fashion. In any case, the manufacturer should be told what percentage of the total applications is represented in the request for proposals.

ANALYSIS OF BIDDERS' PROPOSALS

In studying the bidders' proposals a careful analysis should be made of the several different aspects of each bid. First, the systems submitted must satisfy the requirements for inputs, outputs, and files, and hence be comparable. If the bids do not satisfy the given requirements, they must be returned to the bidder for adjustment. Then, the proposed systems must be studied thoroughly to determine whether they will work.

School districts, as was pointed out earlier, would be wise to consider retaining consultants for verifying the proposals. The time requirements of the machines given in the proposal will have to be checked for accuracy. It should not be expected that timing will be accurate to the millisecond at this stage, since the number and types of program steps required in all cases will necessarily be estimates. Ascertaining the actual time required can be done only when a problem is programmed and run on a particular machine.

Is the equipment adequate to do the job in the time specified? The answer, of course, is determined when the timing estimates are verified. Any serious timing errors can necessitate an adjustment in equipment complement and a resulting adjustment in price.

The proposals should indicate the checking devices that will be employed to insure accuracy of processing. This is especially important when a new or different technique is being proposed and the method of control is not apparent. In most cases, however, if the method of checking is not shown, it is probably one that can be adapted to generally accepted techniques. Care must be taken to determine if all parts of the system are adequately controlled by either stated or implied methods.

If automatic programming languages have been proposed, they should be investigated. If such languages are in use, it is advisable to ask a user how successful they have been. If the languages are not yet in use, a talk with the bidder's programming personnel may help in determining the details of the programming languages and when they will be debugged and ready for use.

If it is expected that a great many applications will be added to the system in the next few years, the equipment's amenability to modular expansions is important. One should probably not plan modular expansions further ahead than five years because the technology is changing so rapidly that in that time a completely new type of hardware is likely to be on the market.

The ability to remove units from the proposed equipment complement is also important. If the proposed complement includes idle time for possible expansion, then the ability to reduce the hardware system to the minimum size to accomplish the immediate work, and subsequently to add to it as expansion of applications requires, can mean a large saving during the period of the initial system installation.

Finally, the reliability of the manufacturer must be investigated. Will he deliver on time? Does he service the machines adequately?

If the equipment recommended by a manufacturer has been successfully used, there is probably little question that it will arrive on the proposed delivery date. However, if the equipment is new and untried, a visit to the manufacturer may be necessary to determine if the quoted delivery date is reasonable in view of the evident progress. In addition, if possible, it is advantageous to consult former customers to determine the manufacturer's past reliability in meeting quoted delivery dates.

Customer service is as important as the equipment itself. A good piece of equipment can be almost useless, especially to an inexperienced user, if the manufacturer does not give adequate service. This service must include the training of customer personnel to program the equipment and to use it effectively, the issuance of up-to-date programming aids and manuals, and the assignment of manufacturer personnel to work closely with the customer to give aid and advice in both systems analysis and programming. Customer service can best be assessed by asking present customers of the manufacturer how satisfied they are with the service provided. It is wise also to try to evaluate whether your informant is overly biased for or against the manufacturer.

If the applications being considered have to be carried out within a certain time limit, the availability of an emergency "backup" machine must be considered. If the manufacturer has one in the area, there probably will be no problem in using it. However, if the use of another customer's machine is contemplated, an agreement should be obtained before the bidder's proposal is accepted.

COMPARISON OF BIDDERS' PROPOSALS

The following are points to be kept in mind in comparing proposals. This discussion assumes that proposals have been analyzed individually and that more than one proposal could do the work satisfactorily.

There is a tendency to judge proposals by comparing the individual characteristics of the hardware. This method of comparison is usually meaningless since, in the separate analysis of the proposal, these separate characteristics of the machines were considered together as a total equipment system which had the capability to solve a complete system problem in acceptable time. Once this is done, there is no reason to compare machines for size of memory, density of tape, speed of tape units, arithmetic speeds, printer speeds, etc. These characteristics are important, but only as they function as a complete system to solve the problem; taken by themselves they are unimportant. In fact, almost any equipment system may have a particular application which is more efficient than other equipment systems—even though its characteristics may not sound impressive when considered separately.

Conversely, machine characteristics that a manufacturer regards as advantages may actually be disadvantages in certain applications. Very few "advantages" are universal. Some printers, for example, rated at a speed of up to four times that of other printers, cannot print certain types of forms as fast as their slower counterparts. Such printers are faster only if their characteristics can be used to advantage in the applications concerned. In summary, the only true test is to compare complete hardware systems designed for a specific application or group of applications.

In comparing proposals, care must be taken to insure that they are intended to accomplish the same work computations, inputs, outputs, key punching, verifying, etc. If they are not, the bids should be adjusted in respect to equipment (and price) so that they are comparable.

DECIDING ON A PARTICULAR PROPOSAL

You should now have before you several comparable bids. One or more proposals can usually be eliminated at once as being entirely inferior to the others. The remaining proposals will have many features such as air conditioning and space that are essentially the same for all. These features can be ignored.

As for the major features, you as the user must decide which ones are the most important. If cost overrides all else, you will select the cheapest system regardless of other features (since it has been established that any of them will do the job). However, other factors, such as promised delivery date, expected service, reports of users of similar equipment, availability of an emergency machine, or individual equipment characteristics may be more important than cost. Other concerns are important to the user but, as a rule, they are not vital enough to influence his decision on whether to accept a proposal. The costs they represent are usually about the same for the various proposals. Only if two or more proposals are nearly equal in every other respect might conditions as these become a determining factor: (1) space and air-conditioning requirements, (2) installation costs, (3) manufacturer's definition of a shift and the method of charging for premium time and downtime, (4) free machine time for program testing.

In short, there are no absolute and universal criteria. The true purpose of the evaluation is to make all the factors and alternatives known to those persons responsible for making the final decision so that they accurately understand the alternatives and actually make the decisions they think they are making. Once this decision has been made, the implementation phase begins.

APPOINTMENT OF A DATA PROCESSING COMMITTEE

The members of the systems study team may continue in their roles under the new guise of a data processing committee. These personnel should function at the staff level. It has been evident from a series of experiences that staff personnel are likely to approach procedures problems with more detachment than are operating personnel. If they neither perform nor supervise the operation being studied, there is less chance that their thinking about the problem on hand will be inhibited by tradition, habit, or personal incentive.

As a result of their systems analysis and work in systems design, the team should have developed extensive knowledge about machines and clerical procedures. They also should have had the opportunity of developing a working knowledge of forms design, principles, and techniques. Their knowledge of the specialized techniques for gathering, organizing, and analyzing data tend to assure that the additional studies they will be called upon to do will be carried out in an efficient manner.

A major outgrowth of this committee's work will be the development of a master file of needed information. It will consist of all of the data needed to operate the information processing system (IPS).

The establishment of a master file is a basic objective of the IPS, and many groups have worked on it. The master file of the Research and Development Center of the California State Department of Education is shown in Appendix III. Other agencies—including the U.S. Office of Education in conjunction with many of the national professional organizations—have also developed files.[2]

DECISIONS REGARDING PROCEDURES

The data processing committee should draw up a list of procedures delineating the scope of the committee's responsibilities. This can be regarded as a statement of its long-range objectives.

Two ingredients are essential to the conduct of the procedures research. They are: (a) policies and objectives that reflect a general recognition among key administrators and the governing board that the study is a continuing activity and (b) a sound plan of organization for carrying on the work. Within this framework the action must take place. It is suggested that the approach be built around the following sequence:

1. Study *procedures* or flow-of-work, not jobs. The basic purpose of most procedures is to co-ordinate effort in order to facilitate action and achieve control. Procedures are but a means to an end.

2. *Pupil Accounting For Local & State School Systems.* U.S. Department of Health, Education, and Welfare. 1964, Washington, D.C.

2. Determine whether the *purpose* or *objective* of the procedure is effective in terms of the desired end to be achieved before giving attention to the intrinsic cost of the means.

3. In seeking opportunities to cut costs or improve performance, analyze the basic *functions* performed before studying individual operations. The purpose of analyzing functions is to determine whether (a) each function is actually necessary, and (b) whether any essential functions can be performed in a basically different, improved, or less expensive way. The test is whether the benefit produced is greater than its cost.

4. By far the most important consideration in any application of data processing is the possibility of producing information not previously available. For instance, by introducing small amounts of additional data in processing associated with standard report card practices, it may be possible to prepare an analysis of student marks which might prove valuable to the staff in curriculum planning.

5. With a similar objective, reports currently prepared for administration should be studied to determine possibilities for further analyzing, summarizing, or recapping data to produce information tailored more precisely to the manner in which it will be used. Detailed listing should also be reviewed to determine the feasibility of listing only items of specific interest or items requiring action.

6. Analyze the *external factors affecting volume of work or complexity* of the procedure. Excessively involved routines should be examined in terms of the basic requirements or policies which the routine intends to satisfy. Excessive complexity may be due to a lack of well defined policies or a laxness in enforcing policies. Reappraisal and modification should be made in the light of the skill and experience of the work force and the cost of perfection to the "nth" degree.

7. Then finally, analyze *individual operations* and the methods by which they are performed. A procedures study should probe for causes, not merely treat effects. Recommendations should reflect practical appreciation of the job to be done and the personnel resources to do it. There is a danger in assuming that the tighter or the more encompassing the controls, the better will be the end result produced. It is as easy to err on the side of developing an unnecessarily precise, and therefore, a wastefully expensive control as it is to develop an inadequate, makeshift one. Developmental efforts should be aimed at creating a simple, workable procedure as distinct from a perfect one.

DECIDING ON APPLICATION SEQUENCES

The director and the district committee now must decide on the sequence in which the applications are to be phased into operation. One of the initial decisions is whether educational applications are to be introduced in the beginning or deferred until later since, as was indicated earlier, the machine requirements and staffing ratios are larger for educational than for financial applications within any given district.

Special conditions in the local situation must be given careful consideration when the sequence of initiating applications is determined. Local factors might not be in harmony with what otherwise might be considered an "ideal sequence." For example, a theoretically desirable sequence might place the payroll application first, whereas the local conditions in a given district might indicate that report cards should be given priority. The latter could be causing difficulties whereas the current payroll could already be functioning satisfactorily. In some districts it might be advisable to override local factors, but they should at least be considered in making decisions concerning the sequence in which applications are initiated.

The current level of employees also should be considered in determining the sequence of beginning applications. If the employees are relatively inexperienced with the type of operations being undertaken, it might be well to start with simple applications and work toward more complex operations. A crew could thus be prepared for the more involved operations while working on the easier jobs.

ESTABLISH THE MASTER SCHEDULE

A critical function in planning and controlling progress is the assignment of personnel to the various pre-installation activities. It is virtually impossible to set a rule of thumb to determine the amount of manpower that will be required to co-ordinate and implement a total data processing system.

The number of people required will depend on the complexity of the applications, caliber of personnel, and the previous method of doing the job. Some large systems have been inaugurated with staffs ranging from five to eighty-five people. On the other hand, some systems have required only from two to five people. Only by evaluating the particular circumstances, can a usable estimate of personnel requirements be evolved.

After thorough planning, dates can be established which will give district administrative personnel the information required to determine alternate district policy with respect to allocation of budget, authorization to employ personnel, and placement of orders for equipment and supplies. Establishment of a systematized schedule will permit a determination of the status of the developments in relation to the progress needed to meet the established completion date.

For our purposes, a schedule is designed to co-ordinate and implement the total program as it relates to the planning, equipment, and personnel needs required to initiate data processing in a school district not previously automated.

PHYSICAL PLANT PLANNING AND SCHEDULING

One of the earliest decisions which must be made in connection with pre-installation planning is the decision regarding the site of the installation. A good many considerations may enter into the making of this decision. Initially, the availability of some particular area may recommend it for consideration. Possibly its suitability as a show place will be relevant.

One important consideration is the extent to which a site may facilitate or hamper the integration of the data processing system with operations which are related to it. Thus, for example, it is necessary to make arrangements for the most efficient delivery or transmission of input information and for the proper disposition of output information.

Over and above such matters as these are the technical problems of physical planning. A good solution to these problems is important to a successful installation. Attention must be given to such factors as entrances and exits, the type of floor and ceiling, the walls (and viewing area they allow), electrical power requirements, air conditioning, etc.

In dealing with these problems, accurate and current information is essential. The engineering personnel of all data processing equipment manufacturers will, if requested, advise and assist customers regarding any problem relative to physical installation.

It is necessary to start preparation of the data processing system site early so as to allow enough time for its completion before the system is delivered. It should be made certain that contractors understand thoroughly all the requirements and specifications for the physical installation of the data processing system. Floors must be strong enough to support the equipment as it is moved. Needless to say, door width, corridor width, and elevators must be sufficient to enable equipment to be moved.

The cost of physical installations depends on many factors—but mostly, on how elaborate or how basic a site is desired by the district. When the layout of the site is final and approved, the lengths of the electrical cables interconnecting the system components should be determined from an accurate scale drawing of the room. The ordering of cables must be done within a specified period of time before scheduled delivery of the system. This time period varies depending on the system being installed.

In addition to readying the chosen site and ordering the equipment, attention should possibly be given to the question of the necessary supplies and peripheral equipment. The designing and ordering of printed forms and cards should be completed early enough to assure that they will be available in time. Also included should be the internal control forms to be used in conjunction with the data processing system for control and scheduling functions. If the system is to use magnetic tapes, the tapes should be ordered early enough for use when the system is installed.

In punch card installations, the necessary control panels must be ordered. This must be done with sufficient lead time to allow wiring of the panels. Other supplies that probably will be needed are files and storage cabinets for printed forms, punch cards, and carts for moving this material into and out of the data processing area. Communications equipment, desks, chairs, and work tables may also be needed.

ESTABLISHING A DELIVERY SCHEDULE

Figure 28 is a time schedule used by the UNIVAC Division of Remington Rand that can be used as a planning time table by any school district converting to a data processing system.

The dates for delivery of machines must be determined after careful study. Factors to be considered would include: (1) manufacturer's production schedule, (2) personnel training needs, (3) initial applications, (4) development of procedures, and (5) the possibility of using equipment at other installations for trial runs. These factors may indicate the desirability of ordering some machines earlier than others in a punch card installation. For example, the keypunch machines would normally be the first machines ordered to allow for the training of personnel and development of master decks or files of information.

Delivery schedules of machines must be related to completion of the physical facilities, employment dates of the staff, and the nature of the functions to be served. If priority emphasis is on fiscal applications, July 1 would be the normal starting date. Educational applications, on the other hand, would not normally begin until approximately September 1. In either case, a trial period should be attempted before dependence on the machines becomes complete.

The commencement of operations should not be delayed by the failure to have the installation completed by the desired date. Should such delay occur, however, a service bureau could be temporarily used or equipment at an existing facility might be rented. It may be economical to use one of these alternatives for the trial period.

Regardless of the immediate availability of the machines, impending fiscal periods, or other considerations, no school district should rush into using data processing machines without proper consideration and planning. The confidence engendered during the early life of the installation will help in securing future co-operation of all personnel. Mistakes due to faulty planning or hasty scheduling may create negative attitudes that would take years to overcome.

PLANNING THE TIME SCHEDULE – THE "COUNTDOWN"

As an aid to planning a realistic time schedule, the activities preceding delivery and installation of the UNIVAC Solid-State System are listed below in sequence by month:

Delivery Minus 10

- Tentative delivery date established.
- Organization charted and UNIVAC Manager appointed.
- Overall objectives defined.
- Announcement made to company employees.

Delivery Minus 9

- Systems analysts and programmers selected.
- Training programs initiated.
- Applications priorities established.

Delivery Minus 8

- Installation site selected and equipment layout planned.
- Budget established.
- Training completed; analysis and systems design initiated for first application.

Delivery Minus 7

- Physical installation plans reviewed by Remington Rand site-preparation engineer.
- Process chart completed; detailed flow charts and experimental programming initiated with feedback to analysts.
- First reviews of systems design with executive committee, department heads, and outside auditors.

Delivery Minus 6

- Systems design and programming continued.
- Forms design initiated.
- Physical installation plans approved; duct work ordered and electrical wiring started.
- Operators selected, and training initiated.

Delivery Minus 5

- Systems and forms design frozen.
- Programming continued and desk checking initiated; first estimate made of daily system utilization.
- Spare parts and test equipment requisitioned.

FIG. 28: *Planning the Equipment Delivery Schedule*

Figure 28 (Continued)

Delivery Minus 4

- Programming completed and testing initiated.
- Test data for comprehensive systems check prepared.
- Conversion plans initiated and conversion runs charted.

Delivery Minus 3

- Systems-check on test data; estimates of daily system utilization revised.
- Systems-check results reviewed for adequacy of audit trail, accounting controls, error recovery, and rerun points.
- Personnel and equipment requirements estimated for conversion of master and reference files.
- Departmental reorganization planned and charted.
- Procedure-writing for affected departments initiated.

Delivery Minus 2

- Program-testing and correction continued; improvements to be incorporated after cut over recorded.
- Final reviews with executive committee, department heads, and outside auditors.
- Tentative schedule for computer operation and preventive maintenance drafted.

Delivery Minus 1

- Cut over and parallel running planned.
- Training initiated for personnel in affected departments.
- Temporary quarters arranged for parallel running.
- Conversion of master and reference files initiated.

Delivery Month

- Equipment installed.
- Systems-acceptance test performed.
- Parallel running initiated.
- Initial application cut over.

Delivery Plus 1

- Management review.
  1. Results compared with objectives.
  2. Budgeted costs compared with actual costs.
  3. Statement of present operating costs drafted.
  4. Recommendations for future activities studied.

FINALIZING THE SYSTEMS DESIGN

Once specific equipment has been ordered, site determination has been made and a date has been set to begin procedures, the target date for completing the systems design must be established.

Actually, a data processing unit should never feel that it has completed its systems design. There should be a constant effort to encourage feedback and to evaluate, replan, and revise systems when it appears advisable.

As used here "finalizing a systems design" means that a minimum of applications have been developed for the installation and inauguration of a processing center. For example, the completion for the payroll application would imply completion of card and form designs and general and operational flow charts. Such a systems design requires co-ordinating the efforts of many individuals and involves gathering and organizing requirements, limitations, goals, and time restrictions, etc. In short, while "finalizing the systems design" should be thought of as a necessary step which must precede initiation of processing, it should also be regarded as a "point of departure" for continuing the evaluation and revision of procedures.

WIRING OR PROGRAMMING SCHEDULE

As systems development determines each application, that application must be scheduled for wiring or programming.

Generally there are two methods which can be applied in assigning manpower to application projects. The first is to assign a given application or program to one person to follow through from start to completion. The primary advantage of this procedure is that only one person carries the entire train of thought; hence, he is fully responsible. A second person, however, should review the work. There is also a decided morale advantage in giving an individual a project which becomes his full responsibility. It gives him an important goal to work toward, and one with which he can honestly and clearly identify himself. His own sense of worthwhileness and pride in achieving his goal will be fully supported by recognition from others. Through this approach the aptitudes and capacities of each individual can be appraised more directly than is possible with the team approach.

The second method of making assignments is to assign one application project to two or more individuals, a team whose members will work together to develop the program. It is recommended that one person on each team be assigned as the team head. The advantages in this approach are: progress toward completion is usually faster and steadier; the abilities and knowledge of more than one person will normally produce better programs; and there is a definite advantage in having more than one person completely familiar with the program during the testing and conversion phases.

This "team" method is to be highly recommended, particularly during the initial phases of the pre-installation period. After the effectiveness of each team member has been assessed, the programming teams can be regrouped. By this time, more will be known in regard to such matters as the specific abilities of individuals, their availability, the job complexity, the size of the programs, how long they will take, and the extent to which problem definition has been completed. In a punch card installation, however, board wiring should be the primary responsibility of one individual with a second person reviewing the work.

In planning personnel assignments it is helpful to draw up a manpower loading chart, an example of which is shown in Figure 29. This type of chart shows at a glance, each person's specific assignment by a job number designation. In the illustrative chart the predicted amount of time for each job is indicated by a line ending with an asterisk (*). It also shows those persons who are scheduled longest and those who will be available first for new assignment. If no one will be available for an assignment which must be made at a certain date, this will be immediately evident. In this event the chart establishes the need for an increase in manpower.

In all cases, sufficient time must be included in the schedule to allow for unforeseen difficulties. Since most of the panels or programs will have to be completed prior to the actual installation of the machines, problems involved in obtaining time for panel or program testing on the machines at other installations must not be underestimated.

CONVERSION

When a data processing system is installed, an organization is faced with the difficult job of changing quickly from old procedures to new data processing procedures. This is a problem of conversion. Although it does not arise until after installation, it must be prepared for in advance. Indeed, an all-inclusive plan for conversion should be initiated at the time that programming or board wiring begins.

The scope of the conversion plan will depend partly on decisions made even earlier, during the final systems design phase of the pre-installation planning. Either of two approaches may be taken at that time in relation to installation date. It may be decided that only some applications will be prepared initially for operation at installation time. It may also be decided that all departments or schools of the district included in these applications will at that time become subject to new data processing pro-

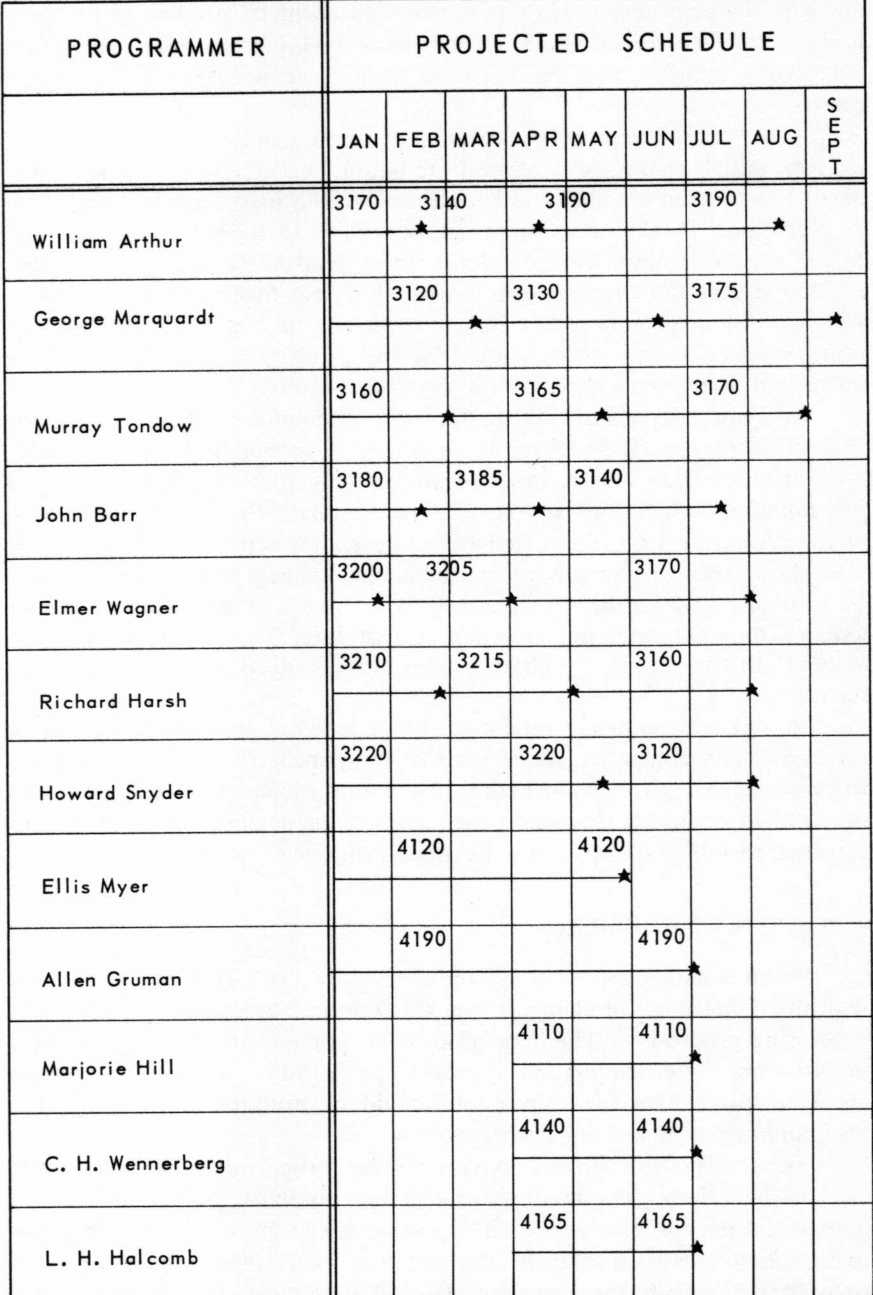

FIG. 29. *Manpower Loading Chart*

cedures. For example, if a mark recording application is one of those in question, the plan may be to include all schools within the district from the outset. In this instance conversion plans must, of course, extend throughout the district.

An alternative approach would be to plan initially for a mark reporting application for just one school in the district and only later to gradually include more schools. This approach, by simplifying each problem, makes it possible to prepare a greater number of applications for operation at installation time. It has the additional advantage of reducing the proportions of the conversion task, since all sectors of the district are not confronted with converting at the same time.

Whichever strategy is adopted, a realistic time schedule for conversion should be developed, based on the amount and type of work to be done as well as on personnel and equipment available to do it. Additional personnel and/or equipment may be needed on a temporary basis to complete preparations for conversion. The job of converting each application should be assigned as a specific responsibility. Some of the specific tasks involved in a conversion operation are listed below:

1. Gathering the data required for the master files.
2. Editing the files for completeness, accuracy, and correct formats.
3. Creating new files and procedures and maintaining them until they are used in production runs.
4. Providing for training machine operators and personnel in the departments which will supply source data and receive process data from the data processing system.
5. Establishing schedules for cut-over to the data processing system.
6. Planning for "pilot" operation.
7. Co-ordinating actual conversion.
8. Cross-checking the results of processing by the two systems (old and new).

If the preparation for a conversion is properly carried out, the conversion itself should occur without difficulty.

Where new procedures are replacing old ones, there are two basic approaches which may be taken at the moment of conversion. The first has been called "parallel" operation. This merely involves the processing of the full volume of current data on both the new system and the old one simultaneously. Parallel operations are usually continued through one complete cycle of processing (e.g., an attendance accounting month). A second approach is called the "pilot" operation. What this means is that the data processing system is immediately put into action, also on a full volume basis using the data from a previous period. In the meantime, current data can be processed by the old procedure. Results of the data processing system can then be compared with the results of the old procedure for the prior period. Output can be checked for accuracy, completeness, and proper handling. Any adjustment of the new procedure which may be necessary can then be made.

Basically what is being accomplished is a testing of the new procedure. Pilot processing tests the entire operation of an application from start to finish. It also provides operational training for data processing personnel since complete applications are run under much the same conditions as will be encountered in actual production runs. In addition, other personnel have the opportunity to prepare input for the data processing system.

The method used in conducting and checking a pilot operation would depend considerably on prior conditions with respect to the applications involved.

The applications may:

1. Have never been done before.
2. Have previously been processed by manual methods.
3. Have previously been processed on punch card equipment.
4. Have previously been processed on a basic data processing system.
5. Have previously been processed on another large data processing system.

In general, all of the above situations require manual checking, editing, and balancing of significant volumes of data. If the application has never been done before, it is necessary to perform a pilot run of the control conditions with sufficient checking to assure that results have been correct. No comparison with previous results is possible in this instance.

If the application has been previously processed manually, a period or cycle should be selected that will provide representative volumes and results for checking purposes. This period or cycle should be one which has already been processed and should be recent enough to assure its having been processed under current policies and procedures.

FORM AND CARD ORDERING SCHEDULE

As used here, the term "form" means any form other than a tabulating card form. "Card" means a tabulating card form of special design tailored to the needs of the operation using it, not a standard stock item of any card manufacturer.

The first step in developing a card and form schedule is to list the various cards and forms required for the application. This list should show each form or card, the estimated time required to design it, the estimated time required to secure the final product, and the stage in conversion where the new card or form must be used. The form and card schedule must be co-ordinated with the other schedules to assure that forms and cards will be ready when needed. The usual time lag between order and delivery runs between six and eight weeks.

Cards and forms should be arranged in order of need. However, the forms are usually designed in reverse order of need. The final products needed, such as report cards, bill warrants, etc., are designed first, and the initial input documents and forms are designed only when all requirements are known.

The form and card schedule represents a time plan. It must be constantly reviewed and kept abreast of the changing conditions of the conversion. Providing columns so that, for each detailed step, the actual date of accomplishment may be inserted beside the plan date on the form, encourages direct comparison of progress with plan.

8

THE ECONOMICS OF THE PROGRAM

Educational data processing, like any other important operation or service, cannot be conducted successfully without a sound financial base. The specific methods of financing data processing installations may differ in the various districts. However, where the money comes from is often less a problem than (1) how it will be spent, (2) how far the district and staff can go with it, and (3) what lessons can be learned about its optimum use.

The third of these issues is, of course, the most significant. Unfortunately, most of the literature that has been written sounds like propaganda for the equipment manufacturers. Out of the many and varied experiences the authors have had in local, county, and statewide data processing operations a body of practical knowledge has been built. This chapter is designed to bring to the school administrator a core of the best methods and best results that will serve as badly needed guidelines for schools. The most valuable financial advice that can be given is that which underscores the best possible use of available funds and some intelligent, hard-rock planning before using them.

The financial outlook of this chapter is largely twofold: (1) it presents the practical experiences of a California state supported pilot data processing project and (2) it discusses implications which those experiences may have for educators, along with carefully considered conclusions and recommendations. Because the majority of school districts have launched their data processing efforts with unit record equipment, the early parts of this chapter focus on this type of equipment.

DISTRICT RESPONSIBILITY

In the normal operation of school districts, educational data processing is, by and large, a district responsibility. The district budget makes provision for this type of service as well as for any other service that is considered important to school operation and administration. Some districts work co-operatively with other districts in providing data processing services; other districts work through the office of the county superintendent of schools; still other districts lease outside equipment and facilities. There are various ways of running the operation, but the responsibility for providing it and meeting whatever costs are involved belongs essentially to the district at the local level.

NECESSITY FOR THOROUGH PLANNING

As it will be shown elsewhere in this chapter, it is imperative that budgetary provisions for data processing be based on serious and intensive planning. A thorough study must be made of the kind and extent of the services to be rendered, the type of equipment and facilities needed, the personnel required, and the overall cost. Sufficient forethought must be given to the possibilities of district growth and corresponding expansion in the data processing operation. Allowance must be made for technological changes in which earlier machines are replaced by newer and better models. To allow no leeway for growth or for change is to invite overloading, severely strained facilities, and possible breakdown of the program.

BENEFITS TO THE SCHOOLS

District budget planners need to take note of the many benefits that accrue to the schools when data processing services are properly used. Actual savings in dollars is one of the benefits, but it may be noticeable only over a period of time.

> The meaningful argument, however, is one of *human economy:* providing for the more professional use of the time of the professional staff, for better guidance and instruction, and for the realization of higher educational goals.[1]

THE REGIONAL CONCEPT

A concept basic to the program of the California state pilot center was that the establishment of regional centers for the processing of school data is feasible. Under this arrangement, several districts within a region can utilize central equipment, staff, and facilities and thereby realize greater budget economy and greater uniformity in procedures and products. State funds might conceivably be allocated for such a purpose.

A concept of this kind has many meaningful implications for students and educators. Since the state pilot installation located in the Richmond, California school district was in large measure an archetype of the proposed regional setup, the concept was tested and applied during the life of the project.

NEED FOR DOCUMENTATION

Data processing staff members generally are in complete agreement regarding the persistent overall need for a technical writer. Such a person

1. "A Report of a Study—Processing Pupil Personnel Data," *Bulletin of the California State Department of Education,* Vol. XXXI, No. 2, March, 1962, p. 92.

would document and, most important, keep up-to-date all detailed procedures. The need for such a person is a major consideration for educators who will be drawing up plans and reckoning costs for data processing programs. "At one time in our installation," a tab supervisor said, "we had all our applications down on paper, but by the time they were ready for use they were obsolete." Another stated: "I recall that during the second year our supervisor spent most of the summer getting procedures written up and printed so that they would be ready for the start of school in the fall. But we changed the systems and processed so differently that everything he wrote was outdated."

An IBM representative told the staff of the pilot center that procedural documentation was imperative. "A good installation," he observed, "cannot operate without either general documentation or detailed procedure. As long as people are carrying important information around in their heads, you are inviting serious problems. If one of the key people leaves, vital information goes with him and you are left with a big hole in your procedures."

UNIVAC representatives have remarked that with proper documentation anyone can come into a data processing installation and function efficiently. "But if you do not have written procedures, no one, regardless of experience, can walk in and process your work."

CUSTOM-MADE PROCEDURES

A continuing problem encountered by data processing installations is the necessity to tailor procedures to accommodate unique and varying requirements in the district. Each school, for example, may have its own testing program, and that program can change from one year to another. Problems are also encountered when different schools use different tests and varying combinations of tests; thus different processing steps are called for. Even if a staff had succeeded in completely documenting what was done for a given district during one year, the documentation would not necessarily be usable in the next school year. On the whole, such tailor-made programs are more expensive than those which are handled similarly for all schools in the system.

UPGRADING OF EQUIPMENT

Another continuing problem is the necessity to make procedural changes when equipment is replaced by new, improved equipment. For example, in the state project, the change from an IBM 602 (slow speed) calculator to an IBM 609 (high-speed) calculator demanded changes in procedure and new card designs. A number of other important replacements during the course of operation carried with them concomitant changes in operation. Despite the costliness of these changes, it has been found that as districts move forward and their operations develop greater compatibility, efficiency increases and unit cost decreases.

PROGRAM BOTTLENECKS

Among the bottlenecks encountered by district data processing centers, one of the most common occurs in mark-sensing. Often, to save money, districts rent a machine with only 10-mark-sense positions on the reproducing punch; this necessitates making multiple passes to mark-sense-punch the test-answer cards and teacher mark-sense report cards.

During the work of the state project staff, the slow workspeed of the 602 calculator was soon identified as a serious handicap in testing operations. Although this machine did an adequate job, its rate of performance was too slow to handle the volume of work within the period of time allotted to the staff. With the 602 it was impossible to maintain a continuing flow of operations from one machine to another; work piled up at several points. The staff succeeded in adding a special device to the IBM 407 tabulating and accounting machine, and the problem was eliminated. Later, the addition of the 609 high-speed calculator brought still greater improvements.

Probably one of the most frustrating bottlenecks that can occur is that of the time-collision of testing and grade-reporting activities.This problem can become particularly acute. As one of the data processors expressed it, "It is unfortunate that poor planning often results in the testing program coinciding with report-card time. Because deadlines have to be met in processing report-cards, the test-answer documents may have to wait many weeks before they can be put on the machines. To a school counselor this might mean a six-week to a two-month delay; in his view, therefore, and in that of the school plant in general, the data processing installation is very slow." This kind of delay is exasperating, and it is not always easy to explain to others the reasons for it.

PROBLEMS OF INTERPRETATION

Data processing staff members need to be aware of problems faced by the school staff in reading and interpreting data processed reports. If a school principal cannot interpret the report submitted to him, the whole thing can end up in the waste basket. A staff member of a district data processing installation recalled the difficulty educators experienced in reading a report produced by an IBM 402 accounting machine. "The print was too big and spread too far apart. When we converted to the IBM 407 tabulating and accounting machine, the school people realized we were printing in English, not in code numbers." Another observer warned: "You must always consider the fact that you are not preparing a report for data processors; you are preparing it for somebody in the school to read and interpret. If you forget this, all your good work may be for naught." Recognition of this problem can help a data processing staff continually to seek ways of making its reports more clear and readable.

With respect to interpretation, the director of information systems can be of assistance in two directions: to the data processors, in outlining what would be most useful at the school level, and to school personnel, in clarifying the functions, capacities, and limitations of data processing equipment and operations. He could also be most helpful in the matter of in-service training—for example, speaking to faculty groups about ways in which they can lend effective co-operation in a data processing venture.

THE ISSUE OF THE SECOND SHIFT

The state pilot project installation in the Richmond California school district was unique in that (1) district operations were run during a full-time day shift and (2) the state project staff worked the machines during a "second shift," or night shift, extending from 5:00 p.m. to 1:00 a.m. While this arrangement was the most practical one for the pilot program in terms of available facilities and centrality of location, certain problems that arose during the state experiment with the two-shift system should be noted here and taken into consideration by educators who will be planning and budgeting data processing operations.

1. The two-shift operation was *not* an integrated system. Each crew had separate functions to perform, and these did not overlap. Therefore, tasks unfinished by the day crew had to wait until the following day, whereas normally the work would have been finished by the day crew in the late afternoon or early evening on an overtime basis. Similarly, overflow from the night shift could not be handled the next day but had to be disposed of after 1:00 a.m. the next evening, and/or during weekends. The operational setup was such that neither crew could relieve the other. Consequently, the day shift suffered a number of delays during busy periods, and the night shift was compelled to put in large amounts of overtime during odd hours.

Despite the separation of goals and functions between the two shifts, and the accompanying irritations, it was fortunate that the personnel on both crews showed mature understanding and maintained friendly relationships with one another during the three years of pilot operations. It cannot be generalized, however, that such maturity and good will could be counted upon in any installation using a non-integrated system of this kind. Rather, personnel problems could very likely turn up along with operational problems.

2. Another problem arose from the fact that school contacts cannot

be made at night. In the words of the director: "The night-shift operation was often delayed for 24 hours because we had to contact a school to obtain missing information or to correct source data. We had to wait until the next day when the schools were in session."

3. The alleged financial advantages of the two-shift system were somewhat offset by the five per cent differential in salary accorded the second shift for working nights.

4. Another financial consideration involved the machines. It was observed by outside company representatives that the financial advantage of being able to use data processing machines on a second-shift basis is often offset by the many problems and difficulties that are bound to crop up.

Machine servicing was also problematical at night. It is a truism that no matter what kinds of machines are involved, each of them has to be serviced at one time or another. In the experience of the state project, machine breakdowns were occasionally handled at night on an emergency basis; but since the servicing company preferred to handle most repairs during daytime hours, it often happened that the school district day shift was seriously crippled while waiting for one or several machines to be repaired. The project staff calculated that the amount of time that machines were shut down for servicing was 1½ to 1¾ times as great on the day shift as it would have been in a single-shift operation.

5. Because of proven drawbacks in second-shift operations, as experienced firsthand by the pilot crew and indirectly by the daytime crew, the project staff and other personnel connected with the program gave frequent consideration to the concept of an integrated two-shift operation versus that of an extended one-shift operation. Varying opinions were offered, with a somewhat heavier preference for the "extension" concept.

It is felt by some that if the setup at the pilot center had been such that both shifts were doing the same or similar work, the two shifts would have been compatible under an integrated system. It is basic that in an integrated two-shift operation one crew can pick up a job where the other leaves off and finish it successfully.

However, lack of co-ordination often interferes. An IBM representative who maintained close contact with the project made the following comment: "When you're talking about pupil-personnel services, you're talking primarily of peaks and valleys. In a normal installation it will be only during the peak periods that you will need to work into a second shift. Generally speaking, district or even regional data processing operations should not be planned around a second shift because there are too many inherent problems. Co-ordination becomes particularly difficult; personnel factors and general supervision are also under fire. If a man on the prime shift doesn't communicate with the corresponding operator on the second shift, it is possible that an entire evening's work could be scuttled.

"Even the integrated two-shift operation causes problems because of peaks and valleys," the staff consultant remarked. "I would say that a valley period should be handled on one shift and a peak on two. And yet this poses staff difficulties. How do you staff a second shift for only peak-period operations?"

One of the IBM representatives suggested that the peak-period problem might be solved by having "overlapping shifts"—actually an extension of the day shift—whereby the work of the installation personnel would be spread out over a longer day without operating a formal second shift. "This arrangement would provide flexibility. When you get over this busy period you can then pull the quitting time back to that of a normal shift operation. To illustrate, your crew might normally work from 8:00 a.m. to 5:00 p.m.; but you expand the working day so that it reaches from 8:00 a.m. to 7:00 p.m. or from 8:00 a.m. to 8:00 p.m. When the peak period has ended, you can bring the hours back to the normal eight."

Some outside representatives felt that the advantages offered by the two-shift system are basically mythical. Rather than have simple machinery doing double-time work it is economically and operationally more sound to use a larger, more advanced machine, such as a computer, that can do all the work during the day.

Although the pilot project could not avoid the second-shift system, the staff agreed, upon the close of its three-year program, that (1) a second-shift operation of the non-integrated type has many serious problems, some of them inherent in the system; (2) even a well-integrated two-shift operation, though more efficient than the one without integration, would not eliminate all the difficulties, nor could it be guaranteed to run smoothly; and (3) the extended day-shift concept appeared to be the most practical with respect to operations and the most economical with respect to school financing.

Budgetary provisions for educational data processing centers are usually "heavy on equipment and light on personnel." An important point here is that wherever this is the trend or practice, *extra funds* need to be included for personnel to handle overtime and peak-period problems, special demands, or possible emergencies.

USE OF OUTSIDE SERVICES

An important factor that should not be overlooked by those who will be planning and budgeting data processing programs involves the possible use of machine services outside the school district. For example, a district enrolling 15,000 students might arrange to have its student scheduling and its testing done by an agency or center beyond its boundaries. Either a portion of a job may be done this way, or all of it. The California pilot project used an IBM 1401 electronic computer at two places some distance from the center.

Sufficient thought should be given to this aspect of the program because the extent of usage of outside facilities will certainly have a bearing on the amount and type of equipment that is to be installed and utilized in a district's installation. Efforts must be made to gauge realistically what will be done inside the district and what, if anything, should be done on the outside. Budget plans should reflect the differences and provide for what is required.

BREAKDOWN OF COSTS

On the basis of the experience gained by the California state pilot project, the staff personnel estimated that data processing for a school population of 35,000 would cost only about $2.28 per student for pupil-personnel services This was the figure computed after breaking down the following costs for a given year: equipment, $33,000; materials and supplies, $10,000; salaries, $37,000. Behnk[2] found that an average per pupil cost of $2.00 is charged when applications are centered in either the student or financial account areas. An average cost of about $3.00 per pupil was found when the center was processing both student and financial records for member schools. Table IV shows per pupil costs for machine rental and miscellaneous expenses in school districts of various sizes as reported by Behnk.[3] Table V indicates personnel costs—number of machines and applications.[4] As can be seen, the overall costs in the California project and the costs reported by Behnk in his survey of schools in New York State are quite similar. It cannot be emphasized too strongly that these figures do not represent the total picture. Costs vary in the initial stages and in periods of change and experimentation. The variety of services offered controls the cost. Therefore, these figures should not be viewed as appropriate for all school situations.

MACHINE UTILIZATION

In any data processing installation, the factor of *machine utilization*—the actual amount of use a machine gets—is of paramount importance. It is impossible to have *all* machines running productively all the time; this would call for 100 per cent usage. It is unavoidable, moreover, that certain pieces of equipment, by their very functions or purposes, must remain idle for certain periods of time.

On the other hand, much time is wasted and many investment dollars are lost because of poor equipment planning. Personnel who are new in the

2. Behnk, W., "Results of a Data-Processing Survey," *Journal of Educational Data-Processing,* Vol. I, No. 1, May 1964.
3. *Ibid.*, p. 7.
4. *Ibid.*

TABLE IV
DATA PROCESSING SURVEY
PER PUPIL COSTS—MACHINE RENTAL AND MISCELLANEOUS EXPENSES

Enrollment K-12	Average Machine Rental	Average Per Pupil Cost of Machine Rental	Average Misc. Expense	Average Per Pupil Cost for Misc. Expense	Average Total Expenditure	Average Per Pupil Cost for Total Expenditure	Average Equipment Cost for D. P. Room
Under 3,999	$5,410	$1.89	$9,273	$3.24	$14,683	$5.13	$1,089
4,000 to 7,999	5,838	1.06	12,655	2.30	18,493	3.36	1,483
8,000 to 11,999	9,045	.87	15,654	1.51	24,699	2.38	1,113
Over 12,000	17,630	.89	23,294	1.33	43,924	2.22	2,990
Average Total All Installations	9,053	.98	15,773	1.71	24,826	2.69	1,652

TABLE V
PERSONNEL COSTS—NUMBER OF MACHINES AND APPLICATIONS

Enrollment K-12	Average Salaries				Average Total Personnel Costs	Average No. of Data Processing Machines	Average No. of Applications
	D. P. Manager	Machine Operator	Keypunch Operator	Machine & Keypunch Operator			
Under 3,999	$7,100	$3,500	$3,900	$4,037	$6,910	5	13
4,000 to 7,999	6,740	4,140	3,307	4,153	9,828	6	10
8,000 to 11,999	8,000	4,000	4,100	4,018	14,494	7	11
Over 12,000	7,357	4,227	3,485	4,400	21,150	9	11
Average Total All Installations	7,216	4,139	3,543	4,152	13,110	7	11

field are often apt to utilize a sequential series of machines for one operation at a time. When the cards leave the first machine and are going through the second, the first machine stands idle; when the cards reach the third machine, the first and second machines stand idle; and so on. Good planning would try to utilize simultaneously as many machines as possible and to narrow the margin of idleness to a reasonable minimum. New material should be coming into the first machine very shortly after a given batch has left it for the second machine.

In the experience of the state project, the per cent of utilization was low at certain times and surprisingly high at others—ranging from below 25 per cent to as high as 50 per cent. While percentages of 40 or 50 might appear rather low, actually at the center they were high. Most installations measure machine usage by recording the time that elapses between the start of a machine operation and the end of it. At the center, however, the staff installed on each piece of equipment a special clock that automatically recorded its true running time. Every time a machine stopped running for any reason whatever, its clock stopped counting. Thus a percentage derived from this technique showed considerably greater machine utilization than did an identical score derived from the overall method of measurement.

Because it was the very nature of the state project to strive for the most efficient techniques possible in order to help the schools, it was to be expected that its rate of machine utilization would be comparatively high. The staff was able to average nearly twice the average rate elsewhere.

Utilization, of course, depends to a great extent upon the kind of application to be conducted, the type of operation to be performed, the specific pieces of equipment required by a given operation, rates of speed, range of usability for certain machine sequences, machine conditions and maintenance, replacements or additions of equipment, and other operational factors. It also depends upon school needs, the time of the school year, the depth and breadth of the services requested, channels of communication, presence or absence of co-ordination, growth in attendance, curriculum expansion, changing or upgrading of student activities, administrative changes, and other factors in the school setting. It should also be noted that (1) each machine has a use capacity that is different from that of any other machine in an installation (barring duplication of equipment) and (2) there can be a great variation in the amount, the timing, and the quality of *input*—i.e., whether information arrives in a reasonably orderly job sequence, or whether it bunches up in a convergence of two or more jobs at one time.

All these factors affect machine use for better or for worse, and thus there can be no such thing as 100 per cent utilization. Neither can it be said that the effectiveness of an installation depends upon the per cent of actual machine utilization. The more important consideration is that the data processors in a district or regional installation strive to program machine operations in such a way that the equipment is put to the best possible use.

Equipping an installation is usually based on realistic criteria, such as school needs and available funds; these can be grappled with. Once the equipment is on site, however, the criteria for operational techniques, although just as realistic, are usually more numerous and more difficult to perceive with clarity. If the data processors will take the time and trouble, not only prior to job runs but, during *any time* they can beg, borrow, or steal, to establish ways and means of improving machine use—reducing idle standing, doing several operations simultaneously wherever feasible, redistributing work loads, altering a program to eliminate or reduce strain on equipment, and the like—and if these efforts are consistent and commensurate with machine ability, then what the district spends on the installation will be justified. Other things being equal, over a period of time the expenditure will prove to have been a wise investment.

SPACE CONSIDERATIONS

The amount of space required by a data processing installation must be calculated both on the basis of available finances and on that of potential operation. Can the installation make use of an already existing structure, or must a new building be provided, or new space added to an existing building? These and other possibilities must be studied carefully to determine what will best accommodate the amount of equipment, working space, and storage necessary for the installation and yet come within the budgetary allowance.

The space turned over to the state project was an area adjoining the data processing installation in the basement of the Richmond city schools' administration building. It contained two small offices, a conference and working room, a files section, counter space, and storage facilities. The adjacent installation area that housed the machines was available to the state personnel in the late afternoon and evening hours, beginning at 5:00 p.m. The total floor space, including that of both the machine area and the adjoining area for the state staff, was approximately 1,200 square feet. This space was not expanded during the entire three-year program.

Considering the total student population receiving data processing services (nearly 35,000), the project personnel regarded the total floor space at the center as inadequate. They estimated that the space should have been half again larger. Most trying was the rather limited storage space in proportion to the work that was done and the materials that were handled.

THE PROBLEM OF EQUIPMENT VERSUS PERSONNEL

One of the most important factors in the operation of an educational data processing installation is the need to establish on the most realistic basis possible the correct proportion of personnel to the amount of equipment—i.e., on a basis that will combine economy with efficiency. There have been instances in which school districts installed poor equipment and hired too many people to operate it; in other cases the equipment was good, but there were too few persons on hand to run it. Districts have also hired too small a staff in proportion to the complexity of the machinery to be managed; or if the staff was in just the right proportion, one or several of the members were not expert operators. All of these examples can do much to slow down operations; in some cases they can seriously damage the program.

Although the right proportion of equipment to personnel is not easy to calculate and calls for much planning ahead of time, experience has shown that (1) the equipment should be of high grade; and (2) the staff should be small in number but truly competent. Within the budgetary framework of a district, efforts should be made to upgrade the equipment as time goes on but to maintain a small staff of experts, rather than stumble along with mediocre, inadequate equipment and hire more personnel to straighten out the clutter.

It should be noted that school districts of the same type and size will not necessarily evince the same rate of EDP production nor utilize the same number of personnel. Rate of output depends primarily upon two factors: (1) the number of applications to be conducted and (2) the type of equipment that is to be used. Interdistrict variations with respect to these factors are common. For example, a district with a student population of 15,000 may use equipment of high-production ability to process low-quantity applications. Obviously this district can get along with less personnel than the one with an equal population that uses equipment of low-production ability to process applications of high quantity. A district serving 20,000 students and using limited equipment might process a small quantity of work at a slow rate of production while another district of comparable size using high-speed equipment could turn out a large amount of work at a much faster rate. It is important for budget planners to estimate the best possible combination of equipment, personnel, and workload on the basis of district needs for data processing and available funds to meet those needs.

Much thought and research should go into the selection of equipment. While there is a tendency among some districts to want plentiful equipment but to balk at hiring people, the equipment itself should be chosen on the basis of the number of students to be served, the potential growth of the district and the present and future needs of the program. In some situations it might be better to begin with a highly complex but very efficient machine rather than try to serve a sizable school population with one or several machines of slower speeds and lesser abilities. The equipment at the Richmond center had been augmented and improved over a period of 10 years to a relatively high degree of machine sophistication; and yet there were few changes in staff—an increment of perhaps one person in three or four years. While a small, tightly knit staff is greatly to be desired, a district launching an educational data processing installation must make certain that every member of that staff is completely qualified. There must be no exceptions to this rule; the machines can never be any better than the men who run them.

DISTRICT SIZES, TYPES AND EQUIVALENTS

The magnitude of an educational data processing program—its plans, its facilities, its personnel—and the funding of that program are, or should be, in direct ratio to the size and type of school district the program is to serve. No program can be efficient or even practical if it does not fully consider this ratio.

In districts that have only elementary schools, needs for data processing services are more limited than those in districts with higher levels. While at the secondary level there are intensive grade-reporting activities, regular attendance accounting and student scheduling, quite an extensive testing program, and usually a large number of student activities, in the elementary district there are few if any grade-reporting problems, the attendance-accounting approach is entirely different, student scheduling is absent, testing is done on a smaller scale, and pupil activities are fewer and less sophisticated. In a high school district, processing is done for all students; in an elementary district, only a portion of the pupil population is involved and the amount of work is minimal by comparison.

A district that has both elementary and secondary schools is still another type. Its needs differ from those of either the elementary or the secondary district. On the basis of master records, the bulk of data processing operations in a unified school district is usually concerned with grades seven through twelve. It should be borne in mind, therefore, that serving a high school district of 5,000 students would be equivalent to serving a unified school district of a much larger population—perhaps 10,000 to 12,000, depending on the extent of the secondary level. By the same token, a high school district of 2,000 to 3,000 student enrollments could require more data processing than a unified district of 5,000.

Currently, in terms of work involvement, it can be said that in the field of school business services there is at least twice as much data processing generated by each student in the secondary school as there is by each pupil in the elementary school, and that in the field of pupil-personnel services there is about three times as much.

DATA PROCESSING OPERATIONS AND DISTRICT SIZE

In the sections that follow, the requirements of a data processing installation according to district size will be explored. The discussions and recommendations will be based on the following premises:

1. The type of organizational framework is that of the unified school district which is composed of students in grades K-12.

2. The content of data processing work has to do with pupil-personnel activities.

3. The area of pupil-personnel services is confined primarily to such major applications as attendance accounting, grade reporting, and test scoring, and to certain by products of unit-record reports.

On these bases, installation requirements will be considered in terms of equipment, staff, and other specific needs as well as the costs that are likely to be entailed in the requirements. Several categories of school district size will be cited as levels of reference.

Student Population: 5,000

The project staff estimated that for a unified school district of approximately 5,000 students, the necessary data processing equipment should consist of (1) a keypunch, (2) a verifier, (3) a sorter, (4) an interpreter, (5) a reproducing punch, (6) a tabulator, and (7) possibly a collator. The processing staff should comprise at least two full-time employees—one to operate the keypunch and the tabulating machine, one to do both types of work and be able to attend to machine wiring as well—and a third employee to act as a back-up operator for each of the two regulars on the basis of such part-time assignments as might be needed. Looking forward to the time when the installation would have an augmented staff, the regular man who is also a wiring expert would be a potential "tab supervisor."

The rental cost for equipment in a district of this size and type would range between $400 and $900 per month, allowing for variations in the number and kinds of applications attempted. An average cost might be $600 or $700.

In regard to salaries, the prevailing rates in industry must be considered. However, these can be equated to salary schedules in school districts. In this case the wage for the back-up man would possibly be equal to the beginning wage in the district; the wage for the keypunch and tab operator, will range between the top figure paid to an intermediate clerk upward to the top rate paid to a senior clerk; the wage for the wiring overseer/machine operator (potential tab supervisor), will possibly equal that of a trained professional accountant.

When a district takes a square look at its growth possibilities and finds them promising, its administrators should not balk at hiring a man who is so well trained in machine operation and machine wiring or programming that he can eventually manage a crew of men in the capacity of data processing manager; and they should pay this man a wage that is good enough and fair enough in relation to his abilities to enable him to stick with his job and not leave it for better pay. Clerks can come and go, and so, perhaps, can the keypunch operators. But the manager (or potential manager) means very much to the continuity of operations in an installation of this kind; if his salary is meager, he will not last long, and the program is in for trouble. A more detailed discussion of this was contained in chapter 6.

Usually the first year of operation in a district data processing program is the most expensive because it entails the installation of equipment and getting the program off the ground, which in turn involves certain losses of economy due to lack of experience on the part of the staff and lack of understanding and familiarity on the part of the schools. As the staff becomes more capable and more efficient, as the equipment comes under smoother control, as the program rids itself of awkwardness, needless steps, and "bugs," the operation will become more economical.

It should be stressed that the initial installation of equipment should be made with a realistic prognosis as to future growth in the district. On the basis of student population trends, community conditions, the financial outlook, and other factors closely tied in with growth potential, the district (1) should provide data processing facilities at the outset that will be able to handle some of the estimated increases in district services; and (2) should make long-range budgetary allowance for costs of equipment (and possibly personnel) that may have to be added because of district expansion.

It is often more economical, in the long run, to install equipment of reasonably high ability so that growth increases can be met with a minimum of difficulty. If growth comes to a district that has installed equipment of low ability, there is much expense involved in converting from one type of machine to another, in redesigning card forms, control panels, and so on—even in just stopping work on one machine in order to plan for conversion to another.

Student Population: 10,000

A unified school district of this size that is going into data processing for the first time should have EDP personnel and facilities equivalent to those of a district with 5,000, but with this important refinement: the tabulating and accounting machine should be one that has greater abilities. Generally, in this situation the tabulator would be doing a good deal more than financial accounting; it would also be doing pupil-personnel jobs involving a large amount of alphabetical data. Although the staff size would be about the same, additional part-time help might at times be required.

Machine rental costs would be approximately the same as those for districts having between 5,000 and 10,000 enrollees; possibly there would be a slight increase in costs due to the acquisition of a higher-ability tabulator. Staff salaries would be approximately the same.

There may be some instances in which a district of this size, particularly one that has already accumulated some experience in data processing, may require more than has been specified here—more equipment and additional staff to accommodate an intensive, productive program. However, the estimates given here are made for purposes of comparison; they are concerned with an *average beginning* district, not with EDP oldtimers—nor with "balls of fire" on the one hand or "foot-draggers" on the other.

As was suggested earlier, the district's administrators need to give careful consideration to potential district growth when they plan the installation. If it is determined that the growth potential is great, it may be necessary to install more extensive equipment to handle this growth and to provide a slightly larger staff.

A seasoned data processing veteran estimates that a *high school* district serving 10,000 to 15,000 students is likely to have a volume of work equal to that of a unified school district of 25,000 students and also would have the same variety of applications to perform.

Student Population: 15,000

In a unified school district of roughly 15,000 students, the equipment should consist of about the same number and types of pieces as required by the districts of 5,000 and 10,000, except that the tabulator should definitely be of higher ability and greater power and a calculating machine might be added.

The EDP staff would normally comprise a data processing manager, a machine operator, and two keypunch operators. While the number of staff members would depend to a large extent upon the number and type of applications in the district and whether or not the volume of work would be high or low, this estimate poses an average.

The range of machine rental expenses in districts of this size would be fairly broad. Typically, the monthly costs would range between $1,500 and $2,500. This estimate takes into consideration the variations that would occur from district to district in the amount of work that would be done. The salaries of the processing staff would be approximately equivalent to those of staff members in districts of 5,000 to 10,000 enrollments, but the total salary expenditure would be greater because of the additional personnel.

Here again, allowance should be made in the initial plans for district growth so that equipment can be upgraded and personnel added as needed. Possible staff additions, of course, would be minimal by comparison with possible equipment changes or additions.

Student Population: 25,000 or More

In a unified school district containing 25,000 or more students, the needs for data processing services are typically greater and more complex. In districts of this type and size, the trend is away from mechanized equipment with slow-to-moderate speeds and toward electronic equipment of high speeds and optimum ability. While monthly costs for renting electronic machines would be greater and the salaries paid to key personnel for programming, analysis, and management would be generally higher, the increased expenses would be considerably offset, over a period of time, by the elimination of several pieces of prior equipment, by a small, tightly knit staff of well-trained technicians and expert professional men, and by increased efficiency in operations. In proportion to the much greater volume of work to be done, there would be very little increase in staff. The staff would be highly specialized and limited in number. Space requirements would ordinarily be minimal because the new electronic machine would replace two or more pieces of non-electronic equipment.

By the third year in the state pilot program, when the center had benefited from two full years of valuable experience and was operating at a high level of efficiency, the installation (which served 35,000 pupils) consisted of the following IBM equipment: two keypunches (types 024 and 026), a verifier, the 084 sorter (replacing the slow-speed 083), the 088 high-speed collator (replacing the earlier 077), the 407 tabulator (for tabulating, accounting, and printing), the 519 reproducing and summary punch (linked to the 407), the 609 high-speed calculator (replacing the slow-speed 602), the 557 interpreter, a burster for splitting forms apart, a decollator for unwinding carbons, a wiring table, and various related appurtenances.

For an installation using similar or equivalent equipment and serving approximately the same total school population, the technical staff would typically consist of two tab operators, one data processing manager, and one or more keypunch operators; the professional staff would consist of a director of information systems and an assistant director.

If a school district using equipment approximating the center's third-year facilities converts to high-powered automation and brings in an electronic computer (a small to medium-size but highly capable machine), the equipment eliminated by the conversion would usually be the tabulator, the calculator, and the collator. The recommended technical and managerial staff would then consist of two keypunch operators, one console operator (a technician), one or possibly two programmers, and a data processing manager. The programmer and the manager would of course be highly trained specialists.

As recommended in Chapter 6, over and above the installation staff there should be a district director of information systems who would superintend the overall data processing program; co-ordinate district plans, requests, and schedules; act as liaison man between the center and the schools; prepare written instructions and procedures to assist school personnel; and set up in-service training to improve the EDP program. Ordinarily this official would be chosen from the higher echelon of district administration.

The rental costs for maintaining an installation of this magnitude, on the basis of a computer system, would amount to approximately $3,750 per month, or $45,000 per year. Variations in these figures would correspond to certain variations in equipment, such as a smaller type of computer and/or slightly different pieces of non-electronic equipment in the operating system. "For example," as one of the project staff explained, "if you stripped down to a smaller computer, with an external storage device known as the disk pack, the rental for the computer itself would amount to about $2,000 per month, and the use of necessary peripheral gear would boost the total rental to about $3,000."

The two keypunch operators would be paid the same rate as in districts serving 5, 10 and 15 thousand students (Table V, p. 112). A slightly higher wage, approximately $6,500–$7,000, would go to the console (computer) operator. The programmer, a highly specialized technician, would typically receive an annual salary in the neighborhood of $8,500–$9,000. The data processing manager, on the basis of his broad responsibilities and in-depth training, would receive an annual wage approximating $10,000.

CO-ORDINATORS AND DIRECTORS

The California pilot project made use of a rather unique job category —that of district co-ordinator, a professional man (a school man) who had a liaison relationship between the center and the district he represented. While the district co-ordinator performed extremely valuable services during the state program, the cost of maintaining him was not really a part of the center's actual data processing costs. In existing independent EDP installations, however, the "co-ordinator" may actually be the man in charge of the overall program and may be known by one of a variety of titles. School district administrators, for the sake of uniformity and clarity, should use the title of "director" for the professional person who heads up their data processing centers. Titles notwithstanding, the cost of paying a professional man to maintain overall charge of a data processing program may or may not be computed as part of the actual costs of data processing, depending on local administrative practices and local budgeting.

REGIONAL OPERATIONS

School men across the country are becoming excited over a new and different type of EDP installation envisioned as a *regional* center, which would be established to serve two or more school districts within a given region. It should be apparent that the equipping, staffing, and funding of such an installation would be different in some respects from the bases of establishing a district center at the local level, although operationally there would be many similarities. The California pilot project was a regional program in a number of ways. Even though the financing of the state experiment was different, the program and the operations were much the same as would be those of future regional systems in a state.

In an EDP center of regional magnitude, equipment and staff would be upgraded so that the best possible service could be given to the co-operating districts. Costs would be shared; funds might also be allocated by the state to assist the program. A further discussion of this is to be found in Chapter 15, "Organizational Implications."

PART III

Typical Educational Applications

9

MARK REPORTING

It is the intent of this chapter to describe how factual report card data can be presented to students, parents, and staff in the most meaningful fashion. In addition, it proposes to show how these data can be used in conjunction with other student data to present a longitudinal view of the student and his performance as related to his ability and subject achievement.

Similar patterns for mark reporting are being widely used both by schools that use manual systems and by those employing automated systems. These patterns provide for the following practices:

1. Receiving or preparing lists of class enrollments.
2. Recording attendance, absence, and tardiness data.
3. Assigning marks for student achievement; rating students on effort, behavior and the like.
4. Reporting marks at intervals to students, parents, and school offices.
5. Posting marks to cumulative records.
6. Preparing honor lists.
7. Making mark adjustments.
8. Making special reports.

Report cards are generally issued quarterly, but some schools report at the end of each six-week period. In either instance the work has to be accomplished within a restricted period.

Schools that have data processing equipment usually use it to print their report cards. In many cases not only has grade reporting been one of the most important applications attempted by local data processing installations, but often proves to be one of the most beneficial. Of all the major applications, moreover, mark reporting has most often had the most far-reaching effects with respect to changing and improving the educational program.

PREPARATION

Before beginning the machine application of issuing mark reports, or any other major application for that matter, time has to be spent in planning the application and laying the groundwork for its operations. Planning includes conferring with teachers, counselors, and other administrators so that their best thinking can be included in the planning. This should be followed by a comprehensive in-service training program for those who will actually be engaged in the operation or who will receive data as a result of the operation.

A great deal of time will be taken up in designing workable cards and other forms, and in drafting lists of course offerings and, most important, developing procedures to be followed. An example of such procedures, which can serve as a guide for local districts interested in developing a procedural handbook, is to be found in Appendix II.

If the report card application is to work smoothly, it is important that all schools in the district agree upon a common title and a common number for each course offered within the district. If they cannot, additional staff and machine time will have to be spent in accommodating the varieties of demands. With tight deadlines this may delay the delivery of accurate report cards.

A broad variety of forms from other districts should be examined and thoroughly discussed before proposals are adopted for the district's final forms for the report-card application and for the report card itself.

Two methods of preparing the report card application are indicated below:

1. Prior to the end of the first marking period in the school year, the master schedule of classes and the individual student programs should be obtained and converted for data processing (in schools doing automated student scheduling, this information would already be on hand). At the close of the marking period the teacher should receive from the data processing center one deck of cards per class, each card representing a student. These cards, which should identify both the individual student and the class to which he belongs, should be specifically designed so that the teacher can transcribe the necessary mark data from the roll book to the card by filling in mark-sense spaces ("bubbles") on the card with an electrographic pencil. These cards should then be returned to the center, where they will serve as a source of information for printing the report cards. Earned credits can be automatically reported each semester. Procedural steps in this operation are shown in Figure 30.

2. A report sheet is prepared by the data processing center and sent to the classroom teacher. This sheet lists the students' names in alphabetical order with other identifying data, and leaves blank spaces for marks. The teacher indicates the mark, which might involve a plus or minus sign; final examination marks; citizenship marks; and effort ratings (these can also be incorporated in the previously mentioned system). The form is then returned to the data processing center. The procedural steps in this operation are shown in Figure 31. Once data is transferred to punch cards, further processing is easily accomplished.

Als note Flow Chart

APPLICATION

Mark Reporting

Step 1.

Data Processing department will furnish mark card each marking period for each student in each class.

Step 2.

Each school will receive the cards arranged alphabetically by class, by teacher.

Step 3.

School clerk distributes cards to teachers.

Step 4.

Teachers mark-sense marks and citizenship if necessary.

Step 5.

School clerk checks to make sure all teachers have returned their cards at the scheduled time. Cards are returned to the data processing dept.

Step 6.

Data processing department will machine process the mark-sensed mark cards.

Step 7.

Report cards are printed alphabetically by grade. Cards are burst and sent to schools. School clerk folds, staples, and mails mark cards.

Step 8.

A mark analysis is run by course by teacher and sent to schools.

Step 9.

Class-size analysis is run by course by school.

Step 10.

Perm record labels are run alphabetically by grade and sent to schools. School clerk posts records to student perm record.

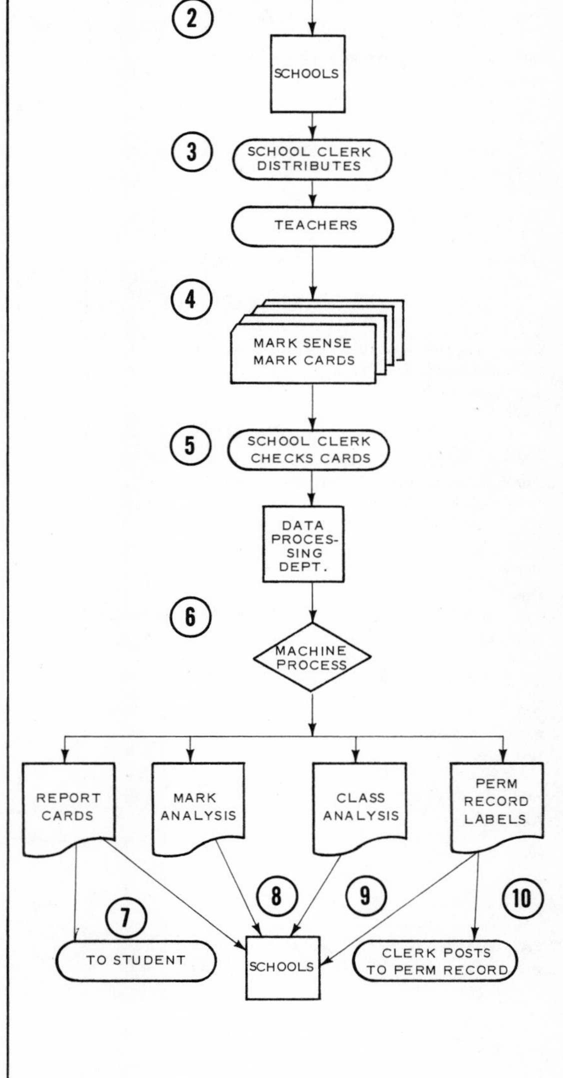

FIG. 30. *Procedural Steps for Mark Reporting—Card Oriented*

APPLICATION

Mark Reporting

Step 1.

Data processing department will furnish a mark sheet for each teacher for each class taught.

Step 2.

Each school will receive the mark sheets arranged alphabetically by teacher.

Step 3.

Clerk distributes sheets to teachers.

Step 4.

Teacher records letter mark and additional comments.

Step 5.

School clerk checks to make sure all teachers have returned their sheets at the scheduled time. Sheets are returned to the data processing department.

Step 6.

Data Processing Department will keypunch and process the resulting punch cards.

Step 7.

Report cards are printed alphabetically by grade. Cards are burst and sent to schools. School clerk folds, staples, and mails report cards.

Step 8.

A mark analysis is run by course by teacher and sent to schools.

Step 9.

Class-size analysis is run by course by school.

Step 10.

Perm record labels are run alphabetically by grade and sent to schools. School clerk posts records to student perm record.

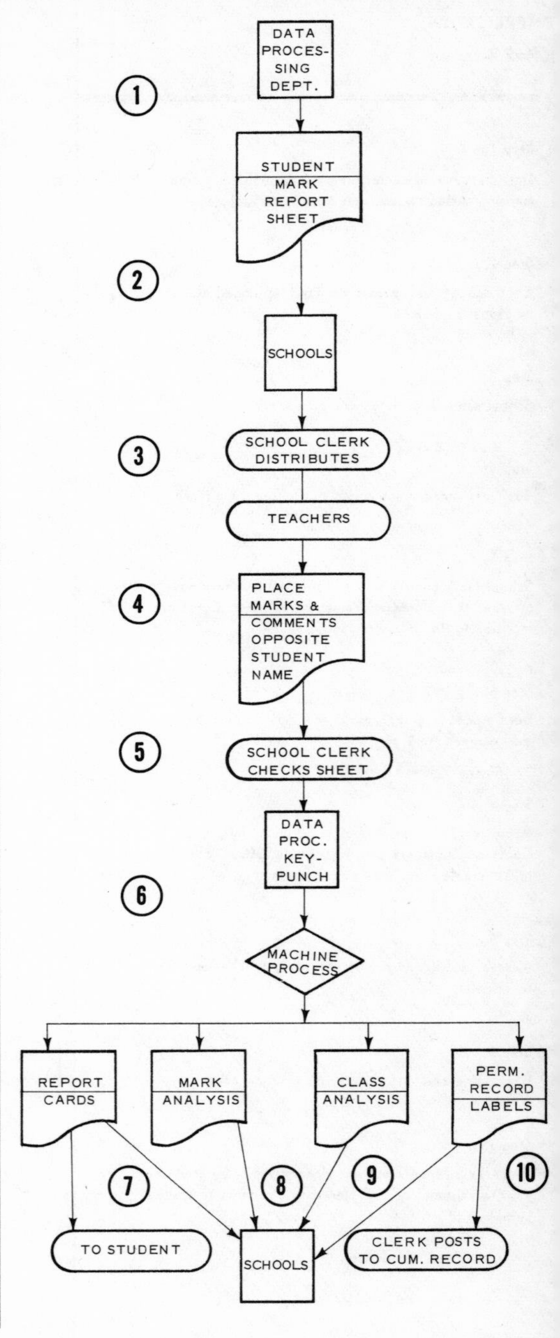

FIG. 31. *Procedural Steps for Mark Reporting—Document Oriented*

CONDUCTING THE APPLICATION

Once a method is decided upon and forms selected, it is time to begin operations. For the first round, parallel operation—wherein the manual and automated systems are conducted simultaneously—are recommended. In such an operation the staff goes ahead with the usual manual operation. In addition, a few selected teachers (volunteers) also go through the mechanized operations. This becomes a simulation study in that the operation can be conducted and evaluated without the pressures of actual production deadlines. During this simulation period there should be frequent meetings in which the data processing staff and school staff air their difficulties and agree on practical solutions.

In an operation center where unit record or card processor equipment is used, it is necessary to utilize the teacher class card that was developed during the scheduling and registration operation and combine it with the student's class card from the same operation. The information from these two cards is brought together through a process called "interspersed gang punching" to create a new and different type card known as the teacher mark-sense card. In a computer operation utilizing magnetic tapes, the teacher and student files would be kept together in a unified record on class assignments.

When using unit record equipment, the newly created teacher mark-sense cards need to be sorted alphabetically by period and merged with teacher class cards; the latter are placed in front of class groups. So that the information is readable to school staffs, the cards are run through an interpreter which prints the punched information on the card.

A computer system can punch out the teacher mark-sense card directly from the scheduling and registration tape. This card too, would have to be run through the interpreter to be understandable to the lay person.

No matter which system is used, the card decks are then delivered to the school. Clerical staffs are responsible for seeing that the cards are distributed to the appropriate teachers, making sure that each faculty member keeps a class master card in front of the teacher mark-sense cards for that class.

In the actual task of reporting marks, teachers are asked to enter scholarship results on the mark-sense cards by filling certain spaces or "bubbles" on each card; in this way they can indicate marks ranging from A through F, "incomplete," or "no mark." The teacher mark-sense card used in the California pilot project is shown in Figure 32. You will note that on this card the teacher is also able to specify from one to four explanatory comments by filling spaces in a second column; next to the spaces in this column is a key word which stands for an entire comment regarding the student's achievement, conduct, or habits. A complete list of comments is to be found on the face of the report card itself. A somewhat similar card used in the Indianapolis schools is shown in Figure 33. When all the cards have been marked, they are returned to the center for further processing. The usual procedure is to have a reproducing punch machine "sense" the cards at the rate of 100 cards per minute and punch the cards accordingly. Various other sorting and merging operations are carried on with unit record equipment until the decks of cards are in proper order and the report cards are ready for printing. A com-

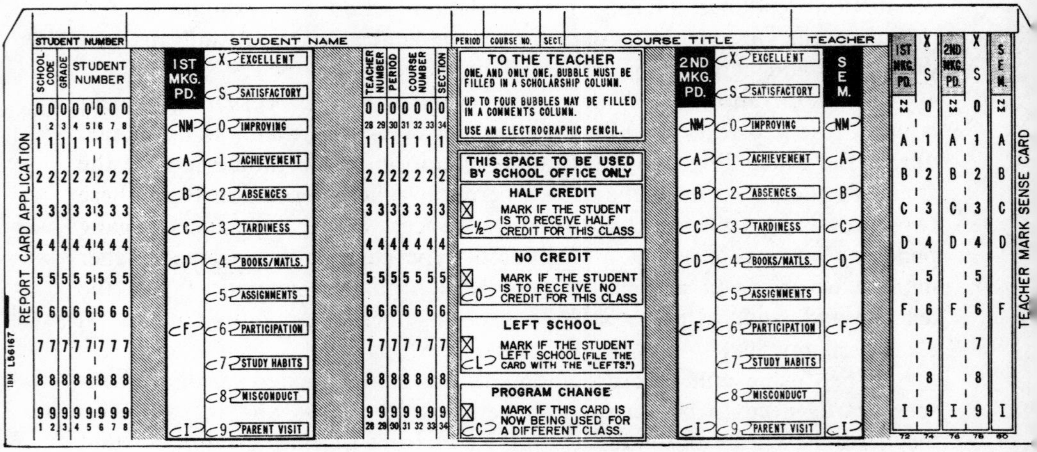

FIG. 32. *Teachers' Mark-Sense Marking Card Used in California State Pilot Project*

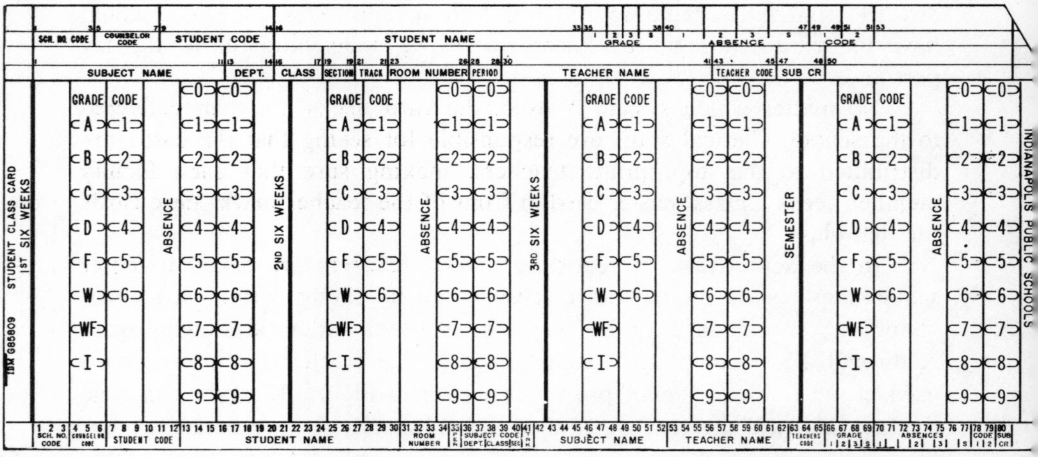

FIG. 33. *Teachers' Mark-Sense Marking Card Used in Indianapolis Schools*

RICHMOND UNION HIGH SCHOOL DISTRICT

REPORT CARD

School Name	School Term	Counselor	Gr.	Adv.	Student Name
HARRY ELLS HIGH	FALL 1962	RUSH E	10	208	WHITAKER ESTHER

EXPLANATION OF MARKS

A — Outstanding achievement
B — Good achievement
C — Satisfactory achievement
D — Minimum achievement
F — Failure due to unsatisfactory achievement
I — Incomplete due to justifiable absence

EXPLANATION OF COMMENTS

X — Progress is excellent
S — Progress is satisfactory
0 — Showing some improvement
1 — Achievement is not up to apparent ability
2 — Absences are affecting school work
3 — Tardiness is affecting school work
4 — Books/materials are not brought to class
5 — Assignments are not being completed
6 — Participation in class work is poor
7 — Study habits need improving
8 — Student misbehaves in class
9 — Please contact teacher through counselor

PER.	COURSE	MARKS 1	MARKS 2	MARKS Sem.	Comments	TEACHER	Credits
1	FRENCH 1	A				ARCHIBALD B	
2	TYPING 1	A				MACCRACKEN V	
3	BUSINESS MATH	C				HANNAH M	
5	BIOLOGY	C				SLIFKY R	
6	PE GIRLS	B			1	BJUGSTAD E	
7	ENGLISH 2	C				WOODSON B	

Normal credits for a semester are 30. You may keep this card for your records.

Speediflo ® Moore Business Forms, Inc. e

.01

FIG. 34. *Report Card Used in California State Pilot Project*

WILLIAMSVILLE CENTRAL SCHOOL
Secondary School Progress Report

1

MARKS	CITIZENSHIP	EFFORT
A = 94-100 B = 85-93 C = 72-84 D = 65-71 E = INCOMPLETE F = BELOW 65	1. COMMENDABLE 3. UNSATISFACTORY 2. SATISFACTORY 4. CONFERENCE WITH PARENT REQUESTED CITIZENSHIP: RESPECTS AUTHORITY AND SCHOOL REGULATIONS. ACCEPTS CRITICISM. IS COURTEOUS. TAKES GOOD CARE OF SCHOOL MATERIALS AND EQUIPMENT. PARTICIPATES IN CLASSRM. ACTIVITY. ACCEPTS RESPONSIBILITY. THINKS FOR HIMSELF.	1. SUPERIOR 2. ADEQUATE 3. DOES NOT PAY ATTENTION 4. ASSIGNMENT POORLY OR NOT DONE 5. DOES NOT BRING REQUIRED MATERIALS TO CLASS 6. PARENT REQUESTED TO CONFER WITH TEACHER

MAIL TO

STUDENT NAME JONES, GOMER

PERIOD ENDING		
MO	DA	YR
1	15	63

CREDIT
C - CERTIFIED
R - REGENTS
S - SCHOOL

FIRST SEMESTER		1ST PERIOD			2ND PERIOD			3RD PERIOD			SEMESTER AVERAGE	MID YR. OR FINAL EXAM	FINAL MARK	CREDIT
SUBJECT	TEACHER NAME	MARK	CITIZENSHIP	EFFORT	MARK	CITIZENSHIP	EFFORT	MARK	CITIZENSHIP	EFFORT				
U S HISTORY	NAZAR, J	D	2	2										
APPLIED SCI	SELLECK, A	F	2	3										
PE BOYS	KAMB, R.	D	2	2										
ENGLISH 3	HEWES, C	D	2	2										
GEN MATH 2	ONEILL, E	C	2	2										
METAL 1	WASDEN, M	C	2	2										

			ATTENDANCE REPORT											
			1ST PERIOD				2ND PERIOD				3RD PERIOD			
GRADE	STUDENT NO.	HOME ROOM TEACHER	½ DAYS ABSENT LEGAL	½ DAYS ABSENT ILLEGAL	TIMES TARDY LEGAL	TIMES TARDY ILLEGAL	½ DAYS ABSENT LEGAL	½ DAYS ABSENT ILLEGAL	TIMES TARDY LEGAL	TIMES TARDY ILLEGAL	½ DAYS ABSENT LEGAL	½ DAYS ABSENT ILLEGAL	TIMES TARDY LEGAL	TIMES TARDY ILLEGAL

SECOND SEMESTER		4TH PERIOD			5TH PERIOD			6TH PERIOD			SEMESTER OR YEARLY AVERAGE	FINAL EXAM	FINAL MARK	CREDIT
SUBJECT	TEACHER NAME	MARK	CITIZENSHIP	EFFORT	MARK	CITIZENSHIP	EFFORT	MARK	CITIZENSHIP	EFFORT				

			ATTENDANCE REPORT											
			4TH PERIOD				5TH PERIOD				6TH PERIOD			
GRADE	STUDENT NO	HOME ROOM TEACHER	½ DAYS ABSENT LEGAL	½ DAYS ABSENT ILLEGAL	TIMES TARDY LEGAL	TIMES TARDY ILLEGAL	½ DAYS ABSENT LEGAL	½ DAYS ABSENT ILLEGAL	TIMES TARDY LEGAL	TIMES TARDY ILLEGAL	½ DAYS ABSENT LEGAL	½ DAYS ABSENT ILLEGAL	TIMES TARDY LEGAL	TIMES TARDY ILLEGAL

SCHOOL PASSING GRADE
65%

SEE OTHER SIDE

FIG. 35. *Report Card Used in Williamsville Central School District* puter system would be progammed to organize the data in proper sequence and then print the reports without human intervention.

PRODUCTION OF REPORT CARDS

The output document, the report card itself, takes various forms. A common format used by the five participating school districts in the California pilot project is shown in Figure 34. Another used by the Williamsville Central District in New York is shown in Figure 35.

It is possible to print from one to six legible copies of this document. Usually four is all that is necessary. Depending on the equipment used, the forms can be printed at a rate ranging from 50 lines per minute (IBM series 50 punch card equipment) to over 1,000 lines per minute (computer based system). After the machine runs, the original copies can be split off from the long coil of joined forms; these single original copies are distributed to the students. The three carbon copies can be separated from the coil in such a way that three different report cards (for three different students) comprise one 8½ x 11 inch carbon sheet. Thus three carbon sets of triple-section sheets are made available. This technique can save many hours of clerical drudgery involved in bursting the forms singly. This arrangement also makes it possible for school staffs to bind the 8½ x 11 inch sheets in binders to be used for reference by the counselor and various offices and departments within each school.

The teacher mark-sense cards can also be used to prepare pressure-sensitive labels as shown in Figure 36. These can be used in posting the students' marks on their cumulative records.

RELATED OPERATIONS

Within the mark-reporting application certain operations are required to handle student program changes, departures from school, new enrollments, and the like. These all have a bearing, of course, on the reporting of marks.

Student Program Changes

Students do not stay put. As soon as you think you have them scheduled they change their programs—and on what seems to administrators as mere whims. Whatever the case, it causes a great many headaches. In some schools up to 60 per cent of the student body request program changes during the year. One way to facilitate record keeping and to keep from being inundated by slips of paper used in class changes is to make multiple use of the teacher mark-sense card.

To change a student's program, a school office staff member removes the appropriate punch card from the desk assigned to the course which the student is dropping, marks a bubble labeled "program change" on the teacher mark-sense card as used in the California project (which, as you remember, has been returned by the center to the school) and places that card behind the class master card for the new course in which the student is enrolling. At the next marking period, the teacher of the new course can enter the student's marks on the card although it still contains the identity of, and the marks pertaining to, the course that was dropped. In subsequent processing, the course identification will be corrected by sub-

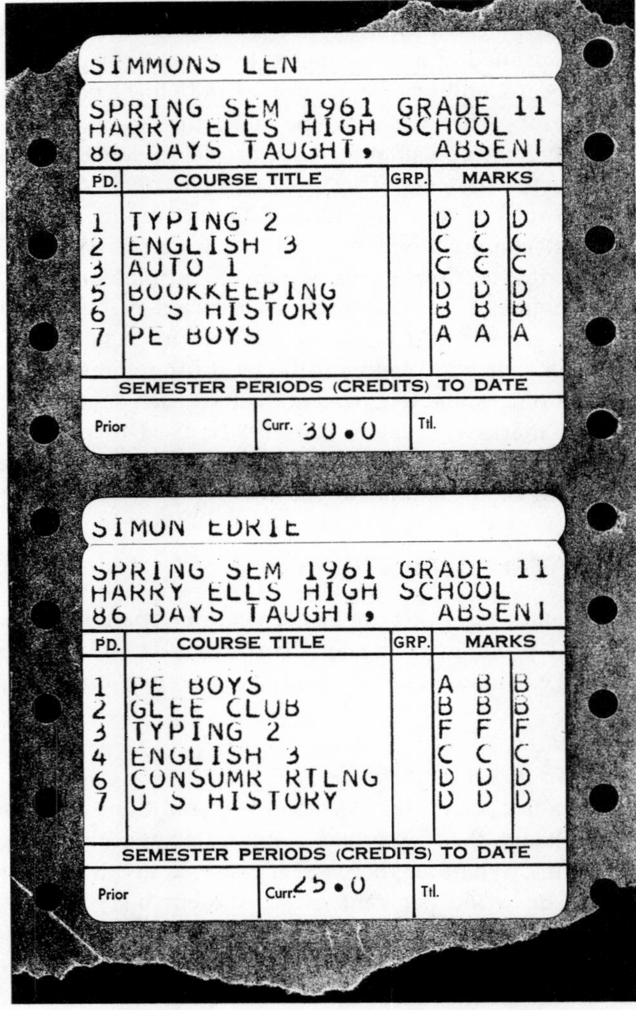

FIG. 36. *Pressure-Sensitive Labels Used for Recording Student Marks*

stituting the information contained in the class master card that precedes the old card in the deck.

Departure from School

When students leave school, the office staff should remove all their cards from the deck, mark a special bubble on the teacher mark-sense card labeled "left school," and file the cards in a separate section of the deck.

New Arrivals

When new students enroll in a school, the data processing center should be notified of this fact by means of the attendance application. A set of teacher mark-sense cards containing only student-identifying data should then be produced automatically for each new enrollee and delivered to the school. The office staff should file these cards behind the appropriate class master cards in the deck.

BY-PRODUCTS OF THE APPLICATION

From the automation of grade reporting, several useful by-products emerge. A district staff should be able to develop these by-products on the basis of data derived from the punch cards used in the preparation of report cards. The most important of these derivations are (1) mark analysis, or analysis of student marks; (2) class-size analysis; and (3) relationship of marks to other educational data.

The first by-product of immediate importance to a school emerges from a series of operations by which student achievement is analyzed and reported in detail. The data that form the substance of the mark-analysis reports are those submitted to the center by the individual schools at mark reporting times. These data pertain primarily to the ability grouping of homogeneously grouped classes; the marking of student achievement; and teacher comments on student performance, behavior, and habits. Symbols for student marks and teacher comments, and the explanations of these symbols, have already been shown in the reproduced report card in Figure 34, on page 131. The following major mark-analysis reports can be produced by a typical data processing center.

Analysis of Student Marks

In a mark-analysis report, the name of each student is generally listed in descending sequence by mark-point average within a grade level with a minor total after each grade and an intermediate total by school. Multiple copies can be produced for delivery directly to the school.

In this analysis, students taking a course for half-credit receive an 0.5 count in the number of marks in order to weigh such a mark properly

RICHMON

MAR

HELMS JUNIOR HIGH

SCHOOL NAME

FORM 31 - M3 (REV. 7/63)

GRADE / TCHR. NO.	STUDENT NUMBER / PD., COURSE NO., AND GROUP	STUDENT NAME / TEACHER NAME	COURSE TITLE	ABILITY N	ABILITY AVG. %	ACHIEV. N	ACHIEV. AVG. %	NUMBER X,S,Ø	1	2
08	21798-G	DAVIS BEVERLY						1		
08	23877-B	DIAZ MICHAEL							2	
08	24759-B	DORADO ANTONIO						3		
08	33138-G	GARRETT SHEREL						1		
08	35028-B	GOLDEN CLIFTON						1	1	
08	36508-G	GREGG LANA						2		
08	38619-G	HAMILL ROSEMARY						2	1	
08	46053-G	INGRAHAM CASSANDRA						1		
08	48321-B	JOHNSON CHARLES 10						2	1	
08	52479-B	LAMET CHRISTOPHER						1	1	
08	52983-G	LARRICK SUSAN							1	
08	58023-G	MATTESON JANE						1	1	
08	58779-G	MCBREEN BETH						2		1
08	60291-G	MEADERS CAROL						1		
08	69237-B	PERRY MODDY						2	2	
08	71568-G	PRICE MARY J						2		
08	76671-G	ROSBY PATRICIA						3		
08	82656-B	SLUSHER RANDALL						1	3	
08	83790-G	SNOUFFER SANDRA						1	1	
08	86877-B	STUART DONNIE						3		
08	93240-B	VROOM DENNIS						2		
08	96327-B	WILDE MICHAEL						1	1	
08	96831-G	WILLIAMS MARY						1		
08	97587-G	WILSON SANDRA						3		
08	28035-B	ERWIN WILLIAM							1	1
08	45738-G	HURST SHERRY						2		1
08	59031-B	MCCLAFLIN CARL						2		
08	82971-B	SMITH JOSEPH						1	4	
08	00945-G	ALEXANDER DANA						1		
08	05544-B	BARNEY DENNIS						1		
08	08757-G	BILLS KATHLEEN						2		
08	11529-B	BROWN ROGER						1		
08	12411-B	BUCKLEY DENNIS						1	1	
08	14994-B	CASH JAMES						1		
08	19278-G	CORREIA KATHLEEN						1		
08	25798-B	DUNHAM HERMAN						2		
08	26649-B	ECHOLS MARK							1	
08	29988-B	FLYNN MICHAEL						3	1	
08	30996-B	FRACISCO WILLIAM						1	1	
08	35847-G	GRCINA TERESA								
08	36603-B	GRIFFIN STUART						2	2	
08	37233-G	GUILLORY CAROLYN								
08	37359-B	GULLEDGE JAMES						2	1	
08	43848-B	HOLTZCLAW DOUGLAS						1	1	
08	44541-B	HORTON WENDELL						2	1	
08	45297-G	HUDSON GWENDA						1		
08	51219-G	KNIGHT CLARA						3		
08	54117-G	LEONARD SHARON						2		
08	69678-G	PETTIT LORRIE						2	1	
08	70338-B	POLING JOHN						2		
08	71505-G	PRICE BRENDA						2		

FIG. 37. *Student Mark-Analysis Report*

SCHOOLS
ANALYSIS

NOV/08/1963
MARKING DATE

F COMMENTS						NUMBER OF MARKS					MARK PERCENTAGES					GRADE POINT AVG.
4	5	6	7	8	9	# A's	# B's	# C's	# D's	# F's	% A's	% B's	% C's	% D's	% F's	
			1			1.0	2.0	2.0	1.0		17	33	33	17		2.5
			3				3.0	3.0				50	50			2.5
						1.0	2.0	2.0	1.0		17	33	33	17		2.5
							3.0	3.0				50	50			2.5
		1	2			1.0	2.0	2.0	1.0		17	33	33	17		2.5
							3.0	3.0				50	50			2.5
							3.0	3.0				50	50			2.5
			1				3.0	3.0				50	50			2.5
						1.0	1.0	4.0			17	17	66			2.5
			1				3.0	3.0				50	50			2.5
	2		2				3.0	3.0				50	50			2.5
						1.0	1.0	4.0			17	17	66			2.5
				1			3.0	3.0				50	50			2.5
						1.0	1.0	4.0			17	17	66			2.5
							3.0	3.0				50	50			2.5
							3.0	3.0				50	50			2.5
							3.0	3.0				50	50			2.5
			1	1		1.0	2.0	2.0	1.0		17	33	33	17		2.5
						1.0	1.0	4.0			17	17	66			2.5
						1.0	1.0	4.0			17	17	66			2.5
							3.0	3.0				50	50			2.5
	1		3			1.0	1.0	4.0			17	17	66			2.5
			1			1.0	1.0	4.0			17	17	66			2.5
							3.0	3.0				50	50			2.5
	2		2			1.0	1.0	5.0			14	14	72			2.4
						1.0	1.0	5.0			14	14	72			2.4
1		1	2			1.0	3.0	2.0		1.0	14	43	29		14	2.4
	2	1		3		1.0	2.0	3.0	1.0		14	29	43	14		2.4
			2				2.0	4.0				33	67			2.3
	1	1	1	1		1.0	1.0	3.0	1.0		17	17	49	17		2.3
	1						2.0	4.0				33	67			2.3
			1			1.0	1.0	3.0	1.0		17	17	49	17		2.3
	1		1	3		1.0	1.0	3.0	1.0		17	17	49	17		2.3
							2.0	4.0				33	67			2.3
							2.0	4.0				33	67			2.3
						1.0		5.0			17		83			2.3
	2						3.0	2.0	1.0			50	33	17		2.3
			1			1.0	1.0	3.0	1.0		17	17	49	17		2.3
		1				1.0	1.0	3.0	1.0		17	17	49	17		2.3
1	1	1	1				3.0	2.0	1.0			50	33	17		2.3
			1				2.0	4.0				33	67			2.3
				1			3.0	2.0	1.0			50	33	17		2.3
			1				2.0	4.0				33	67			2.3
	1		1			1.0	1.0	3.0	1.0		17	17	49	17		2.3
			1				3.0	2.0	1.0			50	33	17		2.3
			1			1.0	1.0	3.0	1.0		17	17	49	17		2.3
							2.0	4.0				33	67			2.3
			1				3.0	2.0	1.0			50	33	17		2.3
			1				3.0	2.0	1.0			50	33	17		2.3
						1.0	1.0	3.0	1.0		17	17	49	17		2.3
							2.0	4.0				33	67			2.3

RICHMOND

MARK

PORTOLA JUNIOR HIGH
SCHOOL NAME

FORM 31 - M3 (REV. 7/63)

GRADE	STUDENT NUMBER	STUDENT NAME		ABILITY		ACHIEV.		NUMBER			
TCHR. NO.	PD., COURSE NO., AND GROUP	TEACHER NAME	COURSE TITLE	N	AVG. %	N	AVG. %	X,S,Ø	1	2	3
001	1-301-	ABEL C	MECH DRAW 1	28	62	28	69	3			
001	3-408-4	ABEL C	ARITHMETIC							1	
001	4-050-3	ABEL C	GEN BUSINESS	20	41	20	39	1		1	
001	6-050-6	ABEL C	GEN BUSINESS	33	55	33	55			1	
001	7-050-5	ABEL C	GEN BUSINESS	26	50	26	44	1		1	
					COMMENTS			BY	SCHOLARSH		
							4	5			
							21				
							45			2	
							6			1	
										1	
			TEACHER	TOTALS-			76	5		4	
**********	**********	**********	**********	*****	*****	*****	*****	*****	*****	*****	*****
002	1-408-5	ANDERSON K	ARITHMETIC							2	
002	3-809-6	ANDERSON K	WORLD HIST 2	25	75	25	75				
002	5-408-7	ANDERSON K	ARITHMETIC								
002	6-809-5	ANDERSON K	WORLD HIST 2	24	51	24	54				
002	7-408-5	ANDERSON K	ARITHMETIC								
					COMMENTS			BY	SCHOLARSH		
							3				
							17				
							76				
							27			1	
							4			1	
			TEACHER	TOTALS-			127			2	
**********	**********	**********	**********	*****	*****	*****	*****	*****	*****	*****	*****
003	1-809-4	ANDERSON P	WORLD HIST 2	16	38	16	33	2	3	1	
003	2-809-8	ANDERSON P	WORLD HIST 2	32	91	32	94			1	
003	3-809-3	ANDERSON P	WORLD HIST 2	19	23	19	24	4		1	
003	6-990-	ANDERSON P	LIBRARY ASST	3	76	3	83				
003	7-809-7	ANDERSON P	WORLD HIST 2	30	78	31	81	4	11		
					COMMENTS			BY	SCHOLARSH		
							18				
							32	1	1		
							11	8	7	1	
							3	1	6		
										2	
			TEACHER	TOTALS-			64	10	14	3	
**********	**********	**********	**********	*****	*****	*****	*****	*****	*****	*****	*****
004	1-511-	BARTRAM A	FRENCH 1	30	86	30	87	3	1		
004	3-511-	BARTRAM A	FRENCH 1	25	90	25	93	1			
004	5-510-	BARTRAM A	CONV FRENCH	1	31	1	27	3		1	

FIG. 38. *Teacher Mark-Analysis Report*

CHOOLS

NALYSIS

11/06/1963

MARKING DATE

COMMENTS					NUMBER OF MARKS					MARK PERCENTAGES					GRADE POINT AVG.
5	6	7	8	9	# A's	# B's	# C's	# D's	# F's	% A's	% B's	% C's	% D's	% F's	
3	3		4		3	11	11	3	1	10	39	38	10	3	2.4
7	6	2	3			2	15	6	2		8	60	24	8	1.7
6	8	2	6		3	1	10	7	2	13	4	44	30	9	1.8
7	8	5	12		1	8	18	9	2	3	21	47	24	5	1.9
2	12		7		2	4	7	18		6	13	23	58		1.7
RK. COLUMN AT LEFT INDICATES NO COMMENTS USED.															
					9										
			5			26									
	2		13				61								
19	29	5	12					43							
6	6	4	2						7						
25	37	9	32		9	26	61	43	7	6	18	42	29	5	1.9
**															
6			2		1	3	14	8	5	3	10	45	26	16	1.6
	2				2	4	17	5	1	7	14	59	17	3	2.0
						7	12	5	1		28	48	20	4	2.0
						1	21	8	2		3	66	25	6	1.7
6	1	3	2			2	12	7	6		7	45	26	22	1.4
ARK. COLUMN AT LEFT INDICATES NO COMMENTS USED.															
					3										
						17									
							76								
2	2		1					33							
10	1	3	3						15						
12	3	3	4		3	17	76	33	15	2	12	53	23	10	1.7
**															
11	4	10	1			4	10	5	1		20	50	25	5	1.9
5	1	2			11	20	2		1	32	59	6		3	3.2
7	2	6	1	1		1	15	9	2		4	56	33	7	1.6
					4					100					4.0
5	15	7			3	14	13	4		9	41	38	12		2.5
ARK. COLUMN AT LEFT INDICATES NO COMMENTS USED.															
					18										
2	3		1			39									
9	9	10					40								
13	7	12	1					18							
4	3	3		1					4						
28	22	25	2	1	18	39	40	18	4	15	33	34	15	3	2.4
**															
2	3	3	2		8	13	10	1	1	24	40	30	3	3	2.8
1		1			10	12	3	1		38	46	12	4		3.2
7	2	4			6	5	12	6	2	19	16	40	19	6	2.2

RICHMON

EL CERRITO HIGH
SCHOOL NAME

MAR

FORM 31 - M3 (REV. 7/63)

GRADE / TCHR. NO.	STUDENT NUMBER / PD., COURSE NO., AND GROUP	STUDENT NAME / TEACHER NAME	COURSE TITLE	ABILITY N	ABILITY AVG. %	ACHIEV. N	ACHIEV. AVG. %	NUMBER X,S,Ø	1	2
056	2-009-	PHILLIPS W	APPLIED ART							
056	3-009-	PHILLIPS W	APPLIED ART							
056	4-009-	PHILLIPS W	APPLIED ART							1
056	7-009-	PHILLIPS W	APPLIED ART							
056	8-009-	PHILLIPS W	APPLIED ART							
020	4-019-	FINK E	ART					11	6	1
020	9-019-	FINK E	ART					10	1	
042	1-019-	LORING E	ART						1	2
042	2-019-	LORING E	ART						2	4
042	6-019-	LORING E	ART							
042	7-019-	LORING E	ART					2	1	1
042	3-035-	LORING E	COMMERCL ART					13	6	2
017	1-040-	ELKIND S	STAGECRAFT					5		
										ART
030	2-052-	HALLIGAN P	BOOKKEEPING					1		1
057	4-052-	RICE B	BOOKKEEPING							
057	6-052-	RICE B	BOOKKEEPING							
031	3-054-	HALLINAN A	BUSINESS ENG							
037	7-054-	JONES H	BUSINESS ENG							
033	9-056-5	HILL R	BUSINESS MATH							
075	3-056-6	WORTHINGTON N	BUSINESS MATH							1
075	5-056-5	WORTHINGTON N	BUSINESS MATH					1		6
075	9-056-5	WORTHINGTON N	BUSINESS MATH					2		2
024	3-062-	GOMSHAY P	COMMERCL LAW					4		
024	7-062-	GOMSHAY P	COMMERCL LAW					2		

FIG. 39. *Course Mark-Analysis Report*

SCHOOLS

ANALYSIS

NOV/08/1963
MARKING DATE

F COMMENTS						NUMBER OF MARKS					MARK PERCENTAGES					GRADE
4	5	6	7	8	9	# A's	# B's	# C's	# D's	# F's	% A's	% B's	% C's	% D's	% F's	POINT AVG.
	1		1	1		1	4	10	5	4	4	17	41	21	17	1.7
	2			2			9	7	5	4		36	28	20	16	1.8
	6			5			8	9	6	6		28	30	21	21	1.7
	5		6	8		1	9	8	3	11	3	28	25	9	35	1.6
	5		4	4			6	9	2	5		27	41	9	23	1.7
COURSE TOTALS-						2	36	43	21	30	2	27	32	16	23	1.7
	8					7	12	11	6		19	33	31	17		2.6
	1	1		2		3	9	11	1		13	38	45	4		2.6
	4					6	9	8	6	1	20	30	27	20	3	2.4
	11	5		4			8	12	10	4		24	35	29	12	1.7
	4			2		3	8	11	3	1	12	31	41	12	4	2.3
	7	1		1		7	13	8	1	1	23	44	27	3	3	2.8
COURSE TOTALS-						26	59	61	27	7	14	33	34	15	4	2.4
	8			4		6	8	12	11	1	16	21	31	29	3	2.2
COURSE TOTALS-						6	8	12	11	1	16	21	31	29	3	2.2
						8	12	2			36	55	9			3.3
COURSE TOTALS-						8	12	2			36	55	9			3.3
EPARTMENT TOTALS-						42	115	118	59	38	11	31	32	16	10	2.2
	17		3			1	7	19	8	1	3	19	53	22	3	2.0
1	2		1			4	8	12	8	2	12	24	34	24	6	2.1
						2	7	14	9	2	6	21	41	26	6	1.9
COURSE TOTALS-						7	22	45	25	5	7	21	43	24	5	2.0
						10	18	8		1	27	48	22		3	3.0
	5	2	5		3	1	6	18	9		3	18	53	26		2.0
COURSE TOTALS-						11	24	26	9	1	15	34	37	13	1	2.5
						1	6	14	4		4	24	56	16		2.2
	4					6	6	10	3	2	22	22	38	11	7	2.4
1	4		3			3	5	13	8	7	8	14	37	22	19	1.7
			1			4	5	8	4	4	16	20	32	16	16	2.0
COURSE TOTALS-						14	22	45	19	13	12	19	40	17	12	2.0
						4	7	5	14	1	13	23	16	45	3	2.0
		1	2			2	6	16	8	1	6	18	49	24	3	2.0
COURSE TOTALS-						6	13	21	22	2	9	20	33	35	3	2.0

in the mark-percentage and mark-point average. In all other reports every mark counts as 1.0 regardless of the credit involved. Figure 37 shows such an analysis.

Analysis of Teacher Marks

A teacher mark-analysis report is designed to analyze each class taught by a particular teacher. A minor total is recorded for each teacher, an intermediate total for the school, and a major total for the district. Again, multiple copies can be produced by the center for the school and for the central administration. Figure 38 shows a copy of this report.

Analysis of Course Marks

A course-mark analysis takes into account each class taught in a particular course. A minor total is recorded after the last line of that course offered in a given school, and a major total after the final card for that school. Figure 39 shows this report.

Analysis of District Marks

In a district mark-analysis report each class taught in a particular course is analyzed. A minor total is recorded after the last card of that course offered in a given school, an intermediate total after the last card of the same course offered in all schools, and a major total at the end of that subject area listed for all schools.

Schools offering the same course follow each other in school-number sequence so that marks for that course are immediately comparable from school to school. In addition, when the cards are sorted for this report, the total cards can be sorted with the data cards and then summarized in the same manner as are the data cards. Thus each subject-area total card can be listed, with a district total for that particular subject area. This permits immediate comparison for subject-area totals among schools.

Multiple copies can be prepared for routing to all schools and to the central administration. This report is shown in Figure 40.

The mark-analysis reports serve a number of valuable purposes. For example, they enable administrators and teaching faculties to get both a sharper and broader view of student achievement, trends in course-work difficulty, school marking practices, and other factors involving student performance and the effectiveness of the instructional program. Analysis also can do much to reduce the amount of work that once was required in the construction of lists of student honors and failures.

Class-Size Analysis

Once the mark-analysis phase of the center's work is in operation, another by-product of mark reporting becomes possible. This is the class-size analysis wherein each class in a particular course offered within a school is analyzed according to size.

The request for this type of analysis is usually generated from the board of education, which is concerned with class-size increases, especially in academic areas. Such increases often result from tightened financial circumstances.

In most districts, reports pertaining to the class-size have been prepared manually, but the difficulty in obtaining sufficient data and the great amount of clerical work involved in summarizing the data have made this an expensive procedure. Moreover, the class-size categories can not be precise enough to present a really accurate picture.

At least two types of class-size reports are possible: one, according to school; the other, a district report with all schools combined. Both reports can be printed on four-part forms. Each school can receive one copy of the report for that particular school, and the remaining three copies of all school reports can be sent to the central district administration. Copies of the district report can also be circulated throughout the individual schools in the district. These class-size reports are shown in Figures 41 and 42.

The class-size analysis reports can prove useful to board members and administrators because they provide summarized data regarding the range and distribution of class sizes by meaningful classifications. Teachers are frequently assigned to schools on the basis of formulas designed to provide logical class sizes in different types of courses, but the specific teaching assignments are established by the local school administrator. The efficiency of the principal in making teacher assignments is, of course, made evident by means of class-size analysis.

This type of report also provides objective data to substantiate or refute various claims regarding class sizes and teacher workloads. Class-size analysis can give both the building administrator and the district administrator a truly effective tool for maintaining the most equitable balance of classes.

RELATIONSHIP OF MARKS TO OTHER EDUCATIONAL DATA

The mark each student receives has importance in itself; however, combined with other pertinent information, it provides essential information to teachers, counselors, and school administrators.

As a result of the automated mark-reporting system, each teacher can receive a list of his students with marks earned in all courses. Teachers often find this information of value in instructional planning. The school counselor can have prepared for his use a special report concerning the relationship between a student's achievement test scores reflecting his intellectual ability, and his marks. With proper planning, such a report

RICHMONI

MAR

RICHMOND UNION HIGH SCH DIST
SCHOOL NAME

FORM 31 - M3 (REV. 7/63)

GRADE / TCHR. NO.	STUDENT NUMBER / PD., COURSE NO., AND GROUP	STUDENT NAME / TEACHER NAME	COURSE TITLE	ABILITY N	ABILITY AVG. %	ACHIEV. N	ACHIEV. AVG. %	NUMBER X,S,Ø	1	2
13	531		SPANISH 1							
27	531		SPANISH 1							
29	531		SPANISH 1							
31	531		SPANISH 1							
32	531		SPANISH 1							
38	531		SPANISH 1							
42	531		SPANISH 1							
60	531		SPANISH 1							
65	531		SPANISH 1							
67	531		SPANISH 1							
27	532		SPANISH 2							
31	532		SPANISH 2							
32	532		SPANISH 2							
60	532		SPANISH 2							
65	532		SPANISH 2							
27	533		SPANISH 3							
31	533		SPANISH 3							
32	533		SPANISH 3							
65	533		SPANISH 3							
27	534		SPANISH 4							
31	534		SPANISH 4							
32	534		SPANISH 4							
65	534		SPANISH 4							
							MODERN	LANGUAG		
13	610		GEN MUSIC							
27	610		GEN MUSIC							
29	610		GEN MUSIC							
38	610		GEN MUSIC							
42	610		GEN MUSIC							
60	610		GEN MUSIC							
65	610		GEN MUSIC							
67	610		GEN MUSIC							

FIG. 40. *District Mark-Analysis Report*

SCHOOLS

NALYSIS

06-13-63

MARKING DATE

F COMMENTS						NUMBER OF MARKS					MARK PERCENTAGES					GRADE POINT AVG.
4	5	6	7	8	9	# A's	# B's	# C's	# D's	# F's	% A's	% B's	% C's	% D's	% F's	
COURSE TOTALS-						254	332	311	174	67	22	30	27	15	6	2.5
						8	28	36	9	2	10	34	43	11	2	2.4
						34	22	15	2		46	30	21	3		3.2
						18	27	22	8	1	24	35	29	11	1	2.7
						8	24	22	18	26	8	24	22	18	28	1.7
						5	14	21	18	5	8	22	33	29	8	1.9
						6	15	16	3		15	38	39	8		2.6
						5	22	24	5	1	9	39	41	9	2	2.4
						35	35	32	19	1	28	29	26	16	1	2.7
						25	34	41	24	14	18	25	30	17	10	2.2
						4	9	17	13	2	9	20	38	29	4	2.0
COURSE TOTALS-						148	230	246	119	52	19	29	30	15	7	2.4
						28	32	18	1		35	41	23	1		3.1
						23	38	61	40	15	13	21	35	23	8	2.1
						22	47	37	33		16	33	27	24		2.4
								1					100			2.0
						27	78	75	37	10	12	35	33	16	4	2.3
COURSE TOTALS-						100	195	192	111	25	16	31	31	18	4	2.4
						8	9	7			33	38	29			3.0
						5	27	30	16	5	6	33	36	19	6	2.1
						8	21	19	8		14	38	34	14		2.5
						29	26	26	14	1	30	27	27	15	1	2.7
COURSE TOTALS-						50	83	82	38	6	19	32	32	15	2	2.5
						4					100					4.0
						3	4	8	1		19	25	50	6		2.6
						6	8	3	6		26	35	13	26		2.6
						12	7	6	1		46	27	23	4		3.2
COURSE TOTALS-						25	19	17	8		35	28	25	12		2.9
EPARTMENT TOTALS-						1031	1529	1421	728	249	21	30	29	15	5	2.5
						49	40	14	3		46	38	13	3		3.3
						3	31	19	15	11	4	39	24	19	14	2.0
						23	38	49	23	4	17	28	35	17	3	2.4
						19	38	18	14	1	21	42	20	16	1	2.7
						17	38	61	42	20	10	21	34	24	11	1.9
						18	61	15	1		19	64	16	1		3.0
						2	15	18	16	4	4	27	33	29	7	1.9
						14	27	70	31	4	10	18	48	21	3	2.1
COURSE TOTALS-						145	288	264	145	44	16	33	30	16	5	2.4

HARRY ELLS HIGH SCHOOL

SCHOOL OR DISTRICT NAME

SCHOOL CODE	COURSE NUMBER	COURSE TITLE	AVERAGE CLASS SIZE	TOTAL STUDENT COURSE ENROLL-MENT	TOTAL NUMBER OF CLASSES	*= MEDIAN 1 - 12	13 - 14	15 - 16
32	020	APPLD ART	26	104	4			
32	021	APPLD ART ADV	22	22	1			
32	040	ART	27	80	3			
32	041	ART ADVANCED	24	24	1			
32	060	COMMERCL ART	24	24	1			
			25	254	10			
32	115	BOOKKEEPING	33	99	3			
32	120	BUSINESS ENG	30	119	4			
32	125	BUSINESS MATH	27	164	6			
32	130	COMMERCL LAW	34	34	1			
32	135	CONSUMR RTLNG	33	131	4			
32	140	MACHINE CALCN	28	138	5			
32	150	OFFICE PRACT	29	116	4			
32	155	RECORD KPG	29	88	3			
32	160	STENOGRAPHY 1	30	89	3			
32	161	STENOGRAPHY 2	22	44	2			
32	170	TRANSCRIPTION	22	44	2			
32	180	TYPING 1	34	369	11			
32	181	TYPING 2	32	127	4			
			30	1562	52			
32	230	ENGLISH 2	33	530	16			
32	231	ENGLISH 2X	30	59	2			
32	232	ENGLISH 3	31	245	8			
32	233	ENGLISH 3X	34	34	1			
32	234	ENGLISH 4	31	309	10			
32	235	ENGLISH 4X	36	36	1			
32	251	GENERAL ENG 2	25	148	6			
32	252	GENERAL ENG 3	30	89	3			
32	253	GENERAL ENG 4	28	28	1			
32	260	DRAMA 1	21	42	2			1*
32	270	JOURNALISH 7	23	23	1			
32	272	JOURNALISM YB	21	21	1			
32	280	ORAL ENGLISH	27	53	2			
32	291	READING	25	50	2			
			30	1667	56			1
32	310	HOMEMAKING 2	27	54	2			
32	311	HOMEMAKING 3	22	22	1			
32	320	CLOTHING 1	26	51	2			
32	321	CLOTHING 2	25	49	2			

FIG. 41. *Class Size Analysis Report—School*

CLASS SIZE ANALYSIS

PAGE ______ FALL SEM PERIOD ENDING

DISTRIBUTION OF NUMBER OF CLASSES BY SIZE

17 - 18	19 - 20	21 - 22	23 - 24	25 - 26	27 - 28	29 - 30	31 - 32	33 - 34	35 - 36	37 - 38	39 - 40	41 - 42	43 - +
				3*	1								
		1*											
			1	1*			1						
			1*										
			1*										
		1	3	4*	1		1						
							2*		1				
				1		1*	1	1					
		1	1	1*		1	1	1					
								1*					
						1		2*	1				
			1	1		3*							
				1	1*		2						
					1	1*	1						
					1	1*	1						
		2*											
		2*											
							2	7*	2				
					1		1*	1	1				
		5	2	4	4	8	11*	13	5				
					1		3	9*	3				
					1*		1						
			1			3*	1	3					
								1*					
				1	1	4*		2	2				
									1*				
	1		2*	1	2								
					1		2*						
					1*								
					1								
			1*										
		1*											
			1*			1							
			1*		1								
	1	1	6	2	9	8*	7	15	6				
				1*	1								
		1*											
			1*		1								
			1*	1									

423

RICHMOND UNION HIGH SCH DIST

SCHOOL OR DISTRICT NAME

SCHOOL CODE	COURSE NUMBER	COURSE TITLE	AVERAGE CLASS SIZE	TOTAL STUDENT COURSE ENROLL-MENT	TOTAL NUMBER OF CLASSES	* = MEDIAN 1 - 12	13 - 14	15 - 16
27	496	ANALYTIC GEOM	10	10	1	1*		
31	496	ANALYTIC GEOM	20	20	1			
32	496	ANALYTIC GEOM	18	18	1			
65	496	ANALYTIC GEOM	10	10	1	1*		
		COURSE TOTALS	15	58	4	2*		
	TOTALS-MATH.		29	10941	372	4	2	3
13	510	CONV FRENCH	32	160	5			
27	510	CONV FRENCH	26	104	4			
29	510	CONV FRENCH	26	52	2			
38	510	CONV FRENCH	34	34	1			
42	510	CONV FRENCH	28	112	4			
60	510	CONV FRENCH	32	254	8			
67	510	CONV FRENCH	26	52	2			
		COURSE TOTALS	30	768	26			
13	511	FRENCH 1	37	73	2			
27	511	FRENCH 1	30	118	4			
29	511	FRENCH 1	22	22	1			
31	511	FRENCH 1	32	64	2			
32	511	FRENCH 1	31	31	1			
38	511	FRENCH 1	12	12	1	1*		
42	511	FRENCH 1	22	44	2			
60	511	FRENCH 1	29	116	4			
65	511	FRENCH 1	30	60	2			
67	511	FRENCH 1	24	24	1			
		COURSE TOTALS	28	564	20	1		
27	512	FRENCH 2	28	85	3			
31	512	FRENCH 2	29	146	5			
32	512	FRENCH 2	34	101	3			
60	512	FRENCH 2	1	1	1	1*		
65	512	FRENCH 2	25	100	4			
		COURSE TOTALS	27	433	16	1		
27	513	FRENCH 3	24	24	1			
31	513	FRENCH 3	26	77	3			
32	513	FRENCH 3	31	61	2			
65	513	FRENCH 3	31	31	1			
		COURSE TOTALS	28	193	7			

FIG. 42. *Class Size Analysis Report—District*

LASS SIZE ANALYSIS

16
PAGE

NOV/06/1963
PERIOD ENDING

DISTRIBUTION OF NUMBER OF CLASSES BY SIZE

8	19 - 20	21 - 22	23 - 24	25 - 26	27 - 28	29 - 30	31 - 32	33 - 34	35 - 36	37 - 38	39 - 40	41 - 42	43 - +
	1*												
1*													
1	1												
5	8	13	20	42	52	58*	57	49	31	21	6		1
			1		1	2*							1
			1	1*	2								
			1*			1							
								1*					
		1	1*			1				1			
					1	2	2*	2		1			
		1*				1							
		2	4	1	4	7*	2	3		2			1
									1*	1			
				1	1*		1	1					
		1*											
					1*					1			
							1*						
		1*	1										
				1	1*	1		1					
					1*		1						
			1*										
		2	2	2	4*	1	3	2	1	2			
					1	2*							
			1		1	1*		2					
								2*	1				
			2*	2									
			3	2	2*	3		4	1				
			1*										
			1	1*	1								
						1*	1						
							1*						
			2	1	1*	1	2						

R/D CENTER
CALIFORNIA STATE DEPARTMENT of EDUCATION

TEST SCORE TO PERFORMANCE ANALYSIS

TEST IDENTIFICATION | TEST DATE | SCHOOL NAME | SCHOOL ADDRESS | DATE | COUNSELOR

INT TEST SCORES XXXX XXXX XXXX	STUDENT NAME	TEST SCORES-AREA				MARK AVERAGE BY AREA				AREA INDICATED BELOW NEEDS FURTHER ATTENTION
		LANG	READ	ARITH	TOTAL	LANG ARTS	MATH	SOCIAL SCI	TOTAL GPA	
	AMOS, JOHN F.	7	6	7	7	2.72	2.61	3.19	2.85	
	CHATTERY, LADY B.	8	8	7	8	2.37	3.52	2.68	2.77	LA SS BELOW EXPECTANCY
	DEVER, CARL P.	4	4	3	4	3.21	3.31	3.69	3.42	ALL FAR ABOVE EXPECTANCY
	EVANS, THOMAS R.	4	3	9	6	1.82	3.62	1.59	2.08	TOT GPA BELOW EXPECTANCY
	PRYZNEWSKI, WENISLAUS O.	7	7	8	7	2.81	2.23	2.97	2.74	M BELOW EXPECTANCY

EXPLANATION
FAR BELOW EXPECTANCY
BELOW EXPECTANCY
ABOVE EXPECTANCY
FAR ABOVE EXPECTANCY

FIG. 43. *Test Score to Performance Analysis Report*

can flag students whose actual achievement in the classroom is short of their potential. Many times such a report may reflect ineffectual teaching as much as so called underachievement. Figure 43 shows such a report.

For the building administrator, special reports can be compiled for the student body as a whole. It becomes meaningful for the principal to know that thirty-seven eleventh graders are three years retarded in reading and that other grade levels have similar problems. A special "education intelligence" report can provide him with these students' mark point averages and test scores. Having the specific students' names and supplementary information about each one, including health and behavior data, is much more meaningful to the principal than having teachers and department chairmen complaining that this generation of kids "just can't read." He is now armed with facts to act in developing remedial programs or in modifying the curriculum for these handicapped students. A somewhat similar report can provide the district administrator with total district information about reading handicaps in relation to marks received as well as breakdowns for each individual school.

The possibilities for specific reports is almost unlimited provided a basic system for data collection has been well organized and implemented.

As can be seen, many and varied reports can be generated from the collection of basic data. It is important to establish a system that will not only collect information, but develop the information in a way that it can best serve the administration, faculty, and student body.

10

TEST SCORING AND REPORTING

The purpose of testing is to obtain data that can be used in improving the instruction, distribution, and adjustment of individual students. Testing is a means to an end. In far too many school districts across the country that end is considered to be fulfilled when a list of test scores is presented to the teacher; any use that is made of the results is then left to the initiative of the individual teacher.

Traxler has stated that it is axiomatic in the guidance field that every school should have a carefully planned program for using the results of all tests given to pupils.[1] The first step in this program is to provide each counselor, teacher, and school administrator with a copy of the test results which are of special concern to that particular staff member. The second step is to record the results cumulatively on some meaningful and comparable basis, such as scaled scores, stanines, or percentiles. The test scores should be merely one of several important parts of a comprehensive record form which covers several years and contains a digest of pertinent information about each pupil.

Detailed information about the use of such cumulative records in relation to data processing will be carried in the chapter on cumulative records. Along with the cumulative record system there should be a continuous in-service training program designed to educate the school staff in the preparation and use of such records. It is important that school personnel realize that using objective data in solving the problems of students can be one of the largest single contributing factors in individualizing instruction and in making the total school program more meaningful.

SCORING PROCEDURES

If a testing program is to be of any great value in the work of a school, it is necessary that the tests be scored accurately and quickly and the results be reported to teachers, counselors, and administrators in a form that they can and will use. Unless the whole program is carefully planned, there is danger that the scoring of tests will be allowed to drag over a period of several months until the faculty and administration, as

1. Arthur Traxler, *Techniques of Guidance*. New York: Harper & Brothers, 1957.

well as the students, have lost all interest in them. A still more serious danger is that of inaccuracy of scoring.

In general, there are three ways of scoring after the test has been administered—local hand scoring, local machine scoring, and scoring by a scoring agency. Let us consider briefly what is involved in each plan.

Local Hand Scoring

If the tests are to be scored at the local school, the personnel to do the scoring must be selected. Probably the most common, but certainly the least satisfactory procedure, is to have the teachers or counselors do the scoring. The teacher may be a good instructor but a very poor scorer. Counselors and teachers, with their many other tasks, usually are less efficient scorers than office clerks. Since the salaries of teachers and counselors are higher than those of clerks, it is obviously poor economy to use them for scoring. Since this is a treatise on machine operations, we will dispense with the idea of hand scoring.

Local Machine Scoring

One of the earliest mechanical developments in scoring objective tests was the production of an electrical, test-scoring machine by IBM. It is known as the IBM 805-Test-Scoring Machine. This machine makes use of the fact that a mark made by a soft lead pencil will pick up an electric current. Instead of indicating his answers in a test booklet in the usual manner, the pupil records them on an answer sheet similar to the one shown in Figure 44. Each side of the standard answer sheet provides for answers to 150 questions, usually with a maximum of five choices to each question. There is room on the sheet for a total of 700 marking positions. Instead of writing the number of the answer he chooses in a designated place, as is done in the ordinary objective test, the pupil indicates the number of his choice by penciling a heavy mark between printed lines.

Machine detection is based on the direct contact of electrical reading brushes with the graphite marks; recognition, by the density of the marks; and scoring, by the cumulative electrical effect of a number of marks in a known area. The output of this machine is controlled by the ability of the operator to insert answer sheets and manually record scores one at a time.

The development of this machine was a significant advance over the manual method, but it was not enough to effectively meet the ever-increasing enrollment in school population for elementary, secondary schools and colleges. The 805 Test-Scoring Machine was a revolution in its day, but it had limited flexibility and potential.

Subsequent to the development of the IBM 805-Test-Scoring Machine, IBM manufactured a larger machine known as the 9902. This

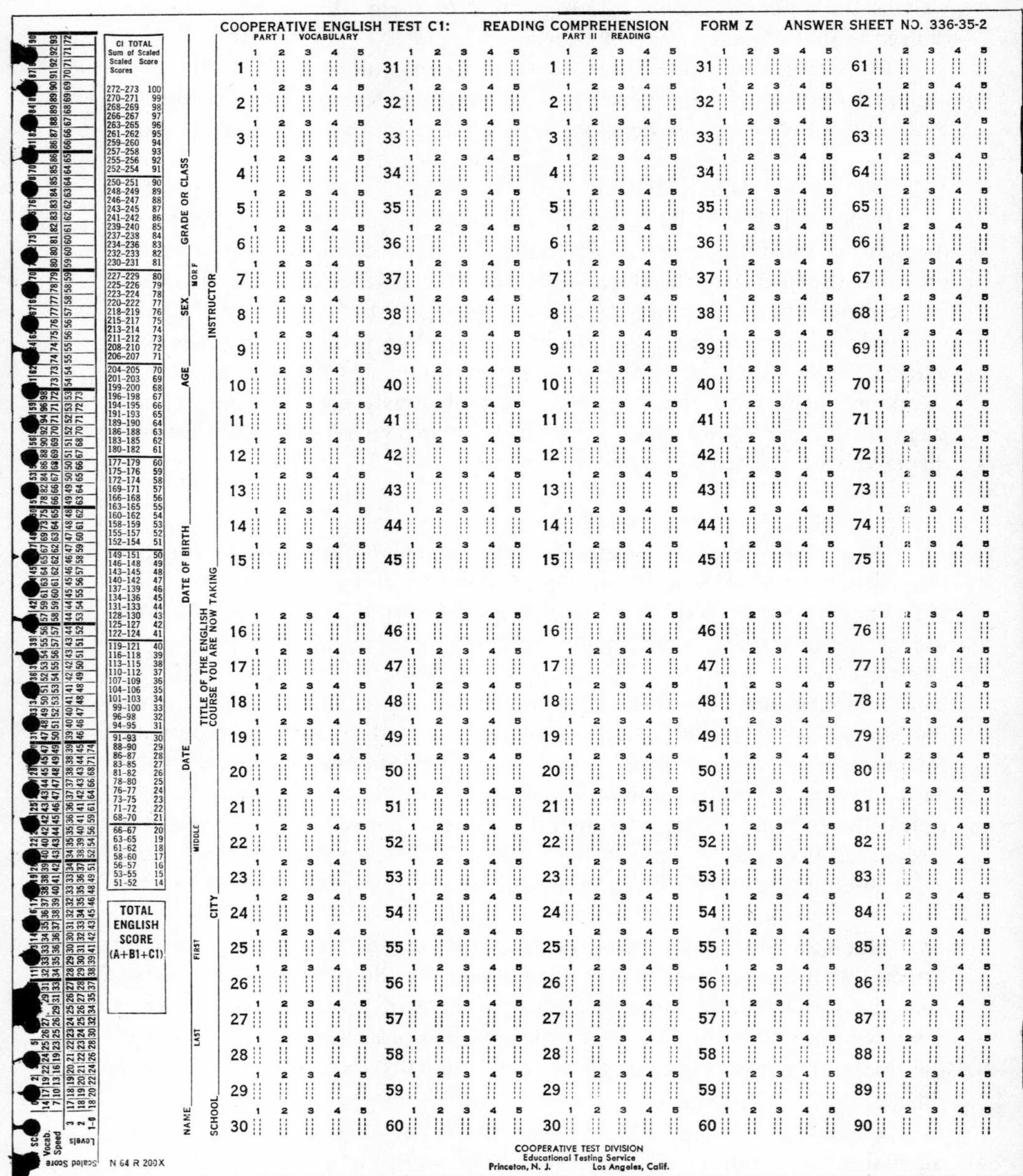

COOPERATIVE ENGLISH TEST C1: READING COMPREHENSION FORM Z ANSWER SHEET NO. 336-35-2

PART I VOCABULARY — PART II READING

CI TOTAL Sum of Scaled Scores	Scaled Score
272–273	100
270–271	99
268–269	98
266–267	97
263–265	96
261–262	95
259–260	94
257–258	93
255–256	92
252–254	91
250–251	90
248–249	89
246–247	88
243–245	87
241–242	86
239–240	85
237–238	84
234–236	83
232–233	82
230–231	81
227–229	80
225–226	79
223–224	78
220–222	77
218–219	76
215–217	75
213–214	74
211–212	73
208–210	72
206–207	71
204–205	70
201–203	69
199–200	68
196–198	67
194–195	66
191–193	65
189–190	64
186–188	63
183–185	62
180–182	61
177–179	60
175–176	59
172–174	58
169–171	57
166–168	56
163–165	55
160–162	54
158–159	53
155–157	52
152–154	51
149–151	50
146–148	49
143–145	48
140–142	47
137–139	46
134–136	45
131–133	44
128–130	43
125–127	42
122–124	41
119–121	40
116–118	39
113–115	38
110–112	37
107–109	36
104–106	35
101–103	34
99–100	33
96–98	32
94–95	31
91–93	30
88–90	29
86–87	28
83–85	27
81–82	26
78–80	25
76–77	24
73–75	23
71–72	22
68–70	21
66–67	20
63–65	19
61–62	18
58–60	17
56–57	16
53–55	15
51–52	14

TOTAL ENGLISH SCORE (A+B1+C1)

NAME — LAST — FIRST — MIDDLE — DATE — DATE OF BIRTH — AGE — SEX M OR F — GRADE OR CLASS

SCHOOL — CITY — TITLE OF THE ENGLISH COURSE YOU ARE NOW TAKING — INSTRUCTOR

Scaled Score — Levels — Vocab. — Speed

N 64 R 200X

COOPERATIVE TEST DIVISION
Educational Testing Service
Princeton, N. J. Los Angeles, Calif.

FIG. 44. *Typical 805 Test Answer Sheet*

machine was cumbersome and had built in inaccuracies and was never too successful.

A number of educational agencies across the country, especially E. F. Lindquist at the University of Iowa, continued searching for new and better methods of test scoring. In recent years a number of new and startling developments have taken place which have allowed educators to completely update their scoring techniques and provide for faster and more reliable service. However, until 1959 there was no one system that could be utilized by a local school district which allowed tests to be scored and processed by the same general purpose data processing equipment that processed the school district's business and other pupil-personnel applications.

During the 1959–60 school year, a new system of test scoring was devised and developed for use in the Richmond, California schools and later in the pilot project of the California State Department of Education It was called FAST, a short title or acronym for "Fully Automatic Scoring Technique."[2] It took the form of a test-answer card and was first used in a school testing program in the spring of 1960.

Test scoring, using the FAST system, is accomplished through the use of an IBM *card* instead of an *answer sheet*. The card is designed with sets of mark-sense "bubbles." Each set is identified by a test-item number, and contains a certain number of responses. Figure 45 illustrates a number of different FAST cards. The bubbles are so arranged that the card is read vertically rather than horizontally. Both the front and back of the card can be used. There are usually two vertical columns of response bubbles running down each face of the card, and each set of responses is normally four or five positions wide to allow for choice of answer. As many as 27 items can be accommodated per vertical column of items, so with two sets of columns on front and back, a theoretical maximum of 108 test items can be accommodated on a single card. Since the card must be identified in some manner to distinguish it from those with similar but slightly different designs, normally at least two item sets are sacrificed for this purpose so that the maximum number of items included in a design actually might be 106.

Recent announcements by IBM and by the Digitek Corporation have given hope that new test scoring devices will now provide faster and more powerful test-scoring potential and can pave the way for more effective operations. IBM has announced the 1230 test-scoring machine as a logical successor to the IBM 805 test-scoring machine. This new machine involves a totally new concept in test scoring. Instead of special electro-

2. The FAST System was invented and developed by Charles F. Wilkes, Chief Accountant for the Richmond City Schools.

Computer Test-Answer Cards (not for std IBM)

FAST CARD
FORM 15-1
© Copyright 1962, C. F. Wilkes
Fully Automatic Scoring Technique
DIRECTIONS
FILL ONLY ONE BUBBLE FOR EACH ITEM. USE ONLY THE SPECIAL PENCIL. PRESS FIRMLY TO MAKE GLOSSY BLACK MARKS. ERASE COMPLETELY ANY MARKS TO BE CHANGED. DO NOT MAKE ANY EXTRA MARKS ON THE CARD.
SAMPLE A
TEST I-SECTION A
TEST I-SECTION B
GO ON TO THE NEXT COLUMN
STOP WAIT FOR DIRECTIONS
BE SURE YOUR MARKS ARE HEAVY AND BLACK
MAKE NO EXTRA MARKS ON THE CARD.
ERASE ANY MARKS TO BE CHANGED.
IBM L56062
FAST CARD
FORM 17-77
© Copyright 1962, C. F. Wilkes
Fully Automatic Scoring Technique
DO ALL FIGURING ON SCRATCH PAPER
TEST A-I
PRESS FIRMLY TO MAKE GLOSSY BLACK MARKS. USE ONLY THE SPECIAL PENCIL. FILL ONLY ONE BUBBLE FOR EACH EXERCISE.
DO NOT MAKE ANY EXTRA MARKS ON THE CARD. DO NOT MARK THE TEST BOOKLET. ERASE COMPLETELY ANY MARKS TO BE CHANGED.
GO ON TO NEXT COLUMN
STOP-END OF TEST A-I
IBM L55975
FAST CARD
FORM 26-2
© Copyright 1962, C. F. Wilkes
Fully Automatic Scoring Technique
SAMPLE QUESTIONS
START HERE
GO ON TO NEXT COLUMN
GO ON TO OTHER SIDE
IBM L56006

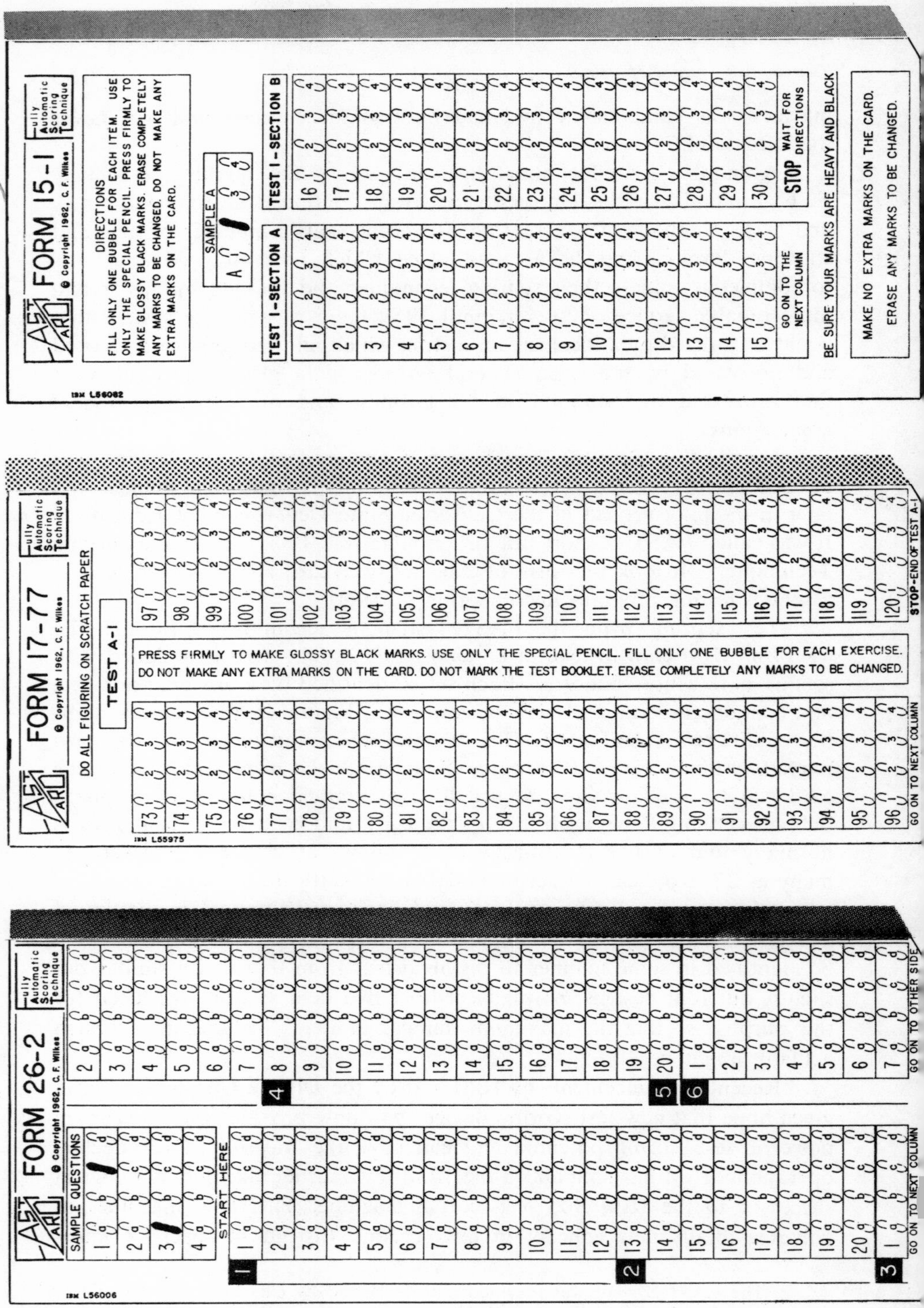

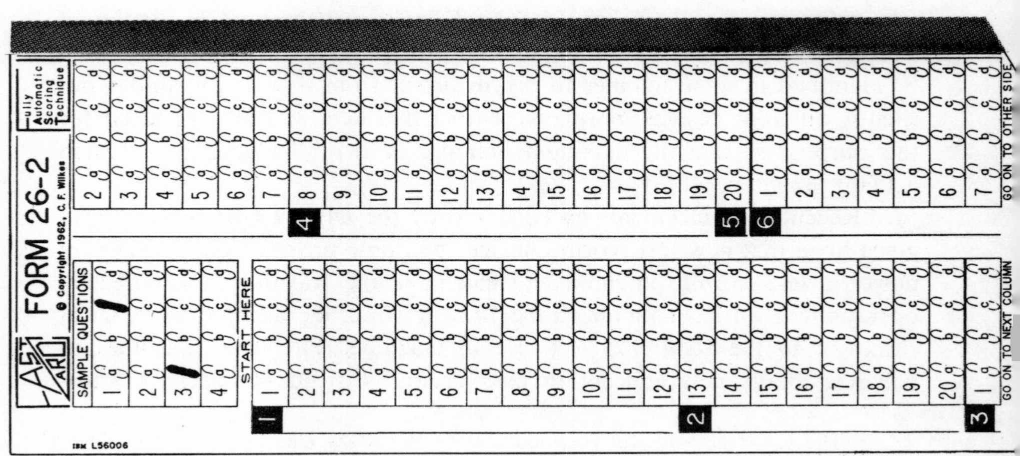

FIG. 45. *Samples of FAST Answer Cards*

FIG. 46. *IBM 1230 Test Scoring Machine*

FIG. 47. *Digitek 100 Test Scoring Machine*

graphic pencils to make electrically conducted marks, ordinary black lead pencils can be used. There is no longer the risk that someone may use the wrong kind of pencil since any soft-lead pencil will do.

The answer sheets used for this machine are different too. They are printed in red or brown because the optical reading process is insensitive to these colors. They are not larger but they can handle more questions and answers. The new answer sheet has up to 1,000 response positions, more than ever before. In this new form, response positions are laid out horizontally instead of vertically, there is room for either 400 two-part questions, 203 four- or five-part questions, or 106 ten-part questions. A vertical row of tiny marks on the right-hand border is reserved for programming processing instructions.

Both the IBM 1230 and the Digitek test-scoring machines have an operator's console through which test-scoring action can be controlled. Here switches, dials, and buttons are set up to electronically store correct answers and scoring instructions, to set the number of responses to a question, to select the scoring formula, to detect incorrect marking, to direct output, and to check operating accuracy. Figure 46 illustrates the IBM 1230 scoring machine and Figure 47 the Digitek 100 test-scoring machine.

Instead of scoring 400 tests an hour as on the 805 scoring machine, these machines operate at over 1200 sheets an hour. Through the use of electronics, the machine does no "guesswork." When the reading heads of these devices "see" a normal mark in a normal position, the mark is electronically registered as such. If the mark is weak or if heavy erasing is detected, the answer sheet will be automatically rejected for correction. If double marking is reflected, the sheet will be rejected, and the item will either be eliminated from the score or scored wrong—whichever the operator has selected.

The results, as read by the reading device, speed to counters. Here they are accumulated and, one at a time, counted for rights, wrongs, omits, rights minus wrongs, or rights minus a fraction of wrongs. The printer prints the group and total results in the margin of the answer sheet. Scored answer sheets go to a stacker; rejected sheets to a different stacker. Answer-sheet identification number and response results can then be punched into cards if desired.

The IBM 1230 Optical Mark Scoring Reader, as it is called, comes in three versions. One version will score tests and print information on the test answer sheet itself. The second version will punch a card with summary information which later can be processed on either punch card or computer equipment for final tabulation. A third version reads directly from the test-scoring machine into the memory of an electronic computer.

The Digitek machine also comes in a variety of models; it can punch cards or record on magnetic tape for computer processing.

Scoring By a Service Agency

Many schools are now taking advantage of the scoring services provided by various outside agencies. This plan insures accuracy of scoring and statistical work, and relieves the local school of a great deal of routine work. Also the service agencies today utilize very fast electronic data processing machines. Illustrative of some of the systems available today are the Science Research Associates Inc., Docutran System and the Scribe System of the Educational Testing Service. The unique SRA Docutran Service applies components of special design built for SRA. The most notable advance in this equipment is a high-speed photoelectric document-reading machine which scans one or both sides of a pencil-mark answer sheet and converts the marks of more than 5,000 positions to electronic impulses. These impulses produce output to a high-speed card punch or directly into the computer core memory for processing and output to magnetic tapes or an on-line printer. Although the system eliminates the need for punch cards, these can be prepared automatically and inexpensively at the speed of 5,280 per hour should the district's program require them or if the district wishes to do additional punch card processing.

The Educational Testing Service's Scribe System consists of three major components: a paper-handling assembly, a processor, and a card punch. For test scoring, these components collectively sense or "read" pencil-marked responses and translate them into numerical, alphabetical, or score response data, perform simple counting operations, and transcribe this information into punched cards in the following manner:

Answer sheets are introduced into the paper handling assembly and, by means of an electronic scanning system, the name of each student, his school, date of birth, test taken, and any other identification data that have been coded on his answer sheet are "read." As the paper is carried further along, Scribe reads the sudent's responses to test questions and communicates this information to the processor. Storing this information in its magnetic core memory, the processor selects the appropriate key (set of answers) for the test taken, and compares it with a student's responses. The numbers of right, wrong, and omitted responses are then totaled and these figures, together with the necessary identification data, are punched into cards. (Scribe II operates in a similar manner, but it has both a card punch and a magnetic tape output and can thus transcribe information either to cards or to tape.)

Scribe can perform this entire operation in little more than half a second. On a single answer sheet, it can score up to six different tests, in any order, at a rate of nearly 100 sheets a minute. Because Scribe can hold the answers to as many as 24 different tests in its memory, it can score an assortment of answer sheets each containing a different selection of tests. This eliminates the need for a pre-sorting of answer sheets into sub-

HOGAN JR HIGH CTMM

STUDENT NAME	M.A. LANG	N-LANG	TOTAL
OLSON IRWIN JR	157	191	174
PAULSEN RICHARD K	147	202	175
PELLEGRINI VINCENT	157	202	180
PODPLESKY CHARLENE	126	156	141
PODPLESKY SUSAN	198	195	197
POLLARD RICHARD	154	191	173
POPLEON GENE E	154	160	157
PORTER DORMAN L	123	160	142
ROBINSON RHONDA J	200	164	182
ROUTH MICHAEL	214	218	216
SAMANSKY EDWARD J	144	195	170
SCHREIBER TERESA	152	188	170
SCHWARTZ DANA K	154	191	173
SERVANTE ANTHONY L	157	160	159
SHANKLES DONALD M	136	137	137
SHANLEY J MICHAEL	202	152	177
SHAW GLEN E	164	126	145
SHAWHAN CHARLES V	139	131	135
SHEROUSE PATRICIA	144	149	147
SHIREY DONNA L	172	152	162
SHIRLEY LINDA K	147	140	144
SIMONS TERRY H	160	137	149
SMITH ALANA J	157	156	157
SMITH GEORGE S	160	172	166
SMITH LINDA R	157	152	155
SMITH RODJIE M	180	156	168
SOUTHERLAND RONNY L	184	164	174
SPEHAR HARRY R	139	191	165
STAMPER SUZANNE	157	168	163
STANDISH BEVERLY	149	191	170
STANLEY DARLENE F	176	172	174
STEHLE RANDOLPH C	200	218	209
STEPHENSEN JUDY A	210	210	210
SULLIVAN PATRICIA A	164	188	176
SWEET MICHAEL J	131	202	167
TAYLOR JAMES E	149	145	147
THOMAS CHARLES	117	124	121
TREADWAY ROBERT	192	168	180
TULLETT MARY E	134	160	147
VAUGHAN MICKIE	131	137	134
VILLARREAL ROGER	200	164	182
WALKER MARY A	172	156	164
WHITESELL GEORGE W	212	222	217
WIGGINS JOAN E	164	172	168
WILLIAMS KENNETH D	144	191	168
WILLIAMS L FAYE	147	168	158
WILLIAMS NANCY J	154	172	163
WINNIFORD LINDA D	180	184	182
WIRBICK LARRY	164	160	162
WOODALL ANGELINE L	160	202	181
WOODALL RACHAEL L	180	120	150

FIG. 48. *Class Roster of Test Scores*

SEC FEBRUARY 1961 TESTING

I.Q. LANG	I.Q. N LANG	I.Q. TOTAL	I.G.P. LANG	I.G.P. N-LANG	I.G.P. TOTAL
87	106	97	7.8	10.2	9.0
85	116	101	6.9	12.5	9.7
91	117	104	7.8	12.5	10.2
73	90	82	5.2	7.7	6.5
123	121	122	10.7	10.5	10.6
84	104	94	7.5	10.2	8.9
85	88	87	7.5	8.0	7.8
67	86	77	5.0	8.0	6.5
114	94	104	11.5	8.3	9.9
133	135	134	13.8	14.3	14.1
78	105	92	6.7	10.5	8.6
86	107	97	7.3	10.0	8.7
89	110	100	7.5	10.2	8.9
85	86	86	7.8	8.0	7.9
77	77	77	6.0	6.2	6.1
114	85	100	12.5	7.3	9.9
97	74	86	8.3	5.2	6.8
76	72	74	6.2	5.6	5.9
86	89	88	6.7	7.1	6.9
102	90	96	9.0	7.3	8.2
84	80	82	6.9	6.3	6.6
94	80	87	8.0	6.2	7.1
92	91	92	7.8	7.7	7.8
94	101	98	8.0	9.0	8.5
90	87	89	7.8	7.3	7.6
104	90	97	9.5	7.7	8.6
105	94	100	9.8	8.3	9.1
80	109	95	6.2	10.2	8.2
94	100	97	7.8	8.7	8.3
88	113	101	7.1	10.2	8.7
102	100	101	9.2	9.0	9.1
118	129	124	11.5	14.3	12.9
125	125	125	13.4	13.4	13.4
97	111	104	8.3	10.0	9.2
76	117	97	5.6	12.5	9.1
84	81	83	7.1	6.7	6.9
64	68	66	4.5	5.1	4.8
111	97	104	10.3	8.7	9.5
78	93	86	5.8	8.0	6.9
77	81	79	5.6	6.2	5.9
106	87	97	11.5	8.3	9.9
101	91	96	9.0	7.7	8.4
121	127	124	13.6	14.9	14.3
93	97	95	8.3	9.0	8.7
83	110	97	6.7	10.2	8.5
87	99	93	6.9	8.7	7.8
92	102	97	7.5	9.0	8.3
103	105	104	9.5	9.8	9.7
91	88	90	8.3	8.0	8.2
90	113	102	8.0	12.5	10.3
101	67	84	9.5	4.8	7.2

FORM 31 - R4 (REV. 7/63) ®

RICHMOND

REPORT OF

GRANADA
SCHOOL NAME

STUDENT NAME	VRENA %/ST-9		VERB. REAS. %/ST-9	NUM. ABIL. %/ST-9	ABSTR. REAS. %/ST-9	
ACHICA FELICIANO	02%-1		02%-1	08%-2	03%-1	
ADAMS DWAYNE	31%-4		50%-5	17%-3	86%-7	
ALLEN BARBARA	02%-1		12%-3	01%-1	47%-5	
ALLEN SHIRLEY #	74%-6		88%-7	45%-5	89%-8	
ALLISON DORIS	07%-2		25%-4	05%-2	44%-5	
AMIE JESSIE 8	14%-3		12%-3	25%-4	21%-3	
ARCHIE CAROLYN	02%-1		03%-1	05%-2	41%-5	
ARNOLD PERLINE	02%-1		03%-1	02%-1	13%-3	
ASAZAWA GARY	39%-4		50%-5	30%-4	55%-5	
AVERY DEBORAH	02%-1		08%-2	01%-1	11%-3	
BALLARD WILLIAM	46%-5		30%-4	63%-6	13%-3	
BANKS JOSEPHUS	49%-5		53%-5	45%-5	50%-5	
BATES WILLY	02%-1		01%-1	08%-2	03%-1	
BELVIN ANGELA	23%-4		25%-4	25%-4	53%-5	
BELVINE ANGELITA	29%-4		25%-4	35%-4	27%-4	
BENNETT MATTIE	49%-5		40%-5	60%-6	16%-3	
BERRY ROBERT #	89%-8		99%-9	17%-3	88%-7	
BLACKMORE HENRY	36%-4		07%-2	67%-6	18%-3	
BLADE LINDA	20%-3		12%-3	35%-4	34%-4	
BOLDS JEFFREY	01%-1		01%-1	01%-1	13%-3	
BOLES WILHELMINA	31%-4		30%-4	35%-4	36%-4	
BOLLING JERRY	39%-4		20%-3	60%-6	58%-5	
BOOKER CHERYL	31%-4		12%-3	55%-5	50%-5	
BOSTIC CAESAR	05%-2		20%-3	03%-1	18%-3	
BOYER KATHLEEN	02%-1		08%-2	01%-1	03%-1	
BRACKENRIDGE ROBERT	05%-2		10%-2	08%-2	58%-5	
BRICE CAROLYN	49%-5		55%-5	45%-5	53%-5	
BRIM DIANE	05%-2		05%-2	13%-3	22%-3	
BRITT BARBARA	01%-1		02%-1	02%-1	06%-2	
BROCK KIRK	01%-1		01%-1	03%-1	13%-3	
BROWN CANDACE	20%-3		45%-5	07%-2	29%-4	
BROWN JANIS	34%-4		15%-3	55%-5	22%-3	
BROWN NORMA	23%-4		12%-3	40%-5	03%-1	
BRYSON ORENE 8	05%-2		20%-3	05%-2	27%-4	
BUTLER LARRY	17%-3		25%-4	17%-3	29%-4	
BUTLER WALTER				01%-1	14%-3	
BYIAS STANLEY	11%-3		04%-2	25%-4	03%-1	
CALHOUN RUBY	07%-2		12%-3	13%-3	15%-3	
CAMPBELL GERALD	17%-3		15%-3	25%-4	34%-4	
CARLSON WAYNE A	51%-5		73%-6	25%-4	65%-6	
CARPENTER LARRY	39%-4		81%-7	01%-1	39%-4	
CARTER BETTY	34%-4		20%-3	50%-5	06%-2	
CHANG THOMAS #	81%-7		79%-7	75%-6	80%-7	
CHAVEZ VICTOR	54%-5		76%-6	25%-4	19%-3	
CHELENEDOS JERRY	20%-3		20%-3	25%-4	27%-4	
CHENEY LYDIA	11%-3		05%-2	30%-4	12%-3	
CHRISTIAN ZORA	05%-2		20%-3	05%-2	60%-6	
CLAIBORNE JOYCE	17%-3		12%-3	30%-4	29%-4	
CLAUDIO LEONARD	61%-6		60%-6	60%-6	86%-7	
COBBS GREGORY	23%-4		45%-5	09%-2	86%-7	

FIG. 49. *Class Roster of Differential Aptitude Test*

SCHOOLS

TEST RESULTS

8 (GRADE) | (GROUP) | DEC-1963 (DATE TESTED)

MECH. REAS. %/ST-9		SPACE REL. %/ST-9		SPELL-ING %/ST-9		SEN-TENCES %/ST-9		CLER. SP&ACC %/ST-9	
15%-3		01%-1		62%-6		03%-1		20%-3	
41%-5		63%-6		23%-4		54%-5		10%-2	
32%-4		52%-5		33%-4		11%-3		07%-2	
99%-9		62%-6		87%-7		44%-5		62%-6	
14%-3		40%-5		46%-5		41%-5		07%-2	
01%-1		19%-3		23%-4		01%-1		02%-1	
09%-2		13%-3		28%-4		34%-4		24%-4	
01%-1		19%-3		14%-3		01%-1		50%-5	
41%-5		89%-8		28%-4		69%-6		50%-5	
50%-5		17%-3		11%-3		08%-2		01%-1	
04%-2		50%-5		64%-6		34%-4		55%-5	
41%-5		54%-5		41%-5		34%-4		12%-3	
05%-2		08%-2		05%-2		03%-1		03%-1	
14%-3		55%-5		34%-4		12%-3		26%-4	
22%-3		58%-5		56%-5		01%-1		24%-4	
32%-4		60%-6		63%-6		56%-5		06%-2	
34%-4		90%-8		95%-8		92%-8		09%-2	
03%-1		36%-4		23%-4		59%-5		03%-1	
14%-3		65%-6		10%-2		12%-3		04%-2	
13%-3		15%-3		47%-5		03%-1		10%-2	
07%-2		01%-1		54%-5		46%-5		09%-2	
11%-3		73%-6		67%-6		03%-1		09%-2	
40%-5		46%-5		77%-7		01%-1		16%-3	
24%-4		41%-5		05%-2		29%-4		40%-5	
71%-6		19%-3		00%-1		06%-2		04%-2	
55%-5		66%-6		38%-4		54%-5		07%-2	
62%-6		37%-4		93%-8		49%-5		70%-6	
19%-3		35%-4		24%-4		06%-2		06%-2	
32%-4		04%-2		17%-3		01%-1		05%-2	
05%-2		07%-2		20%-3		03%-1		03%-1	
65%-6		31%-4		59%-5		19%-3		24%-4	
43%-5		81%-7		53%-5		19%-3			
22%-3		37%-4		00%-1		15%-3		10%-2	
19%-3		29%-4		00%-1		01%-1		02%-1	
04%-2		30%-4		05%-2		26%-4		06%-2	
03%-1		10%-2		26%-4		03%-1		12%-3	
04%-2		17%-3		15%-3		51%-5		07%-2	
16%-3		21%-3		46%-5		01%-1		09%-2	
15%-3		12%-3		44%-5		21%-3		05%-2	
41%-5		17%-3		96%-9		69%-6		29%-4	
36%-4		81%-7		57%-5		17%-3		14%-3	
22%-3		24%-4		44%-5		12%-3		21%-3	
41%-5		75%-6		94%-8		85%-7		09%-2	
24%-4		71%-6		58%-5		29%-4		00%-1	
15%-3		53%-5		15%-3		03%-1		12%-3	
28%-4		37%-4		22%-3		01%-1		65%-6	
25%-4		54%-5		00%-1		24%-4		33%-4	
32%-4		19%-3		00%-1		26%-4		16%-3	
41%-5		91%-8		80%-7		46%-5		12%-3	
74%-6		65%-6		65%-6		51%-5		02%-1	

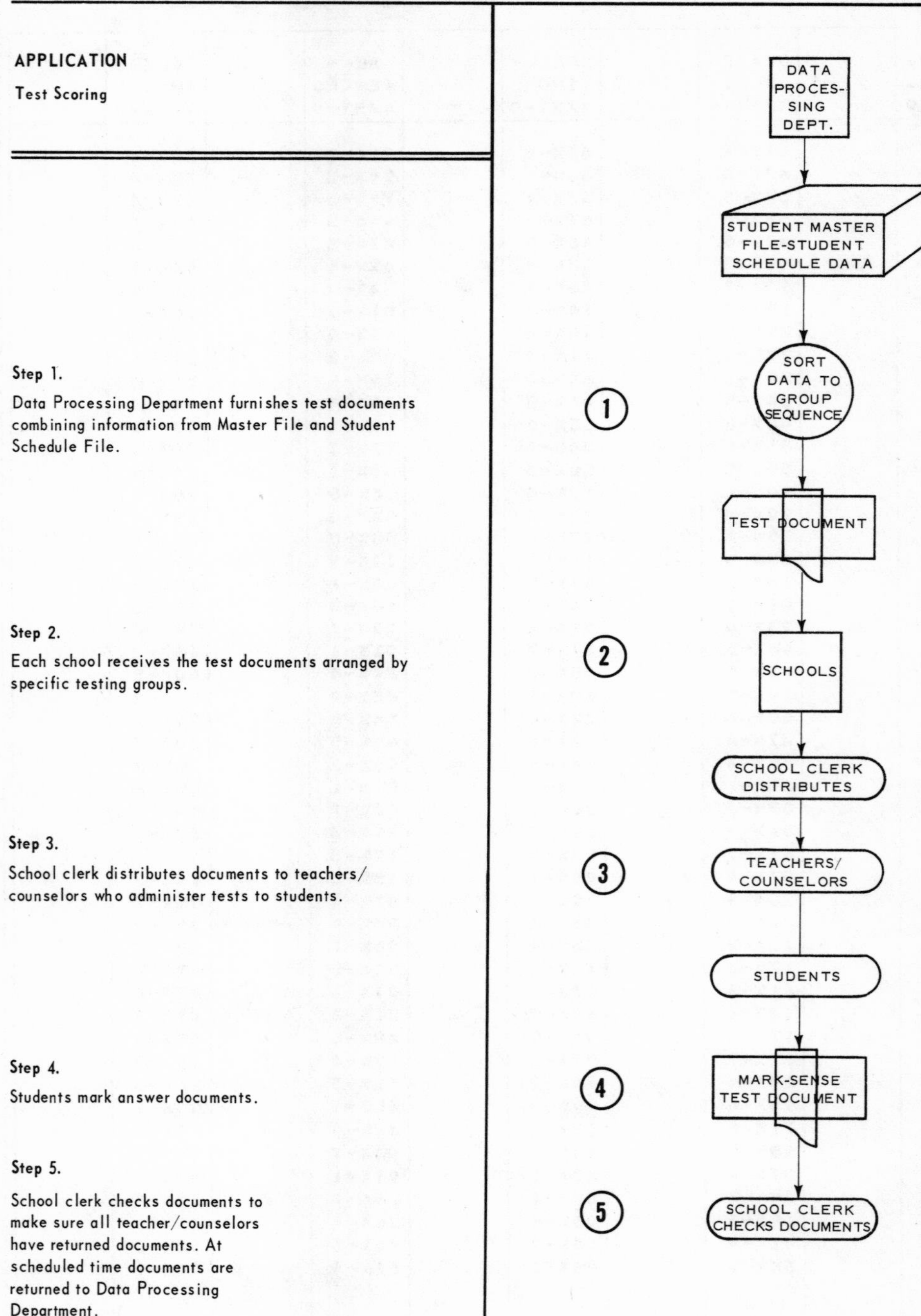

FIG. 50. *Procedural Steps for Test Scoring*

APPLICATION

Test Scoring

Step 6.

Test documents are converted to machine language and processed. Appropriate norms tables are introduced. Data punched into cards to be sent to State.

Step 7.

Student profile cards are prepared.

Step 8.

Test rosters are prepared by various test groups.

Step 9.

Test rosters are prepared by schools.

Step 10.

An item analysis of achievement tests is prepared.

Step 11.

Pressure sensitive labels for the student cumulative record are prepared.

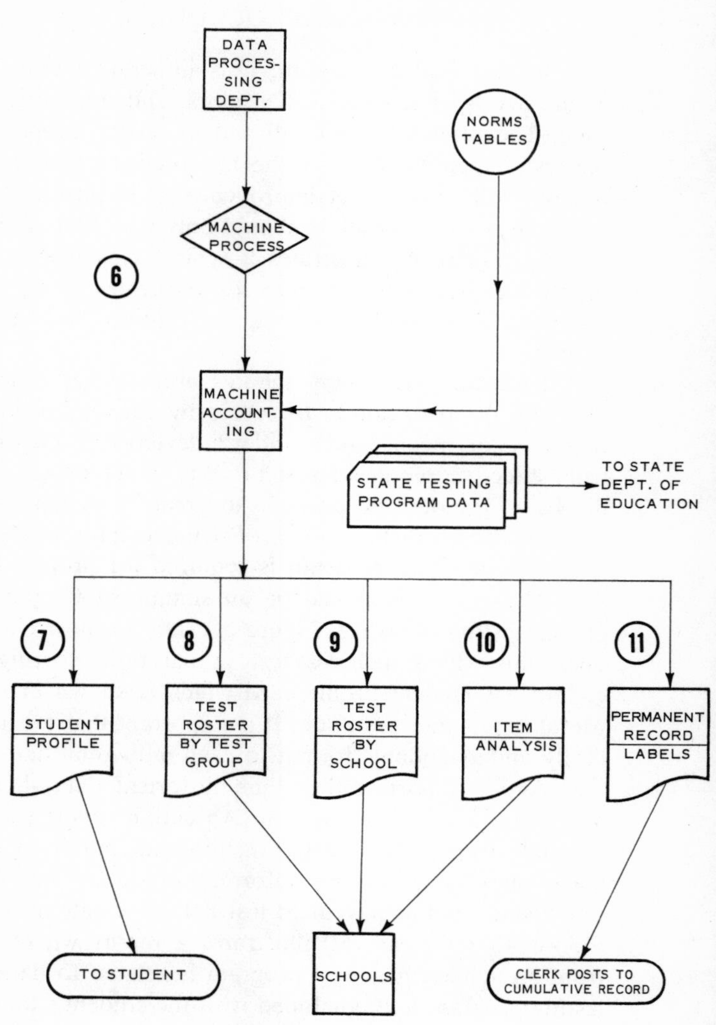

ject categories such as French, mathematics, English, or physics. It also enables students to use the same answer sheet for an entire half-day of testing.

RECORDING PROCEDURES

In any testing program, it is imperative that the results be placed in the hands of teachers, counselors, and administrators as soon as possible. Too often a school will end its testing program with the scoring of the tests, apparently under the mistaken impression that the mere taking of tests will bring about improvements. Returning a roster of test results to teachers and counselors should only be a first step in the total reporting process. Figure 48 illustrates a typical class roster of test scores for an intelligence test while Figure 49 illustrates a report of the Differential Aptitude Test combining both percentiles and stanines on a common format.

Unfortunately, many schools are satisfied with just preparing class lists and the distribution of scores by classes, together with medians and quartiles, or means and standard deviations. This is not adequate for a truly effective reporting system. With data processing equipment at our disposal, it should be possible to create a system that is able to quickly summarize and distill a mass of detailed information, making information available in whatever detail is required for proper decision-making.

The emphasis should be on summarized reports rather than routine clerical listing of scores. Figure 50 shows a flow chart of a school district operation which includes test preparation, scoring, and reporting procedures. A student profile card which is shown in Figure 51 can also be useful in test interpretation. It is important that test data be reported in an easily understandable format to each individual like this.

Action reports rather than historical data should be emphasized in developing a reporting system. An action report should draw information not only from a current testing program but from other sources such as mark reporting, and this information should be further combined with intelligence and achievement test data to create a more meaningful report. Figure 43 on page 150 illustrates a report where the basic information from an achievement test program is related to data from the intelligence testing program and combined with the student's total mark-point average. It should be noted that this type of action report takes into consideration the fact that counselors, teachers, and administrators are not often well trained in statistics; therefore data should be presented in a simple straightforward manner. The reporting device used is that of a simple stanine scale. It should also be noted that at the far right-hand side of this report is a written statement indicating to the educator who receives this information pertinent data which calls for action on his part. A school

STUDENT NAME		GRADE	STUDENT NUMBER	SCHOOL	TESTING PROGRAM	DATE TESTED
ANDERSON DIANA	007	6	00050-G	15	GRADE 6 FALL TESTING	DEC63

TEST NAME AND FORM	TEST RESULTS	TEST PROFILE
HENMON-NELSON 3-6	88%ILE	*****************************
PARAGRAPH MEANING	76%ILE	*************************
WORD MEANING	83%ILE	***************************
ARITH. REASONING	NO TEST	
ARITH. COMPUTATION	NO TEST	

INDIVIDUAL TEST RECORD

FAST Test Results

BELOW AVERAGE AVERAGE ABOVE AVERAGE

FIG. 51. *Student Test Profile Card*

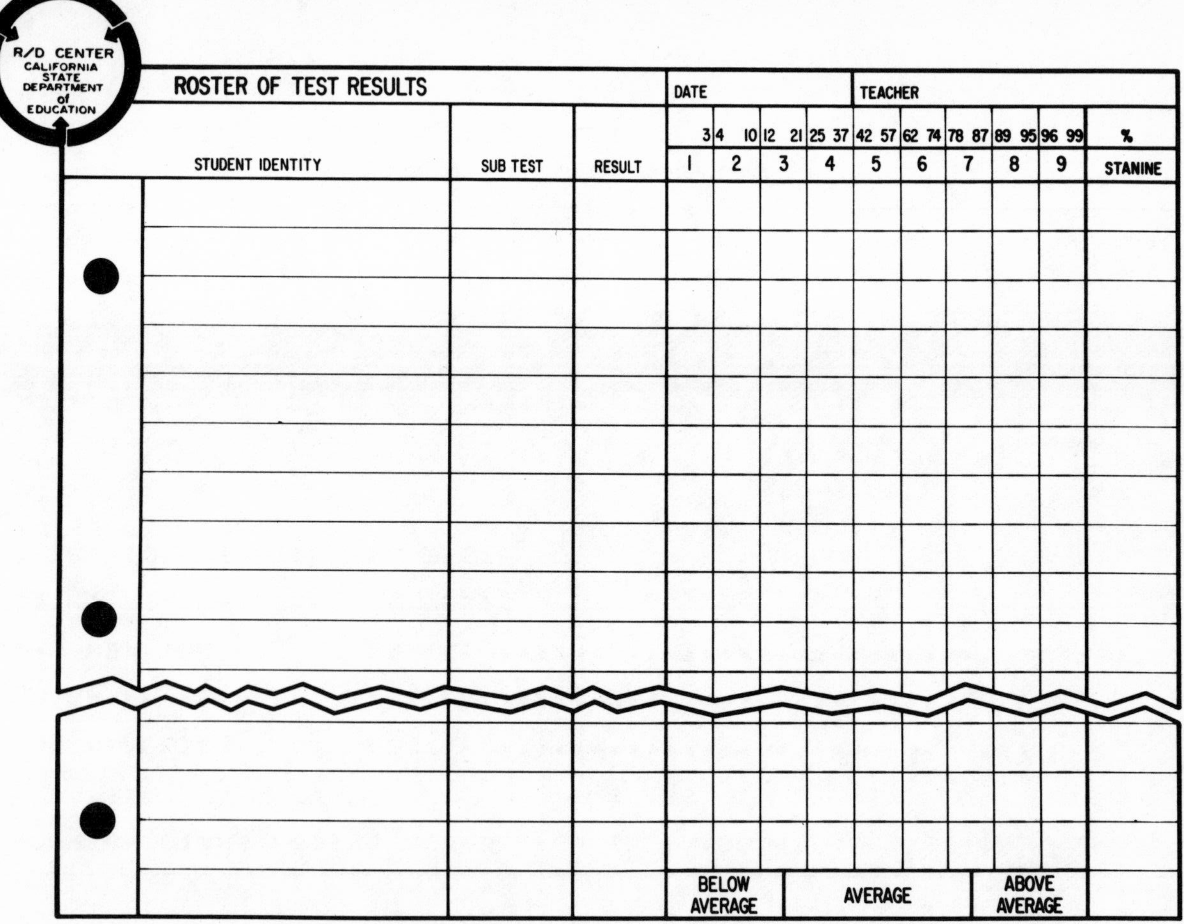

FIG. 52. *Roster of Test Results*

administrator looking at this report can tell that his school is out of step with other schools in the district, or that certain departments within his school have abnormal marking practices, or students in his school are not living up to their potential. Similar and related information is available to the counselor for each of his students and to the teacher for each and everyone of her students.

A specially prepared teacher report is illustrated in Figure 52. In this report, for the first time, detailed information is made available to, and directed at, the teacher. It is not a simple roster of test results but a detailed and meaningful report that will enable the teacher to individualize her classroom instruction.

GUIDELINES FOR LOCAL TEST-SCORING OPERATIONS

If your school district is going to use data processing equipment for test scoring, the following suggestions are offered as guidelines:

1. Local district test scoring can be more accurate and efficient if back-up use of a computer is made available for further processing after the actual answer sheets or cards have been scored.

2. Insofar as it is possible, test scoring should be scheduled so as to avoid an extreme peak time, e.g., report card preparation. If business applications are to be processed, additional scheduling problems might occur and should be taken into consideration.

3. All computer programs, control panel setups, and procedures should be thoroughly prepared, tested, and retested *prior* to the time they must be used for live data.

4. There is need for tight controls on the quality of input data. If the cards or documents are not marked correctly or are not submitted in proper procedural order, data processing operations can become snarled.

5. Promises of completion dates for test-processing jobs should be made with the utmost conservatism. No one complains when results come early; there are many complaints when results come late.

6. Only competent personnel should be employed, and they should be well paid; this holds true for all other areas of personnel in the data processing field. It is important that employee turnover be reduced to a negligible minimum, and continuity of staff be assured. In the long run, it is not the hard work, the system, or the methods, but the *personnel* who will make or break an installation. Foresight on this point has its rewards.

11

ATTENDANCE ACCOUNTING

Of all the major areas of EDP application in education, the accounting of pupil attendance is perhaps the most rewarding, primarily because attendance data usually form the basis for the apportionment of state funds for school operation. It also provides the facility for compiling meaningful analyses of patterns of pupil attendance and the evaluation of entries and withdrawals, including dropouts, in the school setting.

TWO TYPES OF ATTENDANCE ACCOUNTING

There are two main types of attendance accounting: apportionment and control. Apportionment accounting is a daily count of how many pupils attended school for any given segment of that day, and generally is reported on a monthly or less frequent basis to the apportioning agency. This is a straightforward process that lends itself to automation. Figure 53 shows a report used for this purpose.

The control type of accounting is an administrative tool used to keep track of all pupils for each and every period; it provides the information to answer such questions as "I just saw Johnny Jones walking down the street. Was he marked absent this period?" This type of attendance accounting, even though maintained by most schools, rarely has been automated successfully.

GENERAL PROCEDURE

For either system, most schools start the accounting cycle by using a method which provides for the gathering of pupil absence information, period by period, on some type of reporting form. Teachers record the names of absent students on forms that are collected by monitors each period. The monitors converge on the attendance office with all of the forms for immediate recording on the pupil's master attendance card. One variation of the method uses the first period forms to compile a master roster of the day's absentees. This roster is distributed to the teachers so that only "new" absences need be reported during the succeeding periods of the day. Another variation has every teacher record every absence each period on the attendance form; in this case a master roster is not prepared for distribution.

In either case, the attendance office staff records the daily absences on a document or card bearing the student's name. Figure 54 shows several types of recording cards. The cards or documents can be pre-printed and identified from the student master file data thus saving considerable clerical time in the attendance office. The data cards can be accumulated in the office for a complete attendance period before being sent to the data processing center.

This procedure allows the various monthly and yearly reports to be prepared accurately and easily. These reports can include the preparation of the attendance register for the teacher (see Figure 55) as well as a statistical breakdown of enrollment at the beginning of the attendance period, of new entries by entry type, returnees, withdrawals, end-of-attendance period enrollment, days of attendance, days of absence by the type of absence, and summaries and totals for each category.

PREPARATION

Although attendance accounting is almost a universal practice, the methods and procedures used for this application vary greatly from district to district, and from school to school. Therefore, prior to establishing an automated system for processing attendance data, it would be advisable to spend adequate time in planning the application.

It has been mentioned in Chapter 9 that the teachers, counselors, and administrators affected by these procedures should be involved in the planning of the conversion to a new system. It is equally important, with regard to attendance, to involve the clerical staff in the orientation and in-service training programs for this new system.

Since accuracy is extremely important in this application, considerable thought and planning must be devoted to developing an efficient system. The Richmond Pilot Project staff constructed a manual of procedures for attendance clerks that also served as a ready reference for teachers, counselors, and administrators. It contained step-by-step explanations of the following points:

1. Materials provided for the schools at the beginning of the attendance accounting year.
2. Special procedures to be followed during the first month.
3. Procedures for handling newly enrolled pupils.
4. Maintenance of pupil cards.
5. Principles and procedures for marking an absence.
6. Procedures for disenrolling pupils.
7. Explanation of the left codes which indicated why pupils dropped school.

▼ DISTRICT OR SCHOOL

SCHOOL MONTH	SCHOOL CODE	GRADE	SCHOOL, DISTRICT OF RESIDENCE, TEACHER NAME	CURRENT			
				BOYS	GIRLS	TOTAL	DAYS TAUGHT

FIG. 53. *Attendance Accounting Apportionment Report*

ATTENDANCE REPORT

PAGE | FISCAL YEAR

CHOOL MONTH				SCHOOL YEAR TO DATE				
DAYS NOT ENROLLED	DAYS ABSENT O. T. I. O. Q.	DAYS OF APPORT'MT ATTEND.	TOTAL DAYS	DAYS TAUGHT	DAYS NOT ENROLLED	DAYS ABSENT O. T. I. O. Q.	DAYS OF APPORTION'MT ATTENDANCE	TOTAL DAYS

2199

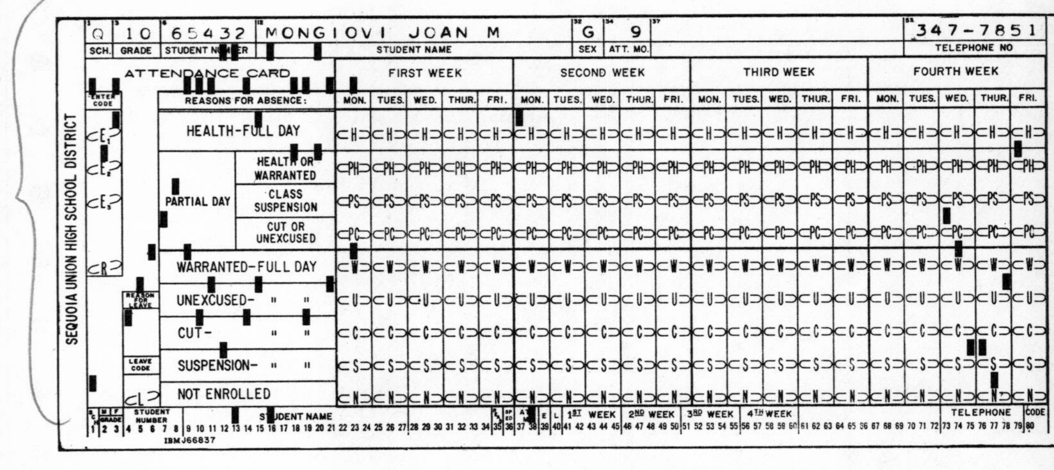

SEQUOIA UNION HIGH SCHOOL DISTRICT

SCH.	GRADE	STUDENT NUMBER	STUDENT NAME	SEX	ATT. MO.	TELEPHONE NO
Q	10	65432	MONGIOVI JOAN M	G	9	347-7851

ATTENDANCE CARD

ENTER CODE	REASONS FOR ABSENCE:		FIRST WEEK MON.	TUES.	WED.	THUR.	FRI.	SECOND WEEK MON.	TUES.	WED.	THUR.	FRI.	THIRD WEEK MON.	TUES.	WED.	THUR.	FRI.	FOURTH WEEK MON.	TUES.	WED.	THUR.	FRI.
E1	HEALTH-FULL DAY		H	H	H	H	H	H	H	H	H	H	H	H	H	H	H	H	H	H	H	H
E2	PARTIAL DAY	HEALTH OR WARRANTED	PH	PH	PH	PH	PH	PH	PH	PH	PH	PH	PH	PH	PH	PH	PH	PH	PH	PH	PH	PH
E3		CLASS SUSPENSION	PS	PS	PS	PS	PS	PS	PS	PS	PS	PS	PS	PS	PS	PS	PS	PS	PS	PS	PS	PS
		CUT OR UNEXCUSED	PC	PC	PC	PC	PC	PC	PC	PC	PC	PC	PC	PC	PC	PC	PC	PC	PC	PC	PC	PC
R	WARRANTED-FULL DAY		W	W	W	W	W	W	W	W	W	W	W	W	W	W	W	W	W	W	W	W
REASON FOR LEAVE	UNEXCUSED- " "		U	U	U	U	U	U	U	U	U	U	U	U	U	U	U	U	U	U	U	U
	CUT- " "		C	C	C	C	C	C	C	C	C	C	C	C	C	C	C	C	C	C	C	C
LEAVE CODE	SUSPENSION- " "		S	S	S	S	S	S	S	S	S	S	S	S	S	S	S	S	S	S	S	S
L	NOT ENROLLED		N	N	N	N	N	N	N	N	N	N	N	N	N	N	N	N	N	N	N	N

SCH 1 · M F GRADE 2 3 · STUDENT NUMBER 4 5 6 7 8 · STUDENT NAME 9–35 · 36 · ATT. 37 38 · E 39 · L 40 · 1ST WEEK 41–45 · 2ND WEEK 46–50 · 3RD WEEK 51–55 · 4TH WEEK 56–60 · 61–72 · TELEPHONE 73–79 · CODE 80

IBM J66837

SCH. CODE	GRADE	STUDENT NUMBER	B/G	STUDENT NAME	BIRTH-DATE MONTH	YEAR	ADVISORY	DIST. OF RES.	NEW	CHANGE	LEFT

SCHOOL CODE	GRADE	STUDENT NUMBER Y/8= BOY X/8= GIRL	STUDENT NAME -19 COLUMNS- LAST NAME, FIRST NAME, MIDDLE INTL.	BIRTH DATE MO.	YR.	ADVISORY ROOM NUMBER	DIST. OF RESIDENCE	LEFT CODE
0 0	0	0 0 0 0 0	0 0 0 0 0 0 0 0 0 0 0 0 0 0 0 0 0 0 0	0	0 0	0 0 0	0 0	0
1 2	3	4 5 6 7 8	9 10 11 12 13 14 15 16 17 18 19 20 21 22 23 24 25 26 27	28	29 30	31 32 33	34 35	36
1 1	1	1 1 1 1 1	1 1 1 1 1 1 1 1 1 1 1 1 1 1 1 1 1 1 1	1	1 1	1 1 1	1 1	1
2 2	2	2 2 2 2 2	2 2 2 2 2 2 2 2 2 2 2 2 2 2 2 2 2 2 2	2	2 2	2 2 2	2 2	2
3 3	3	3 3 3 3 3	3 3 3 3 3 3 3 3 3 3 3 3 3 3 3 3 3 3 3	3	3 3	3 3 3	3 3	3
4 4	4	4 4 4 4 4	4 4 4 4 4 4 4 4 4 4 4 4 4 4 4 4 4 4 4	4	4 4	4 4 4	4 4	4
5 5	5	5 5 5 5 5	5 5 5 5 5 5 5 5 5 5 5 5 5 5 5 5 5 5 5	5	5 5	5 5 5	5 5	5
6 6	6	6 6 6 6 6	6 6 6 6 6 6 6 6 6 6 6 6 6 6 6 6 6 6 6	6	6 6	6 6 6	6 6	6
7 7	7	7 7 7 7 7	7 7 7 7 7 7 7 7 7 7 7 7 7 7 7 7 7 7 7	7	7 7	7 7 7	7 7	7
8 8	8	8 8 8 8 8	8 8 8 8 8 8 8 8 8 8 8 8 8 8 8 8 8 8 8	8	8 8	8 8 8	8 8	8
9 9	9	9 9 9 9 9	9 9 9 9 9 9 9 9 9 9 9 9 9 9 9 9 9 9 9	9	9 9	9 9 9	9 9	9
1 2	3	4 5 6 7 8	9 10 11 12 13 14 15 16 17 18 19 20 21 22 23 24 25 26 27	28	29 30	31 32 33	34 35	36

8/62

IBM L56121

DAYS OF ABSENCE OTHER THAN ILLNESS OR QUARANTINE

FIRST WEEK M	T	W	T	F	SECOND WEEK M	T	W	T	F	THIRD WEEK M	T	W	T	F	FOURTH WEEK M	T	W	T	F	DAYS NOT ENROLLED
1	1	1	1	1	1	1	1	1	1	1	1	1	1	1	1	1	1	1	1	0 1
1	2	3	4	5	6	7	8	9	10	11	12	13	14	15	16	17	18	19	20	

THIS SPACE TO BE USED FOR NEW STUDENTS ONLY

THE COUNSELOR NAME AND ALL DATA AT THE TOP OF THE CARD MUST BE PROVIDED FOR EACH NEWLY ENROLLED STUDENT. ______ COUNSELOR-LAST NAME & INITIAL

TEST DATA ON NEWLY ENROLLED STUDENTS WILL BE INCORPORATED IN DISTRICT REPORTS IF PROVIDED BELOW.

DISTRICT TESTING PROGRAM	DATE TESTED ______ MONTH-YEAR	______ NAME OF INTELLIGENCE TEST	______ I.Q.
______ NAME OF ACHIEVEMENT BATTERY	RDG. TEST ______ % RANK	MATH. TEST ______ % RANK	LANG. TEST ______ % RANK
D.A.T. BATTERY	V.R.+ N.A. ______ % RANK	VERB. REAS. ______ % RANK	NUM. ABIL. ______ % RANK	ABST. REAS. ______ % RANK
MECH. REAS. ______ % RANK	SPACE RELNS. ______ % RANK	LANG. SPELL. ______ % RANK	LANG. SENT. ______ % RANK	CLER. S.&A. ______ % RANK

ATTENDANCE CARD 2 3 4 5 6 7 8 9 80

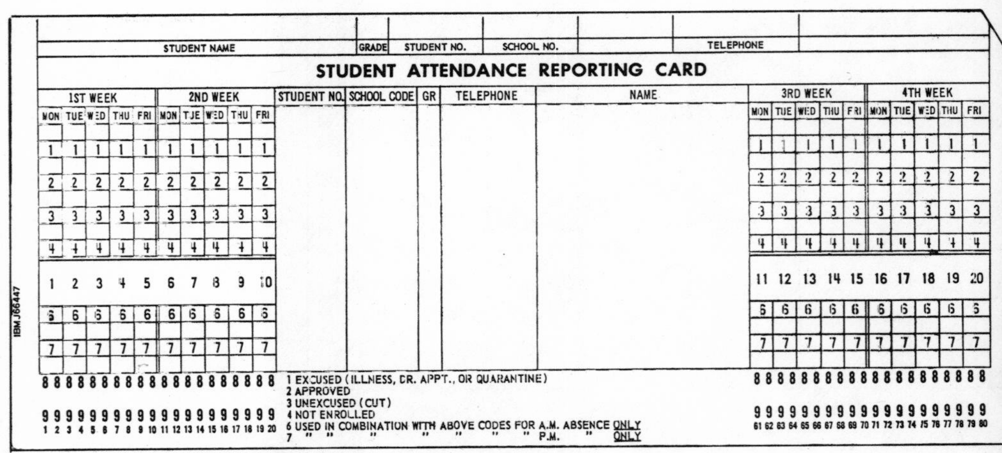

STUDENT NAME	GRADE	STUDENT NO.	SCHOOL NO.		TELEPHONE

STUDENT ATTENDANCE REPORTING CARD

1ST WEEK MON	TUE	WED	THU	FRI	2ND WEEK MON	TUE	WED	THU	FRI	STUDENT NO.	SCHOOL CODE	GR	TELEPHONE	NAME	3RD WEEK MON	TUE	WED	THU	FRI	4TH WEEK MON	TUE	WED	THU	FRI
1	1	1	1	1	1	1	1	1	1						1	1	1	1	1	1	1	1	1	1
2	2	2	2	2	2	2	2	2	2						2	2	2	2	2	2	2	2	2	2
3	3	3	3	3	3	3	3	3	3						3	3	3	3	3	3	3	3	3	3
4	4	4	4	4	4	4	4	4	4						4	4	4	4	4	4	4	4	4	4
1	2	3	4	5	6	7	8	9	10						11	12	13	14	15	16	17	18	19	20
6	6	6	6	6	6	6	6	6	6						6	6	6	6	6	6	6	6	6	6
7	7	7	7	7	7	7	7	7	7						7	7	7	7	7	7	7	7	7	7

8 8 8 8 8 8 8 8 8 8 8 8 8 8 8 8 8 8 8 8 — 8 8 8 8 8 8 8 8 8 8 8 8 8 8 8 8 8 8 8 8

9 9 9 9 9 9 9 9 9 9 9 9 9 9 9 9 9 9 9 9 — 9 9 9 9 9 9 9 9 9 9 9 9 9 9 9 9 9 9 9 9

1 2 3 4 5 6 7 8 9 10 11 12 13 14 15 16 17 18 19 20 — 61 62 63 64 65 66 67 68 69 70 71 72 73 74 75 76 77 78 79 80

1 EXCUSED (ILLNESS, DR. APPT., OR QUARANTINE)
2 APPROVED
3 UNEXCUSED (CUT)
4 NOT ENROLLED
6 USED IN COMBINATION WITH ABOVE CODES FOR A.M. ABSENCE ONLY
7 " " " " " " " " P.M. " ONLY

IBM J66447

FIG. 54. *Cards Used for Recording Student Absences*

8. Procedures for pupils who enroll and leave within the same reporting period.

9. Procedures for pupils who leave and return during the same reporting period.

10. Procedures for handling cases where pupils are assigned to home teachers.

11. Procedures for handling situations where pupils have been assigned to or are returned from the juvenile authorities.

12. Procedures for changing student data in the attendance office file.

13. Procedures for correcting errors in marking absence.

14. Procedure for submitting the reports for processing at the end of each attendance period.

15. Procedures for handling the attendance control form to reconcile the pupil accounting forms sent to the data processing center with the number delivered to the school for the following attendance period.

16. The maintenance of attendance registers and reports.

17. Methods to be used in handling the various report forms.

Such a reference manual should contain a flow chart, an explanation of the overall attendance accounting procedures, and illustrations of the various cards, forms, and reports that will be used in the general process. All district personnel should be briefed well ahead of the time when the attendance application will come into being, and all staff members affected by it, including clerical staff, teachers, counselors, and administrators, should know the significance of the procedures and the manner in which they will affect their established methods and procedures. Finally, in addition to the various pre-operation conferences that should be held in the schools and the data center and following the distribution of copies of the reference manual, school personnel should feel free to call the data center for assistance in clarifying any problems that still might be bothering them. They also should be encouraged to call for assistance whenever special problems arise.

DESCRIPTION OF SYSTEMS / TRADITIONAL PUNCHED CARD

As developed in the typical card oriented installation, the attendance-accounting application is basically a card-counting system. The system typically uses the widely accepted porto-punch-type card illustrated in Figure 54. Each card in the attendance deck (1) represents a student who is enrolled during all or part of the school month, and (2) contains "porto-punch" perforations that enable attendance clerks to punch holes indicating "apportionment absence" and/or the number of days the student was not enrolled in school during the given month.

FIRST PRINT LINE

3

DISTRICT NAME | SCHOOL

PUPILS NUMBER	B/G	PUPILS NAME: BOYS	GIRLS	TOTAL	E/L	FIRST WEEK: M.	T.	W.	TH.	F.	SEC… M.	T
061450	2	WINSOR MARY			L							
061500	2	WINTEROWD JEANETTE										
061700	1	WOLD ROBERT J										
061800	1	WOOD LARRY ALLAN										
061900	1	WOODSON CHARLES E										
062000	1	WOOLFORD ALAN										
062100	1	YBARRA TONY										
062150	1	YENOKIDA GORDON										
062200	2	YOUNG GLADYS										
062300	2	ZAVATTERO CAROL										
062400	2	ZAVATTERO JOAN										
		322	301	623								

E = ENTER
L = LEAVE

FIG. 55. *Attendance Register*

ATTENDANCE REGISTER

ME | SCHOOL CODE | SCHOOL MONTH | FISCAL YEAR | GRADE | PAGE

ND WEEK			THIRD WEEK					FOURTH WEEK					TIMES T		DAYS NOT ENROL'D AND/OR NOT EXCUSED		DAYS ABSENT EXCUSED		DAYS APP. ABSENCE		TOTAL DAYS ABSENT		DAYS OF APPRN. ATT.		TOTAL DAYS TAUGHT	
W.	TH.	F.	M.	T.	W.	TH.	F.	M.	T.	W.	TH.	F.	CUR	Y.T.D.	CUR	Y.T.D.	CUR	Y.T.D.	CUR	Y.T.D.	CUR	Y.T.D.	CUR	Y.T.L.	CUR	Y.T.D.
					1	1	1	1	1	1	1						7	7			7	7	18	18	18	18
						1											1	1			1	1	18	18	18	18
																							18	18	18	18
																							18	18	18	18
																							18	18	18	18
																							18	18	18	18
3	3	3	3												4	4					4	4	14	14	18	18
																							18	18	18	18
				1							1						2	2			2	2	18	18	18	18
																							18	18	18	18
																							18	18	18	18
												CUR		251		21		228		81		581		10861		
					yearly total to date →							YTD		251		21		228		81		581		10861		
												CUR		1								1		89		
												CUR		1								1		1		
												CUR		103		21		78		43		245		3811		
												CUR		30				45		16		91		2438		
												CUR		55				54		17		126		2574		
												CUR		61				51		5		117		1950		
												YTD		251		21		228		81		581		10861		

ATTENDANCE CODES

A = SCHOOL APPROVED
U = UNEXCUSED

X = EXCUSED (ILLNESS; QUARENTINE, ETC.)
T = TARDY OR PART DAY ABSENCE

N = NOT ENROLLED

At the end of each month, the cards are machine-counted and the total is multiplied by the number of days in the school month to determine the total of "pupil days" possible. Days of absence (for reasons other than illness or quarantine) and "days not enrolled" are subtracted from the total of pupil days. The remainder constitutes the days of apportionment attendance during the month and is the figure that is used in claiming state apportionment funds.

Because any mistake in handling could result either in overclaiming state funds or in the loss of funds to which the district is entitled, school people are urged to take special care in preparing the cards for processing. It must be pointed out that there has to be one card, and one card only, in the deck for each student, regardless of his attendance record during the school month.

MAJOR STEPS IN THE OPERATION

The principal steps involved in conducting the attendance-accounting operation are illustrated in Figure 56.

1. Every month the processing center provides each school with a student attendance deck of cards. The deck contains one porto-punch card for each student enrolled in the school.
2. At the end of the school month the attendance clerk punches, on the card representing each student involved, a hole for each day of unexcused absence.
3. After the cards are appropriately prepared at the school, they are sent to the center for processing.
4. The student cards are then machine counted; the total number is multiplied by the number of teaching days in the month.
5. The number of unexcused absences and the "days not enrolled" are subtracted from the total of students-times-teaching days. The balance represents the average daily attendance upon which the district would base its claim to apportionment funds from the state.
6. As indicated in the monthly attendance deck that was processed, corrections for new enrollees and/or for students who left school are made in the student master deck maintained in the data processing center.
7. A new monthly attendance deck is prepared and sent to each school —the deck again containing one card for every student enrolled in the school.

COMPILATIONS OF ATTENDANCE DATA

After the basic machine operations are carried out at the center, the data processors compile and send to each school an Attendance Register

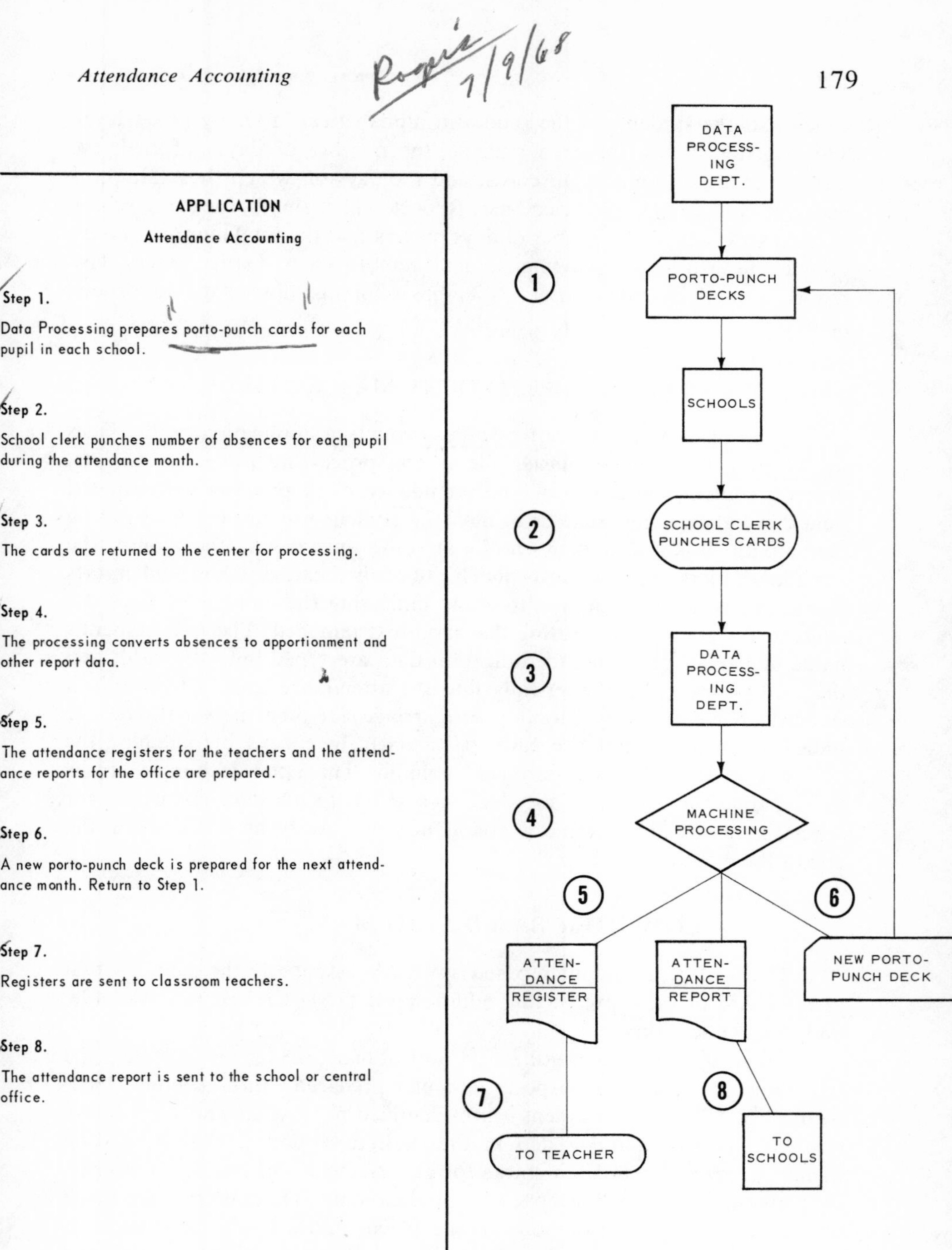

FIG. 56. *Procedural Steps for Attendance Accounting*

which lists the students at the school in alphabetical order by grade level. This register shows, for each student, the number of days enrolled, the number of apportionment absences, and the days on which those absences occurred. In addition, an Attendance Report, which shows, for every school in the district, the total number of days present and the total number of days of unexcused absence is compiled and sent to each district office. This report is used by the district as its basis for claiming state apportionment aid.

UPDATING THE STUDENT MASTER FILE

Some districts use the attendance-accounting application as the basis for keeping the student master file in the processing center up-to-date. When a student leaves school, the attendance clerk punches a perforated hole that indicates the number of days the student was not enrolled during that month. When a student enrolls at some time during the month, the attendance clerk types a porto-punch attendance card for him and inserts it into the deck again. Again, the hole indicating the number of days the student was not enrolled during that month is punched. The new student's name and other personnel identification data are typed onto the card, and the card is inserted alphabetically into the attendance deck. Changes in a student's name (e.g., by adoption or marriage) or other personal data are indicated on the attendance card, particularly by means of punching the "0" hole in the "days-not-enrolled" column. The latter technique serves to "separate the card from the deck"—a signal to the data processors for special attention at the time the attendance data are being processed at the end of the month.

A COMPUTER BASED SYSTEM

The goal of a computer based system is essentially the same as that of the EAM process, except that additional data should become available, and in much less time.

One proposed system utilizes an optical mark-reader for collecting the basic data from a dual purpose computer-prepared "turn-around" document (Fig. 57). This document is pre-identified for teacher and school, and has the students' names listed in the desired sequence. Following each name are spaces to indicate marks for achievement and teacher comments on performance, as well as space for absence data. These entries are made with a pencil or pen in the appropriate places. On a Friday afternoon, at the conclusion of the attendance period, the documents are collected and processed, and new documents, with cumulative data, are ready for the teachers to use the following Monday morning.

BY-PRODUCTS OF THE APPLICATION

By-products of the attendance accounting system can be numerous, but one of the most important is the availability of data on why students drop out of school. Whenever a student leaves school during an attendance month the counselor or administrator has the opportunity to indicate by a code the reason for the pupil's leaving. After each attendance accounting period these cards can be separated in the data center for analysis. Reports can then be prepared for the district by school, by grade, by reason, and any other category.

Dropout Data

Dr. John F. Putnam, a specialist in Educational Records and Reports in the United States Office of Education has said

> The staggering proportions of the school dropout problem have emphasized the educator's need for a way of analyzing the problem in an objective and unemotional manner. Educators need sound information about the nature of dropping out so that they can learn both how to encourage potential dropouts to stay in school long enough to graduate, and how to determine the special needs of students who *must* drop out.[1]

By developing compatible systems for collecting such information, studies on a statewide and nationwide basis can be constructed. Dr. Putnam has been working for four years on a project that has involved over 250 representatives of ten national organizations interested in improving methods and procedures for collecting and using educational information in the area of pupil accounting. The codes developed as part of this project are presented in Appendix IV, and appear to be a logical way for collecting enrollment data on pupils..

Intelligence Reports

An effective attendance accounting system can provide leads for the guidance staff that may help solve the dropout problem. By identifying developing patterns of irregular attendance, the staff may be able to work more intensely with potential dropouts at a time when there is still hope for preventing the situation from reaching the point of no return. Figure 58 illustrates a new type of attendance report. This report can be prepared to identify those students who were absent more than the "acceptable" number of times during the current month, or on a cumulative basis for the school year to date. This would be an exception-type report and would list only those students who qualified as irregular attendees. Any developing pattern of absences, such as all Monday and Friday absences, would be

1. *School Life,* U.S. Office of Education, Washington, D.C., Nov., 1960.

PAGE NO.

INSTRUCTIONS (PLEASE FOLLOW CAREFULLY)

IBM H91219

1. MARK POSITIONS AS IN UPPER RIGHT CORNER
2. USE # 2 PENCIL ONLY
3. DO NOT MARK BEYOND HEAVY GREEN LINE ON RIGHT SIDE OF PAGE
4. ERASE COMPLETELY IF ANY CHANGES ARE MADE
5. THIS STUB IS FOR TEACHERS RECORD—

NAME	TOTAL EXCUSED	TOTAL UNEXCUSED	A B C
COMMENTS	GRADES		PLUS MINUS W
NAME	TOTAL EXCUSED	TOTAL UNEXCUSED	A B C
COMMENTS	GRADES		PLUS MINUS W
NAME	TOTAL EXCUSED	TOTAL UNEXCUSED	A B C
COMMENTS	GRADES		PLUS MINUS W
NAME	TOTAL EXCUSED	TOTAL UNEXCUSED	A B C
COMMENTS	GRADES		PLUS MINUS W
NAME	TOTAL EXCUSED	TOTAL UNEXCUSED	A B C
COMMENTS	GRADES		PLUS MINUS W
NAME	TOTAL EXCUSED	TOTAL UNEXCUSED	A B C
COMMENTS	GRADES		PLUS MINUS W
NAME	TOTAL EXCUSED	TOTAL UNEXCUSED	A B C
COMMENTS	GRADES		PLUS MINUS W
NAME	TOTAL EXCUSED	TOTAL UNEXCUSED	A B C
COMMENTS	GRADES		PLUS MINUS W
NAME	TOTAL EXCUSED	TOTAL UNEXCUSED	A B C
COMMENTS	GRADES		PLUS MINUS W
NAME	TOTAL EXCUSED	TOTAL UNEXCUSED	A B C
COMMENTS	GRADES		PLUS MINUS W
NAME	TOTAL EXCUSED	TOTAL UNEXCUSED	A B C
COMMENTS	GRADES		PLUS MINUS W
NAME	TOTAL EXCUSED	TOTAL UNEXCUSED	A B C
COMMENTS	GRADES		PLUS MINUS W
NAME	TOTAL EXCUSED	TOTAL UNEXCUSED	A B C
COMMENTS	GRADES		PLUS MINUS W
NAME	TOTAL EXCUSED	TOTAL UNEXCUSED	A B C
COMMENTS	GRADES		PLUS MINUS W
NAME	TOTAL EXCUSED	TOTAL UNEXCUSED	A B C
COMMENTS	GRADES		PLUS MINUS W
NAME	TOTAL EXCUSED	TOTAL UNEXCUSED	A B C
COMMENTS	GRADES		PLUS MINUS W
NAME	TOTAL EXCUSED	TOTAL UNEXCUSED	A B C
COMMENTS	GRADES		PLUS MINUS W

FIG. 57. *Computer-Prepared Attendance Accounting Document*

ATTENDANCE AND MARK REPORTING

DO NOT MARK BEYOND THIS LINE →

CLASS NUMBER

REPORTING PERIOD

TEACHER

PAGE NUMBER

DO NOT MARK

D F 1 2 3 4 5 TOTAL ABSENCES M T W T F M T W T F
COMMENTS
I Ø 6 7 8 9 10 UNEXCUSED ABSENCES M T W T F M T W T F

D F 1 2 3 4 5 TOTAL ABSENCES M T W T F M T W T F
COMMENTS
I Ø 6 7 8 9 10 UNEXCUSED ABSENCES M T W T F M T W T F

D F 1 2 3 4 5 TOTAL ABSENCES M T W T F M T W T F
COMMENTS
I Ø 6 7 8 9 10 UNEXCUSED ABSENCES M T W T F M T W T F

D F 1 2 3 4 5 TOTAL ABSENCES M T W T F M T W T F
COMMENTS
I Ø 6 7 8 9 10 UNEXCUSED ABSENCES M T W T F M T W T F

D F 1 2 3 4 5 TOTAL ABSENCES M T W T F M T W T F
COMMENTS
I Ø 6 7 8 9 10 UNEXCUSED ABSENCES M T W T F M T W T F

D F 1 2 3 4 5 TOTAL ABSENCES M T W T F M T W T F
COMMENTS
I Ø 6 7 8 9 10 UNEXCUSED ABSENCES M T W T F M T W T F

D F 1 2 3 4 5 TOTAL ABSENCES M T W T F M T W T F
COMMENTS
I Ø 6 7 8 9 10 UNEXCUSED ABSENCES M T W T F M T W T F

D F 1 2 3 4 5 TOTAL ABSENCES M T W T F M T W T F
COMMENTS
I Ø 6 7 8 9 10 UNEXCUSED ABSENCES M T W T F M T W T F

D F 1 2 3 4 5 TOTAL ABSENCES M T W T F M T W T F
COMMENTS
I Ø 6 7 8 9 10 UNEXCUSED ABSENCES M T W T F M T W T F

D F 1 2 3 4 5 TOTAL ABSENCES M T W T F M T W T F
COMMENTS
I Ø 6 7 8 9 10 UNEXCUSED ABSENCES M T W T F M T W T F

D F 1 2 3 4 5 TOTAL ABSENCES M T W T F M T W T F
COMMENTS
I Ø 6 7 8 9 10 UNEXCUSED ABSENCES M T W T F M T W T F

D F 1 2 3 4 5 TOTAL ABSENCES M T W T F M T W T F
COMMENTS
I Ø 6 7 8 9 10 UNEXCUSED ABSENCES M T W T F M T W T F

D F 1 2 3 4 5 TOTAL ABSENCES M T W T F M T W T F
COMMENTS
I Ø 6 7 8 9 10 UNEXCUSED ABSENCES M T W T F M T W T F

D F 1 2 3 4 5 TOTAL ABSENCES M T W T F M T W T F
COMMENTS
I Ø 6 7 8 9 10 UNEXCUSED ABSENCES M T W T F M T W T F

D F 1 2 3 4 5 TOTAL ABSENCES M T W T F M T W T F
COMMENTS
I Ø 6 7 8 9 10 UNEXCUSED ABSENCES M T W T F M T W T F

D F 1 2 3 4 5 TOTAL ABSENCES M T W T F M T W T F
COMMENTS
I Ø 6 7 8 9 10 UNEXCUSED ABSENCES M T W T F M T W T F

D F 1 2 3 4 5 TOTAL ABSENCES M T W T F M T W T F
COMMENTS
I Ø 6 7 8 9 10 UNEXCUSED ABSENCES M T W T F M T W T F

R/D CENTER
CALIFORNIA STATE DEPARTMENT of EDUCATION

IRREGULAR ATTENDANCE REPORT

SCHOOL NAME	SCHOOL ADDRESS	/ / DATE OF ATTENDANCE PER.	COUNSELOR

STUDENT IDENTIFICATION	ABSENCES THIS		PATTERN					RELATED FACTORS					NOTES
	MONTH	YEAR	M	T	W	T	F	INT	READ	ARITH	LANG	CURRENT GPA	

FIG. 58. *Irregular Attendance Report*

displayed on a cumulative basis, and this would give the school staff another clue to investigate. Academic aptitude and achievement test data and the current mark-point average also would be displayed so the staff can determine if these related factors were of significance in the absence pattern. The report could be prepared in multiple copies for distribution to all offices concerned, such as the attendance supervisor, guidance staff, and vice principal.

In summary, the attendance accounting application can save the schools a great deal of time in gathering the basic information needed to claim state apportionment funds. It can also serve as the medium for collecting needed information on the mobility and stability of pupils. Perhaps even more important is its capability to compile data on dropouts that could lead to the development of programs and the general restructurng of curricula to stem the growing tide of wasted opportunity.

12

REGISTRATION AND SCHEDULING

Building a master schedule for a modern secondary school and registering and scheduling students remain as two of the most complex and time-consuming tasks confronting today's educators. Austin and Gividen[1] state that the staff should keep in mind that any schedule is a device which is useful only to the degree that it allows students and teachers to work together more efficiently than they could without it or with a different one. According to these authors, no amount of schedule redesign can, of itself, make good teachers, good methods, or a good learning situation. But new and imaginative schedule design and implementation can result from healthy staff studies of the educational program, and these changes enhance opportunity for better learning. The above statement serves to place scheduling in its proper role—as an aid to effective learning—and also calls for involvement of the total school staff in the planning and development of new scheduling designs.

There are two distinct phases of the scheduling process. One centers around the educational process and is concerned with local philosophy as it pertains to such things as curricular offerings, school time patterns, large group-small group instruction, heterogeneous versus homogeneous grouping, and school-within-a-school arrangements. The second phase involves the actual construction of a master schedule and the assignment of students to this schedule. It is in the latter area that educational data processing techniques and equipment are effective and efficient aids to school personnel. The use of data processing, while lifting much of the clerical burden from the scheduling process, also permits more experimentation and thereby often leads to an improved environment for learning.

EDUCATIONAL CONSIDERATIONS

It is not the purpose of this chapter to explore thoroughly the many options open to educators as they study the scheduling process. However, a historical summary of developments in this area will serve to bring the problem into focus.

Since the early 1900's the traditional school day has consisted of

1. Austin, David B. and Gividen, Noble, *The High School Principal and Staff Develop the Master Schedule*. New York: Bureau of Publications, Teachers College, Columbia University, 1960.

classes scheduled four to five times weekly, meeting from forty to forty-five minutes each day. This arrangement was made necessary by the Carnegie Unit, a basis for entrance to most colleges. Laboratory and vocational courses typically met for two or three periods.

Some alterations of this approach occurred with the advent of the core program, which allotted longer blocks of time to related subject matter areas, a concept concentrated in the junior high schools.

However, Dr. Conant[2] recommended a return to the traditional day. He felt that a seven or eight period day, with periods as short as forty-five minutes, permitted academically talented students to secure a variety of needed academic courses.

MODERN APPROACHES

Current research and literature reveal the extent of the efforts to implement new ideas in scheduling. These have resulted in significant changes in staff utilization and in organization for instruction. Such concepts as team teaching, non-graded schools, flexible scheduling of classes with time patterns constructed of varying "modules" of time for each subject or student in each academic area reflect growing trends in secondary schools. For a review of these new approaches the reader is encouraged to read the bulletin entitled "Changing Secondary Schools."[3]

GATHERING STUDENT DATA

The preparation of the schedule for programming students starts with the collection and analysis of pertinent information about the school, students, staff, and physical facilities.[4] The decisions to be made and the data to be gathered are basic to the process, regardless of what method is used or what automatic processing equipment is employed.

The educational plan developed for each student as part of the regular counseling process reflects the long-range goals of the student based on his interests and abilities. Specific data needed to initiate the scheduling process include:

1. Student name, grade, sex.
2. List of present subjects taken.
3. Subjects requested for next year.
4. Alternates for elective subjects.
5. Credits earned to date toward graduation.
6. Signature of counselor and parent or guardian.

2. James B. Conant, *The American High School Today*. New York: McGraw-Hill Book Co., 1959, p. 64.

3. "Changing Secondary Schools," *Bulletin of the National Association of Secondary School Principals,* May, 1963.

4. Austin and Gividen, *op. cit.* (n. 1), p. 15.

For grouping or tracking, it may also be desirable to include ratings of the student's aptitude and achievement.

ANALYSIS OF DATA

The following aids to building the master schedule can be obtained from an analysis of student requests:

The course tally reflects the total number of pupils requesting each course in the curriculum, and may show totals by grade or sex if desired.

A *course* for this purpose is defined as a unit of subject matter in which all sections are mutually interchangeable when assigning pupils to classes. If it makes a difference to which section a pupil is assigned, that section should be defined as a separate course.

The determination of *sections* of a given course is obtained by dividing the number of students requesting the course by the desired class size. From this process "singletons" (single-section courses), "doubletons" (two-section courses), and "multiple-section courses" are identified.

The *conflict matrix* (an example of which is in Fig. 65, pp. 200-201) is a two-way table of course requests listing the number of pupils who have requested every possible pair of courses. For "singletons," this is the number of potential conflicts of two courses scheduled in the same period.

BUILDING THE MASTER SCHEDULE

With the above data available, it is now possible to plan for the effective and efficient use of teacher talents, available space within the school plant, and the time patterns most suitable for the arrangement of curricular offerings. According to Austin and Gividen, the task of combining the various resources and needs within a secondary school to produce a schedule of classes with a minimum of conflict and a maximum of individualized student programming has been likened to that of playing five games of chess simultaneously.

The most effective manual procedure is to secure a large slotted board with the period blocks running along the edge in one direction and the teaching staff arrayed in the other direction. Tabs representing each section of the master schedule (a *section* of a course is defined as a particular class usually taught by one teacher and meeting at a specific time and in a specific room) are prepared and can be easily moved about the slots as the schedule is built. The conflict matrix is a necessity at this time to aid in the proper placement of sections so as to insure a minimum of conflict.

A room utilization chart is necessary to plot the use of facilities and to illustrate rooms available for instruction.

The following are the desired outcomes of this process:

1. A master schedule showing all sections to be offered, the time block assigned to each, the room assignment, and the teacher in charge.
2. A master list of teacher assignments, room use, and departmental offerings.

SCHEDULING OF STUDENTS

The task that now remains is to assign students, according to their educational program, to the constructed master schedule. In this process, the classes must be balanced according to predetermined limits, grouping considered, and a final student schedule of classes produced. Depending on the size of the school, this task can take from two weeks to five or six weeks of professional and clerical time. It is obviously a sizable task.

USING DATA PROCESSING TECHNIQUES IN SCHEDULING

In this section, the use of data processing techniques in scheduling will be described. Early attempts to automate this area included the use of both hand punched cards and of the standard machine processed punched cards. Today's electronic computers, with their immensely greater speed and flexibility, have opened whole new horizons for educators.

As these methods are explained, the basic premises and principles outlined in Chapter 3, "Anatomy of Data Processing" will be utilized, regardless of the system employed.

HAND PROCESSING OF CARDS

Two systems that have had widespread use throughout the country are the McBee Keysort Cards and the E-Z Sort Cards. Both systems employ the method of hand punching coded scheduling information arranged around the margin of the cards. Once properly punched, the cards can be separated by placing a long needle in the appropriate hole and lifting out the desired cards.

PUNCHED CARD METHOD

The punched card is readily adaptable to student scheduling and has been widely used for this purpose in both secondary schools and colleges.

As in other data processing applications, coding is an important part of the operation. Courses to be offered are grouped by department and coded, usually with a three to five digit number.

Counselors, referring to a student's three or four year educational plan, select courses for the coming year. Figures 59 and 60 illustrate two cards used in the registration process. In Figure 59, the requested course and code number are written on a pre-identified student card. Fields in the card are set aside for each major subject area. In Figure 60 course codes are mark-sensed according to selected subjects.

By using the sorter and selecting appropriate punches in the various card columns, it is possible to obtain course tallies for each course offered. A conflict matrix may also be prepared using the sorter.

Two basic approaches are open to schools using punched card equip-

FIG. 59. *Card Used to Record Course and Code Number*

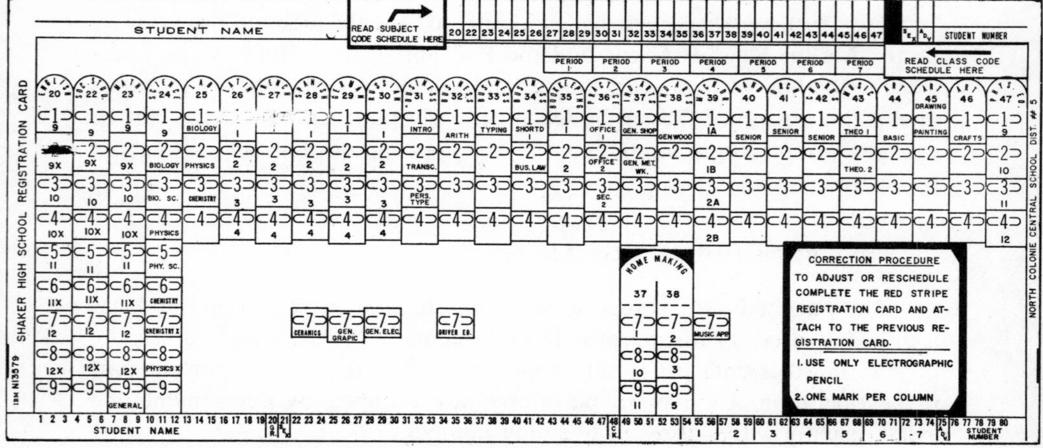

SHAKER HIGH SCHOOL REGISTRATION CARD

STUDENT NAME

READ SUBJECT CODE SCHEDULE HERE

READ CLASS CODE SCHEDULE HERE

STUDENT NUMBER

NORTH COLONIE CENTRAL SCHOOL DIST. # 5

HOME MAKING

CORRECTION PROCEDURE

TO ADJUST OR RESCHEDULE COMPLETE THE RED STRIPE REGISTRATION CARD AND ATTACH TO THE PREVIOUS REGISTRATION CARD.

1. USE ONLY ELECTROGRAPHIC PENCIL

2. ONE MARK PER COLUMN

IBM N13579

FIG. 60. *Card Used to Mark-Sense Selected Courses*

ment for scheduling. They are the *bin* or *tub file* method and the *sorter* method. IBM describes the bin plan in its General Information Manual on Public Education Student Records.[5]

Once the school's master schedule has been constructed, punched cards are prepared. One card is prepared for each section in the master schedule and contains teacher name and number, course name and number, period and room number. From these teacher master cards, the required number of subject cards are prepared to represent available seats in all sections.

Each small deck of cards representing a section in the master schedule is placed in a tub file or bin.

Using the registration cards as a guide, subject cards for each student are pulled for the course listed. Care is taken to pull courses having only single or double sections first; when multiple section courses are pulled, it is important to keep sections balanced. A different colored card placed after each 10 available seats will serve to alert the clerk or counselor to keep sections balanced. Once a student's program is complete, the subject cards are placed behind the registration card, and the student's name and number are gang punched into his subject cards.

This method of scheduling is commonly used in secondary schools and has found wide acceptance in colleges and universities. In the collegiate application, prospective students for a course pick up pre-punched cards at a registration desk. When all cards are gone, the section is closed. The student may then use his card as an admission to each class.

A variation of the bin plan using the punched cards is the "sorter method." In this plan, the registration cards are sorted according to a priority list of courses (singletons, doubletons, tripletons, etc.). As each card course code is sorted, the appropriate subject cards are merged behind the student registration cards, and the student's name and number are gang punched into the subject cards. The plan involves no hand pulling of cards and schedules courses on a priority basis making certain that difficult courses are scheduled first.

The multiple use of punched cards is dramatically illustrated in the scheduling process. Subject cards may now be sequenced in period order by student and used to print locator cards in multiple copies for the opening of school. Re-sequencing of the cards into section order will permit the printing of class lists, home room lists and study hall lists. The subject cards may then be used as mark gathering documents in the preparation of student report cards.

Behnk has recently illustrated the data flow in a scheduling system.[6] Figure 61 represents this data flow.

5. *Public Education Student Records,* General Information Manual, International Business Machines, New York, N.Y. 1959.

6. Behnk, William E., *Educational Data Processing, A Modern Approach to Pupil and Financial Accounting,* New York State Department of Education, 1963.

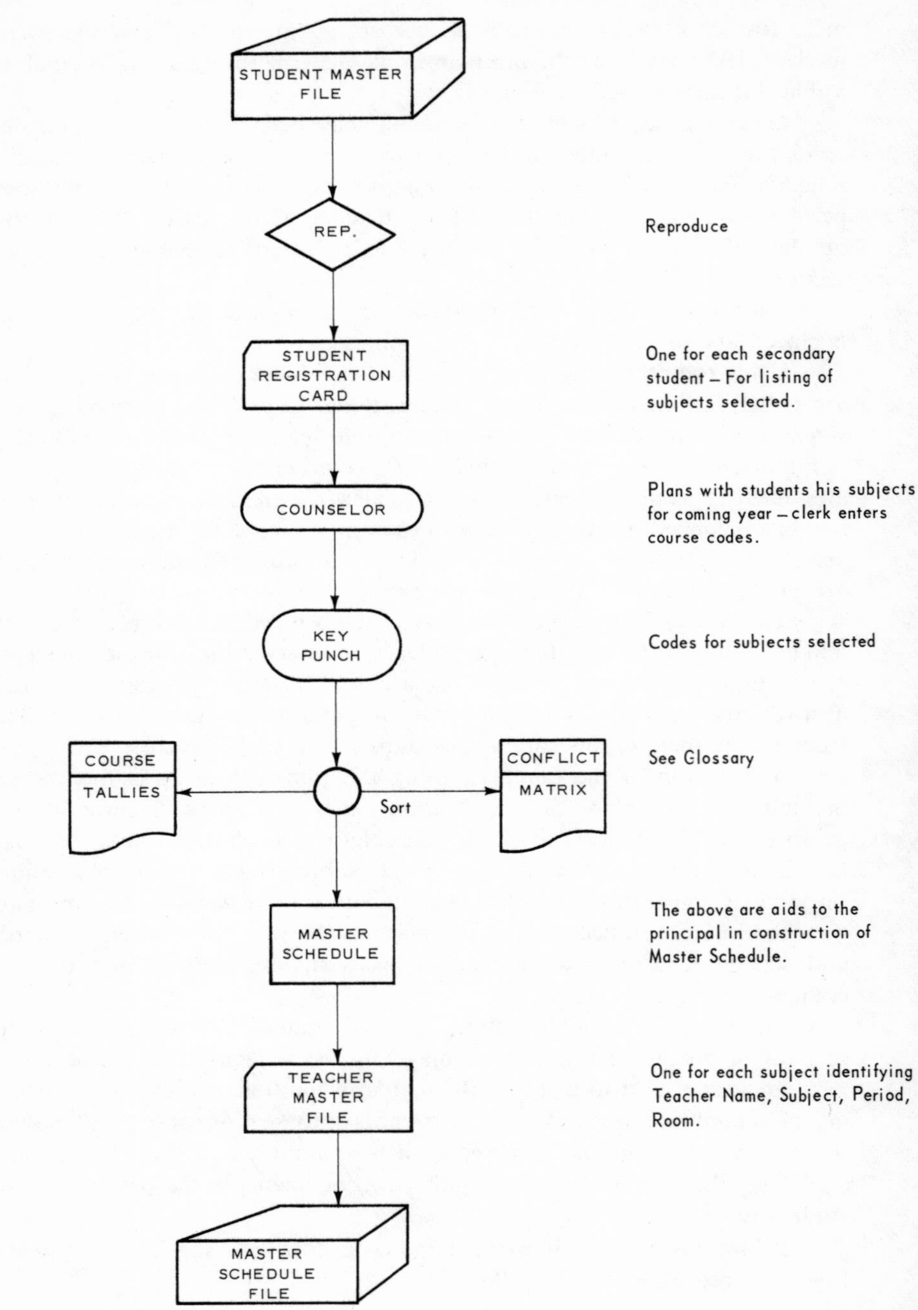

FIG. 61. *Procedural Steps for Secondary Student Scheduling*

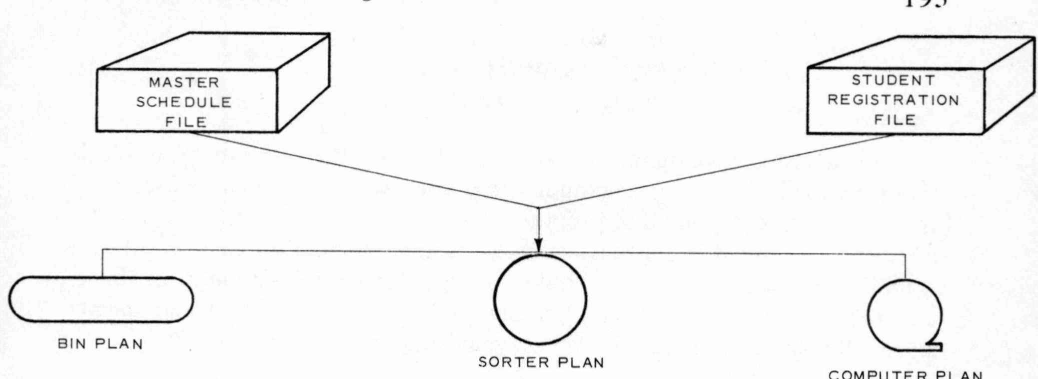

Student scheduling is similar in principle, regardless of scheduling plan used. The student registration file is matched against the master file, with the goal of reserving an available seat in a class for each student selecting the particular subject. The operation of each plan will be discussed in detail in a scheduling bulletin.

Output in each plan consists basically of student subject cards containing: name of student and teacher, subject title, room number and period — one card for each student per subject scheduled.

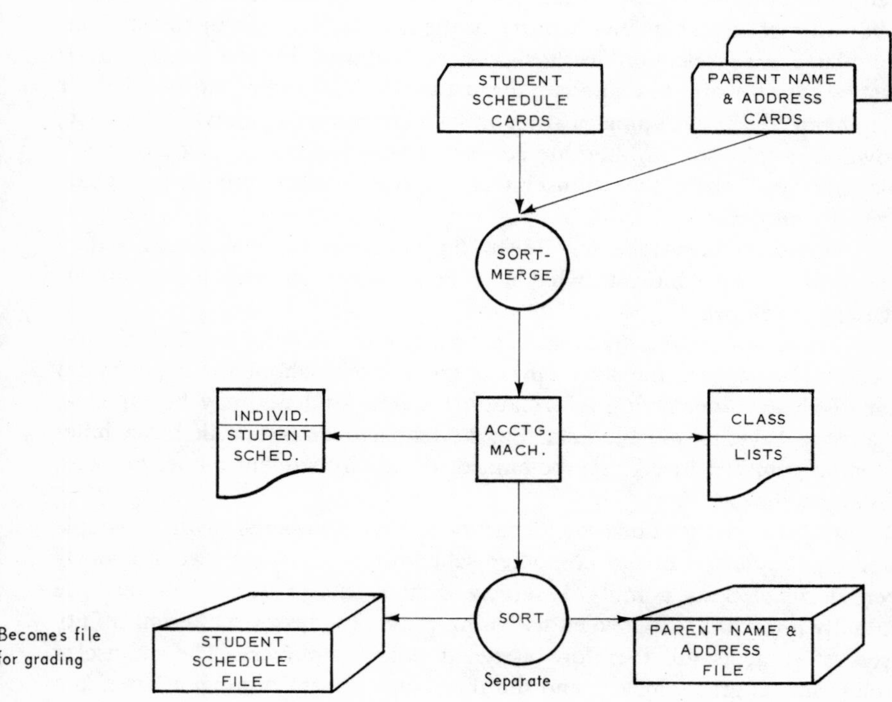

ELECTRONIC COMPUTERS AND STUDENT SCHEDULING

Its decision-making ability and speed make the computer an ideal tool for solving the many scheduling problems that face modern educators. It is only in recent years that programs have been written that assign pupils to classes contained in a predetermined master schedule. Pioneer efforts to actually construct a master schedule, to allow for flexible modules of time, and to make student and teacher assignments, are in the development stages. It is important that all of these concepts be fully explored.

DATA COLLECTION IN A COMPUTER SYSTEM

As scheduling techniques become more sophisticated, the need to develop data collection systems to provide accurate and detailed input into the system becomes necessary. The goals of any system are to reduce the paperwork of administrators, counselors, and school clerks by using machine methods. However, the control of the input must be in the hands of educators and must reflect their philosophy. For instance, if it is desirable to have direct counselor involvement in the course selection of the student, then the course selection form should be initiated by the counselor. It must be easy for him to complete, it must contain the facility to provide for tracking or ability grouping of students by curriculum or individual course, provide for selection of alternate courses if certain electives are not available, and also allow the counselor to express teacher preference where necessary in individual cases.

The following systems will illustrate approaches to the problem of data collection and also indicate what may be expected as refinements in this area are developed:

System A—Figure 62 illustrates the use of an 8½″ by 11″ Course Selection Form with the total curriculum of each school for a particular year displayed. Identifying information for new students may be typed in to serve as basic master file data. For students currently enrolled, machine-prepared gummed labels may be affixed to identify student name, number, grade, etc.

Subjects are grouped by department and numbered with a simple three-digit code for use in computer scheduling. A course has previously been designated as a unit of subject matter such that all sections are mutually interchangeable when assigning pupils to classes. Different ability levels of subjects are therefore assigned unique numbers. The counselor circles each course selected, and the three-digit course number is then key punched in a student card.

The new optical mark-readers appearing on the market today, such as

'64–'65 STUDENT COURSE SELECTION FORM Please Print in Block Letters **WASHINGTON UNIFIED DISTRICT**

STUDENT NAME (Last, First, Middle Initial)	Counselor No.	Home Rm. No.	PARENT/GUARDIAN NAME (First Initial and Last Name)		
	Counselor Name		STREET AND NO.	CITY	PHONE NO.
GRADE SEX DATE OF BIRTH					

100 ENGLISH 1
101 ENGLISH 1C
102 ENGLISH 2
103 ENGLISH 2C
104 ENGLISH 3
105 ENGLISH 3C
106 ENGLISH 4
107 JOURNALISM 1
108 JOURNALISM 2
109 DRAMA
110 PUB SPKG

200 LEADERSHIP 1
201 LEADERSHIP 2
202 WEST CIVIL
203 WEST CIVIL C
204 US HISTORY
205 US HISTORY C
206 AMER GOVT-EC
207 AMER GOVT-EC C

300 GEN MATH
301 ARITH
302 ALGEBRA 1
303 ALGEBRA 2
304 GEOMETRY
305 TRIG-ADV MATH
306 CONSUMER MATH

400 BOYS PE 1
401 BOYS PE 2
402 BOYS PE ADV
403 GIRLS PE 1
404 GIRLS PE 2
405 GIRLS PE ADV
406 CADETS 1
407 CADETS 2
408 CADETS 3
409 CADETS 4

450 GEN SCI
451 GEN SCI C
452 BIOLOGY
453 BIOLOGY C
454 PHYSIOLOGY
455 CHEMISTRY
456 PHYSICS
457 PHOTOGRAPHY

500 SPANISH L 1
501 SPANISH L 2
502 SPANISH L 3
503 SPANISH L 4
504 SPANISH L 5

600 GEN BUS
601 TYPING 1
602 TYPING 2
603 SHORTHAND 1
604 SHORTHAND 2
605 BOOKKEEPING
606 BUS PRAC
607 CLER PRAC
608 BUS LAW
609 BUS ARITH
610 MERCHANDISING
611 DUPLICATING

700 WOOD SHOP 1
701 WOOD SHOP 2
702 WOOD SHOP 3
703 WOOD SHOP 4
704 METAL SHOP 1
705 METAL SHOP 2
706 METAL SHOP 3
707 IND DRAW 1
708 IND DRAW 2
709 IND DRAW 3
710 ARCH DRAW
711 IND MATH
712 ELECTRICITY

800 HOMEMKG 1
801 HOMEMKG 2
802 HOMEMKG 3
803 HOMEMKG 4
804 SR HOMEMKG
805 BOYS FD & FAB

850 ART 1
851 ART 2
852 ART 3
853 ART 4
854 ARTS & CRAFTS
855 CRAFTS 1
856 CRAFTS 2
857 PHOTOGRAPHY

900 BAND 1
901 BAND 2
902 BAND 3
903 EAND 4
904 CONCERT BAND
905 INTER INSTRU
906 BEG INSTRU
907 GEN MUSIC
908 CHOIR 1
909 CHOIR 2
910 CHOIR 3
911 CHOIR 4
912 CHORUS 1
913 CHORUS 2
914 BOYS CHORUS
915 GIRLS CHORUS

950 SPECIAL ED 9
951 SPECIAL ED 10
952 SPECIAL ED 11
953 SPECIAL ED 12
954 LIB ASST 1
955 LIB ASST 2
956 LAB ASST
957 OFFICE PRAC
958 STU BODY BOOKS
959 AUD-VIS ASST 1
960 AUD-VIS ASST 2

INSTRUCTIONS FOR SPECIAL HANDLING

ALTERNATES (If necessary)
Code Elective to be substituted
E_1, E_2, E_3

A_1 ____________

A_2 ____________

A_3 ____________

TEACHER ASSIGNMENT INSTRUCTIONS

1. ____________

2. ____________

I approve the above outlined program and understand that once this is accepted, changes can be made only in cases of extreme hardship or educational need.

STUDENT'S SIGNATURE ____________

PARENT'S SIGNATURE ____________

COUNSELOR'S SIGNATURE ____________

FIG. 62. *Course Selection Form*

the IBM 1230 and the Digitek, can be readily adapted to collect data for student scheduling. The form illustrated in Figure 62 could be designed for a mark-reader and the counselor would simply be required to make a single mark next to each subject selected. These sheets would then be processed by machine to produce either punched card output or output connected directly to the computer.

System B—Figure 63 illustrates a mark-sensed card used in data collection. This card was designed by Charles Wilkes of the Richmond, California, Public Schools and is part of the "SOCRATES" Scheduling Sys-

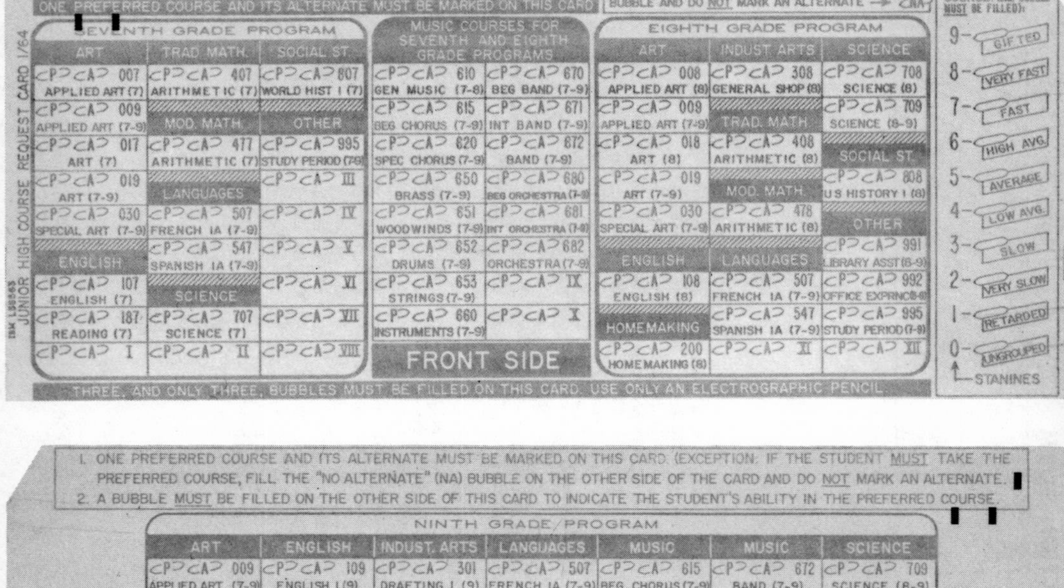

JUNIOR HIGH COURSE REQUEST CARD 1/64 — IBM L50563

SCH CD | GRADE | STD/PRNT NO | B/G | STUDENT NAME (ENTER IF SPACE IS BLANK)

ONE PREFERRED COURSE AND ITS ALTERNATE MUST BE MARKED ON THIS CARD

IF THE STUDENT MUST TAKE THE PREFERRED COURSE AND NO ALTERNATE IS POSSIBLE, MARK THIS BUBBLE AND DO NOT MARK AN ALTERNATE → ⊂NA⊃

SEVENTH GRADE PROGRAM

ART	TRAD MATH	SOCIAL ST
⊂P⊃⊂A⊃ 007 APPLIED ART (7)	⊂P⊃⊂A⊃ 407 ARITHMETIC (7)	⊂P⊃⊂A⊃ 807 WORLD HIST I (7)
⊂P⊃⊂A⊃ 009 APPLIED ART (7-9)	MOD. MATH	OTHER
⊂P⊃⊂A⊃ 017 ART (7)	⊂P⊃⊂A⊃ 477 ARITHMETIC (7)	⊂P⊃⊂A⊃ 995 STUDY PERIOD (7-9)
⊂P⊃⊂A⊃ 019 ART (7-9)	LANGUAGES	⊂P⊃⊂A⊃ III
⊂P⊃⊂A⊃ 030 SPECIAL ART (7-9)	⊂P⊃⊂A⊃ 507 FRENCH IA (7-9)	⊂P⊃⊂A⊃ IV
ENGLISH	⊂P⊃⊂A⊃ 547 SPANISH IA (7-9)	⊂P⊃⊂A⊃ V
⊂P⊃⊂A⊃ 107 ENGLISH (7)	SCIENCE	⊂P⊃⊂A⊃ VI
⊂P⊃⊂A⊃ 187 READING (7)	⊂P⊃⊂A⊃ 707 SCIENCE (7)	⊂P⊃⊂A⊃ VII
⊂P⊃⊂A⊃ I	⊂P⊃⊂A⊃ II	⊂P⊃⊂A⊃ VIII

MUSIC COURSES FOR SEVENTH AND EIGHTH GRADE PROGRAMS

⊂P⊃⊂A⊃ 610 GEN MUSIC (7-8)	⊂P⊃⊂A⊃ 670 BEG BAND (7-9)
⊂P⊃⊂A⊃ 615 BEG CHORUS (7-9)	⊂P⊃⊂A⊃ 671 INT BAND (7-9)
⊂P⊃⊂A⊃ 620 SPEC CHORUS (7-9)	⊂P⊃⊂A⊃ 672 BAND (7-9)
⊂P⊃⊂A⊃ 650 BRASS (7-9)	⊂P⊃⊂A⊃ 680 BEG ORCHESTRA (7-9)
⊂P⊃⊂A⊃ 651 WOODWINDS (7-9)	⊂P⊃⊂A⊃ 681 INT ORCHESTRA (7-9)
⊂P⊃⊂A⊃ 652 DRUMS (7-9)	⊂P⊃⊂A⊃ 682 ORCHESTRA (7-9)
⊂P⊃⊂A⊃ 653 STRINGS (7-9)	⊂P⊃⊂A⊃ IX
⊂P⊃⊂A⊃ 660 INSTRUMENTS (7-9)	⊂P⊃⊂A⊃ X

FRONT SIDE

EIGHTH GRADE PROGRAM

ART	INDUST ARTS	SCIENCE
⊂P⊃⊂A⊃ 008 APPLIED ART (8)	⊂P⊃⊂A⊃ 308 GENERAL SHOP (8)	⊂P⊃⊂A⊃ 708 SCIENCE (8)
⊂P⊃⊂A⊃ 009 APPLIED ART (7-9)	TRAD. MATH	⊂P⊃⊂A⊃ 709 SCIENCE (8-9)
⊂P⊃⊂A⊃ 018 ART (8)	⊂P⊃⊂A⊃ 408 ARITHMETIC (8)	SOCIAL ST.
⊂P⊃⊂A⊃ 019 ART (7-9)	MOD. MATH	⊂P⊃⊂A⊃ 808 US HISTORY I (8)
⊂P⊃⊂A⊃ 030 SPECIAL ART (7-9)	⊂P⊃⊂A⊃ 478 ARITHMETIC (8)	OTHER
ENGLISH	LANGUAGES	⊂P⊃⊂A⊃ 991 LIBRARY ASST (8-9)
⊂P⊃⊂A⊃ 108 ENGLISH (8)	⊂P⊃⊂A⊃ 507 FRENCH IA (7-9)	⊂P⊃⊂A⊃ 992 OFFICE EXPRNC (8-9)
HOMEMAKING	⊂P⊃⊂A⊃ 547 SPANISH IA (7-9)	⊂P⊃⊂A⊃ 995 STUDY PERIOD (7-9)
⊂P⊃⊂A⊃ 200 HOMEMAKING (8)	⊂P⊃⊂A⊃ XI	⊂P⊃⊂A⊃ XII

ESTIMATE THE STUDENT'S ABILITY IN THE PREFERRED COURSE. (ONE BUBBLE MUST BE FILLED):

9- GIFTED
8- VERY FAST
7- FAST
6- HIGH AVG.
5- AVERAGE
4- LOW AVG.
3- SLOW
2- VERY SLOW
1- RETARDED
0- UNGROUPED
STANINES

THREE, AND ONLY THREE, BUBBLES MUST BE FILLED ON THIS CARD. USE ONLY AN ELECTROGRAPHIC PENCIL.

1. ONE PREFERRED COURSE AND ITS ALTERNATE MUST BE MARKED ON THIS CARD. (EXCEPTION: IF THE STUDENT MUST TAKE THE PREFERRED COURSE, FILL THE "NO ALTERNATE" (NA) BUBBLE ON THE OTHER SIDE OF THE CARD AND DO NOT MARK AN ALTERNATE.
2. A BUBBLE MUST BE FILLED ON THE OTHER SIDE OF THIS CARD TO INDICATE THE STUDENT'S ABILITY IN THE PREFERRED COURSE.

USE AN ELECTROGRAPHIC PENCIL ONLY

NINTH GRADE PROGRAM

ART	ENGLISH	INDUST. ARTS	LANGUAGES	MUSIC	MUSIC	SCIENCE
⊂P⊃⊂A⊃ 009 APPLIED ART (7-9)	⊂P⊃⊂A⊃ 109 ENGLISH I (9)	⊂P⊃⊂A⊃ 301 DRAFTING I (9)	⊂P⊃⊂A⊃ 507 FRENCH IA (7-9)	⊂P⊃⊂A⊃ 615 BEG CHORUS (7-9)	⊂P⊃⊂A⊃ 672 BAND (7-9)	⊂P⊃⊂A⊃ 709 SCIENCE (8-9)
⊂P⊃⊂A⊃ 019 ART (7-9)	⊂P⊃⊂A⊃ 110 ENGLISH DRAMA (9)	⊂P⊃⊂A⊃ 321 METAL I (9)	⊂P⊃⊂A⊃ 508 FRENCH IB (8-9)	⊂P⊃⊂A⊃ 620 SPEC CHORUS (7-9)	⊂P⊃⊂A⊃ 680 BEG ORCHESTRA (7-9)	SOCIAL ST.
⊂P⊃⊂A⊃ 030 SPECIAL ART (7-9)	⊂P⊃⊂A⊃ 111 ENGLISH JOURN (9)	⊂P⊃⊂A⊃ 341 WOOD I (9)	⊂P⊃⊂A⊃ 511 FRENCH I (9)	⊂P⊃⊂A⊃ 650 BRASS (7-9)	⊂P⊃⊂A⊃ 681 INT ORCHESTRA (7-9)	⊂P⊃⊂A⊃ 809 WORLD HIST 2 (9)
BUSINESS	⊂P⊃⊂A⊃ 190 READING (9)	TRAD. MATH	⊂P⊃⊂A⊃ 547 SPANISH IA (7-9)	⊂P⊃⊂A⊃ 651 WOODWINDS (7-9)	⊂P⊃⊂A⊃ 682 ORCHESTRA (7-9)	OTHER
⊂P⊃⊂A⊃ 050 GEN BUSINESS (9)	HOMEMAKING	⊂P⊃⊂A⊃ 411 ALGEBRA I (9)	⊂P⊃⊂A⊃ 548 SPANISH IB (8-9)	⊂P⊃⊂A⊃ 652 DRUMS (7-9)	⊂P⊃⊂A⊃ XIX	⊂P⊃⊂A⊃ 990 STUDY HALL (9)
⊂P⊃⊂A⊃ XIII	⊂P⊃⊂A⊃ 201 HOMEMAKING IA (9)	⊂P⊃⊂A⊃ 431 GEN MATH I (9)	⊂P⊃⊂A⊃ 551 SPANISH I (9)	⊂P⊃⊂A⊃ 653 STRINGS (7-9)	⊂P⊃⊂A⊃ XX	⊂P⊃⊂A⊃ 991 LIBRARY ASST (8-9)
⊂P⊃⊂A⊃ XIV	⊂P⊃⊂A⊃ 202 HOMEMAKING IB (9)	MOD. MATH	⊂P⊃⊂A⊃ 552 SPANISH 2 (9)	⊂P⊃⊂A⊃ 660 INSTRUMENTS (7-9)	⊂P⊃⊂A⊃ XXI	⊂P⊃⊂A⊃ 992 OFFICE EXPRNC (8-9)
⊂P⊃⊂A⊃ XV	⊂P⊃⊂A⊃ 203 HOMEMAKING I (9)	⊂P⊃⊂A⊃ 481 ALGEBRA I (9)	⊂P⊃⊂A⊃ XVII	⊂P⊃⊂A⊃ 670 BEG BAND (7-9)	⊂P⊃⊂A⊃ XXII	⊂P⊃⊂A⊃ 995 STUDY PERIOD (7-9)
⊂P⊃⊂A⊃ XVI	⊂P⊃⊂A⊃ 205 HOMECRAFTS (9)	⊂P⊃⊂A⊃ 491 GEN MATH I (9)	⊂P⊃⊂A⊃ XVIII	⊂P⊃⊂A⊃ 671 INT BAND (7-9)	⊂P⊃⊂A⊃ XXIII	⊂P⊃⊂A⊃ XXIV

MAKE NO EXTRA MARKS ON THE CARD

IBM L50564

THREE, AND ONLY THREE, BUBBLES MUST BE FILLED ON THE ENTIRE CARD (BOTH SIDES COMBINED).

FIG. 63. *Mark-Sense Card Used for Data Collection*

tem[7] to be described later. The basic design of the card has had wide usage as a data collecting instrument. The counselor has only to mark a single bubble for each course. This mark is then converted by a computer into a three-digit numeric code, which is then used by a computer in the actual scheduling.

Wilkes has incorporated two features in this card that are somewhat unique. (1) Each course has two possible bubbles, a "P" (preferred course) or an "A" (alternative course). The counselor marks one or the other depending on the preference of the student. (2) Bubbles are provided for rating the expected ability of the student in his preferred course, according to a nine-point scale, if grouping is to be performed. A bubble is also provided for ungrouped courses where rating is not required. This feature is related to the scheduling system in which each class specified in the master schedule is coded to indicate the lowest ability which is to be included, and the highest ability to be included. Only if the student fits within the range specified is he considered for grouping.

These two systems are examples of attempts to aid administrators, counselors, and teachers in proper placement of students. Systems are rapidly becoming available that will consider current progress of a student in a course, latest standardized test data, and present placement. With these data, computers can recommend placement for each student in his program for the following year—subject, of course, to the counselor review and approval.

COMPUTER ASSIGNMENT OF STUDENTS

The phases of the scheduling process have been outlined in an earlier section of this chapter, regardless of the system used. As will be evident, however, the use of computer systems will permit greater speed and flexibility, and will provide schools with more detailed information for planning curricular offerings and building the master schedule.

The number of computer scheduling systems in use has grown in the past few years. The majority of programs have been written for large scale computers with extremely large memory size. There is one exception which will be discussed later.

The development of computer programs has been financed either by large universities, usually with outside research grants, or by private manufacturers of data processing equipment. The programs developed by universities are usually available to other educational institutions having access to the required hardware. Programs developed by manufacturers are

7. Wilkes, Charles F., *Socrates Student Scheduling System*, Richmond, California Public Schools, 1964.

usually only available through service bureaus using the manufacturers' equipment. For example, the IBM Corporation pioneered the field with the introduction of the CLASS (Class Loading and Student Scheduling System) Program, for use on the IBM 7070, 7074 and 7040. This program is available through the IBM computer service centers.

An outstanding scheduling program developed by G. Ernest Anderson in a project underwritten principally by the School and University Program for Research and Development at Harvard University, Cambridge, Massachusetts, has found wide acceptance. This program, written for the IBM 7090 and 7094 will be described here in some detail as an illustration of computer scheduling. Some of the output illustrations used here were produced on the IBM 7040 with programs modified by the staff of the Research and Development Center in Educational Data Processing of the California State Department of Education. They were assisted by the staff of the Sacramento, California, County Office of Education.

INPUT DATA

From the Student Course Selection Form (Fig. 62 on page 195) a single punched card (course detection card) containing identifying student information and up to 10 course requests is obtained for each student. A course master deck is also prepared containing a card for each course offered by the school. Computer processing of this data will quickly and accurately produce the following information:

1. *Course tallies*—the number of pupils requesting each course in the curriculum.
2. *Course Request Verification* (Fig. 64)—a listing of the courses requested by each student to verify the accuracy of the course selection card.
3. *Course Conflict Matrix* (Fig. 65)—a display of the courses by number, both horizontally and vertically. The intersection of the same course numbers represent the simple tally for the course (the diagonal represents all tally numbers). The remainder of the array reflects the number of students registered for two separate subjects offered in the matrix schedule.

It is evident that the above information will be invaluable in determining staff needs, ordering textbooks and supplies, and preparing the master schedule.

MASTER SCHEDULE INFORMATION

Once the master schedules have been formulated, schools prepare a Master Schedule Coding Form (Fig. 66) which will describe in detail each section of the master schedule including such information as: course number, meeting time, semester designation, minimum and maximum seats, teacher name, teacher number, and room number. This information

```
I.D.        NAME              COURSE NR COURSE TITLE   SEX YR HOMEROOM COUNSELOR PERIOD BLOCKED

         ANTROBUS WILLIAM D   975       LUNCH           1   9            0
                              101       ENGLISH 1
                              454       PHYSICAL SCI
                              204       WORLD HIST
                              506       SPANISH 1
                              301       ALGEBRA 1
                              402       PE 1 BOYS

I.D.        NAME              COURSE NR COURSE TITLE   SEX YR HOMEROOM COUNSELOR PERIOD BLOCKED

         BAHR CANDACE T       975       LUNCH           2   9            0
                              101       ENGLISH 1
                              454       PHYSICAL SCI
                              204       WORLD HIST
                              801       HOMEMAKING 1
                              302       GEN MATH 1
                              403       PE 1 GIRLS

I.D.        NAME              COURSE NR COURSE TITLE   SEX YR HOMEROOM COUNSELOR PERIOD BLOCKED

         BALL WYATT R         975       LUNCH           1   9            0
                              101       ENGLISH 1
                              454       PHYSICAL SCI
                              204       WORLD HIST
                              703       MECH DR 1
                              301       ALGEBRA 1
                              402       PE 1 BOYS

I.D.        NAME              COURSE NR COURSE TITLE   SEX YR HOMEROOM COUNSELOR PERIOD BLOCKED

         BAYS SUE A           975       LUNCH           2   9            0
                              101       ENGLISH 1
                              454       PHYSICAL SCI
                              204       WORLD HIST
                              703       MECH DR 1
                              302       GEN MATH 1
                              403       PE 1 GIRLS
```

FIG. 64. *Course Request Verification*

CROSS TALLY EAST NICOLAUS

CDI	503	600	601	602	603	604	605	606	607	700	701	702	703	704	705
100	0	0	8	0	0	0	0	0	0	8	0	0	0	0	1
101	0	1	31	0	1	0	0	0	0	1	0	0	0	2	4
102	0	0	11	10	2	8	8	4	3	0	0	0	0	3	7
103	0	0	2	1	2	4	5	9	1	0	1	0	0	3	5
104	0	0	4	0	0	0	2	0	0	7	0	3	0	1	1
105	0	0	13	0	0	0	1	0	0	1	2	2	2	11	6
106	0	0	3	1	0	0	0	0	0	0	2	0	0	6	2
107	0	0	9	1	0	0	0	0	0	1	2	0	0	6	4
108	0	0	2	5	2	4	6	4	1	0	0	0	0	0	1
109	0	0	1	2	0	0	3	3	0	0	0	0	0	1	5
200	0	0	11	0	0	0	0	0	0	15	0	1	0	0	1
201	0	1	43	0	1	0	0	0	0	2	0	2	1	9	7
202	0	0	15	10	2	8	9	4	3	0	1	0	2	10	11
203	0	0	7	4	3	10	11	14	1	0	10	3	0	15	6
204	0	0	5	0	0	0	0	0	0	7	0	1	0	0	2
300	0	0	16	0	0	1	1	1	0	9	4	3	1	11	5
301	0	1	17	0	0	0	1	0	0	8	0	0	0	1	3
302	0	0	13	0	0	1	0	0	0	0	0	0	0	1	2
303	0	0	6	0	0	0	1	2	0	0	0	0	0	0	4
304	0	0	0	0	0	1	0	3	0	0	0	0	0	1	3
400	0	1	31	0	1	4	2	6	0	16	11	6	2	31	19
401	0	0	42	14	4	14	18	12	4	0	0	0	0	0	6
450	0	1	25	1	0	1	1	0	0	1	1	0	0	1	1
451	0	0	1	0	0	1	1	5	0	0	0	0	0	2	5
452	0	0	5	0	0	0	1	1	0	0	0	0	0	1	4
453	0	0	6	0	0	0	0	0	0	8	0	0	0	2	0
500	0	0	6	0	0	0	0	0	0	6	0	0	0	1	4
501	0	1	19	0	0	0	0	0	0	0	0	0	0	2	0
502	0	0	2	0	0	0	0	1	0	0	0	0	0	0	0
503	0	0	0	0	0	0	0	0	0	0	0	0	0	0	0
600	0	1	0	0	0	0	0	0	0	0	0	0	0	0	0
601	0	0	73	0	0	4	1	3	0	4	2	3	1	9	6
602	0	0	0	14	1	8	8	2	4	0	0	0	0	0	0
603	0	0	0	1	5	2	4	1	0	0	1	0	0	0	0
604	0	0	4	8	2	18	8	3	2	0	1	1	0	3	2
605	0	0	1	8	4	8	20	3	2	0	1	0	0	1	0
606	0	0	3	2	1	3	3	18	0	0	3	2	0	4	2
607	0	0	0	4	0	2	2	0	4	0	0	0	0	0	0
700	0	0	4	0	0	0	0	0	0	17	0	0	0	0	0
701	0	0	2	0	1	1	1	3	0	0	11	2	0	10	1
702	0	0	3	0	0	1	0	2	0	0	2	6	0	3	0
703	0	0	1	0	0	0	0	0	0	0	0	0	2	1	1
704	0	0	9	0	0	3	1	4	0	0	10	3	1	31	9
705	0	0	6	0	0	2	0	2	0	0	1	0	1	9	25
750	0	0	0	0	0	0	0	0	0	0	0	0	0	0	0
751	0	0	0	0	0	0	0	0	0	0	1	0	0	1	0
752	0	0	3	0	0	0	0	0	0	1	0	0	0	0	0
753	0	0	2	0	0	0	0	0	0	0	0	0	0	2	1
754	0	0	4	0	0	2	1	3	0	0	3	0	0	6	1
800	0	0	6	0	0	0	0	0	0	0	0	0	0	0	0
801	0	0	11	0	0	0	0	0	0	0	0	0	0	0	2
802	0	0	3	2	0	1	2	0	1	0	0	0	0	0	0
803	0	0	1	3	1	5	7	7	0	0	0	0	0	0	0
850	0	0	10	1	1	1	3	3	0	1	5	2	0	11	4
851	0	0	3	6	1	4	5	2	2	0	0	0	0	0	0
900	0	0	0	0	0	0	0	0	0	0	0	0	0	0	0
901	0	0	0	0	0	0	0	0	0	1	0	0	1	0	1

FORM 6613 GV

FIG. 65. *Course Conflict Matrix*

750	751	752	753	754	800	801	802	803	850	851	900	901	902
3	4	0	0	0	13	0	0	0	0	0	1	0	6
0	0	3	2	0	0	7	0	0	4	1	0	0	8
0	0	0	1	3	0	0	4	0	0	5	0	0	6
0	0	0	0	3	0	0	0	10	1	3	0	0	0
2	3	1	1	0	4	1	1	0	4	1	0	1	5
1	2	2	1	0	0	3	0	1	9	1	1	1	1
0	1	0	3	3	0	0	3	1	2	3	0	0	0
0	0	0	1	1	1	2	3	2	6	5	1	0	0
0	0	0	0	1	0	0	2	4	0	2	0	0	1
0	0	0	0	1	0	0	2	2	0	3	0	0	0
5	7	1	1	0	17	1	1	0	3	1	1	1	10
1	1	5	3	0	0	12	1	0	14	3	0	0	9
0	0	0	3	5	0	0	7	1	2	8	1	1	6
0	1	0	1	9	0	0	1	16	9	9	0	0	3
3	3	1	1	0	7	0	0	0	0	0	1	0	5
3	5	3	2	5	11	2	0	1	9	0	0	2	5
3	3	3	2	0	6	1	0	0	3	1	1	0	10
0	0	0	1	2	0	2	0	0	0	0	0	0	4
0	0	0	0	1	0	0	1	0	0	0	0	0	4
0	0	0	0	1	0	0	0	3	0	1	0	0	0
6	9	6	8	11	0	0	0	0	15	0	0	2	19
0	0	0	0	3	17	12	8	17	12	18	2	0	8
1	1	1	1	0	0	6	0	0	4	0	0	0	7
0	0	0	0	2	0	0	0	7	0	2	0	0	0
0	0	0	0	0	0	0	0	0	0	0	0	0	3
2	4	0	0	0	10	0	0	0	2	0	0	1	5
0	3	2	1	0	5	2	0	0	0	0	0	0	4
0	0	0	1	3	0	1	2	0	3	1	0	0	5
0	0	0	0	0	0	0	0	0	1	0	0	0	0
0	0	0	0	0	0	0	0	0	0	0	0	0	0
0	0	0	0	0	0	0	0	0	0	0	0	0	0
0	0	3	2	4	6	11	3	1	10	3	0	0	7
0	0	0	0	0	0	0	2	3	1	6	0	0	0
0	0	0	0	0	0	0	0	1	1	1	0	0	0
0	0	0	0	2	0	0	1	5	1	4	0	0	3
0	0	0	0	1	0	0	2	7	3	5	0	0	2
0	0	0	0	3	0	0	0	7	3	2	0	0	0
0	0	0	0	0	0	0	1	0	0	2	0	0	0
0	0	1	0	0	0	0	0	0	1	0	0	1	4
0	1	0	0	3	0	0	0	0	5	0	0	0	1
0	0	0	0	0	0	0	0	0	2	0	0	0	1
0	0	0	0	0	0	0	0	0	0	0	0	1	0
0	1	0	2	6	0	0	0	0	11	0	0	0	2
0	0	0	1	1	0	2	0	0	4	0	0	1	1
6	4	0	0	0	0	0	0	0	0	0	0	0	2
4	9	0	0	0	0	0	0	0	1	0	0	0	0
0	0	6	4	0	0	0	0	0	0	0	0	0	0
0	0	4	8	4	0	0	0	0	1	0	0	0	0
0	0	0	4	14	0	0	0	1	3	0	0	0	2
0	0	0	0	0	17	0	0	0	0	0	1	0	4
0	0	0	0	0	0	12	0	0	6	1	0	0	0
0	0	0	0	0	0	0	8	0	0	3	0	0	0
0	0	0	0	1	0	0	0	17	2	7	1	0	1
0	1	0	1	3	0	6	0	2	27	3	0	0	0
0	0	0	0	0	0	1	3	7	3	18	1	0	2
0	0	0	0	0	1	0	0	1	0	1	2	0	0
0	0	0	0	0	0	0	0	0	0	0	0	2	0

PROGRAM NOTES

MASTER SCHEDULE LAYOUT FORM

Course No.	Time Pattern	S	H	Min.	Max.	Teacher Name	Course Title	Course No	Teacher No.	School Time Pattern	Room No.	School Code
1-3	4-9	10	11	12-14	15-17	20-37	38-51	54-56	57-59	60-64	65-68	75-79

FIG. 66. *Master Schedule Coding Form*

is now keypunched into cards, one card for each section of the master schedule.

COMPUTER SCHEDULING RUNS

The Anderson program will handle two semesters at once, seven or fewer periods per day, and up to 1200 sections divided in any manner among as many as 350 courses. Since individual students are processed sequentially, any number may be handled within the permissible number of sections. On the IBM 7094, the program will process 800 to 1000 pupils per minute on simulation runs and 500 to 800 pupils per minute on production runs. In the simulation scheduling run, (Fig. 67) output is limited to complete information about pupils who could not be scheduled, including such information as number of tries to schedule, courses successfully scheduled, and courses that could not be scheduled. Section balances for each section are provided at the close of the simulation run. From these data, school personnel can make any adjustments necessary on the master schedule or student program to produce the most desirable outcomes.

After two or three simulation runs and prior to the opening of school, a production run should be completed. Output from this run may contain printed results of good schedules as well as the few remaining conflicts (Fig. 68). With a good master schedule and some degree of flexibility in student course selections, a high percentage of students (usually 95 per cent or better) can be accurately scheduled.

If the local educational data processing center has a large enough computer, the final output can be printed directly from the computer tape. If the center uses punched card equipment, cards can be punched from the computer tape at high speed. These cards can then be used to produce all output from the scheduling system, as follows:

1. *Student locator cards*—cards containing basic student information and the daily schedule of each pupil.
2. *Class lists*—lists of students assigned to each section in the school program.
3. *Master schedule list*—a class or section directory (Fig. 69) containing the name of each section, course number, a unique section number (different for every section in the school), teacher name, period, and the seats remaining in each section. This information is valuable in hand-scheduling new students after the opening of school.

A typical sequence of events in the scheduling process is presented in Figure 70. With local modifications, this sequence can be applied to most scheduling operations.

```
                                                                          RUSAW
                                                                         COURSE
                                                                    PREASSIGNED
                                                                            100
                                                                            301
                                                                            400
                                                                            450
                                                                            601
                                                                            707
                                                                         COURSE
CLASS   2 MINIMUM SEATS FULL ENGLISH 1            1000605                    34
CLASS   1 MINIMUM SEATS FULL ENGLISH 1            1001253                    43
CLASS 111 MINIMUM SEATS FULL GEN SCIENCE C        4511656                    38
CLASS 163 MINIMUM SEATS FULL IND DRAW 1           7071301                    73
CLASS 163 CLOSED             IND DRAW 1           7071301                    73
CLASS 133 MINIMUM SEATS FULL GEN BUSINESS         6001954B                   19
CLASS 138 MINIMUM SEATS FULL TYPING 1             6011955                    15
CLASS 138 CLOSED             TYPING 1             6011955                    15
CLASS 137 MINIMUM SEATS FULL TYPING 1             6010134B                   15
CLASS 137 CLOSED             TYPING 1             6010134B                   15
CLASS  87 MINIMUM SEATS FULL GIRLS PE 1           4030306                    72
                                                                   COMBINATIONS
                                                                          SMITH
                                                                         COURSE
                                                                    PREASSIGNED
                                                                            111
                                                                            301
                                                                            400
                                                                            450
                                                                            700
                                                                            854
                                                                         COURSE
CLASS  58 MINIMUM SEATS FULL GENERAL MATH         3002106                    23
CLASS 169 MINIMUM SEATS FULL HOMEMAKING 1         8001501                    29
CLASS 123 CLOSED             SPANISH L 1          5001806                    24
                                                                   COMBINATIONS
                                                                         TILLER
                                                                         COURSE
                                                                    PREASSIGNED
                                                                            100
                                                                            300
                                                                            403
                                                                            450
                                                                            500
                                                                            912
```

FORM 6613 GV

FIG. 67. *Simulation Scheduling Run Output*

```
ERNEST JR             09  00 TRYS=  14 LEVEL= 6 SEQ=   835
  A    B    C    D    E    F    G    N    TITLE
  0    0    0    0    0    0    0
  0    0    3    0    3    0    0    3    ENGLISH 1
  0    0    3    0    0    0    0    1    ARITHMETIC
  3    3    3    0    0    0    0    3    BOYS PE 1
  3    3    3    3    0    0    0    4    GEN SCIENCE
  3    3    3    3    3    3    0    6    TYPING 1
  3    0    0    0    3    0    0    2    IND DRAW 1
  707 DELETED

     NO.  835 PROCESSED

     NO.  839 PROCESSED

     NO.  840 PROCESSED

     NO.  840 PROCESSED

     NO.  840 PROCESSED

     NO.  843 PROCESSED

     NO.  844 PROCESSED

     NO.  844 PROCESSED

     NO.  845 PROCESSED

     NO.  845 PROCESSED

     NO.  848 PROCESSED
EXHAUSTED FOR
MELVIN                09  00 TRYS=   2 LEVEL= 6 SEQ=   850
  A    B    C    D    E    F    G    N    TITLE
  0    0    0    0    0    0    0
  3    0    0    0    0    0    0    1    ENGLISH 1R
  0    0    3    0    0    0    0    1    ARITHMETIC
  3    3    3    0    0    0    0    3    BOYS PE 1
  3    3    3    3    0    0    0    4    GEN SCIENCE
  0    3    0    3    0    3    0    3    WOODSHOP 1
  3    3    3    3    3    3    0    7    ARTS + CRAFTS
  854 DELETED

     NO.  853 PROCESSED

     NO.  853 PROCESSED

     NO.  854 PROCESSED
EXHAUSTED FOR
 JACQUELYN L          09  00 TRYS=  62 LEVEL= 6 SEQ=   858
  A    B    C    D    E    F    G    N    TITLE
  0    0    0    0    0    0    0
  0    0    3    0    3    0    0    3    ENGLISH 1
  0    3    3    3    3    3    0    6    GENERAL MATH
  0    0    0    3    3    3    0    3    GIRLS PE 1
  3    3    3    3    0    0    0    4    GEN SCIENCE
  0    3    0    0    0    3    0    2    SPANISH L 1
  0    3    0    0    0    0    0    1    CHORUS 1
```

```
COMBINATIONS EXHAUSTED FOR 01030

01030 BROOCK S                    527649801 TRYS#   4 LEVEL# 5 SEQ#  24
          COURSE    A   B   C   D   E   F   G   N
PREASSIGNED         0   0   0   0   0   0   0
              31    0   0   0   0   0   3   0   1
              33    3   0   0   0   3   0   0   2
              35    0   0   3   0   0   0   0   1
              36    0   0   0   3   0   0   0   1
             103    0   0   3   3   3   3   0   4
             107    3   3   3   3   3   3   0  18
01030 COURSE 103 DELETED
```

FIG. 68. *Student Scheduling Production Run*

```
030 BROOCK S                       5276498 013M                   244
    BKKP 2-3         GN031 24F           5     PURCELL
    BUS MACH         GN033 45A           3     TOSCHI
    SHORTHAND 2      GN035 45C           7     TOSCHI
    TRANSCRIPTION    GN036 45D           2     TOSCHI
    PE, GIRLS        GN107 50E         GYM     ADD TWELVE
    ENGLISH 3-G      GN 10    G     WELLER
    ENGLISH 3-G      GN 10    B     WELLER

029 BRIDGES F                      5276498 013M                   245
    ENGLISH 4-G      GN013 52A          28     ADD FOURTEEN
    MERCHANDZG       GN037 45F           7     TOSCHI
    HMKG 4-F         GN057  8B          42     GORMAN
    ECON             GN104 12E          31     TAYLOR
    PE, GIRLS        GN107 10          GYM     JOHNSON
    ENGLISH 3-G      GN 10    G     WELLER
    ENGLISH 3-G      GN 10    D1245WELLER
    ENGLISH 3-G      GN 10    C24   WELLER

028 BREWER J                       5276498 013M                   246
    ENGLISH 4-C      GN012  1C          30     BRUNOLLI
    BUS LAW          GN032  4E          08     COOK
    BUS MACH         GN033 45A           3     TOSCHI
    ECON             GN104  6F          31     CURRAN
    PE, GIRLS        GN107 28D         GYM     ROGERS
    ENGLISH 3-G      GN 10    G     WELLER
    ENGLISH 3-G      GN 10    B     WELLER

027 BRESLER H                      5276498 013M                   247
    ENGLISH 4-C      GN012 35E          18     VELGUTH
    PUB SPKG         GN015 21C          33     PALMER
    TRI6/SOLD GEOMGN081 33D             12     SMULLIN
    PHYSICS          GN094 11A          44     KELLY
    ECON             GN104  6F          31     CURRAN
    P E              GN106 18B         GYM     KENNY
    ENGLISH 3-G      GN 10    G     WELLER

026 BRANCO M                       5276498 013M                   248
    ENGLISH 4-G      GN013 52C          12     ADD FOURTEEN
    BYS HMK F        GN061  8A          42     GORMAN
    MECH DRWG 3      GN066 42F          54     RAPPAPORT
    AUTO SHOP        GN069 38D          63     THOMPSON
    ECON             GN104 12E          31     TAYLOR
    PE, BOYS         GN106 51B         GYM     ADD THIRTEEN
```

CLASS	CO.	PER.	SEM	MINS	MAXS	LAST= 883	
1	100	C	3	-6	0	MARRAZZO MR	ENGLISH 1
2	100	E	3	-4	0	CURLEY MR	ENGLISH 1
3	100	E	3	-6	0	MARRAZZO MR	ENGLISH 1
4	101	A	3	8	11	MARRAZZO MR	ENGLISH 1C
5	101	B	3	8	11	MARRAZZO MR	ENGLISH 1C
6	101	D	3	7	10	MARRAZZO MR	ENGLISH 1C
7	101	F	3	0	3	WELLS MISS	ENGLISH 1C
8	102	A	3	2	7	WELLS MISS	ENGLISH 2
9	102	B	3	2	7	WELLS MISS	ENGLISH 2
10	102	C	3	0	6	BUXTON MRS	ENGLISH 2
11	102	D	3	1	7	BUXTON MRS	ENGLISH 2
12	102	E	3	-2	2	FINCHER MRS	ENGLISH 2
13	103	B	3	1	5	CURLEY MR	ENGLISH 2C
14	103	C	3	0	4	CURLEY MR	ENGLISH 2C
15	103	D	3	-1	3	CURLEY MR	ENGLISH 2C
16	104	B	3	2	7	BUCKLES MR	ENGLISH 3
17	104	C	3	1	6	BUCKLES MR	ENGLISH 3
18	104	D	3	-1	4	BUCKLES MR	ENGLISH 3
19	104	F	3	1	6	FINCHER MRS	ENGLISH 3
20	105	A	3	0	2	FINCHER MRS	ENGLISH 3C
21	105	C	3	-1	1	FINCHER MRS	ENGLISH 3C
22	105	D	3	0	2	FINCHER MRS	ENGLISH 3C
23	106	D	3	2	7	WELLS MISS	ENGLISH 4
24	106	E	3	2	7	WELLS MISS	ENGLISH 4
25	107	E	3	0	1	BUCKLES MR	JOURNALISM
26	107	F	3	-2	0	BUCKLES MR	JOURNALISM
27	108	E	3	2	6	BUCKLES MR	JOURNALISM
28	110	E	3	2	14	BUXTON MRS	PUB SPKG
29	111	A	3	1	2	CURLEY MR	ENGLISH 1R
30	200	A	3	8	10	BROWN J MR	LEADERSHIP
31	201	A	3	2	4	BROWN J MR	LEADERSHIP
32	202	A	3	-1	3	CRANDALL MR	WEST CIVIL
33	202	B	3	1	5	CRANDALL MR	WEST CIVIL
34	202	B	3	-1	4	NAGATZ MR	WEST CIVIL
35	202	C	3	-1	4	NAGATZ MR	WEST CIVIL
36	202	D	3	1	3	KUZNETZOFF MR	WESTERN CIV
37	203	D	3	5	9	NAGATZ MR	WEST CIVIL
38	203	E	3	-1	3	NAGATZ MR	WEST CIVIL
39	203	F	3	-1	3	NAGATZ MR	WEST CIVIL
40	204	A	3	3	7	MAES MR	US HISTORY
41	204	B	3	0	4	BROWN J MR	US HISTORY
42	204	C	3	3	7	MAES MR	US HISTORY
43	204	E	3	0	4	MAES MR	US HISTORY
44	205	B	3	-1	3	MAES MR	US HISTORY
45	205	D	3	0	4	MAES MR	US HISTORY
46	205	F	3	-1	3	BROWN J MR	US HISTORY
47	206	B	3	2	3	GYSBERS MR	AMER GOVT E
48	206	D	3	1	2	BROWN J MR	AMER GOVT E
49	206	E	3	1	2	BROWN J MR	AMER GOVT E
50	207	C	3	1	8	GYSBERS MR	AMER GOVT E
51	207	D	3	1	8	GYSBERS MR	AMER GOVT E
52	207	F	3	1	8	GYSBERS MR	AMER GOVT E
53	300	B	3	0	5	PEASE MR	GENERAL MA
54	300	C	3	2	5	AKINS MR	GEN MATH
55	300	D	3	2	5	AKINS MR	GEN MATH
56	300	D	3	1	4	LOUIE MR	GEN MATH
57	300	E	3	1	4	LOUIE MR	GEN MATH
58	300	F	3	-1	4	WHITE MR	GENERAL MA
59	301	C	3	1	5	PEASE MR	ARITHMETIC

FORM 6613 GV

FIG. 69. *Master Schedule List*

PROGRAM NOTES

	1001253	43
	1000605	34
	1001255	43
	1011251	43
	1011252	43
	1011254B	43
	1012056	42
	1022051	42
	1022052	42
	1020303	33
	1020304A	33
	1020705	44
	1030602	34
	1030603	34
	1030604B	34
	1040252	41
	1040253	41
	1040254A	41
	1040706	44
	1050701	44
	1050703	44
	1050704A	44
	1062054A	42
	1062055	42
	1070255	41
	1070256	41
	1080255	41
	1100305	33
	1110601	34
	2000201	21
	2010201	21
	2020551	96
	2020552	96
	2021452	31
	2021453	31
	2021004B	96
	2031454A	31
	2031455	31
	2031456	31
	2041201	32
	2040202	21
	2041203	32
	2041205	32
	2051202	32
	2051204B	32
	2050206	21
	2060852	22
	2060204A	21
	2060205	21
C	2070853	22
C	2070854B	22
C	2070856	22
	3001552	14
	3000053	13
	3000054B	13
	3001104A	12
	3001105	12
	3002106	23
	3011553	14

ALLIED EGRY BUSINESS SYSTEMS, LA

LARGE VERSUS SMALL COMPUTERS IN SCHEDULING

Until very recently, scheduling programs have primarily been written for large-scale computers. Wilkes is now experimenting with SOCRATES (Scheduling of Classes Realized Through Effortless Systemization), a program written for an IBM 1401 card system with only 4000 memory positions. All students are initially scheduled into those classes which can be taken only at one time during the day. Subsequent machine runs are made to schedule students into doubleton and tripleton courses.

By writing the program in a language close to actual machine instructions, and by passing the schedule cards through several times, the system makes it possible to utilize the small-scale computer effectively. Naturally, the time involved is greater, but the unit cost may prove to be more reasonable since this approach presupposes that such a small computer will be available at the local level. The IBM Corporation also has completed scheduling programs for the 1620 computer and the 1440 system with random access disk packs. General Electric has announced scheduling packages for its 200 series computers. Control Data Corporation and UNIVAC offer student scheduling services through their service bureaus.

ADVANCED COMPUTER SCHEDULING PROGRAMS

Earlier programs have assigned students to a predetermined master schedule. In this discussion, school scheduling is considered to be the process of assigning time, rooms, teachers, and students to the classes required by a school's curriculum. One of the best available packages of this type is the program called GASP (Generalized Academic Simulation Program) currently being developed at the Massachusetts Institute of Technology, under a grant from the Educational Facilities Laboratory.[8] This program may be used to compute one or more of the following outputs: (1) the timetable of classes, (2) instructor schedules, (3) room schedules, and (4) student schedules. GASP attempts to simulate the clerical aspects of an ideal manual scheduling procedure and is divided into two segments. In the first segment, a timetable is constructed in which time, classrooms, and instructors are assigned for each class. In the second segment, students are assigned to the classes in the timetable. The segments may be run separately or together on one continuous run.

The GASP approach is one requiring a rather intimate man-computer relationship. The administrator is allowed the luxury of many trials involving small modules of time, complicated student requests, and a varied

8. Holz, Robert E., *School Scheduling Using Computers,* Massachusetts Institute of Technology, April, 1964.

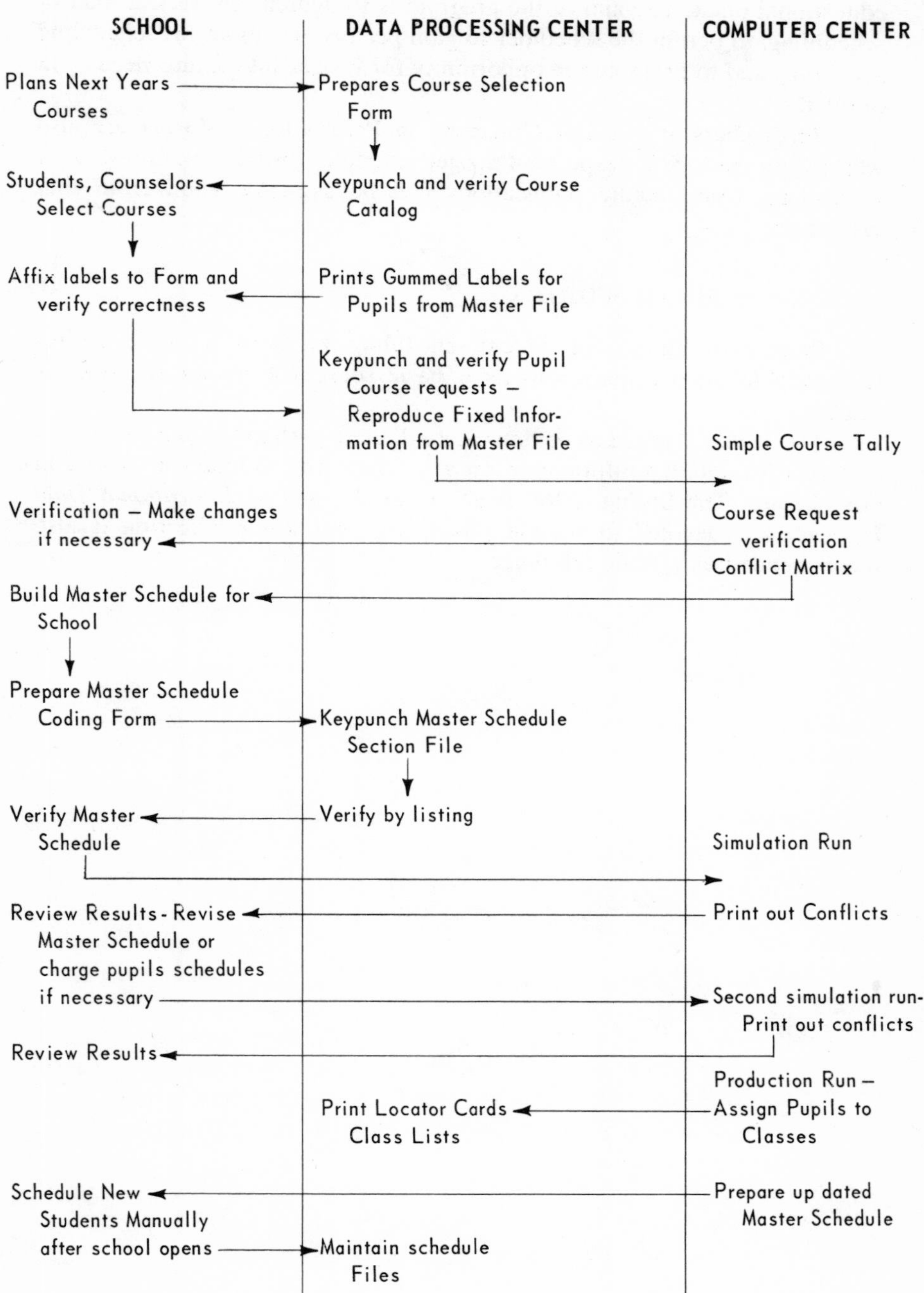

FIG. 70. *Sequence of Events in Pupil Scheduling Process*

educational plant. The aim of the program is to lighten the clerical load of scheduling, to permit the scheduler to gain perspective about his scheduling problems, and to promote the opportunity for insight into future needs and problems.

Researchers at Stanford University in Palo Alto, California are also working on the broader aspects of master schedule construction and student scheduling. Undoubtedly publications will be available soon from that institution.

A FINAL WORD

Progress in automated student scheduling has been dramatic. Its relationship to other applications as a basic source of master file data is evident.

The reader is urged to communicate directly with individuals or manufacturers for detailed information on any scheduling program discussed in this chapter. The Spring, 1964 issue of the *Journal of Educational Data Processing* is devoted to student scheduling, and this publication is also recommended as a basic reference.

13

CUMULATIVE RECORDS

Cumulative records are essential to a good educational program. They should contain some continuity of information on the development of each child throughout his school life. Moreover, the educational system should provide a means of recording and using this information to improve instruction and guidance services.

The proper maintenance and use of cumulative records are particularly important in today's school. The average pupil will have at least 45 different teachers from the time he enters school until he has graduated from junior college. If his family moves often, as so many do, he will have even more teachers. This movement of pupils from school to school is to be expected in an urban-industrial society. And since, in such conditions, contacts between pupils and teachers often are of short duration, teachers need assistance in getting quickly acquainted with pupils. Good cumulative records can be used to advantage for this purpose.

BASIC PURPOSE OF CUMULATIVE RECORDS

Good cumulative records are essential to the proper use of the basic elements that are present in any effective guidance program. Two sets of variables stand out as essential to every activity aimed at providing good guidance services for the secondary school student:

1. Data concerning the individual—abilities, interest, aptitudes, experiences, and background;
2. Information about the area in which he must make choices and plans.

The need for sound guidance, moreover, is heightened by the current national shortages in manpower. There is a direct and significant relationship between the effectiveness of guidance services and the directions that high school graduates take or will be taking in the pursuit of occupational goals.

What the guidance counselor, or the teacher, or any person who has contact with the student learns about the student, is useful not only to himself, but also has value for others, provided the information is made available to them. Unless this vital information is recorded on cumulative records and passed along whenever the student enters another school, its value is lost.

Stewart and Workman[1] began a study on the student's cumulative record with a strong belief in the value of such records as a basis for co-operative educational undertaking by all school personnel. They thought that a major potential of the cumulative record was the invaluable aid it could be to a school guidance program. Indeed, they found it difficult to see how there could be effective functioning of any aspect of the educational program without using the cumulative records for such purposes as discovering special talents and identifying incipient behavioral or educational problems of the students.

In their study of secondary schools, Stewart and Workman revealed that the records are not used to their full extent by teachers and other staff members. In fact, many of them do not use the records at all, preferring to base their thinking and their decisions simply upon their own experiences in teaching the young. Also, perusal of relevant literature indicated to them that surprisingly little research has been done on the use of cumulative records. The research that has been done has been concerned only with the nature of the data included in the records and the kinds of forms used to accumulate these data. There is practically no information concerning the extent to which records are used or the factors related to such use.

The teacher's lack of confidence in the usefulness of the information in the student's cumulative record is justified to a large degree. In general, the records are kept in a rather haphazard fashion. The teacher may have to sift through any number of pieces of paper in order to obtain a test score or some other type of information. Such a state of affairs would seem to discourage their use by all but the most conscientious teachers.

Furthermore, in assembling cumulative records, the amount of information to be screened and recorded for all students in an average high school constitutes no small task. Because of the pressure of more urgent activities, the teacher tends to be lax when making entries in the records. The entries are made in a hurried manner, or the material is simply inserted into the student's folder, or these materials may even be stacked away in some closet never to find their way into the cumulative records.

Stewart and Workman reported that, although little is actually being done to improve the use of the cumulative records, the current forecast for improving their use is good. Administrators voiced an awareness of the need for improvement of the records and for in-service training in their use. Counselors also appeared to be aware of the shortcomings of the records and the obstacles to be overcome if teachers are to make more adequate use of them.

1. Stewart, L. H. and A. D. Workman, *The Student's Cumulative Record—Unachieved Potential*. Sacramento: California State Department of Education. 1963. (Based on a study conducted at the University of California, Berkeley, 1961-1962.)

These two investigators recommended that school administrators who want to see more use made of the cumulative records must (1) make these records more accessible to teachers, (2) maintain them in such a way that rapid perusal will yield the required data, (3) provide more complete information, and (4) reduce the clerical work necessary to the maintenance and use of the records.

NATIONAL BEGINNINGS AND DEVELOPMENTS OF THE CUMULATIVE RECORD

In 1928 the American Council on Education designed the "cumulative record" as a guidance instrument and urged the schools and colleges of the nation to adopt it, or one similar to it, for the maintenance and beneficial use of personnel data.[2] So that the records could be interchanged and used effectively by many agencies, the Council stressed the need for uniformity of content and data-gathering procedures. Since that time, the use of the cumulative student record has become widespread, and abundant literature concerning it has sprung up. Strang[3] and Traxler,[4] among others, have written comprehensive reviews of works published in this field.

STATE CUMULATIVE RECORDS

Informational files on pupils and students, generally in the form of a state cumulative record, have been used in our nation's schools for some years. In some states the state departments of education, assisted by staff members throughout the state, have compiled and published handbooks on cumulative records. The function of these handbooks is primarily to assist school personnel in developing adequate, uniform records and effective ways of handling them.

STATE LEGISLATION

The importance of student personnel information has been officially underscored by legislation in many states. The state of California enacted on July 1, 1960 a law which stated that a cumulative record *must* be maintained for every pupil and student in the public schools of the state. It further required that the "recorded information should be similar to

2. *Cumulative Record Folders for Schools and Colleges.* Committee on the Revision of Cumulative Records. Washington, D. C.: American Council on Education, 1947.

3. Ruth Strang, *Counseling Technics in College and Secondary School.* New York, Harper and Brothers, 1947.

4. Arthur E. Traxler, *Techniques of Guidance.* New York, Harper and Row, 1957.

that provided for by the form known as the California Cumulative Record."[5]

In many of the states, upon the request of any district receiving a new student, the student's cumulative record has to be brought up to date and forwarded to the new district. The object of these regulations is to bring about, on the basis of firm guidelines, greater accuracy and better communication in the maintenance and handling of pupil personnel data.

MECHANICS AND PROBLEMS OF RECORDING DATA

One of the greatest obstacles to the improvement of guidance practices is the vast amount of paperwork necessary to carry out any large-scale guidance program. Pertinent data on identification and registration, attendance, scholastic progress, health status, home background, social adjustment, interests and plans, attitudes, special activities, and other factors in the school life of each boy and girl must be gathered, assembled, and made readily available. In many instances vital data do not reach the classroom teacher or the counselor in time to be of any real help. What is needed in the average school district is a system in which in-process information is easily available and reports are furnished when they are *news,* not history. All this involves a much greater amount of clerical manipulation than is often imagined.

The initial handling of student information should include both the collection of data and their subsequent entry into some type of student record. Such personnel data collection involves the gathering of information that is required for basic documents, and these documents vary considerably from school to school. Examples of such documents are test-reporting forms, report cards, various honor and failure lists, attendance accounting, registration forms, and others too numerous to mention.

Frequently it is found that information from these basic documents is collected from so many sources that one phase of the initial handling function becomes an accumulation of *related* data. In districts providing data processing services, once the data have been collected and related, they can then be processed and recorded easily.

Putting data to work in the form of "educational intelligence" is probably the most important part of the data gathering, processing, and reporting cycle. At this point perhaps a differentiation should be made between data, information, and educational intelligence. Data is simply the collection of raw information. Information is the manipulation of data in the form of a roster or a report. Educational intelligence is the manipula-

5. *Handbook on California Cumulative Records,* Bulletin of the California Department of Education, Volume XXV. No. 5, July, 1956.

tion of the data so that the information generated is a combination of the specific data plus other information that has been stored in the files. This combination of information can be utilized to generate an "action" type of report which has specific meaning for the person receiving it. Information is of no use if it cannot be used effectively by the counselor when he works with his students. The data must be meaningful, and the counselor must be informed regarding their proper utilization. Data processing, too, must be geared (1) to the needs of the school and (2) to the ability of the school staff to use the reports wisely and well. It is axiomatic that reports and statistics should not be issued just for the sake of reports and statistics.

USE, MISUSE, AND LACK OF USE

The problems and tasks of organizing, maintaining, and using pupil personnel data have plagued the nation's schools almost without letup. Wide variations in district policies and lack of uniformity both as to content of student information and as to appropriate methods of putting it to use have been thorns in the sides of our nation's educators and guidance personnel. Data kept by one district are frequently not comparable to data kept by another. Transcript forms are commonly kept separately from cumulative record folders. Data gathering itself is often a haphazard, hit-or-miss operation. Seldom, if ever, are attempts made to analyze or correlate the data so that they can be used profitably.

It has been brought out in numerous reports that *decisions must have their basis in information*—that comprehensive, accurate, and timely data upon which decisions need to be based are vital to the success of any guidance program. It is of utmost importance that these data—these tools for decision-making—be put into the hands of the counselor and the student at the time when decisions are to be made.

That these vital tools are actually lacking in many places, at many times, and to a surprising extent, was born out by Stewart and Workman[6] as well as by the California State Advisory Committee on Integrated Data Processing.

RECENT INNOVATIONS IN CUMULATIVE RECORDS

School districts in recent years have been producing a gummed or pressure-sensitive label containing test scores and student marks for use on some type of cumulative record. Even school districts using manual procedures are receiving pressure-sensitive labels from the major test companies as a part of their test-scoring and reporting services. A major

6. *Op. cit.* (n. 1), p. 47.

problem has been the placing of this information on a record form not designed originally for such purposes.

As school districts have come to use data processing more and more they have moved toward better record-keeping forms. Many districts have moved toward a new academic record form which is divided into seventh- and eighth-grade reports on one side, and reports for grades nine through twelve on the other. Figure 71 shows a form used in the Vallejo, California Senior High School while Figure 72 shows a comparable form used in the Napa Union High School, Napa, California. Spaces left blank on these documents allow for the placement of pressure-sensitive labels. These labels are used in a section provided for recording semester marks and also in a section for reporting standardized test scores. It becomes a simple and rapid matter for a clerical person to fill out the identifying data on one portion of the card and then to place the mark labels and test-score labels in the appropriate spaces.

This combination of a special record form and the use of adhesive labels makes it possible for student information involving scholastic status and standardized testing to be well organized, well integrated, and readily accessible. In many districts that use such a technique it is found to be totally successful. On the one hand, much time and labor has been saved by the uniformity and integration achieved; on the other, teachers and counselors gain immediate access to the records they vitally need.

THE COOPERATIVE PLAN FOR GUIDANCE AND ADMISSION

Educational Testing Service (ETS) through its Cooperative Plan for Guidance and Admission (CPGA) makes available to school districts a unique and comprehensive transcript and record-keeping system. By means of a computer, the CPGA is able to store, summarize, retrieve, and communicate meaningful, comprehensive information about students in a quantity and quality hitherto unavailable to the educational community.

The basic purpose of the Cooperative Plan for Guidance and Admission is to help all schools prepare more meaningful descriptions of their students at the point of school-to-college transition. This is done by means of a computer, using as a basis the academic and personal records the students have accumulated while in school.

To bring this about, the school places each student record on two sides of an 8½″ by 11″ form which looks like a test answer sheet. This is the *input* document for central processing; it requires six to ten minutes of clerical preparation. The computer assimilates all this information, processes it, computes useful descriptive statistics, and prepares a document which combines the student's record and the results of the calculations. This is the *output* document. The school that receives this document

F 275

SENIOR HIGH SCHOOL PERMANENT RECORD
Vallejo, California

Vallejo Senior High School
840 Nebraska

SPRING 63 GR 08 ABSENT
DE ANZA HIGH

PD.	COURSE TITLE	GRP.	MARKS		
0	HOMEMAKING		B	C	C
4	SPEC CHORUS		A	A	A
5	ARITHMETIC	6	B	C	C
6	SOCIAL ST	6	C	C	C
8	ENGLISH	6	B	B	B
9	PE GIRLS		B	B	B

Credits Earned .0 | Credit Courses .0 | Grade Points .0

SPRING 63 GR 08 ABSENT
DE ANZA HIGH

PD.	COURSE TITLE	GRP.	MARKS		
0	PE GIRLS		D	C	C
4	ARITHMETIC	5	C	B	B
5	SOCIAL ST	5	C	D	D
6	HOMEMAKING		D	C	C
8	ART		B	B	B
9	ENGLISH	5	B	B	B

Credits Earned .0 | Credit Courses .0 | Grade Points .0

I certify this record to be correct:

Principal/Registrar

Date Entered......

Date of Leaving......

MARKS:	GROUPS:
A—Superior	1—Honors
B—Very Good	2—Col. Prep.
C—Average	3—Terminal
D—Passing	4—Remedial
F—Failure	⌑— Half Credit
I—Incomplete	✱—No Credit

CALIFORNIA STATE REQUIREMENTS:

	Completed	Exempt
Social Studies	......	......
Safety Ed.	......	......
Polio	......	......
Driver Ed.	......	......

B/D | Birthplace City: | State: | Parent or Guardian:

Name: | Address:

STANDARIZED TEST DATA AND COMMENTS:

```
           NOV 1963   GRADE 8
HENMON-NELSON IQ-106 %-65 STA-6
  STANFORD ADV JM   %ILES/STA-9S
     PARA-65%/6          REAS-93%/8
     WORD-32%/4          COMP-85%/7
AVG RDG-49%/5     AVG ARITH-89%/8
    SPELL-63%/6          LANG-46%/5
```

Counselor:...... School Last Attended: ......

Transcripts sent:

(Photo)

FIG. 71. *Academic Record Form Used in Vallejo, California*

______ SEM. 19______ Grade ______

School

COURSE TITLE	MARKS	
1		

SEMESTER PERIODS (Credits) TO DATE

Prior ______ Current ______ Total ______

______ SEM. 19______ Grade ______

School

COURSE TITLE	MARKS	
2		

SEMESTER PERIODS (Credits) TO DATE

Prior ______ Current ______ Total ______

______ SEM. 19______ Grade ______

School

COURSE TITLE	MARKS	
3		

SEMESTER PERIODS (Credits) TO DATE

Prior ______ Current ______ Total ______

______ SEM. 19______ Grade ______

School

COURSE TITLE	MARKS	
4		

SEMESTER PERIODS (Credits) TO DATE

Prior ______ Current ______ Total ______

______ SEM. 19______ Grade ______

School

COURSE TITLE	MARKS	
5		

SEMESTER PERIODS (Credits) TO DATE

Prior ______ Current ______ Total ______

______ SEM. 19______ Grade ______

School

COURSE TITLE	MARKS	
6		

SEMESTER PERIODS (Credits) TO DATE

Prior ______ Current ______ Total ______

______ SEM. 19______ Grade ______

School

COURSE TITLE	MARKS	
7		

SEMESTER PERIODS (Credits) TO DATE

Prior ______ Current ______ Total ______

______ SEM. 19______ Grade ______

School

COURSE TITLE	MARKS	
8		

SEMESTER PERIODS (Credits) TO DATE

Prior ______ Current ______ Total ______

LAST NAME FIRST MIDDLE ☐ BOY ☐ GIRL

ADDRESS— STREET CITY STATE

BIRTHDATE BIRTHPLACE— CITY AND STATE

PARENT/OR/GUARDIAN

Date Entered	School From	Moved To	Date Left

STANDARDIZED TEST DATA

I certify that the information recorded hereon is correct:

Date ______

Signed ______
PRINCIPAL

School ______

NAPA UNION HIGH SCHOOL - NAPA, CALIF. NPS—104A **ACADEMIC RECORD -- GRADES 7 & 8**

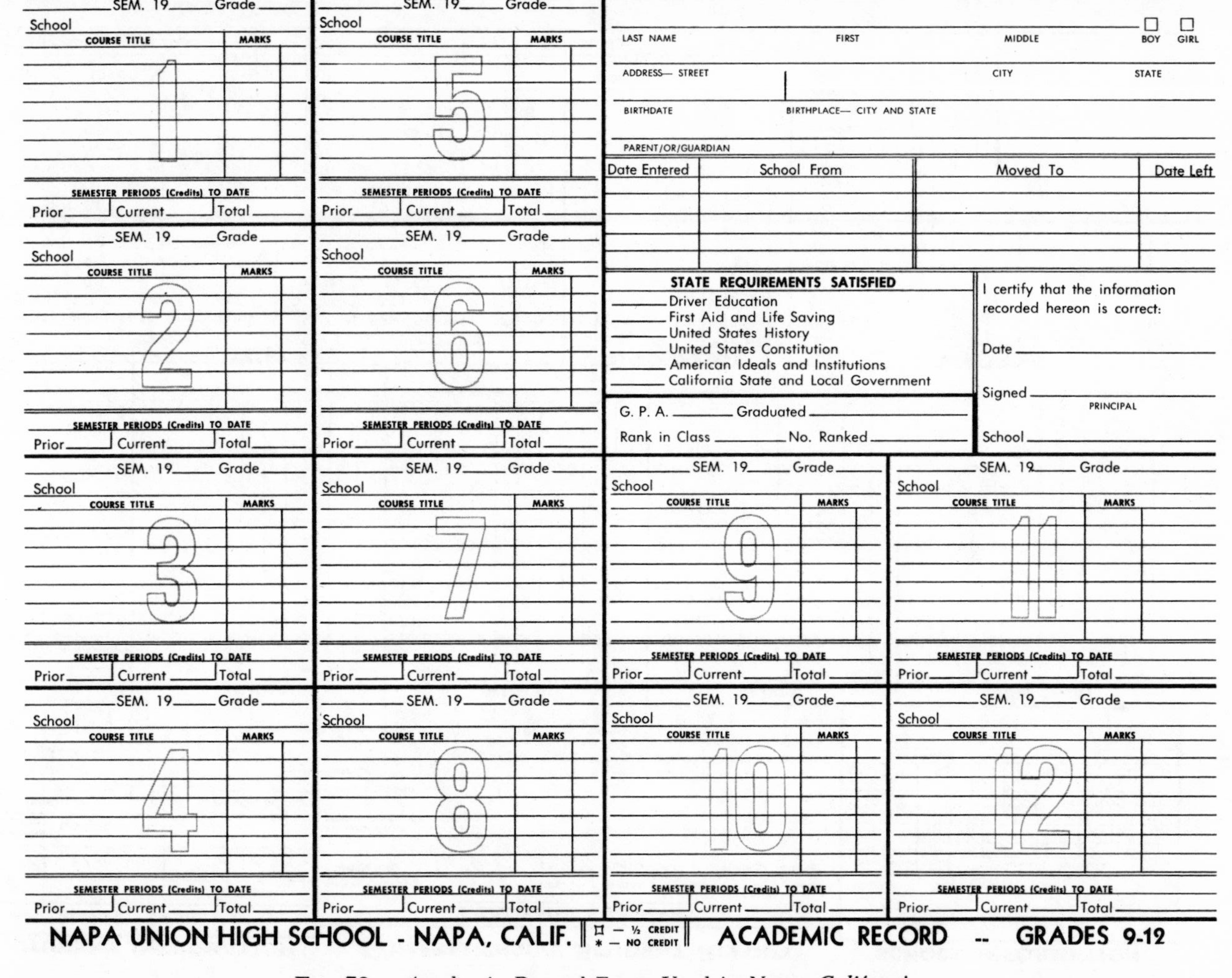

SEM. 19 ____ Grade ____
School
COURSE TITLE	MARKS
1	

SEMESTER PERIODS (Credits) TO DATE
Prior ____ Current ____ Total ____

SEM. 19 ____ Grade ____
School
COURSE TITLE	MARKS
2	

SEMESTER PERIODS (Credits) TO DATE
Prior ____ Current ____ Total ____

SEM. 19 ____ Grade ____
School
COURSE TITLE	MARKS
3	

SEMESTER PERIODS (Credits) TO DATE
Prior ____ Current ____ Total ____

SEM. 19 ____ Grade ____
School
COURSE TITLE	MARKS
4	

SEMESTER PERIODS (Credits) TO DATE
Prior ____ Current ____ Total ____

SEM. 19 ____ Grade ____
School
COURSE TITLE	MARKS
5	

SEMESTER PERIODS (Credits) TO DATE
Prior ____ Current ____ Total ____

SEM. 19 ____ Grade ____
School
COURSE TITLE	MARKS
6	

SEMESTER PERIODS (Credits) TO DATE
Prior ____ Current ____ Total ____

SEM. 19 ____ Grade ____
School
COURSE TITLE	MARKS
7	

SEMESTER PERIODS (Credits) TO DATE
Prior ____ Current ____ Total ____

SEM. 19 ____ Grade ____
School
COURSE TITLE	MARKS
8	

SEMESTER PERIODS (Credits) TO DATE
Prior ____ Current ____ Total ____

LAST NAME ____ FIRST ____ MIDDLE ____ ☐ BOY ☐ GIRL

ADDRESS— STREET ____ CITY ____ STATE ____

BIRTHDATE ____ BIRTHPLACE— CITY AND STATE ____

PARENT/OR/GUARDIAN ____

Date Entered	School From	Moved To	Date Left

STATE REQUIREMENTS SATISFIED

____ Driver Education
____ First Aid and Life Saving
____ United States History
____ United States Constitution
____ American Ideals and Institutions
____ California State and Local Government

G. P. A. ____ Graduated ____
Rank in Class ____ No. Ranked ____

I certify that the information recorded hereon is correct:

Date ____
Signed ____ PRINCIPAL
School ____

SEM. 19 ____ Grade ____
School
COURSE TITLE	MARKS
9	

SEMESTER PERIODS (Credits) TO DATE
Prior ____ Current ____ Total ____

SEM. 19 ____ Grade ____
School
COURSE TITLE	MARKS
10	

SEMESTER PERIODS (Credits) TO DATE
Prior ____ Current ____ Total ____

SEM. 19 ____ Grade ____
School
COURSE TITLE	MARKS
11	

SEMESTER PERIODS (Credits) TO DATE
Prior ____ Current ____ Total ____

SEM. 19 ____ Grade ____
School
COURSE TITLE	MARKS
12	

SEMESTER PERIODS (Credits) TO DATE
Prior ____ Current ____ Total ____

NAPA UNION HIGH SCHOOL - NAPA, CALIF. ⌑ — ½ CREDIT * — NO CREDIT **ACADEMIC RECORD -- GRADES 9-12**

FIG. 72. *Academic Record Form Used in Napa, California*

COMPREHENSIVE STUDENT REPORT

STUDENT INFORMATION

NAME: WARNER, NATALIE B

SEX	BIRTH DATE	STATE OF BIRTH
F	8/ 6/48	GA

PARENT OR GUARDIAN: WARNER, WILLIAM

CURRICULUM	HEALTH FR	HEALTH SO	HEALTH JR	HEALTH SR	PHYSICAL DISABILITY
ACADEMIC	0	0	0		

DAYS ABSENT FR	SO	JR	SR	DAYS TARDY FR	SO	JR	SR
5	2	3		0	0	1	

ACADEMIC SUMMARY

RANK IN CLASS DATA	POINTS	UNITS	AVERAGE	RANK	GROUP SIZE	% ILE STANDING
COMPLETE CLASS:	72.3+	19	= 3.80	4	IN 430	= 99
ACADEMIC GROUP: (ACADEMIC COURSES ONLY)	60.5+	16	= 3.78	4	IN 260	= 99
COMPLETE CLASS WEIGHTED:	77.3+	19	= 4.07	3	IN 430	= 99

COMPOSITE TEST: PRELIMINARY SCHOL APT T

VERBAL TEST SCORE	MATH TEST SCORE	CONVERTED VERBAL COURSE SCORE	CONVERTED MATH/SCIENCE COURSE SCORE	CONVERTED ALL COURSE SCORE	VERBAL COMPOSITE	MATH/SCIENCE COMPOSITE	ALL COURSE COMPOSITE
62	65	71	71	74	64	66	67

SCHOOL INFORMATION

SCHOOL NAME: ROCKY HILL H S

LOCATION: ATLANTA, GA

CLASS PD (MIN)	MEETING WEEK	WEEKS /YEAR	PASSING	HONORS	COL REC	D	C	B	A
55	5	36	70	90	87	70	79	87	95

(MEANING OF GRADES: PASSING, HONORS, COL REC, D, C, B, A)

CEEB SCHOOL NUMBER	CLASS SIZE	GRAD. YEAR	UNITS REQ.	SCHOOL ACCREDITED BY
110170	430	64	18	STATE, REGION

OTHER SECONDARY SCHOOLS ATTENDED	DATE LEFT

ACADEMIC RECORD

AREA	AVERAGE
LANG ART	4.0
FOR LANG	3.5
MATH	3.8
SCIENCE	3.9
SOC STUD	4.0

VERBAL COURSE AVG. 3.7

MATH/SCIENCE COURSE AVG. 3.8

GRADE 9

SUBJECT	1	2	UNIT	GROUP	MISC.
ENGLISH 1	A	A	1		
FRENCH 1	A	A	1		
LATIN 1	B	B	1		
ALGEBRA 1	B	A	1		
GEN SCI 1	A	A	1		
PHYS ED 1	A	B	.50		
MIX CHOR1	A	A	.50		

UNITS TOWARD GRADUATION 6 — GRADE 9 AVERAGE 3.7

GRADE 10

SUBJECT	1	2	UNIT	GROUP	MISC.
ENGLISH 2	A	A	1	HM	
FRENCH 2	A	B	1		
LATIN 2	B	B	1		
PLN GEOM	A		.50		
SLD GEOM		A	.50		
BSCS GRN	B	A	1	HM	
PHYS ED 2	A	A	.50		
MIX CHOR2	A	A	.50		

UNITS TOWARD GRADUATION 6 — GRADE 10 AVERAGE 3.7

GRADE 11

SUBJECT	1	2	UNIT	GROUP	MISC
ENGLISH 3	A	A	1	HM	
FRENCH 3	A	A	1		
FREN CONV	A		.50	HM	CL
TRIGNMTRY	A	A	1		
CHM BND A	A	A	1	HM	
ADV CHEM	A		.50	HM	CL
AM HIST 1	A	A	1		
PHYS ED 3	A	A	.50		
MIX CHOR3	A	A	.50		

UNITS TOWARD GRADUATION 7 — GRADE 11 AVERAGE 4.0

OTHER GRADES

GRADE	SUBJECT	1	2	UNIT	GROUP	MISC
12	CBAP ENGL				H	
12	PHYS SSC				HM	
12	AM GOVT 1					
12	WLD HIST1					
12	PHYS ED 4					
12	MIX CHOR4					
12	PERS TYPE					

UNITS TOWARD GRADUATION — OTHER GRADE AVERAGE

TEST RECORD

GRADE	TEST INFORMATION
9	DIFFERENTIAL APTITUDE NRM:GRD 9 SCOR:% ILE SCHOL 95 , VERB 95 NUMER 90 , ABST 85 SPACE 60 , MECHL 85 CLERL 45 , L-SPL 85 L-SEN 80
9	SCH&COLL ABIL TST LVL3 NRM:GRD 9 SCOR:% BND VERB 96-99, QUANT 99-00 TOTAL 99-99
9	SEQNT TST ED PROG LVL3 NRM:GRD 9 SCOR:% BND READ 92-00, WRITE 83-94 LISTN 73-90, SOC S 89-95 SCIEN 82-95, MATH 86-95
9	CO-OP ACH H S MATH Z NRM: 1 YR ST SCOR:% ILE E ALG 95
10	OTIS QCK-SCR M A GAMMA NRM:GRD 10 SCOR:I Q SCORE 125
11	PRELIMNARY SCHOL APT T NRM:GRD 11 SCOR:STAND VERB 62 MATH 65
11	NATIONL MERIT SCHOL QT NRM:COLLEG SCOR:STAND ENGL 23 MATH 25 SOC S 27 N SCI 15 WORD 19 TOTAL 22

EXTRA-CURRICULAR

ACTIVITY	FR	SO	JR	SR
SOCIAL CLUB		3		
DEBATNG CLB		3	2	
STD COUN BD			2	
JOURNLM CLB	3	3	2	
FUT TEACHRS			2	

WORK RECORD

JOB	FR SUM	FR TERM	SO SUM	SO TERM	JR SUM	JR TERM	SR SUM	SR TERM
CLERCL OCC				1				
CLERCL OCC			17					
ACCT&BOOKP						9		
NURSEMAID	9	1	1	1	9	1		
WRITING								

PERSONAL RECORD	FR	SO	JR	SR
MOTIVATION	1	1	1	
INDUSTRY	1	1	1	
INITIATIVE	1	1	1	
INFLUENCE-LEAD	1	1	1	
CONCERN-OTHERS	1	1	1	
RESPONSIBILITY	1	1	1	
INTEGRITY	1	1	1	
EMOTIONAL STABILITY	1	1	1	

HONORS AND AWARDS

NATL HONOR SOC
LETTER CLUB

John Barr — Prin. — Sept. 3 1963
SIGNATURE — TITLE — DATE

FIG. 73

PRINCIPAL'S RECOMMENDATION

Natalie's interest and ability levels are high in many areas, particularly in biography, marine biology, and foreign languages. At present, she is considering careers in journalism and as a teacher of English or foreign languages.

When her father was killed in an auto accident during Natalie's first year of high school, the chances of attending college for the four Warner children seemed dim. Since that time, her mother has obtained a position with the Family Service Group and with her help and scholarship aid, Natalie should be able to meet her expenses.

At present, Northwestern is Natalie's only choice of college. Her high school faculty feels that she should be able to maintain a high level of scholarship there. It is a pleasure to recommend this serious, wholesome, and unspoiled child who has such a serious desire to continue her education.

9/3/63 — Date | Ethel Thomas — Signature | College Counselor — Title

SPECIAL SYMBOLS

[*] Information insufficient for reporting and computing purposes. Grades and units not included in computations or averages. If an improper composite test entry is coded, summary composites have not been developed.

[#] Information improperly coded or insufficient for reporting purposes. Computations of averages or composites are not affected. If "grade taken" information is not available, grade level average only will be affected.

[&] Additional information not reported due to space or code limitations. Supplementary information should be added by the high school. For courses coded as "other," grade points and units are not included in area averages or academic group calculations.

Colleges have action to take in completion of this Report one year after its receipt. At that time, colleges are to send a transcript of student progress to the Secondary School for completion of its records.

STUDENT INFORMATION

Code #	Days Tardy and Days Absent
0	None
1	One
2	Two
3	3-4
5	5-7
8	8-11
12	12-16
17	17-21
22	22-26
27	27 or more

HEALTH

Code #	Illness Interfered with Studies
0	Not at all
1	To slight degree
2	To moderate degree
3	To appreciable degree
4	To serious detriment of progress.

SCHOOL INFORMATION

Meaning of Grades — The number printed below any grade letter is the lowest grade possible for receipt of that letter grade. **Col. Rec.**—The minimum alphabetic grade for college recommendation. **Grad. Year**—The expected year of graduation. **Units Req.**—The total number of Carnegie Units required for graduation.

ACADEMIC SUMMARY

All Academic Averages are based on assigned values of A=4, B=3, C=2, D=1, and F=O. Rank in Class and Percentile Standing are based on the student's course average (grade points divided by units earned) compared to the course averages of his classmates for each of the separate classifications. **Complete class** data are based on the total class for all courses taken by the students. **Academic group** calculations are presented only for those students in the academic curriculum and are based on academic courses only. **Complete class-weighted** data include all students and all courses. The calculations assign one additional value (A=5, B=4, etc.) for courses tracked as high and high-middle and one less value (A=3, B=2, etc.) for courses tracked as middle-low or low-**Composite test** notes the testing program employed at a school from which composites have been computed.

Converted Verbal Course Score, Converted Math/Science Course Score, and Converted All Course Score place each of these in-school averages on a scale to which composite test scores can be conveniently transposed. After the appropriate test subscores are transposed to this scale, the converted course scores are adjusted by one half the difference in means between class distributions of the course scores and the test scores. From these components, the following composites are developed:

$$\text{Verbal Composite} = \frac{\text{Transposed Verbal Test Score} + \text{Adj. Verbal Course Score}}{2}$$

$$\text{Math/Science Composite} = \frac{\text{Transposed Math Test Score} + \text{Adj. Math/Science Course Score}}{2}$$

$$\text{All Course Composite} = \frac{2\ \text{Trans. Verbal Test Score} + \text{Trans. Math Test Score} + 3\ \text{Adjusted All Course Score}}{6}$$

All composites reflect relative measures of student ability and should not be regarded as direct predictions of college freshman grades. Technical details with regard to adjustments, conversions, transpositions, composites and other computations may be found in the publication "Interpretations from Comprehensive Student Reports"—ETS, 1963.

ACADEMIC RECORD

Field Averages are computed from final grades awarded in all courses taken in separate fields of Language Arts, Foreign Language, Mathematics, Science, and Social Studies. The Verbal Course Average is calculated from final grades in all courses in Language Arts, Foreign Language, and Social Studies. The Math/Science Course Average is calculated from final grades in all courses in Mathematics and Science.

GROUPING

A notation will appear in this space only if students in that course were homogeneously grouped.

Code	Tracking Group	Definition
H	High Group	Advanced Placement (CEEB)
HM	High-Middle Group	Content geared to the above average or superior learner
M	Middle Group	Middle Group
ML	Middle-Low Group	Content adjusted to accomodate a low average learner
L	Low Group	Remedial

MISC.

This column takes note of the following information.

Code	Definition
S	Summer Course
LB	Laboratory Course
TV	Television Course
SM	Seminar Course
CL	Course on College Campus

OTHER GRADES

The "Other Grades" area may include course work from the 8th and/or 12th grade. The column entitled **GRADE** will note the specific grade in which the subject was taken.

TEST RECORD

GR-Grade Taken	%ILE-Percentile
NRM-Denotes the test norm group	IQ-Intelligence Quotient
SCOR-The type of score reported	GRD P-Grade Placement
%BND-Percentile Band	RAW S-Raw Score
STAND-Standard Score	STA 9-Stanine

EXTRA-CURRICULAR ACTIVITIES

Student Performance is rated on the following five point scale.

Code #	Activity
1	President, captain, editor, or group leader doing a high quality job.
2	Other elected officers, appointed officer, a letter man effecting his responsibilities.
3	An effectively contributing participant or varsity member.
4	Member of Junior-Varsity or general participant.
5	A disinterested and uncooperative member.
X	Student participated but was not rated.

WORK RECORD

The work record is divided into Summer and Term classifications for each of the four school years.

Code #	Hours Worked/Week
1	1-8
9	9-16
17	17-24
25	25-32
33	33 #

PERSONAL RECORD

Personal characteristics are rated on a scale one through five, one being the highest possible rating, five the lowest. The characteristics are those on the Personality Record of the National Association of Secondary School Principals. Schools are instructed to average three independent ratings for each trait.

This electronically processed form, developed cooperatively by educators, contains information which the Joint Committee on School-College Relations of NASSP and AACRAO recommends be supplied.

Comprehensive Student Report

SCHOOL NAME: Rocky Hill H.S. Atlanta Ga.

COLLEGE BOARD SCHOOL CODE NO. (6 DIGITS): 110170

STUDENT NAME: LAST Warner FIRST Natalie MIDDLE B.

STUDENT'S DATE OF BIRTH: MONTH 8 / DAY 6 / YEAR '48

STUDENT'S STATE OF BIRTH (MAXIMUM 4 LETTERS): Ga.

MOTHER'S MAIDEN NAME (LAST NAME ONLY): Everett

PARENT OR GUARDIAN'S NAME: LAST Warner FIRST William

TEST NAME		TEST CODE	GRADE TAKEN	TEST NORM	TYPE OF LOCAL SCORE	SUB-SCORES 1	2	3	4	5	6	7	8	9	10
D.A.T.	F	290	9	14		95	95	90	85	60	85	45	85	80	
S.C.A.T.	G	632	9	14		96-99	99-00	99-99.6							
S.T.E.P.	H	641	9	14		92-00	83-94	73-90	89-95	82-95	86-95				
COOP. Alg.	I	239	9	24		95									
OTIS. Q.S. GAM. (EM)		571	10	15		125									
P.S.A.T.	K	600	11	16		62	65								
N.M.S.Q.T.	L	550	11	40		23	25	27	15	19	22				

OTHER SECONDARY SCHOOLS ATTENDED: NAME (MAXIMUM 9 LETTERS) | CITY (MAXIMUM 7 LETTERS) | STATE (MAXIMUM 4 LETTERS) | DATE LEFT MONTH / YEAR

SEX: MALE / FEMALE

PHYSICAL DISABILITY: YES

CURRICULUM: ACADEMIC, AGRICULTURE, COMMERCIAL, GENERAL, TRADE, MUSIC or ART, HOME EC., OTHER

STUDENT PROFILE RECORD Personal Record—SIDE I

PERSONAL CHARACTERISTICS: MOTIVATION, INDUSTRY, INITIATIVE, INFLUENCE-LEAD, CONCERN-OTHERS, RESPONSIBILITY, INTEGRITY, EMO. STABILITY (F, S, J; 1–5)

HONORS & AWARDS (YES): NAT'L. HONOR SOCIETY, LETTER CLUB, SCHOL. SEMI FINALIST, NATIONAL AWARD, STATE AWARD, SCHOOL HONORS, LOCAL AWARD, OTHER

HEALTH SUMMARY / ABSENCE SUMMARY / TARDINESS SUMMARY: FRESHMAN, SOPHOMORE, JUNIOR

WORK RECORD — HOURS PER WEEK (FS, SS, JS; FT, ST, JT) — OCCUPATIONAL CODE: General Clerk; Payroll Clerk; Cafeteria Cashier; Baby Sitting; Reporter

EXTRA CURRICULAR ACTIVITIES — RATING — PARTICIPATED & NOT RATED — ACTIVITY CODE: Social Club; Debating Club; St. Council Board; Journalism; Future Teachers

Be sure each mark is *black* and *completely fills* the answer box.

Cooperative Plan for Guidance and Admission

FIG. 74. *Student Profile Record*

does not need to spend any time calculating rank-in-class, mark-point averages, or other kinds of arithmetic. These calculations are made for the school by the computer.

At the end of the student's junior year, or after each academic year, the person at the school who works with student records, using a manual of procedures and codes, transfers information on each student to the Student Profile Record. If the transfer is done annually, the Student Profile Record can be used as the cumulative record. After this process is completed for all juniors, these input documents are sent to ETS for processing during the summer. At ETS, the information provided by the school is read into the computers. Comprehensive student reports, in multiples of five, are then prepared and returned to the school by the first of September.

Thus, by the start of the new academic year the school district has available comprehensive student reports for its senior class. The original, or top copy, of the form becomes the school's permanent record, and four copies are available as transcripts for college admission, for military service, or for employment. Copies are updated in each case at the time a transcript is requested. The original includes all senior-year data on the student, and becomes his permanent record on graduation. At the time the copy is updated, the principal's or counselor's recommendation is placed on the reverse side of the report in the space provided.

At the present time, about 150 secondary schools in fourteen states are taking advantage of this means for generating more meaningful transcripts on their upcoming graduates. The advent of the computed reports, which contain much more useful information than traditionally provided, seems to be welcomed by college admissions officers.

An operational prototype of the system in Georgia and seven demonstration pilot projects in Arizona, Florida, Indiana, Michigan, Minnesota, Pennsylvania, and Vermont have provided the "proving grounds" for this computer-based communication system. Figure 73 illustrates the Comprehensive Student Report while Figure 74 shows the Student Profile Record.

THE CALIFORNIA GUIDANCE RECORD

Acting under a grant from the Cooperative Research Branch of the United States Office of Education, the Research and Development Team in Educational Data Processing of the California State Department of Education developed a "new type" cumulative record. This record, designed to be used in all of the fifty states, requires no additional input to generate a report. The system is designed so that data in a local district is generated as a result of an ongoing program of guidance and instruction. By placing a new, relatively low-cost mark-reading machine such as the IBM 1230 or the Digitek 100 in each district, the information from standardized

R/D CENTER
CALIFORNIA STATE DEPARTMENT of EDUCATION

CALIFORNIA GUIDANCE REPORT

STUDENT NO.	LAST FIRST MIDDLE STUDENT NAME	YEAR IN SCHOOL	SCHOOL NAME	SCHOOL ADDRESS	CURRENT DATE	COUNSELOR NAME
BIRTH DATE / SEX	PARENT/GUARDIAN NAME	PARENT/GUARDIAN ADDRESS		PREVIOUS SCHOOL NAME	ENTRY DATE	LEFT DATE

HOME TELEPHONE | CONFIDENTIAL DATA | FATHER SEP DEAD OCCUP. | MOTHER SEP. DEAD OCCUP.

COURSE NO.	COURSE TITLE	MARK	CR	DATE COMPLETED

CURRENT MARKING PERIOD

SPECIAL REPORTS

PERFORMANCE SUMMARY
IQ SCORE TOTAL............
ACHIEVEMENT TOTAL SCORE...
GRADE POINT AVERAGE.......
RANK IN CLASS.............
ABSENCES THIS YEAR........

CURRENT TEST PROFILE
TEST NAME DATE OF TEST /

SUB TEST	RESULT	00 02 01 03	04 08 06 10	12 18 15 21	25 33 29 37	42 52 47 57	62 70 66 74	78 84 81 87	89 93 91 95	96 98 97 99
NORM:		1	2	3	4	5	6	7	8	9

COURSE NO.	COURSE TITLE	MARK	CR.	DATE	COURSE NO.	COURSE TITLE	MARK	CR.	DATE	COURSE NO.	COURSE TITLE	MARK	CR.	DATE

STUDENT CURRENT REQUIREMENT EVALUATION

PREVIOUS CREDITS	CURRENT YEAR CREDITS	TOTAL CREDITS	REQ'D AT CURRENT LEVEL	CREDIT DEFICIENCY	CREDITS REQ'D FOR GRADUATION	PERIODS PER WEEK	MINUTES PER PERIOD	MINIMUM PASSING	A= %	B= %	C= %	D= %	ABILITY TRACK PLACEMENT

REMARKS: PRINCIPAL'S SIGNATURE________ DATE OF GRADUATION________

FIG. 75. *California Guidance Report*

tests, mark reporting, attendance accounting, student scheduling and registration, health and psychological services can be read and communicated to a nearby computer (either in the district or in a co-operative regional center) over regular telephone lines. Thus the original documents which were created at the computer center from master records stay physically at the school. Only the information is transmitted.

As the information regarding each student is fed into the computer throughout the year, it is screened for accuracy and then used to update the student's master record kept on magnetic tape. This updated master record is then printed out in six copies each semester as a guidance report. The original copy containing *all* relevant information goes to the counselor. A copy is sent to the administrative offices. A special copy is prepared for teacher reference in a three-ring binder. Another copy is designed for the student and his parents to be used as a basis for yearly conferences with the school counselors. No confidential information appears on the student copy since the area containing it is masked over by a special design of that form.

This form, illustrated in Figure 75, is designed to be issued at the end of each semester and can be used as a uniform college transcript. In addition, this form replaces the typical semester report card by incorporating it as a part of the form itself. The record also deviates from the normal transcripts in that it provides for marks to be listed by subject area rather than by semester. The subject area mark-point average is automatically computed and placed just beneath each specific area. Since dates for the completion of each course are provided, it is an easy matter to reconstruct each semester's courses and marks.

A special area is provided for reporting the latest test scores. As will be noted by inspection, the test score area provides multiple interpretations of test results. In the area provided for subtest results, the publisher's method of reporting his test is listed. Across the top of the form is listed the various percentiles from 0 through 99. Corresponding to the percentiles are the stanine ranks which are listed across the bottom of the test-scoring area. By placing a series of asterisks across the test reporting area, a score may be interpreted in the fashion provided by the test publisher, in percentiles, in percentile bands, and in stanines. Actually this is not an attempt to manufacture a multiplicity of scores but rather to indicate to the teacher a unit score. This does not require that the teacher be an expert in test interpretation, but at one glance it gives her a variety and combination of scores so that the relationship between percentiles, stanines, and the publisher's scores becomes readily apparent. Space is also left on the form for additional information which may be of special relevancy in college admissions.

This form is prepared on one side of an 8½″ by 11″ sheet and contains most of the vital data needed by both the secondary schools and the college admissions officers.

PART IV

Potential for Education

14

IMPACT OF EDUCATIONAL DATA PROCESSING ON SCHOOLS

Change takes time, particularly when it is applied to education. Yet time is the element that today's educators do not have.

Perhaps the greatest impact of educational data processing has been to uncover basic "lacks" in educators. These lacks include some pretty fundamental pieces of the educational puzzle and can be listed as the lack of:

1. understanding of technological capability
2. adequate finances to explore this technology
3. acceptance of change
4. an operational information system
5. an overriding, clear-cut, long-range, all permeating goal or philosophy of education

The age of the computer began in 1946 when ENIAC first was plugged in, and the space age began in 1957 with the orbiting of Sputnik. Educators, after 100 years of relatively static curriculum, suddenly have been faced with a very real—and perhaps terrifying—situation in which change must be brought about right away. The traditional time lag between significant scientific, technological, and social changes and the need to accept and adapt to them has become non-existent. These changes have come about not only in the scientific area but also in the technological and social areas as illustrated by the pressing problems of automation, unemployment, leisure time, and integration.

The entire nation looks to education for the solution to each of these problems, or at least as the agency best suited to provide a solution. Whether this is appropriate or good, will be left to the philosophers and politicians to debate. The main point here is that life is moving too rapidly; educators no longer can do nothing, in hopes that solutions will come with time. In order to do something, hopefully the right thing, a few groups of educators have begun a tentative exploration of paths outside the well worn rut.

In some areas movement has been detected, and one needs to pursue only a few journals to see—"The New Math," "The New Science," "The New Reading," etc. Are these programs merely the result of thrashing about in the dark, wildly grasping at straws to provide the foundation for "The New Educational Structure"? Historians undoubtedly will comment on this.

There is an underlying premise, however, that is so basic that it has been overlooked or rejected by educators for many years. This rejection may be covert or overt, but rejection it is. The premise is: *information about all of the problems in education is available, or can be made available, if an information system is available and in working order.* For too long educators have attached relatively little importance to developing information systems that could provide the facility to generate educational intelligence and, instead, generally have continued to do things the way they always were done—because it is traditional.

Earlier sections on EDP history, anatomy, and systems have documented the ways and means to build information systems. This capability has been available for many years. How many have taken advantage of it? Too few!

There's an old saw about the distaff side of human relations that is meant to reassure the young man who thinks he might lose his girl: like the streetcar, another will be along soon. It may not be far-fetched to identify a parallel to this in public education. Too often educators console themselves for not investigating and adopting educational innovations or for not incorporating new technological developments into the teaching arsenal by rationalizing that, after all, another "gimmick" will be along soon.

This type of thinking has made educators captives of the written word. Since Gutenberg invented movable type in the middle of the 15th century, they have rosily accepted the printed page as the best way to impart knowledge. To be sure, other aids have been recognized—audio visual, for example—as valuable tools that can help us in our job, but their use is regarded as supplemental to the instructional program rather than an integral part of it.

Probably the greatest road block to the acceptance of different ways of doing things is that educators treasure the old seasoned methods and back off from new challenges. Almost everyone in a school district knows how its operations can be improved, but often enough, the improvements are stillborn or not born at all. A variety of reasons, of course, are seized upon. No one is available to plan changes; new proposals may offend somebody; there may not be any room in the budget, and so on.

It is now an established fact that while technological developments have fairly cascaded into the American scene, the organizational patterns of our public schools have not kept pace. Most educators have failed to employ current innovations because we have traditionally adopted the "next streetcar" attitude. When a new technology becomes available to us, we want to see if someone else has determined or demonstrated its feasibility. By the time its potential benefit to the schools is widely accepted, another new development springs up on the horizon; we abandon trial of the prior one because now we must see if the newcomer will prove to be of greater value. While we wait for each new "streetcar" to come along and let each one go by, our students are being deprived of educational aids that could well equip them to cope with the new and challenging space age.

We need somehow to engender an intense, enthusiastic, three-dimensional study of ways in which public education can be tellingly improved. We need to touch off a fire of analysis and evaluation that will sweep across the land and create such excitement, such a passion for renewal, that all of us will be caught up in it. A revolution is what we need; a revolution in modernizing and streamlining the schools is what we must have if we are really to assume the right of educational leadership.

Our passivity, our love affair with the status quo, has led the citizenry and some state legislatures to feel that we have become drifters and that only a few in our profession can boast of realistic programs to educate today's youth. They have become increasingly tired of our lofty pronouncements, our seven cardinal precepts, our vague dreams of Utopia. On all sides they see a highly technological society; but they also see the majority of our schools in the backwash of an ancient time. Small wonder that law-makers step in and mandate new rules to govern our behavior and our practices.

Like animals in the wild, weak men are prey for the strong. Let there be no dispute about it—we have been marked in society's book as the weak. It is not surprising that our public refuses to give us additional financial support for "more of the same thing"; nor is it strange that before they will sanction new funds, they want us to demonstrate, individually as teachers and collectively as school systems, that we can do a far better job than we have done in the past.

What are we doing to revitalize education, to make it strong of sinew and spirit? In some instances—in some areas—new programs have been and are being launched under vigorous leadership. But the record is spotty; our educational leadership, by and large, has responded to the challenge of change either with apathy or with a show of defensiveness. Certainly neither reaction will win the day.

A few states, California for one, have taken bold steps to harness the benefits of automation. In the field of educational data processing, for example, a new breed of educator-technologists have subjected electronic computers to extensive pilot tests, found them worthy of use, and recognized the fact that they can and should be integrated with the instructional and administrative functions of school systems. In areas where this integration has been carried out, the value and quality of pupil-personnel work is being upgraded to a degree that scarcely has a parallel. Automation of this sort, moreover, is producing significant by-products, such as mark analyses, dropout statistics, reports on class sizes, and correlations between ability and achievement. Elsewhere in the nation, mechanized projects of similar nature are underway.

The advent of teaching machines and programed instruction also offers a bright new hope. Foreign language laboratories are making important inroads. Current developments in science equipment and aids to mathematics hold rich promise, to say nothing of fresh approaches in the use of educational television and audio-visual devices and materials.

Whatever the technique, whatever the approach, we can no longer afford to stand on the curbstone, hidebound and slackjawed, letting our chances go by unhailed. We must stop the next streetcar, board it, and move with purpose, insight, and confidence toward the better instructional world of tomorrow.

THE SHORTAGE OF INFORMATION

Dr. Wayne O. Reed, Deputy United States Commissioner of Education, stated in 1960 that:

> Education today is so involved, so changing, and so diverse that even the most professional educator knows it only in part. The interested citizen, no matter how assiduously he studies education, is often deeply perplexed. Only the naïve person or the unscrupulous merchandiser of panaceas dares to claim full understanding.
>
> But complexity and change are not all that present layman and educator with puzzles and problems. If complexity and change were all, we would need only to put the keenest and wisest minds to work at once, and the decisions, clear-cut and unerring, would soon emerge. More thwarting by far than complexity, more unsettling than change—though partly the concomitant of both—is our shortage of information about education.[1]

Dr. Reed has underscored the point that has been advanced time and again by educators and those laymen who are concerned about the current status and the direction of educational trends. Unfortunately there are those who do not recognize that there is a *shortage of information* about education. In many cases we complain about the shortage of funds for financing education, the shortage of teachers, the shortage of classrooms, whereas Dr. Reed states:

> The shortage of information may well be the most serious, the most pervasive, and the most unrecognized educational shortage of all; it may well be the subtle cause of all those other shortages which we clearly recognize as afflicting our schools year after year. This shortage is so subtle that many a man who is troubled by it does not even realize what he lacks.[2]

1. Reed, Wayne O. *School Life,* September, 1960, Vol. 43, No. 1, p. 5.
2. *Op. cit.*

DO EDUCATORS "KNOW"?[3]

It has been pointed out elsewhere that many of the operations in education have been carried on by guess and by gosh. Many of our procedures and practices are based upon tradition rather than reason. Many of our decisions are based upon intuition.

Earlier discussions also have covered the meaning of the word data; that it means information and that it may be represented in many forms. Processing also has been mentioned as the things we do with these data.

If we accept the fact that information systems of some type and sophistication have been in existence for many years, then in all honesty we must admit that the data from these systems have been misused as well as used. As often as not we base our decisions on facts that we have ignored or perhaps on data that have been disguised and hidden.

Let us assume that all school districts are essentially alike and that the chief administrators of each district have the same need for information. It appears reasonable to state that even with existing information processing systems these administrators will get:

1. more data about the district that they have time to use,
2. considerable data that they do not know how to use,
3. data that are dangerous to use,
4. data that are useless,
5. data too late to use,
6. less data than they really need.

Several times throughout this text statements have been made to the effect that the school administrator can be a good administrator only if:

1. he *knows* what he and his district staff have accomplished,
2. he *knows* where he stands in relation to where he planned to be at this point in time,
3. he *knows*, based upon present status and past experience, the direction in which he should be moving and the momentum to use,
4. he *knows*, based upon past experience, that the quantitative and qualitative goals he has established for the future are logical and attainable.

The word "knows" here is distinct from such words as believes, assumes, supposes, or imagines. The connotation is that the necessary facts are in hand, in valid form, and in time.

The disparity between what the school administrator is and what he should be can be resolved, but only if (1) he has the pertinent data re-

3. Material in this section has been adapted from Gill, William A., "ADP in Federal Agencies," *Automatic Data Processing Seminar for Federal Executives,* Washington, D.C.: The Graduate School, U.S. Department of Agriculture, 1961.

quired to evaluate the past and the present on a knowledgeable basis, and if (2) he has the ability to make informed decisions concerning the present and the future of his educational program. It is at point (1) that the administrator is cut off. The system that he heads denies him his potential.

This is a situation which has been with education since its inception, and it is not improving. In fact as schools grow in size, indeed as the United States grows in size, our organization pattern builds layer upon layer of authority in ways that tax the information system itself. Second, efforts to educate the users and producers of educational data, on how to handle those data, have fallen short of the need both in quantity and quality. And third, the tools available for the processing of educational data have in most districts been inadequate. Until the advent of modern data processing equipment, specifically the electronic computer, none of the tools that were available were truly adequate.

RESISTANCE TO CHANGE

As educators become more involved with these modern-day tools it is perhaps to be expected that, as with any innovation anywhere, there will be resistance. This resistance is really resistance to change. The nature, degree, and duration of resistance will vary greatly depending upon the innovation and upon the way it is introduced. Such resistance generally is generated by fear or feelings of insecurity, doubt or mistrust, but generally it is based upon a lack of understanding. Without an understanding of what this change in operating procedures will mean to any given individual, it is natural for that individual to assume the worst—loss of status, salary, and security. The specter of mass displacement by automation is not an unrealistic one to the average worker. In education, however, we have been faced with the problem of a shortage of help at both the certificated and non-certificated levels. It would seem that for the short-range, displacement of help would not be a serious problem. Explaining this to a central office clerk, or to someone who actually is being transferred because of the effects of automation is not as easy as it might appear. These will be continuing problems and ones which we in education will hopefully be able to handle through education.

Evans and Arnstein in *Automation and the Challenge to Education*[4] state that automation may well be considered the second industrial revolution and that it contains:

> . . . a potential for improving human welfare and, at the same time, the ability to add to human hardship. Too often there is a tendency to remember only the marvelous inventions ushered in by the Indus-

4. Evans, Luther H., and Arnstein, George E., Editors. *Automation and the Challenge to Education*. (Symposium) Washington, D.C.: National Education Association, Project on the Educational Implications of Automation, 1962. 200 pp., (NEA Stock number 721-18804).

> trial Revolution and to associate it only with the rise of the modern city, improved transportation, and increased productivity.

The marvels then as the marvels now can be achieved at a painful price for an individual.

Dr. Virgil M. Rogers, director of the National Education Associations project on the Educational Implications of Automation, in a statement to the U.S. Senate subcommittee on Employment and Manpower stated that:

> It should be recalled that the school is part of society, and that one of the major tasks of the school is to prepare young people for meaningful entry into the world of work, as well as to help adults to refine and update old skills, or acquire new skills, so that they can remain employable. It is ironic that the schools are expected to discharge this function on the basis of grossly inadequate information.[5]

Here again is the recurring problem of information, or rather the lack of it, posing problems for education.

Again, from Evans and Arnstein,

> Many of the adverse effects of automation and technological advancement are not inevitable, but can be countered through proper planning. For example, automation creates the need for many high level skills; at present there are a number of unfilled jobs which, if filled, would absorb a considerable portion of the unemployed. With adequate planning and motivation, people could be trained to move up to these positions, thereby leaving room at the bottom for less skilled.[6]

These problems are worthy of consideration by themselves and have been covered in the two publications that were produced by the Educational Implications of Automation Project of the National Education Association: (1) *Automation and the Challenge to Education,* (2) *No Room at the Bottom—Automation and the Reluctant Learner.*

These both pursue the many aspects of the impact of automation on society, with emphasis on the relationship of employment and education in an era of automation. Our concern here is to pursue the impact of automation on education, in terms of how automation can be used to lighten the clerical and routine administrative tasks, and how it can assist educators in preparing pupils for this world of automated work. This will be done by touching lightly on some of the problems that appear to exist

5. Rogers, Virgil M. "Education for Full Employment." *Hearings Relating to the Training and Utilization of the Manpower Resources of the Nation, Nation's Manpower Revolution:* (U.S. 88th Congress, 1st Session, Senate Committee on Labor and Public Welfare, Subcommittee on Employment and Manpower.) Washington, D.C.: Government Printing Office, 1963, pp. 2187-94. (NEA-EIA typescript. October 25, 1963.)

6. *Op. cit.*

and then on some of the projects now in operation that are aimed at solving these problems. While some of these problems and projects will be mentioned briefly now, the following chapters will delve more deeply into each subject.

TOWARD ESTABLISHING INFORMATION SYSTEMS

If it is true that the United States cannot afford to have another generation as ignorant as this, what must we do? One obvious answer is that a modern system of information processing must be developed and that this system must be comprehensive, one that falls into the "total system" category. This system must be able to communicate with other information systems in other districts, regions, or states so that we have, for the first time, an opportunity to compile meaningful data on the status of education at the local, regional, state, and national levels. How can this be done? The solution, while seemingly simple, has been difficult to achieve. How many educators today are able, much less willing, to develop and implement information systems that would provide for the pooling of data and/or machine capabilities with neighboring districts? Field experience has indicated that more and more educators sense the need for such systems and perhaps the time has now arrived for an all-out push toward this goal.

The responsibility for developing systems at the local school level should, of course, be with the local school staff members. Where can they get assistance if they need it? Personnel are available, from county, state and U.S. education offices who are competent in educational and data processing matters. There are also state and national organizations that deal with data processing that are eager to be of service to educational agencies. Some of these are described in chapter 17.

Responsibility is not confined solely to the local school, however. There must be an organized, concerted effort to see that the state education agencies develop information systems that are as comprehensive as those developed at the local level. Many state education agencies have already initiated systems studies on what really is needed in the field of educational information. Great assistance has been provided by the U.S. Office of Education and several of the national professional groups such as the Council of Chief State School Officers and the Commission on Educational Data Systems. Other groups such as the Association for Educational Data Systems and some state education agencies, notably California and Florida, have assumed leadership roles in this field of automated information systems.

A PLAN OF ATTACK

There are several steps to be followed in establishing information systems. First, perhaps, is to attack the widespread indifference to the need for information about education. These informational systems are intangible to the many people who do not have an understanding of why such systems are imperative. There are those who are not only ignorant of such systems' objectives, but who, through misunderstanding, are skeptical of their goals. "Nineteen eighty-four" is approaching rapidly, and many people view organized information as a step to hasten the big brother concept. For this reason, professional education and data processing organizations, citizen organizations, press, legislative bodies, and all who know their importance should join with local, state and federal education agencies to promote an intelligent enthusiasm for better methods of gathering and using information.

Another step will be in the development of sub-systems in which uniform methods would be stressed. Part of this approach would be based on the preparation of handbooks, uniform definitions, and machine processing methods that would facilitate the development of these systems. The U.S. Office of Education has been working along these lines, and several handbooks have been issued that will serve as a basis. In addition, the U.S.O.E. has been developing a Basic Educational Data System that aims at integrating data from many important parts of the educational program.

Leadership in these areas is still greatly needed. In addition, effort should be forthcoming at the local, state, and national levels to pursue uniform and compatible methods for the collection and processing of data.

Investigation of all of the new educational media should be encouraged, so that a better understanding can be developed about the relationship of information systems to educational television, closed circuit T.V., programed learning, "teaching" and auto-instructional machines, the various other visual and audio devices, and data processing equipment.

All of these new techniques, new procedures, new devices, and new media should lead to the development of a more effective educational system and thereby to better and more appropriate utilization of our human resources.

Dr. Virgil Rogers has well summarized these needs:[7]

> 1. Given the increasing complexity of our society, there is an obvious need for better counseling and guidance. Specifically, this means that we must improve the ratio of counselors to students, and that we must upgrade and update the knowledge and information used by counselors. Available information about occupation trends, though far from adequate, should nevertheless reach counselors in greater volume and with greater speed than at present.
>
> 2. More information needs to be developed about occupational trends and current job vacancies, if counselors, school administrators and community leaders are to make meaningful educational plans for their communities and help individual students make intelligent career choices.

7. *Op. cit.*

3. Technical education needs to be further improved and expanded. At the time it was enacted, the Smith-Hughes Act of 1917 provided a major and welcome impetus for the improvement of vocational education. It is good to know that pending legislation [since enacted as PL 88–210] seeks to update the various vocational education acts, that flexibility and broader scope will be added, although it remains to be seen whether even the pending changes will suffice for the schools to develop vocational curricula, courses of study and occupational skills at a level suited to today's, and more particularly to tomorrow's, technology.

4. There is increasing evidence that every member of our society must have competence in such general skills as literacy (comfortable and quick literacy) and number skills, as well as an understanding of the democratic process and human relations. In many schools, this can be accomplished only with the help of auxiliary special services. There is also a need for specialized skills, but these are best developed on a sound, broad basis of general education.

5. If manpower is to be developed in a rational manner, remaining inequalities in educational opportunity must be eliminated. There are enough problems in the distribution of our human resources without adding to them irrational discrimination based on arbitrary grounds.

6. We need to upgrade our current teacher population and teacher education in general. Deplorably, we still certify some teachers without at least a bachelor's degree. A college degree may not be proof of competence, but it does provide some evidence of the breadth and ability we seek to have among our teachers. Even with an appropriate educational background, no teacher can rely on college training alone to maintain the understanding of social and technological changes which he needs to guide his students.

7. A strong case can be made—and should be made—for a flexible curriculum, as one means of keeping up with change.

8. Finally, and this may be of crucial importance, the next generation even more than today's adults must be receptive to change and to the idea that learning is a lifelong process. This has always been desirable; today and tomorrow it is imperative.

INFORMATION SYSTEMS ARE SELF JUSTIFYING

While one does not forget that there is great concern about the possible misuse of information in ways that would be detrimental to the educational programs at all levels, it is equally true that educators have seldom had the information with which to document their position. Data availability alone should justify all of the effort needed to build a system of educational information, one that would provide the capability for transmitting information from kindergarten through university, from local level to national level, and for the interpretation of these data in ways that would advance the cause of education in the eyes of the public. In addition, this system would provide the means for a much needed critical evaluation of the effectiveness of the many and varied curricula now in existence.

The increasing mobility of students is making it imperative that such information be available. There are over 30,000 school districts in the United States, many with a number of schools. There are hundreds of thousands of teachers and millions upon millions of pupils. We must have information about the curriculum, the pupil, the teacher, and the school so that we can truly evaluate our present program while we build a better educational system for tomorrow. The great impact of EDP on education will come from the availability of this information through the use of automated systems and procedures. Wise use of modern technology is crucial if we are to update and improve the substantive aspect of education.

15

ORGANIZATIONAL IMPLICATIONS

In this chapter we will concern ourselves with two distinct but similar types of organization: first, the self-contained information system in which machine capability is available locally and, second, the regional center concept in which the information system is essentially self-contained but relies on hardware capability that is shared with other districts in a region. The personnel needs are essentially the same for both, and will be discussed with the self-contained system. Personnel requirements have already been covered in Chapter 6.

LOCAL OR SELF-CONTAINED OPERATIONS

It is ironic that education, more so than any other field, is forced to operate with wholly inadequate information about its product, about quality control possibilities, about the effectiveness of its program, its staff, and perhaps most important, about its goals.

With the technical equipment now available it is quite possible to build a network for data processing and communications which would bring enormous improvements in the quality of information for administrative planning and control of school districts.

Such a network involves several basic elements. The first is the use of data processing equipment—i.e., computers and electronic input and output devices—for the rapid collection, manipulation, and tabulation of data. The second is highly developed communication links between electronic computers and input-output devices. The third is the proper selection and arrangement of information for planning and control to form a system of reports which will give each administrator the key facts he needs to make decisions. This system of reports should underscore the exceptions and abnormal situations which need the administrator's attention. The final and most important element is an organizational structure that facilitates the management and co-ordination of the entire information system.

If all of these elements are present, a good administrative information system probably exists. Its advantages for the complex organization and interrelated functions of the district are readily apparent. Unfortunately, few of the nation's school districts have developed a truly effective and operational management information system using modern forms of data processing. Computers, it is true, are in wide use in business and industry, and integrated data processing systems have been applied to many types of operations. The difficulty in developing an effective administrative information system in education lies in the third element previously noted; constructing a data processing system that can speedily produce specific tailor-made reports and information when needed by the administration. To do this the personnel associated with the data processing system and those actually in charge of data processing must be intimately acquainted with the informational needs of the administration.

Despite all the advances in data processing, a breakdown in the preparation of the administrative planning and control reports and in their proper utilization is all too frequently observed. The underlying reason is that the systems planners who design data processing programs, and also those who are actually in charge of the systems, are unaware of the exact needs of administration for clear and continuing reports on the total course of the operation. Often expensive and complex data processing equipment is used almost exclusively for electronic record keeping. The preparation of tabulated reports, which are in fact only the results of consolidating raw data records is carried out without reference to the real needs of administration. This type of operation is self-defeating. It negates even the possibility of developing an adequate administrative information system through the use of data processing equipment. No amount of complex manipulation of simple raw data, even with the aid of electronics, can substitute for a carefully conceived system of reports to administration.

The ultimate goal of effective information systems should be to keep all levels of administration completely informed of all developments in the district which affect them. To do this, both the data processing staff and others who feed information into the system should know exactly what data to collect and which to tabulate. Administration, for its part, has the obligation to determine its actual requirements for internal information. Only under the direction of top administration can information specialists be expected to construct the schedule of reports which will keep every individual director or supervisor in the know on all important items.

The reports must be geared to the level of administration which will receive and use them; the higher the administrator, the broader but briefer the report. Reports sent to lower levels in the organization will be longer, more specialized and contain more data. An associate superintendent of schools, for instance, would require a large number of detailed statistics made up periodically for all of the units under his control. The statistical tabulations would be lengthy. A district director or supervisor, on the other hand, would need only the statistical totals of information affecting his distinct operation. The superintendent might need only a broad overview of the entire district. The assistant superintendents, the directors, and supervisors will, of course, require more details whenever an exception—either good or bad—occurs in the operation of units under their control.

Developing such a schedule of information is often difficult. One of the reasons is that in a conventional operation, information is organized on a divisional or departmental basis. In some instances, specialized data are never distributed throughout the department unless specifically requested. In these circumstances a schedule of regular reports for the information of administration is badly needed. If a system is to be effectively designed and effectively used, those operating in staff units must be required to feed data into the system quickly and never to regard specialized data as their own property.

To completely formulate an information system for a school district the following questions should be considered:

1. Why are the data created in the first place?
2. Who is to use them?
3. For what purpose?
4. How does he use them?
5. How much of them does he need?
6. When does he need them?

Unfortunately, the tendency to emphasize immediate benefits can often lead to a very limited processing program. The use of data processing exclusively for limited paperwork projects will not bring about an administrative information system even though it may use electronic data processing. The cost control function, especially, must not be permitted to assume a dominant role. Those who advocate the use of advanced systems techniques and the development of an administrative information system cannot communicate properly with an administration that is primarily concerned with data processing for clerical cost reduction. The prime goal is quality improvement, not cost reduction. The immense benefits to be gained by the use of electronic processing equipment to develop an effective administrative program should not be lost in the pursuit of minor projects.

The first step for a district moving toward a truly effective educational intelligence system, is to appoint a Director of Information Systems. The qualifications and background of such a person have already been described in chapter 6.

The director reports to the superintendent. His rank tops that of line director or supervisor and is on a par with that of an associate superintendent. He must have the prerogative of taking the point of view of the superintendent and pursuing overall district objectives in designing the information system.

Placement of Information Services[1]

It is vital that the position of the Director of Information Systems be established outside any existing division or bureau so that he can pursue overall district objectives and not be limited by parochial views. The director should carry the sole responsibility for furnishing infomation to the administration for the dynamic operation of the district. More than just a reporting function is involved. In effect, the decisions the administration make and the policies they put into effect should flow to the administrative cabinet and division directors through this unit. Associate superintendents and line directors would still manage and supervise in the normal sense of the word.

Undesirable Placement—Business Division

Two typical school districts that have used data processing equipment for performing various functions are represented in figures 76 and 77. In the first district (Fig. 76), data processing is represented as an agency under the assistant superintendent for business. With all due respect for business operations it can be stated fairly that this is not an area that presents great opportunities for dynamic and needed interrelationships with the myriad items of pupil and instructional data. Business operations are straightforward and lend themselves naturally to automated processes. If an information system has been constructed in the business area, and if the automated devices are adequate to process the workload, there will be relatively few problems in managing these business functions.

In an operational setting such as this data processing staff members frequently have been heard to say, "The instructional people have needs for data processing jobs that would be quite easy to handle. We can't get an O.K. to perform these tasks because our division chief says that the financial applications have first priority and that we can get bogged down doing other people's work."

It is understandable that the supervisor of data processing, working at the second or third level in the business division, would not want to become involved with the problems and headaches of processing other people's data. His job is on the "firing line." He has his work to perform, and if he has all of his own problems under control, why should he risk the chance of upsetting his smooth operation just to perform a service for others, particularly if his bosses are not receptive to the idea anyway.

1. Documented histories of success or failure due to organizational structure are hard to find. There are, however, several reliable sources. This section is based on material generated directly from the personal field observations of those involved in the California Pilot Project, and a survey conducted by McKinsey and Company, New York Management Consultants as reported in their pamphlet *Getting the Most out of Your Computer,* by John T. Garrity.

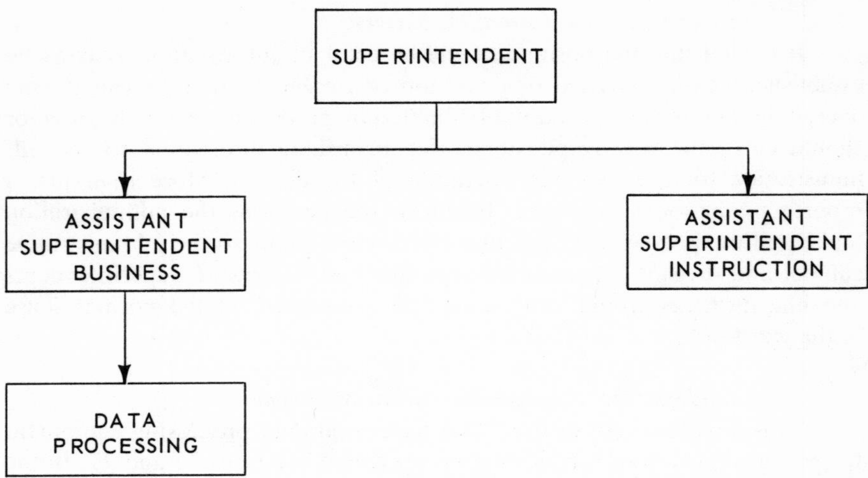

FIG. 76. *Undesirable Placement of Data Processing Center—Business Division*

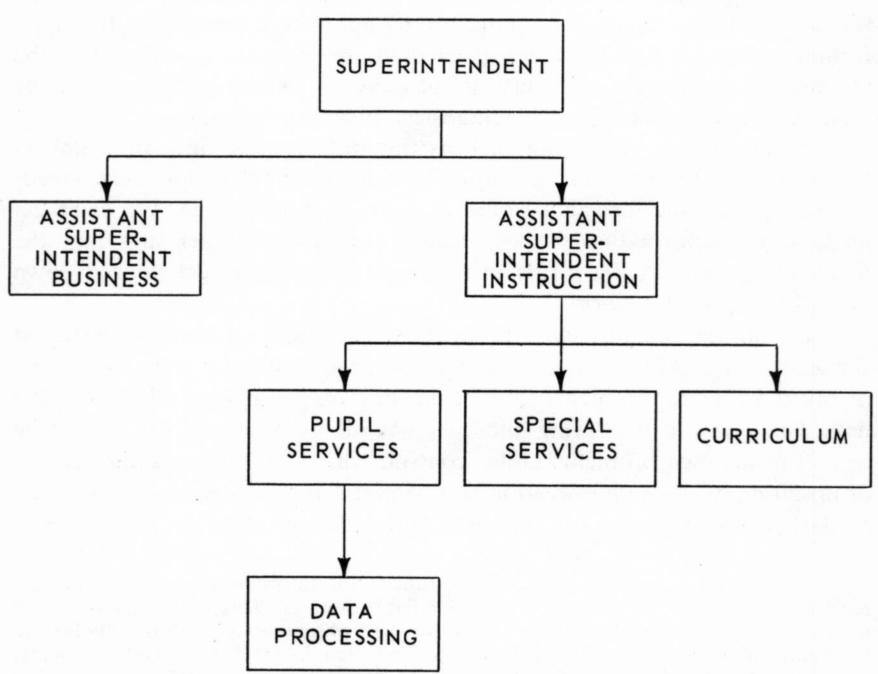

FIG. 77. *Undesirable Placement of Data Processing Center —Instructional Division*

Undesirable Placement—Instructional Division

In the second district (Fig. 77), we find the situation reversed. Here, data processing has developed as part of instruction through pupil-personnel services. The assistant superintendent for instruction is in the same situation as his business counterpart. While many of the applications in pupil-personnel services have been automated or mechanized, little has been done for special services or curriculum and for essentially the same reasons as mentioned above. The data processing staff has certain responsibilities; the bureau of pupil-personnel services has justified hardware and staff on the basis of certain applications, and in order to do the work of others, some shifts would have to take place in budget, personnel, etc. In this situation, even though the data processing is nominally placed on the instruction side, little is done outside of pupil services and nothing is done for business services.

Undesirable Placement—Research Division

These two illustrations are quite typical of the development of data processing in most school districts. A third organizational pattern, one that on first glance has potential merit—which unfortunately is seldom realized—is that shown in Figure 78. In this pattern the assistant superintendents for business and instruction are both without direct responsibility for data processing because the installation has developed as an administrative service under the director of research who reports directly to the superintendent. Machines have been installed as part of the district's research efforts and most frequently are used to run miscellaneous tabulations, analyses of test patterns, and other obscure research applications. This pattern holds more potential promise than the other two because of the direct relationship between the director of research and the superintendent. With direct access to the top man, the research director has an opportunity to develop a system for information that would cut across both business and instruction and would be able to provide all administrators with the type of educational intelligence reports that are desired.

Unfortunately the very nature of the organizational pattern has worked against this goal. One problem is that, as an administrative adjunct, the research budget has never been expanded to adequately cover the extra cost involved in establishing and staffing the data processing installation. In many situations the director himself has been the person who actually runs the machines. He punches cards, sorts, collates, tabulates, and also interprets the reports for research and administrative significance.

Another problem is that the director of research may not fully understand nor appreciate the important implication of the total integrated information system concept, and the superintendent understands it even less well than his director. Without someone at the top management level push-

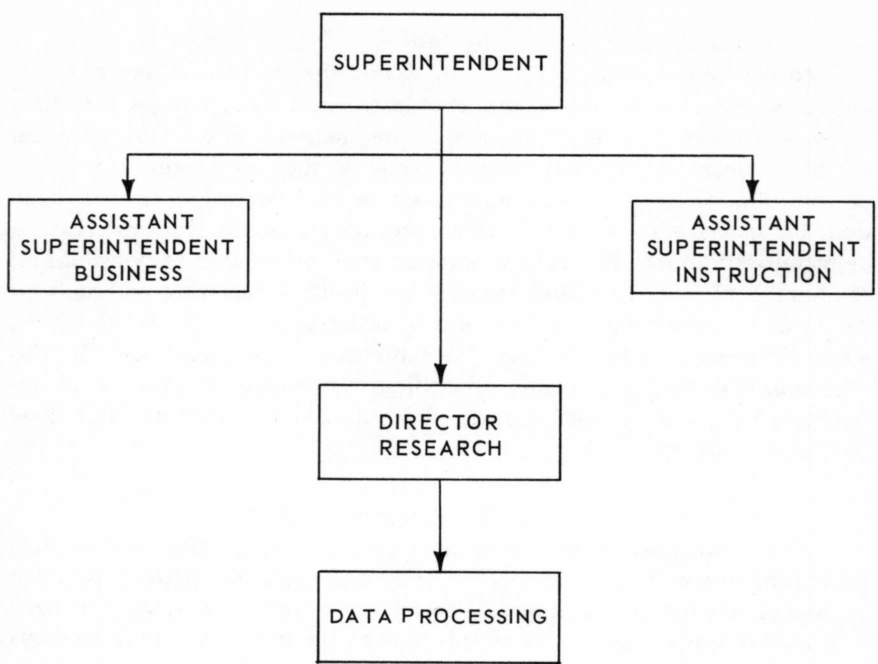

FIG. 78. *Undesirable Placement of Data Processing Center—Research Division*

ing for the establishment of a system, little can be accomplished. Therefore, while association with research may appear to be desirable, the organizational structure often defeats its own purpose.

If we accept the concept that the information system is desirably interwoven throughout the entire district organization and that this information is of vital importance to the effective administration of the district, then it makes considerable sense to require that the management and the co-ordination of the information system be exercised at top management level.

Desirable Patterns

In Figure 79, the most desirable organizational pattern is shown. It reflects the importance attached to the information system by placing the director of the system at the assistant superintendent level rather than at a third or fourth level under the superintendent. *Information* as well has achieved top level status, since it has divisional classification equal to that of business and instruction. For other desirable patterns, see Figures 80 and 81.

Success: More or Less

By categorizing districts with automated systems as "more successful"

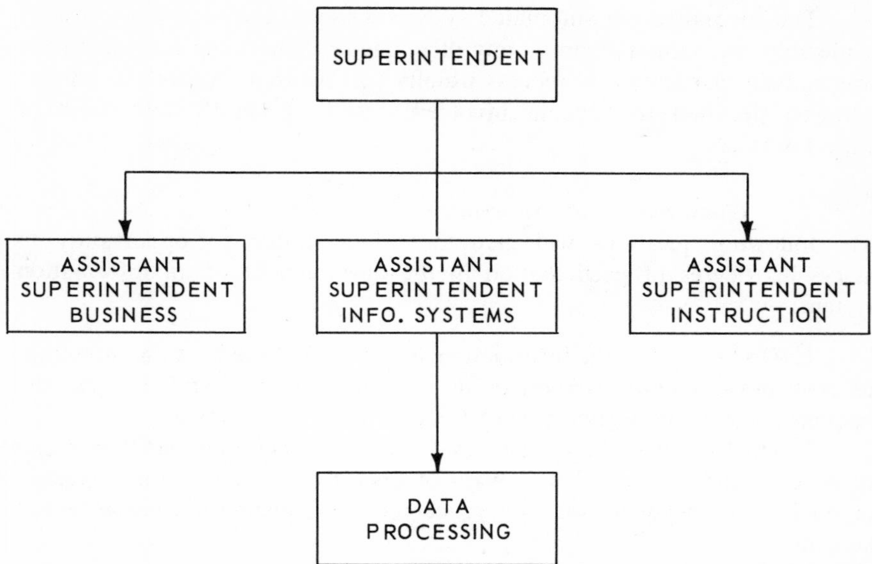

FIG. 79. *Desirable Structure for Information Services*

and "less successful," we can isolate the operational differences between them. The differences, we shall see, can be traced to the administrators' concepts of information and automated systems.

In the "less successful" districts, machines were viewed as highly advanced accounting machines for performing traditional functions faster and at lower cost. Or they were viewed as mysteriously complicated devices that most people could not master, and therefore responsibility was delegated to technicians.

In the "more successful" districts, the information system and the machines were viewed as a major resource to be used in operating the district. The entire system was held no more sacred than any other district activity, and thus was subject to the same management processes.

In addition, both schools and industry having favorable experiences with automation report that clear-cut objectives were established to assure that the system focused on the major problem areas. All activities and plans were reviewed periodically and progress toward goals and tangible results were required.

The higher up the position of the systems director, the more likely the success of the system. The McKinsey Report shows that those companies experiencing above average satisfaction with computerized systems had a computer executive just one level below the chief executive. In those companies reporting only average satisfaction, the computer executive was located two, three, or more levels down.

The success of the automated system is more dependent on top level leadership and support than on any other factor. Where the administration was actively participating, success usually was assured. Where the administration declined to become involved, results generally fell short of expectations.

Questions for the Superintendent

The following questions will give the administrator an opportunity to assess his degree of participation in the development of an information system:

1. Do I devote to the information systems effort the time and attention its cost and potential warrant, or do I neglect my role and delegate the responsibility to the technical staff three or four levels down?
2. Do I see that the information system is functional and that it can be used to find new and better ways of operating the educational system, or do I merely want to use data processing equipment for routine record keeping?
3. Have I insisted on pricing out all proposed areas of the information system, and do I follow up to ensure that each produces a significant return?
4. Have I clearly indicated to my staff that I hold them accountable for seeing that, in running their divisions, they get the most out of the systems?
5. Have I provided the district with the kind of information systems

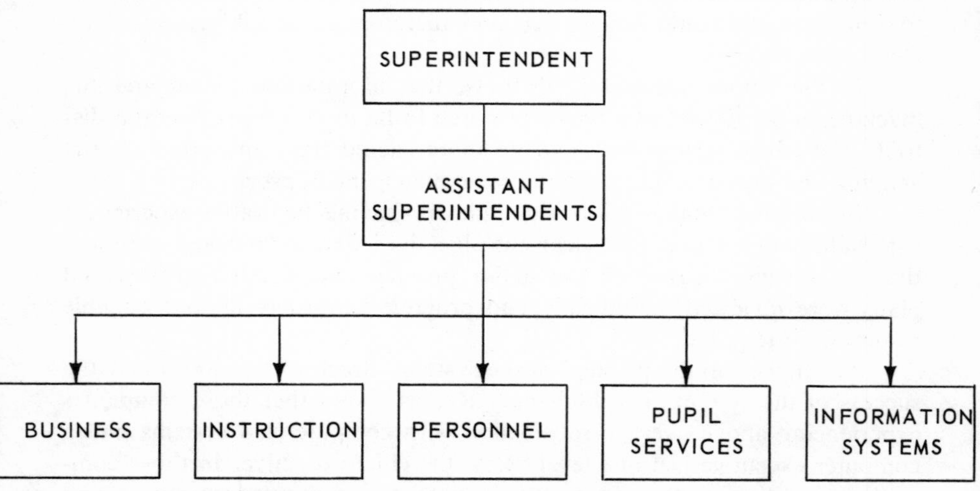

FIG. 80. *Desirable Structure for Information Services*

director needed to get the job done, and have I given him the *support, stature* and *staff* he needs?

In an information system, particularly an automated one, a school district will get only what it pays for. Unless it is willing to pay the price by providing the necessary leadership and taking time to organize, manage, and staff the effort properly, the system will likely be costly and frustratingly non-productive. Where top administration plays its essential role and provides the organizational structure and status, important consequences can follow.

System Benefits

Some mention has been made of the many ways that data processing and information systems can benefit schools. These applications and their costs have been described in some detail. However, we have only alluded to some of the more dramatic aspects of a properly organized information system. Consider that once the basic information processing system has been developed and implemented it is possible to correlate the many items of data that are generated as part of the pupil accounting system, the teacher accounting system, and the curriculum with the heretofore unavailable data that will be flowing from special services areas such as audio-visual and instructional materials.

With the ability to keep track of students and their curricular experiences it is possible to evaluate the effectiveness of new programs not just on a year-to-year basis but from a longitudinal point of view. Such an information system permits detailed accounting for each student for all grades from kindergarten through university, and the analysis of his performance at any given point in the progression can be tied back to any given variable

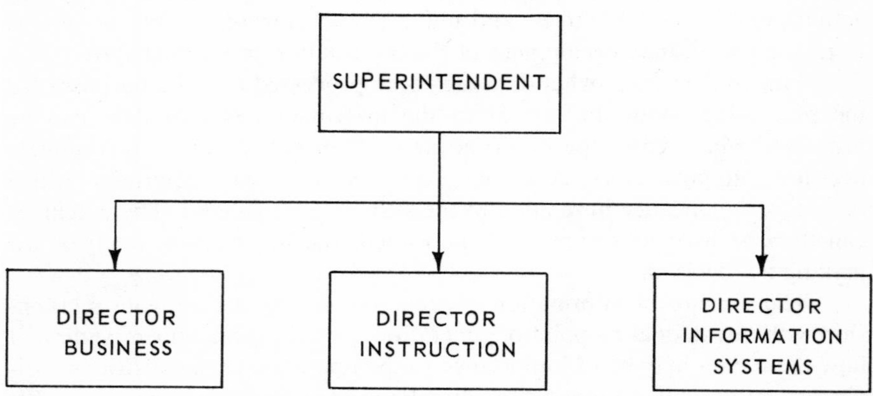

FIG. 81. *Desirable Structure for Information Services*

of any curricular sequence at any particular grade. The possibilities are unlimited and there are undoubtedly districts in the United States that have much more far-sighted or blue-sky programs on the drawing boards or in the process of being implemented. Consider some of the more mundane aspects of school administration.

With the information system capabilities it will be possible to have a true cost accounting of various legislated and special programs that may have reimbursement bases. In the past, reimbursement has been based on the results of limited study or on estimates of the actual cost of such programs. Total information systems will provide the capability to present a comprehensive picture of what the special programs actually cost. In addition, because of the availability of information, legislators can be informed prior to the passage of their bills of the financial implications of their proposal. Again the importance here is that the information would be more complete and accurate than that upon which legislators now base their actions. Certainly educators would be in a much better position to recommend educational policy if they had such complete, accurate, and comprehensive data available to document their statements.

What does all of this mean in terms of the internal organization of the district and what particularly are the implications for the director of information services?

Organizational Benefits

Most districts have found that the system study leading to the establishment of an information processing system clarifies the relationships among the committees that have responsibility for the varied tasks of curriculum development, pupil personnel services, student activities, etc. In most cases the director of information systems finds much of his time devoted to meeting with these committees. Therefore, he is able to provide the local school administrator with many items of data that are of consequence to all the activities of these committees, and ultimately to current school operations. For example, in the development of the information processing system it is necessary to determine what data are to be processed and the purposes for the processing. With the advent of the information system data can be processed with greater speed and accuracy than ever before. To formulate decisions administrators, counselors, and teachers must determine which data have significance in relation to the various jobs at hand. The machines can then be used to secure, as it is needed, the information required for making the decisions.

The director of information systems, because of his intimate relationship with raw data at its point of generation, as well as his understanding of how these data may be of importance to the operation of the district's various programs, is in a unique position. His position becomes more than that of an expediter of reports and/or a brush fire fighter. He has the opportunity to develop in others the visions of the many ways information can be used to improve the total educational system.

Through the use of machine data processing the following information can be generated readily which in many instances will obviate the need for many of the traditional committee activities of teachers:

1. Conducting the school census—districts and schools can obtain abundant and accurate information about the nature and location of school populations both present and future.
2. Establishing student programs and schedules—course programs and class schedules can be set up with with a high degree of efficiency. As by-products of this process, class lists or reports can be compiled accurately that show the names of students and the classes in which they are enrolled, times and locations of classes, the teachers assigned to them, and the credit to be given.
3. Reporting students' marks—quarterly and semester marks can be speedily recorded. Additional readings and reports are possible by-products of this operation. The eligibility lists for athletics, student body, office, scholastic and other activities can be generated as well as the rank and class list, DFI list, and other academic status reports.
4. Evaluating students—group and individual tests on achievement, intelligence, aptitude, and interest can be processed. Effective use of the data thus processed can be made in other guidance procedures and in instruction. The correlations thus generated can be of considerable value to teachers in special subject areas and those that are working with specialized curricula.
5. Identifying and placing students—it is possible to identify and place students according to their abilities, interests, and objectives.
6. Accounting for attendance—evaluating, recording, summarizing, and reporting of attendance data is both feasible and logical at daily, monthly, or less frequent intervals.
7. Recording of data—the analysis of information, the systematic testing of hypotheses, and the summarizing of current information can be greatly facilitated by data processing machines.
8. Reporting—meaningful and accurate information can be readily provided to pupils, parents, teachers, school officials and the community in an appropriate and understandable form.

One of the most important tasks of the director of information systems will be in knowing what types of data these various groups will be requesting and the format in which they will be requested. The original system study would, of course, include working with various teacher, counselor, and administrative groups in specifying such items of information as part of the required output. Planning is a key factor here as is the need for the organization that will funnel this information directly to the man in charge of the information system. All of the committee meetings in the world will be of no value unless decisions are made and recommendations are agreed upon and forwarded to the person who can act on them. If this person is the director of information systems and if he is in a position of sufficient authority to make these decisions, some definite action may be forthcoming. But if the data processing specialist is confined to the business division, or to the instruction division or to some other place where other work has priority, there can be little hope of developing the type of information needed to facilitate district growth.

REGIONAL CENTER OPERATION

Another aspect to consider is the accessibility of machine capability. Whether it is available within a given district or located in a regional data processing center makes little difference to the operation of an information system. Certainly, philosophical, political, and financial factors must be evaluated in the consideration of regional operations.

Until recently, most data-processing systems had been confined primarily to separate school districts. However, the work of such groups as the California State Pilot Project proved that a regional, co-operative venture in education data processing is workable. After three years of experimentation, the California project concluded that large districts—those with an average daily attendance of 20,000 or more—and organized regional groupings that would embrace several districts within each region, could operate data processing systems with foreseeably good results. The size of these centers could be even smaller if instructional applications were included. It further concluded that the regional type of system would offer more advantages than would the separate or local type, regardless of district size, and that the comparison is particularly pertinent to systems used by small and medium-size districts.

Advantages of a Regional System

Among the advantages of the regional system are the following:

1. It is less expensive to furnish and operate one central installation for a region consisting of a number of school districts than to furnish and operate separate installations for each of the same number of districts.

2. The benefits derived from the experiences, developments, and improvements that take place at the processing center in a regional system can be applied to a large number of schools, not just to a few.

3. A high degree of central staff competency is more likely to be realized in a regional system than in a local district system.

4. Greater uniformity of procedures and products can be achieved in a regional venture than among separate district systems.

5. As the depository for regional information, the center would be in a position to conduct various studies of regional scope. It could, for example, compile common types of pupil-personnel records for research and analysis and provide unbiased and confidential analyses of data pertaining to educational functions in many districts.

6. The various districts co-operating in a regional system can contribute valuable suggestions to the total effort. This is true because of the large number of schools participating and the differences that exist among the districts in the system.

Data processing systems in some local school districts have been developed rather haphazardly to meet the pressing needs of each local situation. Despite the hard work of the systems personnel in these districts, certain problems frequently appear, such as inefficiencies due to inadequate equipment and/or a lack of sufficiently trained personnel, failure to integrate properly the data processing applications with the district's educational program, and preoccupation with needs of the moment at the expense of well-planned procedures that would take care of longer range needs. In a regional type of venture, however, these problems would be minimized or removed. Much more thought, for example, would be given to integrating the data processing operations with the educational program everywhere in the region served.

Plans for Establishing Regional Centers

The regional center should be considered as a service organization. Its primary function should consist of providing data processing services which can not be efficiently maintained or operated in local districts. Regional centers could efficiently handle the processing of data from all three of the following types of districts:

Small School Districts

Districts with an average daily attendance of less than 5,000 may wish to send original source documents (such as machine-scored test answer sheets, registration materials, attendance-accounting record cards, grade-reporting rosters, cumulative record entries) directly to the regional center for processing. Although small districts typically do not have sufficient volume to warrant the purchase and use of their own data processing equipment for handling source documents, they could reduce costs and increase efficiency by using the data processing services of the region.

School Districts of Medium Size

Districts with an average daily attendance of from 5,000 to 20,000 typically find justification for minimal data processing equipment, i.e., equipment which is necessary to convert information from source documents into punch card or tape form. In the field of testing, for example, the district would typically have scoring machines, keypunches, and perhaps a sorter, a reproducer, a tabulator, and an interpreter. This equipment allows for punching the data into cards, sorting information for desired groups, and printing rosters of results. Such a district could then submit its punch card data to the regional center for specialized compilation, tabulation, and distribution and for special analysis.

Large School Districts

Districts maintaining a complete line of data processing equipment that allows for a number of operations, including the conversion of basic source material into data processing form, would frequently find it desirable to utilize a regional center for student scheduling, special computational analyses, and complex statistical analysis of data.

Processing Procedures and Reporting Methods

Any educational data processing system, whether district or regional, can run into serious difficulties if (1) the developmental phases of the processing program are not assigned to competent, well-trained personnel, and (2) if quick and effective methods of communication between the central staff and the schools are not established from the outset. However, indispensable to the healthy functioning of a regional data processing system in particular is the willingness of system participants to work out mutual problems, to co-operate, to compromise if necessary, and to consider the progress of all users rather than the gain of a few.

Thus the structure or form of processing procedures and reporting methods should be developed through consensus of the school districts for which the processing will be done. Uniformity of processing design will result invariably in economy, greater speed, and reliability. Part of the regional center's responsibility should be to offer co-ordination and leadership in establishing effective and reliable methods of handling school information.

Criteria for Size and Production

The size and production volume of the regional center should be established on the basis of the following criteria:

1. The maximum volume of data that may be handled within a specified time of need.
2. The equipment needed to accomplish the necessary processing without having excess equipment which would be idle for the major portion of the school year.
3. The acceptance and administration of source data and processing schedules that would make orderly production possible in the regional cen-

ters. If ten schools require 200,000 units of data processing, and the center can process 40,000 units per day, and if all schools send their source material on the first day of the month, some data would have to wait five days for processing. If, however, the schools are administered to send 40,000 units on five consecutive days, processing of school data need not be delayed.

Advisory Planning Committee

An advisory committee composed of members with differing responsibilities is a valuable adjunct to the planning and utilization of a regional data processing system.

A minimal committee in a region of school districts would include such personnel as the following:

1. An administrator (representing the authority to make decisions and recommendations concerning budget approval, personnel assignments, and priority of operation).
2. A supervisor of pupil-personnel services (representing the professional needs and requirements for pupil-personnel records and information).
3. District administrators and teachers (representing the producers and consumers of records and reports).
4. A data processing specialist and programmer (representing the technical skills concerned with utilization of the machines).
5. The regional director of information systems (representing all areas).

It is essential, of course, that each district utilizing the services of the regional center have adequate representation on the advisory committee and contribute to the procedures that will be used and to the form of reports that will be provided.

The advisory committee should be able to review the needed reports or records, the time schedules demanded, the form and content of the source documents, the manner of processing, and the master schedule of operations. The minimal representation suggested here would allow the analysis of data to start with the pupil-personnel needs as defined by the program and to evolve steadily as the various responsibilities and competencies represented on the committee contribute to the plan.

Special Considerations

The following special considerations are proposed for regional data processing systems:

1. *Charges for Services.* The charges for services rendered by cooperatively shared data processing facilities should be based on the actual costs of operation. Processing centers that are administered, planned, and

maintained by public education funds need not operate at the profit that is necessary in private enterprise. Considerable financial savings are possible if appropriate groups or agencies are formed to secure maximum and efficient use of the processing equipment. Educational data processing units are not established to do contract work for private individuals, nor are they in competition with private enterprise. They represent an efficient service organization the purpose of which is to provide, with greater speed and accuracy and at lower cost, the machine processing of heretofore manually processed data.

2. *Channels of Communication.* Continuous communication must be maintained between individuals using pupil-personnel records and the data processing center. Questions concerning the accuracy or meaning of data may recur despite the fact that the same forms and procedures may have been used over a period of years. Any change in forms or in methods of reporting data must be accompanied by thorough in-service education. This will ensure that data are accurately reported on source documents and appropriately used.

3. *Administration of the Regional Center.* The administration of any regional data processing center must be under the direct supervision of a central administrative officer. As pointed out elsewhere in this section, evidence shows that without sufficient authority and proper judicial powers on the part of the administrative head of the local or regional system, data processing operations may be subjected to "pressure politics" in which favoritism or expediency could destroy established procedure, nullify priority, and throw time schedules into confusion.

4. *Ownership of Materials.* Materials handled by the data processing unit may not become the property of the center. As a service unit within an educational system, the data processing group should provide assurance that data will be accurately and efficiently processed and that the results will be returned to the submitting school or agency as its own property for distribution and interpretation. The processing center can be the *custodian* of the source documents, cards, and tapes but never the "owner." With the exception of certain types of attendance accounting for financial reimbursement, school data should not become public information and should not be available for general distribution or interpretation without the consent of the school or administrative officer responsible for the data.

5. *Periodic Conferences.* Periodic meetings of data processors and co-operating school personnel for the purpose of compiling suggestions and evaluations should be a necessary function of any regional processing unit. While data processing centers should not dictate what records will be maintained, it is also true that school workers may not be able to visualize the most advantageous procedures through which the processing center can economically and quickly produce the desired end-results. Such conferences will help the processors and the school personnel to achieve mutual benefit.

SUMMARY

Whether a school district uses local or regional data processing equipment, educators who are truly concerned with the value of information must commit themselves to the concept of a total information system and must place the director of this system in a position of adequate authority in the district. Electronics has provided the facility for bringing each of the various subsystems together into an integrated and total systems approach. It is this total systems approach that offers a tremendous gain in school information services. The total integrated systems approach to information includes all elements of information processing in the various departments of the district. It places particular emphasis on the management principles so often verbalized but seldom practiced in school situations.

Whether education will achieve a totally integrated information system will depend greatly on the organizational structure in which the system operates.

16

SIGNIFICANT PROJECTS IN EDP

This chapter makes no attempt to enumerate every important project in EDP. There probably are many worthy endeavors that could be discussed. The projects mentioned, however, do have some significance in that they are of general applicability, have approached a real problem area, and are working methodically toward a solution; each represents either a different problem area, a different organizational structure, or a different approach.

EDUCATIONAL IMPLICATIONS OF AUTOMATION (EIA)

The impact of automated procedures and practices, both *in* and *on* schools and society, is of great interest and concern to all who are committed to the continued development of this country's chief natural resource, the human being. One program which stresses the human being over the machine, is the project on the Educational Implications of Automation (EIA). The National Education Association inaugurated this project in June, 1961, under a grant from International Business Machines Corporation.

The EIA project has tried to shed new light on the impact of automation and other technological change on our society and our schools, to consider ways in which educational agencies can and should respond to present and projected socio-economic changes, and to inform teachers and other citizens of its findings. Specific areas to which the project has directed attention include: changing skill requirements, the role of adult education, and the importance of fundamental skills such as literacy.

Although the EIA project keeps in touch with developments relating to teaching machines, programed learning, and other new educational media, these are not its primary concern. Similarly, the EIA project is not directly concerned with the use of automation and electronic data processing as aids in school administration.

Two major publications have resulted from this project: *Automation and the Challenge to Education* and *No Room at the Bottom—Automation and the Reluctant Learner.*[1]

1. For additional information, write to Educational Implications of Automation, National Educational Association, 1201 Sixteenth St. N. W., Washington 6. D.C.

THE CALIFORNIA RESEARCH AND DEVELOPMENT CENTER IN EDUCATIONAL DATA PROCESSING (R/D CENTER)

A Research and Development Center in Educational Data Processing was established in the California State Department of Education on July 1, 1962. This three-year project is jointly sponsored by the Department of Education and the Cooperative Research Branch of the United States Office of Education.

The Research and Development Center is charged with developing and demonstrating an effective education information system through the use of an electronic computer. Special consideration is being given to pupil-personnel services and curriculum. The emphasis is on the end products proposed and not on the tools needed to create them.

The Research and Development Center has gained additional support through the success of the State Pilot Project in Data Processing. This project concluded its three-year operation in June, 1963. It served 35,000 students in 25 schools in 5 school districts in 5 separate counties. The pilot project realized its primary goal, that of providing co-operatively-developed data processing services for a variety of schools in a large geographic area.

The general purpose of the Research and Development Center is to assist local school districts and to facilitate the state-wide growth of data processing services. Long-range goals include the development of a total, integrated educational data processing system and the establishment of a network of regional data processing centers. The specific purposes of the R/D Center are discussed below.

1. *The design and development of model systems for collecting and handling data.*—The center is developing improved designs for those pupil accounting systems which already use machine processes as well as experimenting with areas not yet adapted to machine data processing. The systems are to provide maximum use of data for guidance purposes, as well as for communication between schools and articulation between the various levels of educational institutions.

Caution is being exercised so that modifications can be made at different levels of local control. Educational objectives and standards will dictate the nature of the processing system rather than vice versa.

2. *The conduct and support of simulation studies.*—It is evident that certain types of complex decision processes can be performed by computer systems more efficiently than by humans. The potential of these techniques in education appears to be great. Efficient use of data would allow educators to make better decisions and allow them to experiment with techniques and solutions before trying them in schools.

3. *Establishment and maintenance of a library and clearing-house of information on educational data processing.*—The growing amount of literature in data processing needs to be reviewed and made available to schools. Much of this literature is available only in sources usually not consulted by educators or is distributed by manufacturers only to their own customers. Channels of communication are being established with other agencies and organizations which are paralleling and duplicating this clearing house function for the larger field of automatic data processing and automation.

4. *Development of proposals for the co-operative establishment of compatible systems.*—Each school district has generally established its own particular system for processing information, usually while under considerable pressure to get work done. There has been little time or encouragement for original and developmental studies of methods themselves. Therefore, a wide variety of inadequate systems have emerged. There is a great need to develop good methods of producing educational information which will meet the varying requirements at local, regional, state, and national levels.

5. *Evaluation and analysis of data processing equipment.*—Recent developments in technology make it increasingly difficult for educators to obtain objective information about existing equipment. Selection and analysis of the characteristics of available equipment can best be performed by an agency such as the R/D Center.

6. *Providing consultation for local school systems.*—Until now school districts that wished to establish or modify a processing system, including those districts already well advanced in data processing, were limited in obtaining help to a few personnel from other districts or to a few manufacturers' representatives who were qualified in educational matters. The Research and Development Center proposes to make available for consultation its widely experienced staff.

7. *The establishment of regional data processing centers.*—Regional centers for processing data are perceived as efficient organizations for the handling of educational data. For the many school districts which do not have sufficient volume to justify a data processing installation, the regional center could handle all processing. The medium-sized districts with minimal data processing installations which allow for the preparation of source data and for limited processing, could submit their punched card data to a regional center for more complete processing—for specialized compilations, tabulations, distributions, and analyses. Large school districts that maintain a complete line of data processing equipment would find regional centers desirable for special computation and complex statistical analyses of the data. Therefore, the regional center would become a service organization providing the data processing services which ordinarily cannot be financed, maintained, or operated in the local district.

Task oriented committees composed of competent field personnel have been appointed to assist the R/D team in its deliberations. Nine committees have been established to study the various aspects of the project. As recommendations are formulated, they will be considered for inclusion in the master plan for stimulating orderly and appropriate growth of educational data processing in California.[2]

COMPUTER-BASED LABORATORY FOR AUTOMATED SCHOOL SYSTEMS (CLASS)

The System Development Corporation (SDC) has recently completed a new facility, designated "CLASS," for the research and development of a complete educational system that would provide optimal learning conditions.

CLASS permits the simultaneous, automated instruction of twenty students, each of whom either receives an individualized sequence of instructional materials adapted to his particular needs or learns in a group mode of instruction mediated by a teacher or computer. Application of modern data processing technology to other functions normally associated with a school district can also be explored with CLASS.

In the CLASS system, each student has a manually operated film viewer containing 2000 frames of instructional material. In addition, he has a response device, linked to the computer, which indicates the sequence of slides to be seen by the student, enables him to respond to questions, and presents knowledge of results to him in the form of coded light.

The computer maintains performance records for all students and makes these records available to the teacher, or counselor, or administrator.

Provision is made for two teachers in CLASS. Each teacher has console facilities which make it possible for her to call up computer-generated displays showing the current progress of any student or group of students. Automatic alarm lights will alert the teacher to students who are performing unsuccessfully in their lesson.

CLASS also permits instruction—in either the individual or group mode—through different media including television, films, and slides as well as conventional lecture and textbook methods.

With such a system the impact of automation on the roles of guidance, instructional, and administrative personnel can be carried out. For example, if immediate and accurate information is provided by the computer on the state of academic knowledge of individual students, what implications does this hold for changing study schedules on a daily basis, for

2. For additional information write to: Research and Development Center in Educational Data Processing; California State Department of Education, 721 Capitol Mall, Sacramento, California 95814.

student advancement requirements, and for homogeneous class groupings?

Liberated from most record-keeping, paper-grading, and the basic necessity of packing students full of factual material, the teacher can concentrate on the extension of student understanding, on stimulating student creativity, on challenging student imagination, and on providing individual help and counsel.

The instructor in the computer-assisted classroom can evaluate his teaching or lecturing ability by seeding his lecture with diagnostic questions and receiving immediate analyses of the group response through his digital display. He may then elect to branch to simpler materials or to alter his approach.

It cannot be assumed that once teachers are liberated from paper-shuffling and have access to automated learning aids, they will know how to use these advantages. Many teachers are going to have to be trained in the effective use of the resulting free time. Some sophistication in variance and factor analysis, some experience in data processing methods and their potential, an understanding of tutoring methods—all of these will be needed by the teacher in the computer-assisted school system.

Training of teachers in the new laboratory will be one of the primary functions. Plans have been laid for bringing school children and experienced teachers into the CLASS facility. By observing learning activities over an extended period of time, meaningful hypotheses for experimentation will be generated, and hopefully this research will have immediate application in real school situations.[3]

NEW ENGLAND EDUCATIONAL DATA SYSTEMS (NEEDS)

Regional cooperation in the Yankee tradition is being demonstrated by the Newton (Massachusetts) Public Schools and the New England School Development Council (NESDEC). NEEDS began on a modest basis in 1960 as the Data Processing Project of NESDEC, and was supported by the School and University Program for Research and Development at Harvard University.

The recent recipient of a large grant from the Ford Foundation, NEEDS' goal is to provide a variety of computerized services to 100 school systems by 1966. In addition to the routine activities of scheduling, preparing report cards and attendance records, and test-scoring, the NEEDS program is designed to train school personnel in the educational application of data processing technology. The project also plans to work co-operatively with the several state educational departments, colleges, and universities in the region.

3. For additional information write to: Education Project; System Development Corporation, 2500 Colorado Avenue, Santa Monica, California.

Some of the project's objectives are to:

1. eliminate the bottleneck around information in school systems due to the traditional procedures of record keeping.
2. provide quick and accurate information for the use of state and federal agencies in their planning and financing of education.
3. establish effective machinery to relate the research of universities to the day-to-day life of the school system.
4. bring technological improvements within the economic range of the public schools.
5. develop a body of personnel with technological skills in both education and data processing.
6. close the gap between the sophisticated level of data processing in business and federal agencies and the currently simple level of school data processing.
7. aid in the revision of state legislation so that the machinery of government will not impede logical and effective change when and where it is indicated.
8. develop in public education the quality control techniques to promote more sophistication in school administration.

While each of the above goals is stated in technical or administrative terms, the overriding aim of the program is to expedite the operating machinery in education to individualize the instruction of each student.[4]

COOPERATIVE PLAN FOR GUIDANCE AND ADMISSION (CPGA)

The Cooperative Plan for Guidance and Admission is an approach to the solution of a pressing educational problem—that of organizing, summarizing, and communicating, in useful ways, all the important knowledge that high schools collect about students. The plan requires the co-operative action of educators and employers on at least a state-wide basis and works toward the following ends:

1. Development of a "common language" and a "universal code" to be used by all schools and colleges to record and transmit information about students.
2. Application of modern electronic techniques (high-speed computers) for summarizing and communicating such information.
3. Evolution of a system for "feedback" of information to the high schools so that they can know the success achieved by their graduates in jobs and college.

4. For additional information write to: New England Educational Data Systems, Cambridge, Massachusetts 02138.

4. Reduction of the costs of student record-keeping while improving its efficiency.

The CPGA plan uses a standardized set of materials to record all educational data about a student, including his extracurricular activities. At the end of the 11th grade, all of this information is manually transcribed to a machine readable document or transmitted via punched cards. During the summer, these data are processed, printed, and returned to the school on a multiple part form. When a student requests a transcript during his senior year, one copy of the form is manually updated, signed, and mailed. This form also provides space for a college or university to enter the student's marks and other information. The form is returned to the high school, thus enabling it to evaluate its educational program.

CPGA is based on a plan developed in Georgia and has received support from the Educational Testing Service (ETS) and the Ford Foundation. ETS also co-ordinated the processing of materials through its computer facility during the developmental stages of CPGA and now is making available the computer programs and procedures to state education departments and universities desiring local use of CPGA.[5]

THE PERT PROJECT

The road from the inception of an educational project to its successful completion is often strewn with good intentions and inadequate planning. To assist educators to become more proficient in the anticipation and handling of scheduling and timing problems, the Cooperative Research Branch of the U.S. Office of Education has granted funds to The Ohio State University to study the educational applicability of PERT—a Program Evaluation and Review Technique.

One of the most significant aspects of PERT is the possibility that it may provide educators with the procedural techniques needed to identify in advance the events and activities that are critical to the completion of a project.

The general purpose of the PERT Project is to investigate the degree to which the PERT technique can be applied to educational research and development activities and to determine whether or not the advantages cited above can be substantiated.

The specific objectives of the project are:

1. To develop from the present "state of the art" of PERT a set of working guidelines for applying the technique to a variety of educational research and development projects.

2. To construct a series of model PERT networks for common and

5. For additional information write to: Educational Testing Service, Princeton, New Jersey.

representative types of educational research and development projects.

3. To apply the PERT technique to specific ongoing projects in order to study the possible improvement in project progress from such application.

4. To derive a series of recommendations regarding the applicability of PERT to educational projects and to disseminate them through publications, seminars, and workshops to potential project directors.[6]

IOWA EDUCATIONAL INFORMATION CENTER

The Iowa Educational Information Center is conducting a project in educational data processing in cooperation with the College of Education of the State University of Iowa, and the Iowa State Department of Public Instruction.

The objective of the program is to provide local school districts with increased capacity to deal with existing intricate and massive data problems and to facilitate educational research by establishing uniformity and availability of data through the application of data processing and computer science. Problems in reporting and analyzing student personnel data, management data, and financial data are being explored.

The program, aimed at the general problem of introducing the use of computer systems into Iowa schools, has three major and related functions:

1. *Research.* Various data processing procedures are being studied to see which ones can be adapted for the Iowa program. Uniform methods and systems for recording information in the state's schools will be worked out so that data for all schools will be in the same form. Once coding systems have been worked out, it will be possible to study, on a state-wide basis, educational problems which could not be undertaken before because of cost or time factors.

2. *Training.* The University plans to offer workshops and courses to train school personnel in the use of data processing.

3. *Service.* Services to be developed using electronic data processing include: Class registration; class scheduling; automatic class loading; locker assignment; auditorium seat assignment; homeroom sectioning; ability sectioning; grade cards; attendance reports; honor and eligibility lists; pupil progress reports; guidance reports; staff certification; teacher assignment; activity fund records; inventory control of textbooks, library materials, and audio-visual equipment; and preparation of budgets, payroll, requisitions, purchase orders, fiscal reports, and bus routes. In addition, services which most Iowa school administrators do not now have—enroll-

6. For additional information write to: The PERT Project, The Ohio State University, 1945 North High Street, Columbus 10, Ohio.

ment projections, building utilization analyses, financial projections, and unit cost analyses—could all be provided through this program.

The Iowa program is voluntary, and schools may take any number of services on a non-profit basis.[7]

TOTAL INFORMATION SERVICE (TIS)

In developing its Total Information Service, the Chicago (Illinois) Board of Education considered two key elements—efficient data collection and economical data conversion procedures—and the total system approach to data processing.

The board has approached the collection and conversion problem in a way few other school districts would consider, entailing a significant departure from established educational methods as well as from the traditional data processing punch card.

It will use an electronic optical character reader, a device that reads typewriting from a standard 8½″ x 11″ piece of paper and then converts the data to magnetic tape for computer processing. Data will be prepared at the local school on typewriters with special type fonts, and the central computer will use identical type in preparing "turn-around" documents that then can be read by the character reader in the school.

Of equal importance is the belief of the board that data processing cannot be efficiently applied to education by bits and pieces. It is hardly sufficient to schedule student classroom activity without identifying the background, abilities, and previous training of the student as evaluation factors for the assignment. Teachers cannot reasonably be assigned without a system determining their education and experience. And material support cannot be rendered unless the related knowledge of budget status, manpower availability, and authority is provided.

The system was initiated early in 1960 after the completion of a comprehensive study conducted by the Board of Education. The study suggested establishment of a system comprising over one hundred subsystems, integrated through a master organization record, covering all elementary and high school activities. Subsequent to the study, activities of the teacher colleges and junior colleges were added. The initial concept was later expanded to include educational research and data processing instruction.

Although implementation has begun in all significant areas, it is recognized that a minimum of five years will be required for completion of scheduled activities.

The original concept of the classroom as a basis for organization

7. For additional information write to: Iowa Educational Information Center, East Hall, Iowa City, Iowa.

and support has been implemented through the creation of organization records, contained in a single file, for each of over seven hundred school facilities. These basic records, containing complete data for each classroom and school, are the focal point for processing all information.

Not only are individual differences in curricula and instruction recognized and provided for, provision is also being made for administration, personnel, finances, research and supporting services. This advanced approach to education has considered *all* known contributing elements.[8]

UNITED STATES OFFICE OF EDUCATION (USOE)

While not a project per se, the USOE is deeply involved in a number of activities that affect EDP projects and procedures. Its function is to provide leadership and co-ordination in the overall field of education, and this includes systems and machine procedures.

For a number of years the USOE has been working with the major national educational associations toward some agreement on the terminology and items of data needed for educational records and reports.

A series of handbooks has been developed to facilitate and improve the collection, maintenance, and reporting of educational information. Handbook I, *The Common Core of State Educational Information,* was published in 1953. It was followed by Handbook II, *Financial Accounting for Local and State Systems,* in 1957 and Handbook III, *Property Accounting for Local and State School Systems,* in 1959. Handbook IV, *Staff Accounting for Local and State School Systems* and Handbook V, *Pupil Accounting for Local and State School Systems,* are currently being written. A handbook concerning items of information related to instructional programs is expected to follow.

Another division of the USOE has been working on a nation-wide basis with a group of educators and has completed the item specifications for a professional personnel data card, the first phase in a Basic Educational Data System (BEDS).

REGISTRATION/SCHEDULING

EDP equipment has provided the means for the implementation of many new and exciting programs. One of the more mundane and exasperating tasks in education is that of constructing schedules for optimum utilization of staff and plant, while providing the individual student maximum latitude in the selection of curriculum.

Several computer programs have been written to assist the educator in constructing a master schedule and placing students into classes. Recent

8. For additional information write to: Director of Data Processing, Chicago Board of Education, Chicago, Illinois.

developments also are pointing toward the actual computer construction of the master schedule within predetermined and administratvely set limits.

Because of their far-reaching implications, these projects were discussed separately in Chapter 12.

PALO ALTO PROJECT

We have discussed state and national organizations and projects concerned with specific tasks such as scheduling. It is appropriate at this point to give an example of how a school district is attempting to meet the challenge of educational data processing.

In the Palo Alto (California) Unified School District the Information Services Department is responsible for preparing all necessary information so that appropriate decisions may be made by school personnel at all levels. Information is viewed in its broadest sense in this school district. As a result, the Information Services Department includes the computer center and is concerned with other technologies, such as teaching machines; the group testing program, which is viewed as a form of objective information for all school personnel; curriculum; instruction and guidance; and several N.D.E.A. projects related to decision-making.

The individual in charge of Information Services is an educator, the reason being that all of the important decisions required to meet the overriding objectives of this department are educational in nature, and as such should be made from an educational frame of reference. The role of the Information Services in Palo Alto is integrated closely with the daily operational aspects and decision-making procedures of the educational system; it is not viewed as an off-line service.

The department is structured into three basic sections: instruction, production, and development.

1. *Instruction.* The instructional section has two missions. The first is to help teach that part of the secondary school curriculum which relates to the computer sciences. This means offering assistance in the teaching of programming and the use of computers. The computer center is used as a lab by the students. The second is to conduct in-service training of staff in the use of computers.

2. *Production.* This section is responsible for producing those services and reports that are part of the ongoing educational process of the school district such as secondary school scheduling, report cards, testing, attendance, library catalogues, personnel data, and a variety of other services.

3. *Development.* This section is responsible for the necessary systems analysis, design, and implementation of any new service. In this section are those people responsible for programming the computer.

From its achievement, thus far, in maximizing the use of computers in education, the Palo Alto organization deserves to be ranked among the better organizations for the computer sciences within education.[9]

PUBLICATIONS ON EDP

There are several worthwhile publications that deal almost exclusively with the educational aspects of data processing, albeit at different levels of sophistication, and in different areas of concern.

1. *Educational Data Processing Newsletter.* Published monthly during the school year by Educational Systems Corporation, this is one of the first and perhaps most comprehensive of the newsletters. For subscription information write: *EDP Newsletter,* System Development Corporation, 2500 Colorado Avenue, Santa Monica, California.

2. *AEDS Bulletin.* Published monthly by the Association for Educational Data Systems, this bulletin covers much of the same materials as the *EDP Newsletter.* It is the official organ of AEDS. For information write AEDS, c/o Florida State Education Department, Tallahassee, Florida.

3. *Project on Information Processing (PIP) Newsletter.* The project of the National Science Teachers' Association (NSTA) at Montclair (New Jersey) State College is concerned with data processing and computer education at the secondary school level. However, through an unrestricted grant from International Business Machines Corporation (IBM), the PIP project staff publishes a bi-monthly newsletter which covers many aspects of data processing in education.

4. *Data Processing for Education.* One of the American Data Processing series, this publication is issued monthly. For information write ADP, 22nd Floor, Book Tower, Detroit 26, Michigan.

5. *Journal of Educational Data Processing.* A quarterly publication, this journal covers in depth the various subjects skimmed by the newsletters. It is an Educational Systems Corporation effort, and subscription information is available from the *EDP Newsletter* (see above).

6. *Educational Data Processing Monograph Series.* Another Educational Systems Corporation endeavor, the Monographs are issued as warranted and generally present an intensive study of a current problem, activity, or event. For subscription information write to the *EDP Newsletter* (above).

9. For additional information write to: Information Services Center, Palo Alto Unified School District, 25 Churchill, Palo Alto, California.

17

THE FUTURE OF EDP IN EDUCATION

Because it has such a short history, it is difficult to say that electronic data processing will have a great future in education. Most of our comparisons are made on the basis of the success or failure of established installations or at least indications from experimental and pilot projects.

If we look for success or even satisfaction with EDP installations in business and industry—much less in schools—we are faced with a startling fact. Approximately one-third of computer installations are relative or outright failures.[1] If we base our expectations on what has happened in the past we are doomed to conclude that approximately one-third of the activity in this area is less than acceptable.

BRIEF HISTORY

Let us look at this in another vein. Some school districts have been involved with automated data processing for twenty to thirty years. These districts started with the EAM equipment, and in some cases have graduated to EDP and the systems approach. Other districts have started with computers and are looking toward the development of total systems. Still others, through lack of foresight, initiative, or planning, have succeeded in mechanizing all of the old manual systems and procedures so that they now have a modern electronic mess. Educators, the group most likely to play the role of the true conservative, have viewed with alarm the headlines that have reported the complete failures or the cases where machines have proved to be less efficient than the older manual system.

Certainly there have been some spectacular failures. Certainly there have been inefficient installations. But there are many more installations that are unqualified successes. Some, because they are so close to home and relatively unspectacular have been overlooked by many educators. We can say that the future of well planned, adequately financed, appropriately staffed, and realistically placed installations appears quite promising. Those districts that are now on the sidelines, watching with interest and, in some cases, anxiety, for the best way to get into the game, or debating whether to get in at all, should look to those districts that have

1. *ADP Newsletter,* Vol. VIII, No. 22, March 30, 1964.

had successful experience. Let them talk with the administrator who, for the first time, has had information available to allow him to truly administer his district, to and then let him determine whether or not automation has a future in education.

A quick look back over the development of all data processing equipment reveals that approximately half a century was required to develop the punch card and EAM equipment to a relatively sophisticated level. Starting in the early 1940's, work was begun on the electronic computer and it took a fifteen-year period to develop the equipment through the first generation of tube computers to the current level of solid state equipment. Essentially we are in the final stages of the second and are entering the third generation of computers.

During the period from the late 1800's through the 1940's, most efforts focused on the technological aspects of machines. Processing of scientific data was the area of greatest concentration of effort. It was not until the early 1950's that business management and some farsighted school administrators began to see that these machines might have considerable impact on operations in their respective fields. During that time more and more consideration was given to the development of systems that would be able to take advantage of EDP, with particular emphasis on source data automation and the various aspects of report design and display.

We are currently in another stage. Society has become aware of the computer and its technological possibilities. A great mass of technical skill has developed which is drawn upon by people from all areas of endeavor. Management science has become more highly developed, and familiarity with the use of EDP is becoming a prerequisite to advancement. Finally, there is a shift taking place now in which educators increasingly appreciate the potential of EDP in the development of plans, programs, schedules, and management intelligence and are less preoccupied with merely mechanizing records and reports. We are approaching Wiener's conception of cybernation in which not only will man's muscles be liberated from the routine drudgery of production but also his brain will be liberated from the routine tasks that are a part of any educational or business establishment.

Hardware will continue to be developed. Recent announcements have indicated that machines are faster, easier to use, and dramatically reduced in size and cost. More manufacturers are looking toward a modular approach in which minimal configurations can be used at the start, and as the workload increases, additional units can be moved in without the need for reprogramming or replacing the entire hardware system. There are great advantages to building along modular lines because the initial cost which is of greatest significance in establishing EDP installations, will be reduced.

THE STATUS TODAY

At this point in the developing field of data processing, educators have enough experience, both good and bad, to be able to distinguish between the outrageous claims that vendors sometimes make and the truly dramatic possibilities that are approaching reality. We are now aware that machines can serve education. We have built some systems that demonstrate this. We are aware of the cost of installing and operating machines and do not at this time expect to create any significant savings by converting to them. The area that we are now approaching is that of total systems, in which the investment for each of the subsystem applications will soon be repaid many fold through the ability to relate and correlate information from the many programs that education operates.

The future use of data processing in education depends upon how well educators can take advantage of the technological capability now available. True, smaller, faster, more economical equipment is being developed, but we are able *now* to do all of the things that we have in the past said we wanted to do if we will only take advantage of existing hardware. The main problem, as we see it, is not that school management personnel are unaware that technology is a useful management tool, but that they are reluctant to get involved with it.

CAVEAT EMPTOR

When applying an existing tool to any new field, goods and services may be oversold or blatantly misrepresented. Enough educators have been involved in data processing problems personally, or know someone who has, to be wary of any situation that could lead to a budget upset, an educational breakdown, or the loss of job status. Recognizing this problem, the California Educational Data Processing Association (CEDPA) sent the following letter to all superintendents in the state:

> Data processing services are recognized as an important part of the educational-administrative field in today's concept of education. The California Educational Data Processing Association was formed to promote this desirable growth. However, the Association considers it timely to alert you to a problem that has emerged.
>
> There are many fine, reputable firms in the data processing field. Unfortunately, there are also a number of data processing firms or agencies that have entered the field with inadequate preparation not only for data processing, but also for the educational applications of data processing. Representatives of some of these agencies are masters of over-statement and of both the "hard" and "soft" sell.
>
> Instances have already been reported in which districts have

> contracted for services that either did not meet specified deadlines, were not delivered in satisfactory form, or did not materialize at all. Delay in receiving contracted materials or services can lead to a disruption of the educational program. Such delays may also cause financial loss and deterioration of confidence in the judgment of educators as well as in electronic data processing. Schools and automation need to present a positive image to the public.
>
> The Association suggests that you consider with due caution any move to automated data processing or to an expansion of an established program. An automated data processing system will be most effective after the total system to be processed has been studied. Such a study should include a consideration of future needs, so that the initial system can be expanded rather than replaced. We also suggest the use of a data processing consultant in your planning—one who can be objective with regard to utilization of equipment and services offered. Our Executive Board will be happy to consult with you concerning the design of such a study.
>
> The Association suggests specifically that any processing agency should agree to the following contractual provisions:
>
> 1. A written itemized list of the data to be processed and the reports to be produced.
> 2. Payment will be made only when all services are provided within the time and conditions specified.
> 3. The contractor may be assessed a penalty for failure to provide the services set forth in the contract.
>
> We also suggest that a contractor's previous clients may be willing to share information on the acceptability of the services rendered to them.

This is a timely warning to all educators, particularly those who are overenthusiastic about everything new that comes along. It also underscores the need for a district to have an educator who is competent in data processing systems, hopefully the local or regional director of information systems.

THE NEXT STEP

We have described the various applications of automation to educational processes. Most of these applications are operational, in the pilot stage, or have at least demonstrated their feasibility in the laboratory. Many of these applications appear to be breakthroughs in the use of technology for educational purposes.

Let us now step into the future and examine some possibilities for which we are technologically but not yet conceptually prepared. Dr. Elmer Wagner, Registrar and Admissions Officer at the University of California at Davis, in a recent, tongue-in-cheek speech to the National Machine

Records Conference painted a startling picture of the typical American college in 1984. While his discussion (part of which follows) centers on higher education, there are many obvious implications for educators at other levels.[2]

On registration day, September, 1984, Joe Doakes, a new freshman applicant, is seen walking up the steps of an ultra-modern building of the University of Utopia. As he approaches the entrance, the doors swing open and a sweet, considerate, motherly voice welcomes him to the University. This voice is Alma Mater, and she bids him to present himself at one of the admissions windows. As he comes close to the window, a partition slides back exposing an array of buttons and lights. One of these buttons is marked "Admissions" and he is advised to punch this button if he wishes admission. He does so.

At once there is seen an application form slowly advancing from one side of an opening in the counter to the other side. Again the motherly voice advises him to provide the requested information on the moving form. He does so, and as the information disappears under the far edge of the opening, the information provided is optically scanned. One of the first items he indicated is his national birth number, and this, when scanned, enables his present information to be related to and checked against information previously stored in the computer (i. e., his entire family record, elementary and secondary school record, test patterns over the years).

It should be pointed out at this point that the State of Utopia has instigated a new procedure which assigns unique special numbers to each and all college preparatory courses so it is possible for the computer to determine quickly the applicant's admissibility by referring to these numbers which have been reported from the secondary school or schools. Consequently, it is not only very easy to determine admission but also to relate these data to previous admittees' experiences and provide predictive success indices for prospective majors in the University.

Let's assume our applicant is a commendable one and admission is successful. The Voice then asks him to insert his hand and forearm into an opening. He does so and a steel bracelet is welded to his wrist. From this bracelet is suspended a key. This key is unique in that no other student has one just like it and of course it can't be lost. The Voice now asks him to report to the bookstore and insert his key in the slot he has "elected" as a major. He leaves the Admissions Office and reports to the bookstore.

As he enters the bookstore, he notes a number of keyholes with the names of the various majors indicated nearby. Our freshman, who has been told that chemistry is his field, inserts his key in the proper keyhole and out slides his entire complement of books,

2. From a presentation at the 1964 National Machine Records Conference.

notebooks, study manual for this particular course, an invitation to review his problems with Alma Mater at any time, as well as various other special pieces of equipment pertinent to this field. Also included is information about his dormitory and the room number to which he has been assigned.

It should be noted that registration as we have known it has long since disappeared. The long lines that used to be so obvious at registration time have been eliminated by computer services. Several features quickly noted are that no registration fees are paid —all students are billed at the beginning of the month to the father's credit account. This was immediately set in motion by the insertion of the key in the bookstore keyhole. Course sectioning is handled by the computer and the problem of large numbers of "directory or address" cards has been eliminated. Departments still need the information but the use of closed TV circuits has been utilized. An identification picture of the student was taken while he was getting his bracelet welded on his wrist and the information-retrieval system is such that by dialing the student's number, the computerized projector shows the student's home address and, since he has just been assigned a local dormitory and room, this too shows as his local address. Any telephone number is of course also included. Hence the student now needs only to report to his dormitory and proceed according to instructions as classes will commence the next day.

He eventually arrives at his room and inserts his key in the keyhole. The door opens and immediately he is taken care of at the office and a further billing is set in motion for board and room. The Voice now speaks up and he is informed of the meal periods, of room regulations, and by this time the scheduling of sections has been accomplished so he is also informed that he is to report to the sections indicated on his TV screen. He is also advised to prepare for the appropriate assignments in each class and that he may make use of the "nocturnal" learning equipment attached to his bed to reinforce his daytime efforts.

The next morning he reports to his first class and enters the room by inserting his key in the keyhole of the door. His seat number is immediately flashed on a little screen as the door opens. He finds his place and seats himself. It should be noted that this seat is not of a variety common in years past. Instead it is more in the form of a booth in which are located a small projector screen, microfilm readers, and an array of buttons in which the three most prominent are "Yes," "No," and "Repeat." As he seats himself, a sign flashes advising him to insert his key in the master control keyhole on his desk. This he does and the console lights up, ready for the class presentation to begin. Incidentally, this also records his attendance in the class. Conversely, non-attendance would serve to prejudice future grade evaluations.

Shortly the lights dim in the classroom as well as in his booth. A sign asks that he put on the earphones lying on the desk and the first presentation begins. Every known inducement to better learning and retention is employed to insure maximum comprehension. Both intrinsic and extrinsic motivation inducements are brought into play, augmented by superb visual and auditory stimuli. Since it has been found that food and sex are the strongest motivational forces, both of these play a predominant role in the lecture presentations.

At any time the student may punch the button "Repeat" and the lecture will be repeated from the last major point. Of course each one of these "repeats" is recorded in the Registrar's Computer. At the close of the lecture period, the student may return at free periods and ask for further "repeats," all of which are recorded and will tend to diminish the final grade evaluation.

Answers to Final Examinations are indicated either by the use of the "Yes" or "No" buttons on the console. If a student feels the need for "hints," he can punch this button and get successively better hints which will be charged against his final grade evaluation. All tests are immediately scored and the student knows his final examination grade before he leaves his desk. Hence the need for multiple copies of final grade reports disappeared quite a number of years ago. Anyone wishing to know about a particular student's record makes use of the closed-circuit TV system, after verification of his authorization for this information has been noted.

As graduation day dawns, the new graduate receives a package in which he finds a small phonograph record and a short strip of magnetic tape. He places the record on a player and hears the speech of a famous person. At the conclusion of the speech, Alma Mater speaks up and with proud, emotional feeling intones:

> "By the powers invested in me, you, Joe Doakes, are hereby awarded the Bachelor of Arts Degree and all the rights and privileges attendant thereto."

The magnetic strip has recorded on it the statement normally noted on diplomas as well as the student's permanent record of work undertaken. This latter portion can be used as a transcript whenever the occasion arises. It will no longer be necessary to order new transcripts from the University, since each prospective employer can make a copy from the original which the student presents.

Having already been assured employment availability upon admission, the new graduate no longer finds that he is entering a "dark" world of earning a living, but at once finds he is in much demand with the attendant high salaries which reflects back into bigger and better alumni relations.

Several interesting sidelights which have not been presented so far are to be noted at this institution. Constant checks on graduation requirements, course advising, and personal adjustment are made by Alma Mater. This motherly, consoling voice inspires students to unbelievable heights so that practically no students become "dropouts."

Dr. Wagner presented this paper not without some degree of humor. At the same time, he noted that many of the descriptions were achievable through use of technological capability currently in existence, and were not merely future speculations. It is important to mention more specifically the concepts stressed by Dr. Wagner. Many educators may dismiss his remarks as pure "Buck Rogersisms" and therefore not to be considered as anything that might be encountered within the foreseeable future.

The most unrealistic part of the entire presentation may lie with the date rather than the content. Our rapidly developing and constantly changing curricula, coupled with a burgeoning student population, are forcing the accelerating acceptance of laboratory and field approved learning techniques. Since technology is no longer a limiting factor, it is quite probable that the more desirable changes mentioned will be widely implemented prior to 1984.

A LOOK INTO THE FUTURE

There are many persons and agencies concerned with analyzing existing systems and updating them to take advantage of technological capabilities available today. Some of these have painted word pictures of things that can be done now, as well as what will be possible within the very near future. Therefore, it might be more appropriate to call this "a look into the present, with extrapolations for the future."

It is projected that by 1970 most data processing installations will be on an on-line real-time basis.[3] This means that all of the information processing equipment will be mobilized to provide immediate access to processing capability as well as immediate output to inquiries.

It is visualized that because of the high degree of equipment sophistication needed to provide this capability, computing utilities will be formed along the lines of the existing public gas, electric and other utilities. Anyone would be able to contract for computing capabilities and data banks. The housewife could balance her budget, the small businessman would be able to maintain inventory control and the student would have access to information in the large computerized library. All of this would be available through a small monthly charge similar to that now being paid for telephones.

Within the next decade the traditional punch card will be used much less frequently.[4] In fact it may vanish completely. It will be replaced by special documents for data collection and input to the computer. The growth of the use of data collection documents will increase spectacularly as less expensive document readers are marketed.

3. Sprague, Richard E. *Electric Business Systems,* Ronald Press, New York, 1962, p. IV.

4. *ADP Newsletter* Vol. IX, No. 5, August 3, 1964.

Services that will facilitate man-machine communication include those that: read typewritten, and in some cases, handwritten, documents; permit voice inquiry and/or voice output a la Alma Mater; accept messages on special typewriter-like consoles and then display the response visually on a television type screen (see Figure 82); "light pens" that allow modification of the material displayed on the screen; traditional teletype and data-phone units that may become as much a part of "gracious living" as the telephone and television.

Another aspect of significance today is the growth of importance of system compatibility, both on an inter- and intra-industry basis. School personnel are in the midst of this problem right now. Business and industry have faced these problems for some time and are working actively to develop compatible systems. The meaning of such systems will be that information will be available in a form that will facilitate cross-referencing in ways that, until now, we only have been able to dream about.

SYSTEMS ASSISTANCE AVAILABLE

A number of agencies, working on related problems have had some

FIG. 82. *Radio Corporation of America Video Data Terminal*

success in building systems that will solve many of the problems described. Some of the projects mentioned earlier have been attacking these problems from a total systems approach. Most, however, have concerned themselves with limited aspects of total systems. In order to move ahead on a broad front, educators have found it necessary and desirable to band together in organizations that are concerned with a global picture of educational data processing.

One of the first of these organizations was the California Educational Data Processing Association. Officially founded in 1961, CEDPA has listed its purposes as:

1. To promote and encourage appropriate use of electronic data processing and computing equipment and techniques for the improvement of education.

2. To bring together for their mutual benefit both operational and professional specialists concerned with educational data processing and representatives from manufacturing and service companies.

3. To provide for sharing ideas, techniques, materials, and procedures among school systems now using or planning to use modern data processing methods.

4. To co-operate with manufacturers, distributors, and operators of educational data processing equipment and supplies to establish and maintain proper technical standards and to meet new needs for specialized devices and systems.

5. To sponsor and engage in research and to publish suitable material relating to educational data processing.

6. To develop professional standards for educational data processing systems and to stimulate the development of adequate programs of instruction and orientation by institutions responsible for the professional training of educators.

7. To promote services which will assist teachers and pupils to recognize and make use of such aspects of data processing as are appropriate for classroom instruction.

8. To promote the general recognition of the vital professional role played by the educational data processing specialist in a modern school system and of the high level of competence required for this role.

Actively pursuing these purposes, CEDPA is now working with regional groups of educators to exchange information about local programs and problems. It meets once a year with the total membership to exchange information on state-wide activities. Working with and through the State Department of Education and its Research and Development Center in Educational Data Processing, the association has also co-sponsored a number of two-day seminars for school executives on the potential of data processing and what it has done and can do for local school districts.

Furthermore, the staff members of the Northern and Southern California County Offices of Education have met on a fairly regular basis to exchange information about problems and procedures at the county operational level.

Through the impetus generated by this growing concern for integrated system development, various school and governmental agencies are in the process of developing a uniform course coding system that will provide flexibility in identifying course content through the use of a numbering system without regard to course titles. Also being developed is a unique school numbering system which would assign one number to each school for all accounting and reporting functions.

Several other states are working toward the development of comparable systems, both individually and through state associations. At the national level is the Association for Educational Data Systems (AEDS), which was formed in 1962 to examine problems on a nation-wide basis. AEDS is working along lines quite similar to those stated in the constitution of the California Association. The United States Office of Education is also concerned with data processing and systems capabilities. Some of their work has been described earlier.

BETTER COMMUNICATION NEEDED

At this point in the development of educational data systems, there is one ingredient lacking, that of an efficient communication system. Many projects and organizations are continuing to replow the same ground. Work that has been completed in one part of the nation is being duplicated in other parts. Several agencies have recognized this need and are working on the possible establishment of a central clearing house on programs, systems, and systems development, so that anyone interested in initiating a data processing project or finding out the state of the art can write or call to obtain answers to his questions.

CONCLUSION

The future of EDP in education appears to be getting brighter each day. Automated systems will continue to play an increasingly important part in the structure of educational organizations. As this happens, more of the clerical and routine paper work will be handled by the machine systems, and teachers, counselors and administrators will find that more of their time will be available to work with pupils. Regardless of increased use of the automated procedures and processes, the future of education still rests in the hands of educators, for only they can determine how effectively automation will be used to better the conditions and the climate for learning.

18

SOME EDUCATIONAL IMPLICATIONS OF AUTOMATION

Electronic data processing systems are only one part of the larger totally integrated-automated-educational system. The ultimate system includes, among other items, auto-instructional and audio-visual laboratories, information storage and retrieval capability, etc. It is assumed, often incorrectly, that as part of the construction of this ultimate system, educators will know how best to use the system. A considerable portion of this text has been aimed at that goal.

Others in business, industry and science have traveled along these same developmental paths. If the system capability—technological or otherwise—is available, and if someone knows how to put this capability into motion, the cycle is complete. No other consideration has been deemed necessary.

But the world has passed this stage. It is incumbent upon all who work in this changing universe to consider not only "can it be done" or "will it work"—but "should it be done" and "what will happen to life and society if it does work."

It is the authors' intent in this chapter to raise some questions about the philosophical and operational bases of modern education and to touch on the implications these may have for the future of education.

A sound philosophy of education must precede a philosophy of automated systems. Without an educational philosophy and the concomitant goals, any attempt at automation would result in merely mechanizing existing operations with the result of doing needless things faster. Educators have frequently, and at great length, concerned themselves with the philosophy of education, but the relationship of their philosophy to the live-school scene is rarely apparent. Philosophy is often confused with tradition, and tradition is frequently built on whim and convenience.

With the advent of computers and automated systems, educators have found themselves forced to relate their ideas to reality, to plot out the connection between the thought and actual practice. For they must submit their goals to the public, a questioning public which may neither understand nor appreciate the role of education, its terms, procedures, and historical sanctity.

Within the context of a sound educational philosophy, automation will be a complex but obedient ally. Information systems and the associated data processing technology will serve the aims of education well. At this point it would be well to explore some of the other implications of automation in education.

"We are now involved in the world's greatest revolution since the industrial revolution. Since that complex age there hasn't been a greater change than that which has come about as a result of the electronic computer and the age of automation. This new revolution has now reached the schools."[1]

While the earlier industrial revolution brought about increased productivity, it also hastened the demise of the craftsman and jack of all trades by emphasizing the production line and segmenting the total job. With segmentation came tedium, boredom, and loss of personal involvement. As with all change, the question arose as to whether the worker had really gained ground in the light of what appeared to be personal devaluation. Educators are apprehensive about what impact EDP may have on the activities and freedom of individuals. It already has been demonstrated that many clerical aspects of education can be done better and faster by machines. Experiments of some magnitude have demonstrated practical applications of team teaching, flexible scheduling, classroom television, auto-instructional machines, and language laboratories. Now, with the introduction of computers, it seems possible to tie all of these new media together, into a self-organizing educational program. This possibility has caused many teachers to look to the future with a fear of personal unemployment. Many non-teaching professional staff members, including administrators, share this concern.

UNDERSTANDING OF TECHNOLOGY IS NEEDED

These attitudes and reactions have caused educators and technologists considerable concern. Without the assistance and encouragement of the great mass of educators, desirable change in information systems would be impossible to accomplish. Therefore, leaders in the field, such as John Caffrey, have said, "The primary need is for education in the techniques and potential values of applying automation to the improvement of educational systems. We cannot exploit these resources to the fullest unless educators at all levels of responsibility, in *both* technical and non-technical assignments, understand what automation implies for education and learn enough about the techniques both to interact intelligently with elements of existing systems and to specify variable objectives for new systems."[2]

It was mentioned previously that great emphasis must be given to the orientation of both certificated and classified personnel to the problems,

1. From a speech delivered by C. H. Wennerberg at the Third Annual Conference of the California Educational Data Processing Association, November 14, 1963.
2. John Caffrey, *"Letter From The President,"* AEDS Bulletin, January 1964, Association of Educational Data Systems, Tallahassee, Florida.

procedures, and probable effects of establishing an information processing system in a school district. The impact of automation on education must be understood. The tremendous potential of this new tool will not be realized until educators learn enough about the technological techniques to be able to visualize not only how the existing system can be made more efficient, but in addition how the interactions of man and machine can eventuate in the development of new and even greater systems for education.

Educators must be alert to prevent technology from determining educational goals. Conversely, they must also be aware of the opportunities that technology presents to achieve these goals in ways that previously were impossible. This implies that all educators at all levels of training must take a second look at their preparation to be sure that somewhere in the teacher training sequence they have been exposed to and have had the opportunity to work with automated systems. To some this will mean a return to the campus; to others, a change of electives; to still others a change in the basic way of thinking. Norbert Wiener has said that the first industrial revolution freed the human arm from being the power of industry. He also stated that the technological revolution will release the human mind from the drudgery that can be done better by machines. In neither instance, does use of the machine imply that man will have other outlets for the use of his arm, nor that he will have other tasks to occupy his mind. The release from routine does not necessarily mean that man will become more creative, intelligent, or happy. The conditions are more favorable but there must be additional conditions met to reach these goals.

Murray Tondow,[3] Director of Pupil Personnel Services, Palo Alto (California) School District, in a memorandum to his school board, stated that:

> The computer sciences represent one of the major scientific-technical-social revolutions that society is now experiencing. Irrespective of what one's role as an adult will be in our society, our students will need an understanding of what this computer revolution is about. We think it has as much meaning to the girl who will become a housewife as to someone who plans to go on to college, whether in the humanities or in the sciences. Unless we provide our students with these opportunities we will not be meeting our responsibilities. Perhaps an important point to make here is that gaining technical competency in the sciences does not necessarily give the student an understanding of the social implications of this equipment.

Applicable here is the statement made by George Arnstein:[4]

3. Project on Information Processing Newsletter. Vol. 1, No. 5 November 1963.
4. *No Room At The Bottom—Automation and the Reluctant Learner,* National Education Association, 1963.

> Automation means that there is *no room* (or very little room) *at the bottom* of the ladder of occupational skills. People must be encouraged to move up that ladder. Upward mobility has always occurred in the United States; today, however, there is a need to adapt quickly to new skills, new attitudes, and new surroundings, not in a generation but often in weeks or months.
>
> Underlying these developments is the phenomenon of change—the rapid development of new industrial patterns and the rapid obsolescence of existing skills. Those who are not left by the roadside by automation are those who can demonstrate their ability to learn new skills and adapt to new situations. But what of those who do not demonstrate this ability? They—the reluctant learners—are our concern. . . . How can we make room for them in a world of technology?

Arnstein is concerned specifically with the reluctant learner both in and out of school. Our concern here parallels his. In business and industry, as well as in education, we have our so-called professionals who are so entrenched in traditional ways of doing things that they shudder even to think about change. When faced with the necessity of becoming involved in change there is a great possibility that they will rebel either overtly or covertly.

Can the new breed of educator-technologist overcome this apathy, lethargy, and resistance? It is mandatory that they be able to, and some procedures have already been suggested for accomplishing it. Local district in-service and orientation sessions on automation and its various instructional offshoots is very important. The teacher-training institutions, moreover, must consider an understanding of automation and its relationship to instructional programs equally as important as a thorough grasp of subject matter and a comprehension of methods. A unit on automation in teacher training preparation would be a positive step forward. Summer workshops are already being offered in special subject areas and other programs are being sponsored by U.S. Office of Education and the National Science Foundation. It is hoped higher education will rapidly accept its responsibility for training all educators for the modern world, and that educators will accept their responsibility for keeping in touch with the times.

UNDERSTANDING OF SYSTEMS IS NEEDED

There are some negative sounding aspects of automation that certainly should be explored The two most frequently mentioned are conformity and control. Both of these are traditionally thought to be the antithesis of education but really they are not. While students, teachers and teaching methods must be allowed the freedom required for the cultivation and nourishment of creativity and human values, conformity and control are necessary ingredients of efficient educational administration and information processing.

Just as all aspects of social interaction require some conformity, so does the use of automation. Automated information systems require agreement about some specific details, such as methods of coding, and formats for input-output. Educators are working toward this goal anyway; consider for example, the proposals for a standard transcript form.

Does this specter of uniformity which implies conformity act as an inhibiting factor in the development of integrated information systems? Does the development of course-coding systems which permit the interpretation of transcripts without the time-consuming, tedious and frustrating aspects of evaluating course titles without any reference point appear to be an unwanted development? Does the establishment of a single unique and permanent identifying number for a school building run contrary to the wishes of school administrators who currently are maintaining a series of files of school numbers in order to be able to enter the appropriate one on any given form? Does the use of this unique school number appear to be distasteful when it provides the capability for returning information about students who formerly have attended a given school and are now progressing through institutions of higher learning?

Does the use of identifying numbers become more attractive if they facilitate the return of data from the myriad local, state, and national programs? Does their use become more attractive if they eliminate the problems caused when data for groups of students are returned to a school with a similar name in another part of the state? Unquestionably, the establishment of compatible or uniform systems offers great advantages to educators who are interested in simplifying administrative processes.

The control aspect is one of some seriousness. Any information system which permits the collection and storage of information about students from enrollment to graduation or, indeed, on citizens from birth to death, is, by its very nature, suspect. But the system is not at fault. It is the *use* of the system that can lead us into difficulty. In education, information might be available to those who oppose certain goals or programs but at the same time educators will have documented evidence to support their contentions, and this, in a sense, would be a first for the field. In the past educators have not been able to fight allegations with fact. For this reason alone, systems may be greatly desired.

There are several other aspects that also must be considered. In thinking about the information needed to administer a school district properly, one must keep in mind that the system needed to present this information is really composed of three aspects.

1. The collection of the source data. This implies that someone knows

what these source data are and those who control these data will release them to the collecting agency.

2. That some method or means of transmitting these data to the processing agency is available, whether by truck, train or transmission line.

3. That the output has been specified as only those reports that are needed by the administration to make the decisions necessary to take appropriate action in the given situation.

Machines and technological devices may or may not have a place in this system. The most important consideration is the information or intelligence that will be produced by the processing system. This end product is what the district administrators must keep foremost in mind. It is all too easy to become enamored with the dramatic and prestigious aspects of computer technology.

Two other points that must be considered in the development of any understanding or philosophy of information processing include immediate versus long-range goals and whether local or regional processing is more desirable.

POSSESSION OF MACHINES NOT REQUIRED

While the total integrated information system has been discussed in the section on systems, it is worth noting here that the immediate problem of getting a program underway, particularly to justify the financial outlay, is a great pressure felt by all who select to tread the path of automation. The purpose, however, of automating the information system is to provide long-range, long-term benefits in data accessibility. Many a long-range goal has been blocked by immediate pressures that diverted all planning to production. Some have solved this problem by separating the system implementation into two parts, one charged with handling all problems involved with the short-term changeover, and the other with long-range, advanced systems planning which is concerned with the future. It is important that the seemingly unattainable long-range goal of a perfect information system be kept in the mind's eye, for when the vision vanishes, all too often any semblance of an information system vanishes also.

Local versus regional processing has been covered in some detail in Chapter 15. Rational thinking is often out of place in a discussion on this point, as is any mention of financial differences in these two types of operations. Seemingly intelligent and well-balanced educators have been observed to react quite violently to any thought that their data and their procedures might be processed anywhere except on their equipment and within the boundaries of their district. There are several reasons advanced for this, all of which assume that it is less costly and more efficient to process data within the confines of a single administrative unit, regardless of the size of that unit.

Perhaps a more rational and, indeed, a more valid approach would be to consider with an open mind the processing capabilities needed to handle the information system of any given school district. Methods for determining the system and hardware needs have already been discussed as have the financial aspects. The logical approach to be taken at this point would be to define and state the problem and to have solutions presented which would best solve the problem. Whether these solutions appear to be traditional is not important because information processing systems in education have traditionally been quite inefficient.

All of this leads to the conclusion that the dream of an educational intelligence system which would provide teachers, counselors and administrators with current, complete, and accurate information for management decisions, and, indeed, for that illusive goal of truly individualized instruction for all pupils, is now within reach because of—heaven forbid—the capability available through the use of machines.

Educators must shake loose from their old ways of thinking and doing and become familiar with the processes and possibilities of the variety of available devices, including computers, automated classrooms, self-instructional and "teaching" machines. They must also become familiar with the collection, processing, storage, and retrieval systems that form the basis for wise utilization of these devices.

If top administration accepts and implements a philosophy that encourages the investigation, experimentation and exploration of these new processes, it should also commit itself to the development of a system for utilizing the many items of data that can help educators make spectacular advances toward this goal of individual instruction.

Viewed in the light of today's changing social and economic atmosphere, a statement by Arnstein is particularly appropriate in pinpointing some often overlooked aspects of education.[5]

> The march of technology calls for bold thinking, for further innovations, and for radical new approaches, including the so-called systems approach which tends to call for solutions appreciably and clearly different from the old-fashioned way of doing things.
>
> . . . there is a need for the acquisition of the basic skills, of reading, arithmetic, and writing, by every person who is or would like to remain a functioning member of our society. Without the ability to read, without the ability to deal with numerical symbols, there are very few opportunities in the world of today and fewer in the world of tomorrow.
>
> . . . on top of a thorough basic education, there must be superimposed specialized skills for those who can take advantage of them and who are needed to move forward the present accomplishments of our society toward new frontiers.

5. From a speech delivered by George Arnstein at the Sixth Annual Conference of the American Driver Education Association, June 27, 1962.

> . . . where lifelong learning used to be a highly desirable aspect of adult life, it has, in the face of technology and automation, become a new imperative.
>
> Beyond this, there are many other implications of automation, but they probably belong more properly in the domain of the economist, the political scientist, the corporate and government administrator, and ultimately, they become the responsibility of the citizens who, acting together, help to shape the policies of this country.

THE REAL CHALLENGE

Educators now have the capability of relating instructional programs to the unique and individual needs of each student. It is the responsibility and duty of educators at all levels to see that this capability is used wisely and to its utmost degree to further strengthen the educational program. Whether this will be accomplished by research in better use of data currently available, by the use of data that now can be collected through these new information processing media, by informing educators in the field of appropriate ways in which they can become users of this technology, by teaching educators to be more intelligent users of information or by all of these, the charge remains that educators must be prepared to meet the real challenge in education today—how to use information systems to benefit the individual pupil.

Data Processing for Educators is intended as a first step in this direction.

Appendixes

Appendix I

DEFINITION AND SPECIFICATIONS FOR POSITIONS IN EDUCATIONAL DATA PROCESSING

DIRECTOR OF INFORMATION SYSTEMS

Definition:

Under general direction, to plan, organize, and supervise educational projects in the application of electronic computers to educational problems in public schools; to plan the work and supervise the staff of the data center; and to do other work as required.

Typical Tasks:

Formulates research project plans and methods of evaluating outcomes of studies of the application of electronic computers to educational problems such as developing model systems, evaluating and analyzing equipment, developing specifications for new equipment, facilitating computer applications by means of programming aids, conducting and supporting simulation studies, and exploring applications of new technology to educational problems; assists in the selection of staff members; plans, organizes, and supervises the activities of the staff; orients staff members in project objectives; arranges and conducts meetings of advisory committees; establishes and maintains a library in educational data processing methods, systems, and equipment; provides consultation to local school systems on the educational application of electronic data processing; develops proposals for the co-operative establishment of compatible systems among local school systems; conducts in-service training of public school personnel; acts as liaison agent to data processing equipment manufacturers' committees; supervises collection and statistical processing of data; analyzes and interprets data; makes progress reports to advisory committees; prepares final reports on research projects; dictates correspondence, answers inquiries, and maintains liaison with other related projects.

Minimum Qualifications:

Possession of a valid administration, supervision, or pupil-personnel services credential or other credential or life diploma of equivalent authorization.

and

Experience: Three years of experience either as a teacher, administrator, supervisor, pupil-personnel worker, or education research worker which will have provided a broad background knowledge of the public schools and the use of data processing equipment.

and

Knowledges and abilities:

Thorough knowledge of: principles, practices, and trends of public education; developments and trends in the fields of data processing.

Wide knowledge of: school curricula; electric and electronic data processing systems and their application to education; research methods and techniques; statistics.

General knowledge of: principles of personnel management and supervision.

Ability to: plan, organize, and direct the work of others; speak and write effectively; secure the friendly co-operation of schools, officials, and others contacted in the course of the work; analyze situations accurately and take effective action.

and

Special personal characteristics: Tact, pleasing personality, and neat personal appearance.

MANAGER OF DATA PROCESSING

Definition:

Under general direction, to plan, organize, and direct either (1) a medium-sized electronic data processing operation; or (2) the machine, control, and filing operations; or (3) systems, programming, and procedures activities of one of the largest electronic data processing operations; or (4) a smaller electronic data processing operation, with responsibility for reviewing the standards and machine utilization of associated data processing systems and providing consultative services; and to do other work as required.

Typical Tasks:

When in charge, plans, organizes, directs, and co-ordinates the activities of a centralized data processing center utilizing an electronic data processing system, peripheral equipment, and supporting electric accounting machines. Directs the development and maintenance of data processing systems, programs, and related machine procedures for maximum utilization of data processing equipment; directs all machine, control, and data processing file operations; consults with departmental administrators on the development, maintenance, and effectiveness of data processing methods; evaluates new data processing equipment and technology for possible use;

reviews operations, analyzes equipment performance, and takes action to correct deficiencies; selects employees; maintains a continuing training program; evaluates the performance of personnel and recommends appropriate action; prepares justifications for staff and equipment in the data processing section budget; develops and maintains effective communications and working relationships with other governmental jurisdictions; provides consultative services on utilization of data processing equipment in a specialized program; prepares correspondence and memoranda.

Minimum Qualifications:

Either I

One year of experience performing duties comparable to those of a Supervisor of Electronic Data Processing, or Accounting-Tabulating Machine Supervisor, or Data Processing Systems Analyst.

Or II

Two years of experience planning, directing, and supervising the work of a large staff in performing varied accounting and statistical functions employing several types of electronic data processing and electric accounting machine equipment.

and

Education equivalent to completion of the twelfth grade. (Additional qualifying experience may be substituted for the required education on a year-for-year basis.)

and

Knowledges and abilities:

Thorough knowledge of: types, capabilities, and operating principles of electronic and electric accounting machine equipment used in maintaining a centralized data processing system.

Wide knowledge of: principles and techniques of programming and procedural work; principles of organization, administration, and management; principles and techniques of personnel management, supervision, and training.

General knowledge of: current developments in the data processing field; accounting practices, methods, and terminology.

Ability to: plan, layout, and co-ordinate a centralized data processing operation and direct the work of a technical staff; co-ordinate the data processing reporting activities of other governmental jurisdictions with the department's programs; analyze administrative problems and make appropriate recommendations; analyze situations accurately and take effective action; speak and write effectively; work co-operatively with others and gain their respect and confidence.

DATA PROCESSING SYSTEMS ANALYST

Definition:

Under general direction, to make studies of the accounting, record keeping, statistical, and other work of state agencies which is or might be done on electronic computers or punch card machines; to recommend needed revisions of data processing systems or to devise and assist with the installation of new systems; and to do other work as required.

Typical Tasks:

Independently or with other analysts makes major studies of the accounting and other office systems of various state agencies; formulates new or revised electronic data processing or punch card machine systems to meet accounting, statistical, and reporting needs; analyzes the feasibility of the application of data processing equipment to specific operations; prepares time and cost estimates and determines unit cost data; analyzes and evaluates existing procedures and proposed changes in operation; prepares factual reports with recommendations based on studies and surveys; prepares work flow charts and designs card forms and report forms; develops detailed machine procedures and wiring diagrams; prepares manuals of operation and guides or assists in the installation of procedures and systems and the training of personnel; studies procedural difficulties and operating problems and advises agencies on their solution; analyzes budget requests for data processing equipment and makes recommendations on their feasibility and necessity; interviews and consults with departmental officials and officers of state agencies.

Minimum Qualifications:

Experience: Three years of supervisory or procedures experience in electronic data processing or punch card machine work, one year of which must have been on full-time assignments in the construction, development, or major revision, and installation of data processing programs, procedures, or systems. In appraising experience more weight should be given to breadth of experience and the candidate's demonstrated ability to devise and install a variety of data processing systems using different makes of equipment than to length of experience.

and

Knowledges and abilities:

Thorough knowledge of: various makes and kinds of equipment used in electronic data processing and punch card operations.

Wide knowledge of: operating principles and methods of various data processing machines and the work possibilities of each.

General knowledge of: accounting principles and procedures; principles of organization, administration, and management.

and

Working knowledge of: office methods, equipment, and procedures.

Familiarity with: statistical methods and procedures.

Skill in: working out methods of coding, punching, or tabulating new or unusual data and making complex tabulations.

Ability to: develop forms and procedures for keeping accounting, statistical, and other records on data processing machines and maintaining adequate controls; prepare questionnaires and interview effectively; establish and maintain co-operative relationships with representatives of public and private organizations; analyze data and draw logical conclusions; speak and write effectively; prepare comprehensive reports and compile manuals of data processing procedures; analyze situations accurately and take effective action.

PROGRAMMER II, ELECTRONIC DATA PROCESSING

Definition:

Under general direction, to participate in the initial planning and to write difficult and complex programs for major projects to be processed by an electronic data processing machine and related equipment; to make necessary program proof tests, revisions, and corrections; to write electronic data processing machine and supporting electric accounting machine operating instructions; and to do other work as required.

Typical Tasks:

Participate in review and definition of problem with particular emphasis on programs assigned; prepares outline logic diagrams and block flow diagrams to indicate essential operations to be performed from initial stages to completion of job; sets up work area in machine by reserving memory positions for input and output areas, temporary storage areas, processing, and controls; develops detailed flow charts for logical machine operation; translates each flow chart step into coded instructions for movement of data in the data processing machine; systematically checks coded program to ascertain if other combinations of instructions would achieve greater flexibility, better machine utilization, or more dependable results; prepares a set of test data for use in testing the program on the data processing machine; does actual testing and correcting of program to avoid errors; prepares a complete set of operating instructions for use by the console operator; on occasion, operates the console in processing programs; trains personnel in console operation and may supervise a group of electronic data processing assistants.

Minimum Qualifications:

Either I

Experience: One year in performing the duties of a Programmer I, Electronic Data Processing.

Or II

Experience: Two years of progressively responsible experience in programming data processing applications for electronic computers;

and

Education: Equivalent to graduation from college. (Additional qualifying experience may be substituted for the required education on a basis of six months' experience being equivalent to one year of college.)

and

Knowledges and abilities:

Thorough knowledge of: clerical processing and mechanical punched card processing techniques and procedures; operation of an electronic computer system and program requirements for conversion of mechanical and clerical processing to the system.

General knowledge of: principles of organization and management; accounting principles and practices.

Working knowledge of: modern office methods and procedures.

Familiarity with: statistical methods and procedures.

Ability to: analyze data and draw sound conclusions; code data flow plan in machine language; analyze situations accurately and adopt an effective course of action; speak and write effectively; prepare clear, complete, concise reports; work co-operatively with others and gain their respect and confidence.

and

Special personal characteristics: Willingness and ability to accept work requiring a high degree of mental concentration.

PROGRAMMER I, ELECTRONIC DATA PROCESSING

Definition:

Under supervision, to assist in programming simple problems and clearly defined segments of large complex programs by preparing block diagrams and writing computer instructions for processing business data on electronic and electric data processing equipment; and to do other work as required.

Typical Tasks:

Participates in the study of electronic data processing applications and the definition of objectives and/or the processing requirements of the applications; translates problem statements and block diagrams into series of coded and detailed operating instructions; assists in preparing block diagrams on complex problems; programs simple problems and clearly defined segments of large complex programs; assists in tests of coded programs and in making revisions to eliminate errors and excess machine time; studies the principles and techniques of programming, and the work processes and methods of the agency; may operate data processing equipment; may analyze machine stoppage and initiate or recommend needed changes.

Minimum Qualifications:

Either I

Experience: Two years in tabulating or electronic data processing work at a level equivalent to a Senior Tabulating Machine Operator or higher.

Or II

Experience: Six months in performing duties comparable to a Programmer Trainee, Electronic Data Processing.

Education: Equivalent to graduation from college. (Successful completion of courses in algebra, geometry, and trigonometry may be substituted for two years of the required education. Experience in the California State Service in the subject matter being processed by electronic data processing equipment may be substituted for the required education on the basis of six months' experience being equivalent to one year of education.)

Or III

Experience: Six months of technical experience in the development of procedures, forms, systems, flow charts, block diagrams, or data processing equipment instructions for conversion of work processes to electronic data processing.

Education: Equivalent to college graduation. (Additional qualifying experience may be substituted for the required education on a basis of six months' experience being equivalent to one year of education.)

and

Knowledges and abilities:

Thorough knowledge of: clerical processing techniques and procedures.

General knowledge of: principles of organization and management; modern office methods and procedures.

Familiarity with: accounting principles and practices; statistical methods and procedures; mechanical punch card processing techniques and procedures; electronic computer systems.

Ability to: analyze data and draw sound conclusions; analyze situations accurately and take effective action; speak and write effectively; prepare clear, complete, concise reports; work with others and gain their respect and confidence.

and

Special personal characteristics: Willingness and ability to accept increasing responsibility and perform work requiring a high degree of mental concentration.

Additional Desirable Qualifications:

Satisfactory completion of recognized courses in electronic computer programming.

ACCOUNTING-TABULATING MACHINE SUPERVISOR II

Definition:

Under direction, to direct the operation of a complete tabulating machine installation maintaining a complex system of records; or to do equivalent level supervisory or procedural work in a larger machine installation; and to do other work as required.

Typical Tasks:

Directs and reviews work, gives instructions, maintains discipline, passes upon problems in supervising a group of employees operating various types of machines in a relatively large, or in a section of a larger, tabulating machine installation and performing related clerical work in performance, and takes or recommends appropriate action; devises or reviews methods of coding, punching, or tabulating new or unusual data; performs the more difficult work in the development of procedures; consults with agency personnel and advises on the possible use of tabulating equipment for accounting and statistical purposes; assigns priorities to work orders to facilitate maximum use of available equipment and to meet work schedules; supervises the preparation of reports; dictates correspondence and memoranda; keeps records.

Minimum Qualifications:

Either I

Experience: One year performing the duties of an Accounting-Tabulating Machine Supervisor.

Or II

Experience: Four years of experience in the operation of tabulating equipment, at least two years of which shall have been in a supervisory capacity. (College training may be substituted for the non-supervisory experience on the basis of one year of education being equivalent to six months of experience.)

and

Education: Equivalent to completion of the twelfth grade. (Additional qualifying experience may be substituted for the required education on a year-for-year basis.)

and

Knowledges and abilities:

Wide knowledge of: various kinds of tabulating equipment, operating principles and methods of the various machines, and work possibilities of each.

General knowledge of: accounting principles and practices; average production rate of machine operators; principles and methods of personnel management and supervision, and planning, organizing, and directing the work of others.

Working knowledge of: different types of office machines.

Familiarity with: statistical methods and procedures.

Skill in: working out methods of coding, punching, and tabulating new or unusual data and making complex tabulations.

and

Ability to: plan, organize, and direct the work of others; develop forms and procedures for keeping records on tabulating equipment and maintain adequate control; analyze situations accurately and adopt an effective course of action; dictate correspondence.

ACCOUNTING-TABULATING MACHINE SUPERVISOR I

Definition:

Under direction, to supervise the operation of a complete tabulating machine installation maintaining a system of records of moderate complexity; or to do equivalent level supervisory or procedural work in a larger machine installation; and to do other work as required.

Typical Tasks:

Directs and reviews work, gives instructions, maintains discipline, passes upon problems in supervising a group of employees operating various types of machines in a tabulating machine installation and performing related clerical work in maintaining records on machine equipment; coordinates machine operations; trains staff, evaluates their performance, and takes or recommends appropriate action; devises methods of coding, punching, or tabulating new or unusual data; assists in the development of complex machine procedures; supervises the preparation of reports; dictates correspondence and memoranda; keeps records.

Minimum Qualifications:

Either I

Experience: One year as a Senior Tabulating Machine Operator.

Or II

Experience: Three years of experience in the operation of tabulating equipment, at least one year of which shall have been in a supervisory capacity. (College training may be substituted for the non-supervisory experience on the basis of one year of education being equivalent to six months of experience.)

Education: Equivalent to completion of the twelfth grade. (Additional qualifying experience may be substituted for the required education on a year-for-year basis.)

and

Knowledges and abilities:

Wide knowledge of: the various kinds of tabulating equipment, of the operating principles and methods of the various kinds of machines and of the work possibilities of each.

Working knowledge of: accounting principles and practices.

Familiarity with: the average production rate of machine operators; the different types of office machines; the principles of supervision, and ability to plan, organize, and direct the work of others.

Skill in working out methods of coding, punching, and tabulating new or unusual data and in making complex tabulations.

Ability to develop forms and procedures for keeping records on tabulating equipment and to maintain adequate control; to analyze situations accurately, and to adopt an effective course of action.

TABULATING MACHINE OPERATOR

Definition:

A Tabulating Machine Operator operates and adjusts sorters, reproducers, collators, tabulators, interpreters, and multipliers; makes standard wiring and other adjustments to tabulating and sorting equipment to permit varied kinds of tabulations and sorts; lifts and moves full trays of tabulating cards; assists with the filing of cards and related data; makes reconciliations, reports, and statements; manually summarizes the tabulated data; may direct the work of other operators and clerks.

Minimum Qualifications:

Experience: Six months of experience in the operation of at least two of the following machines: tabulator, reproducer, collator, multiplier, or sorter.

and

Education: Equivalent to completion of the twelfth grade. (Additional tabulating or clerical experience may be substituted for the required education on a year-for-year basis.)

KEYPUNCH OPERATOR

Definition:

A Keypunch Operator punches information on tabulating cards from accounting or statistical documents or from coded work sheets; verifies punched cards for accuracy; assists in the coding of documents; performs simple sorting or tabulating operations; files and checks tabulated cards; performs related clerical tasks as required.

Minimum Qualifications:

Experience: Six months' experience operating keypunch machines. Ability to punch from average copy at the rate of not less than 7,000 columns an hour with errors in not more than 5 per cent of the cards punched.

and

Education: Education equivalent to completion of the twelfth grade. (Additional full-time clerical experience, including keypunch experience, may be substituted for the required education on a year-for-year basis.)

Appendix II

EXAMPLE OF MARK SECTION OF A PROCEDURAL HANDBOOK

A. *General Information*

The dual purpose class and mark card you have received has appropriately marked bubbles for each quarter's class marks and also citizenship marks for the junior high schools. It should be noted that each mark card covers the entire school year. The mark cards are the basis for report cards, permanent record labels, mark analysis, mark points, and mark point averages. The cards will contain punched and printed information as follows:

1. Student name
2. Alpha number
3. Sex
4. Grade
5. Period
6. Course number
7. Room number
8. Subject
9. Teacher name

B. *Procedures for Schools and Teachers in Mark Reporting*

1. The Data Processing Department will furnish a mark card each marking period for each student in each class.

2. Each school will receive these, arranged alphabetically by course and by teacher, and must deliver them to the teachers. It is important to note that the loss of cards creates a serious problem and that cards must not be bent or damaged.

3. Notify the Data Processing Department immediately of any extra or missing cards so that files can be checked.

4. The teachers will carefully mark-sense the scholarship and citizenship marks in the junior high schools and only the scholarship marks in the senior high schools. Marks are marked in the appropriate quarter or semester section of the card.

5. Electrographic pencils must be used. All marks should be checked back against the roll book for possible error and to determine that there is a card properly mark-sensed for every student in the class.

The most common types of errors are:

a. Incorrect mark mark-sensed
b. Wrong marking period used

c. Card missed
d. Card not furnished
e. Incorrect mark not completely erased

6. When the entire staff has completed the mark cards, the school should box and forward them to the Data Processing Department. There is no need to keep them in order as they will be sorted to student number. They will be counted upon arrival to insure that all have been returned.

C. *Data Processing Department Procedures for Mark Reporting*

1. From the teacher mark-sensed mark cards, there will be made a machine-written mark report. It will be in duplicate and will show the following:

a. Parents' name and address (for mailing)
b. Student's name
c. Period ending
d. Grade
e. Sex
f. School
g. Period
h. Subject
i. Room Number
j. Teacher
k. Scholarship
l. Citizenship

2. Mark reports will be run alphabetically by grade level. The duplicate is a mailable card which will be stripped, folded, stapled, and mailed for high school students. The junior high school mark reports are not to be mailed but returned to schools. Original copies of mark reports are sent to the counseling office of each school.

3. The mark cards will then be sorted and all incomplete marks pulled out. A listing will be made and sent to the respective schools. When the incompletes have been cleared, the marks should be posted on the list and returned to the Data Processing Department for processing. It is suggested that a minimum date be established for making up incomplete marks, as this will hold up printing of transcript information.

4. A mark analysis is then run according to instructor, listing each class and the total number of marks issued in each category.

D. *New Permanent Records*

For all new 10th grade students, the Data Processing Department will originate a new high school permanent record. This will be done at the beginning of each school year. From then on, the junior and senior high schools will prepare by hand, permanent records for all new students that enter school.

E. *Permanent Record Labels*

1. Shortly after the close of each semester, each school will be furnished a permanent record gummed label of marks earned for each student. These labels can be lifted by hand from a gummed roll and fitted in the proper section of the permanent record. Care should be taken with this procedure, as once these labels have been placed on the permanent record, they are very difficult to remove. The permanent record label will have the student's name printed at the top for identification, and when the label is peeled off the gummed roll, it separates itself from that portion of the label which has the student's name printed.

2. The permanent record label will be printed with subject, mark, units, and mark point average. Blank permanent record labels may be obtained from the Data Processing office; it is each school's responsibility to type labels for new students who transfer into the district.

3. Permanent record labels will be run in the order and number requested by schools.

Appendix III

TENTATIVE PROPOSAL FOR CONTENT OF MASTER FILES

FOR USE IN A REGIONAL CENTER PROCESSING PUPIL PERSONNEL DATA

* * * *

MASTER FILE AND CODING SYSTEMS COMMITTEE

RESEARCH AND DEVELOPMENT CENTER

BUREAU OF PUPIL PERSONNEL SERVICES

STATE DEPARTMENT OF EDUCATION

SACRAMENTO 14, CALIFORNIA

* * * *

JANUARY 27, 1964

I - STUDENT MASTER FILE DATA

1.
STUDENT IDENTIFICATION NUMBER - FIRST CHARACTER ALPHABETIC - IDENTIFICATION OF REGIONAL CENTER ISSUING NUMBER, NINE NUMERIC CHARACTERS - SERIAL NUMBER ISSUED AS STUDENT ENTERS SYSTEM FOR THE FIRST TIME. (NO O OR I IN REGION)

```
A123456789
XXXXXXXXXX
        10
```

2.
STUDENT'S FULL LEGAL NAME - LAST, FIRST, AND MIDDLE

```
SMITH, CAROLYN VIRGINIA
XXXXXXXXXXXXXXXXXXXXXXXXXXXXXX
                            30
```

3.
STUDENT'S RESIDENCE ADDRESS

```
2815 HUNTINGTON RD,SACRAMENTO 25,
XXXXXXXXXXXXXXXXXXXXXXXXXXXXXXXXXXXXXXXXXXXXXXXXXX
                                                50
```

4.
AREA CODE AND TELEPHONE NUMBER

```
916IV73202
XXXXXXXXXX
        10
```

5.
SEX

```
F
X
1
```

6.
BIRTHDATE - MONTH, DAY, AND YEAR

```
30245
XXXXX
    5
```

7.
BIRTHDATE VERIFIED

Y
X
1

8.
BIRTHPLACE

SACRAMENTO
XXXXXXXXXX
10

9.
GRADE LEVEL

2
X
1

10.
GRADE POINT AVERAGE - ONE WHOLE NUMBER AND TWO DECIMAL PLACES

327 = GRADE POINT AVERAGE 3.27
XXX
3

11.
RANK IN CLASS - FIRST FOUR DIGITS SHOW STANDING, SECOND FOUR SHOW CLASS SIZE

00230794
XXXXXXXX
4 4

12.
ABSENCE

012
XXX CUMULATIVE ABSENCE
3

01
XX CURRENT ABSENCE
2

13.
PSYCHOLOGIST RECORD AVAILABLE - YES OR NO

N
X
I

14.
SIGNIFICANT MEDICAL HISTORY REPORT AVAILABLE - YES OR NO

Y
X
I

15.
CHILD WELFARE AND ATTENDANCE REPORT AVAILABLE, YES OR NO

N
X
I

16.
SPEECH THERAPIST REPORT AVAILABLE - YES OR NO

N
X
I

17.
SOCIAL WORKER REPORT AVAILABLE, YES OR NO

Y
X
I

18.
MILITARY OR VETERAN STATUS

0
X
I

0 NO MILITARY STATUS
1 VETERAN
2 RESERVIST
3 DRAFT ELIGIBLE
4 4-F
5 DEFERRED

19.
RESIDENT STATUS

I
X
I

I LIVES WITHIN DISTRICT LEGAL BOUNDARIES
2 INTER-DISTRICT PERMIT, NON-PAYING STUDENT
3 INTER-DISTRICT PAYING STUDENT
4 OUT OF STATE PAYING STUDENT
5 FOREIGN STUDENT

20.
MARITAL STATUS

I
X
I

I SINGLE
2 MARRIED
3 DIVORCED
4 WIDOWED
5 LEGALLY SEPARATED

21.
PREVIOUS SCHOOL ATTENDED

39
XX COUNTY OR STATE - ALPHA SERIAL NUMBER
2

741
XXX DISTRICT - THREE DIGIT APPORTIONMENT CODE (999 IF OUT OF STATE)
3

321
XXX SCHOOL - THREE DIGIT APPORTIONMENT CODE (999 IF OUT OF STATE)
3

22.
PREVIOUS DISTRICT NAME

SAN JUAN UNIFIED
XXXXXXXXXXXXXXX
15

23.
PREVIOUS RESIDENCE

WALNUTCREE
XXXXXXXXXX
10

24.
ENTRY DATE INTO THIS SCHOOL DISTRICT - MONTH, DAY, AND YEAR

90561
XXXXX
5

25.
TYPE OF ENTRY

EI
XX USE CODES FROM APPENDIX IV
2

26.
DATE LEFT - MONTH, DAY, AND YEAR

00000
XXXXX
5

27.
REASON FOR LEAVING

*
X
I

* USE CODES FROM APPENDIX IV

28.
PARENT'S OR GUARDIAN'S TITLE - MR., MRS., MISS, HON., REV., DR., ADM., COL., GEN., ETC.

MR.
XXXX
4

29.
PARENT'S OR GUARDIAN'S NAME - LAST, FIRST, AND MIDDLE INITIAL

SMITH, WALKER L
XXXXXXXXXXXXXXXXXXXXXXXXXXXXXX
30

30.
PARENT'S OR GUARDIAN'S ADDRESS (IF DIFFERENT FROM STUDENT)

2815 HUNTINGTON RD, SACRAMENTO 25,
XXXXXXXXXXXXXXXXXXXXXXXXXXXXXXXXXXXXXXXXXXXXXXXXXX
50

31.
LEGAL GUARDIAN RELATIONSHIPS CODE

1
X
1

1 FATHER
2 MOTHER
3 RELATIVE AS GUARDIAN, NOT COURT APPOINTED
4 COURT APPOINTED LEGAL GUARDIAN
5 COURT WARD
6 FOSTER HOME

32.
FATHER'S OCCUPATION - DICTIONARY OF OCCUPATIONAL TITLES CODE

123456
XXXXXX
6

33.
MOTHER'S OCCUPATION - DICTIONARY OF OCCUPATIONAL TITLES CODE

654321
XXXXXX
6

34.
COUNSELOR NAME

JONES
XXXXXXXXXX
10

35.
STATE REQUIREMENTS TO BE COMPLETED - ALLOW ONE PRE-IDENTIFIED SPACE FOR EACH STATE REQUIRED COURSE. LEAVE BLANK UNTIL COURSE IS COMPLETED AND THEN ENTER MARK ATTAINED TO SHOW COMPLETION

BACBBXXXXXXX
12

(SAMPLE SHOWS FIVE COMPLETED COURSES AND SEVEN TO BE COMPLETED)

36.
TEST SCORES

STEP
XXXX TEST IDENTIFICATION
4

B
XX TEST FORM
2

01
XX TEST LEVEL
2

N622
XXXX MONTH, YEAR AND GRADE ADMINISTERED
4

S
X NORM. USED
1

NA
XX SUB-TEST IDENTIFICATION
2

7
X SUB-TEST STANINE
1

NOTE: TEN SUB-TESTS MAY BE ENTERED

37.
COURSES TAKEN AND MARKS ATTAINED

A12345
XXXXXX COURSE IDENTIFICATION
6

C
X MARK ATTAINED
1

6632
XXXX MONTH, YEAR, AND GRADE
4

MARK CODING SYSTEM

A B C D F W WITHDRAWAL
I INCOMPLETE
G WITHDRAWAL-FAILURE
N NO MARK
X AUDIT

CODES USED THROUGHOUT FOR MONTH

1 JANUARY
2 FEBRUARY
3 MARCH
4 APRIL
5 MAY
6 JUNE
7 JULY
8 AUGUST
9 SEPTEMBER
O OCTOBER (ALPHA O)
N NOVEMBER
D DECEMBER

Appendix IV

ENTRY, WITHDRAWAL, AND DROPOUT DEFINITION AND CODE[1]

ENTRY INFORMATION

Type of Original Entry

E1 *Original Entry for the United States*—A pupil who for the first time in the United States or its possessions enters either a public or non-public elementary or secondary school for the regular school term for which the report is made.

E2 *Original Entry Transferred from Another State or Possession*—An entering pupil who previously has entered either a public or non-public elementary or secondary school in another State or possession during the regular school term for which the report is made, and who has not previously entered a school in this State or possession during this regular school term.

Type of Re-entry

R1 *Re-entry from Within the Same School*—A pupil received from another room within the same elementary or secondary school. (This applies only where homeroom registers are kept and used in situations in which the pupil's name has been transferred from one homeroom register to another because of a transfer, promotion, or demotion within the same school.)

R2 *Re-entry from a Public School in the Same Local Administrative Unit*—A pupil received from a public school, located in the same local administrative unit, which he entered earlier in the current regular school term.

R3 *Re-entry from a Non-public School in the Same Local Administrative Unit*—A pupil received from a non-public school, located in the same local administrative unit, which he entered earlier in the current regular school term.

R4 *Re-entry from a Public School in the State, but Outside the*

1. Putnam, John F. and George G. Tankard, Jr. *Pupil Accounting for Local and State School Systems, Handbook V,* State Educational Records and Reports Series, U.S. Office of Education, Washington, D.C., 1964.

Local Administrative Unit—A pupil received from a public school, located in the same State or possession but outside the local administrative unit, which he entered earlier in the current regular school term.

R5 *Re-entry from a Non-public School in the State, but Outside the Local Administrative Unit*—A pupil received from a non-public school, located in the same State or possession but outside the local administrative unit, which he entered earlier in the current regular school term.

R6 *Re-entry from the Same Room in the Same School After Withdrawal or Discharge*—A pupil who returns to the same room in the same school after withdrawal or discharge from this room earlier in the current regular school term, and who has not entered any other school during the intervening period.

R7 *Re-entry from Another State or Country*—A pupil received directly from a school in another State, possession, or country who previously entered a school in this State or possession during the current regular school term.

WITHDRAWAL INFORMATION

Withdrawal information is information about pupils who withdraw from membership in a class, grade, or school by transferring, by completing school work, by dropping out, or because of death. Causes of withdrawal should be recorded for all pupils who withdraw, whether during the regular school term or between regular school terms.

Transfer

A pupil who leaves one class, grade, or school and moves to another class, grade, or school is referred to as a "transfer." Each pupil who transfers from one elementary or secondary class or school to another during a regular school term, or between the completion of one regular school term and the beginning of the next, is identified with a designation selected from items T1-T4.

Additional subcategories under existing headings may be developed as deemed appropriate for use in individual school systems. For example, it may be desirable to include subcategories under items T2, T3, and T4 for pupils sent or transferred by legal authority to residential correcttive institutions where they take part in instructional programs which can be applied toward the completion of elementary or secondary school programs.

Information about a pupil who transfers from an elementary school to a secondary school or from a junior high school to a senior high school is included under items T2 to T4. Information about a pupil completing high school is included under Completion of School Work.

A pupil who transfers from college, adult education, and elementary or secondary summer school may be identified as a transfer by the symbol "T" without further classification.

T1 *Transfer Within the Same School*—This applies where homeroom registers are kept. The pupil's name is transferred during the regular school term from one homeroom register to another because of a transfer, promotion, or demotion within the same school.

T2 *Transfer to a Public School or Other Instruction Under Public School Supervision in the Same Local Administrative Unit.*

T3 *Transfer to a Non-public School Located Within the Same Local Administrative Unit.*

T4 *Transfer to a School Outside the Local Administrative Unit.*

Completion of School Work

School work is considered completed when the pupil graduates from a high school (grade 12) or junior college, completes a terminal program, or otherwise fulfills the requirements for a prescribed program of studies. Mid-year or year-end transfer to a higher grade within the same school is not considered as completion of school work.

C1 *Graduated From High School or Junior College*—The pupil receives a diploma or degree as formal recognition for the successful completion of a high school or junior college program of instruction.

C2 *Completed Terminal Program*—The pupil receives a certificate as formal recognition for the successful completion of a junior college or adult education terminal program.

C3 *Completed Other School Work*—The pupil completes school in an approved manner other than that included under C1 and C2 above and receives a certificate of attendance or a certificate of completion, gains recognition for work as a high school post-graduate, is accepted for early admission to a college or university, or receives other recognition. A pupil receiving a high school equivalency diploma or a high school equivalency certificate is not considered as a withdrawal and therefore is not included under this item.

Dropout

A dropout is a pupil who leaves school, for any reason except death, before graduation or completion of a program of studies and without transferring to another school.

The term "dropout" is used most often to designate an elementary or secondary school pupil who has been in membership during the regular school term and who withdraws from membership before graduating from secondary school (grade 12) or before completing an equivalent program of studies. Such an individual is considered a dropout whether his dropping out occurs during or between regular school terms, whether his dropping out occurs before or after he has passed the compulsory school attendance age, and, where applicable, whether or not he has completed a minimum required amount of school work.

Reason for Dropping Out

The explanation as to why a pupil dropped out of school. *The one most significant reason* should be indicated for each pupil dropping out of school; additional reasons may be maintained if desired.

D1 *Physical Illness*—The pupil left school because of a physical illness.

D2 *Physical Disability*—The pupil was excused from school attendance because of a physical impairment or handicap of a permanent or semi-permanent nature.

D3 *Mental Illness*—The pupil was excused or required to leave school because of mental illness.

D4 *Mental Disability*—The pupil was excused from school attendance because of insufficient mental ability for successful participation in the educational program of the school system.

D5 *Behavioral Difficulty*—The pupil was required to withdraw from school because of behavioral difficulty.

D6 *Academic Difficulty*—The pupil left school or was required to leave because of academic difficulty.

D7 *Lack of Appropriate Curriculum*—The pupil left school because the curriculum was not appropriate for his needs.

D8 *Poor Pupil–Staff Relationships*—The pupil left school because of poor relationships with members of the school staff.

D9 *Poor Relationships with Fellow Pupils*—The pupil left school because of poor relationships with fellow pupils.

D10 *Dislike of School Experience*—The pupil left school because of an active dislike of one or more aspects of his school experiences other than those expressed in items D6 through D9. Any such area of dislike should be specified.

D11 *Parental Influence*—The pupil left school as a result of parental encouragement to do so.

D12 *Need at Home*—The pupil left school to help with work at home.

D13 *Economic Reasons*—The pupil left school because of economic reasons, including inability to pay school expenses and inability of parents to provide suitable clothing.

D14 *Employment*—The pupil left school to seek or accept employment, including employment required to support parents or other dependents.

D15 *Marriage*—The pupil left school because of marriage.

D16 *Pregnancy*—The pupil left school or was required to leave because of pregnancy.

D17 *Other Known Reasons*—The pupil left school or was required to leave for some known reason, other than those of items D1 to D16. Any such reason should be specified, e.g., no school available, excessive distance from home to school or to school bus route, etc.

D18 *Reason Unknown*—The pupil left school for a reason which is not known.

D19 *New Residence, School Status Unknown*—The pupil left school upon moving to a new residence; it is not known if he entered a new school.

Death of a Pupil

W1 *Death*—The pupil died.

GLOSSARY

Words have played an important role in our developing society, and they are of particular significance in the fields of education and data processing. This glossary is presented in an attempt to clarify and define the terms in current use in these two fields.

The authors felt that an extensive glossary was desirable to provide both the experienced worker and the novice with the verbal tools needed to comprehend the language used in these special areas.

The terms relating to education were drawn primarily from the glossary in the *Pupil Accounting Handbook for Local and State School Systems,*[1] and the automation terms were drawn primarily from the *Automatic Data Processing Glossary.*[2]

ADP—See *processing, automatic data.*

ALGOL—*ALGO*rithmic *L*anguage. See *language, algorithmic.*

ALU—*A*rithmetic and *L*ogical *U*nit. See *unit, arithmetic.*

Access, Immediate—Pertaining to the ability to obtain data from, or place data in, a storage device, or register directly without serial delay due to other units of data, and usually in a relatively short period of time.

Access, Random—(1) Pertaining to the process of obtaining information from, or placing information into, storage where the time required for such access is independent of the location of the information most recently obtained or placed in storage; (2) pertaining to a device in which random access, as defined in definition 1, can be achieved without effective penalty in time.

Accounting Machine—See *tabulator.*

Activities, Student Body—Non-course activities for pupils, such as entertainments, publications, and clubs, that are managed or operated by pupils under the guidance or supervision of staff members.

Address, Absolute—An address which indicates the exact storage location where the referenced operand is to be found or stored in the actual machine code address numbering system. Synonymous with "specific address" and related to *code, absolute.*

Address—(1) An identification, represented by a name, label, or number, for a register or location in storage. Addresses are also a part of an instruction word along with commands, tags, and other symbols. (2) The part of an instruction which specifies an operand for the instruction.

Administrative Unit, Local Basic—An administrative unit at the local level which exists primarily to operate public schools or to contract for public school services. Normally, taxes can be levied against such

1. John F. Putnam and George G. Taukaud, Jr. *Pupil Accounting for Local and State School Systems.* Washington, D.C.: U.S. Department of Health, Education, and Welfare, Office of Education (State Educational Records and Reports Series: Handbook V) 1964.

2. *Automatic Data Processing Glossary.* Washington, D.C.: Executive Office of the President, Bureau of the Budget, 1962.

Administrative Unit (*Cont'd.*)
units for school purposes. These units may or may not be coterminous with county, city, or town boundaries. This term is used synonymously with the term "school district."

Algebra, Boolean—A process of reasoning, or a deductive system of theorems using a symbolic logic, and dealing with classes, propositions, or on-off circuit elements. It employs symbols to represent operators such as AND, OR, NOT, EXCEPT, IF . . . THEN, etc., to permit mathematical calculation. Named after George Boole, famous English mathematician (1815–64).

Alphabetic-numeric—The characters which include letters of the alphabet. numerals, and other symbols such as punctuation or mathematical symbols.

Alphameric—A contraction of *alphanumeric* and alphabetic-numeric.

Alphanumeric—a contraction of alphabetic-numeric.

Analog—The representation of numerical quantities by means of physical variables; e.g., translation, rotation, voltage, or resistance. Contrasted with *digital.*

Analog computer—See *computer, analog.*

Analysis, Systems—The examination of an activity, procedure, method, technique, or a business to determine what must be accomplished and how the necessary operations may best be accomplished.

Analyst—A person skilled in the definition of and the development of techniques for the solving of a problem; especially those techniques for solving problems on a computer.

Application—The system or problem to which a computer is applied. Reference is often made to an application as being either of the computational type, wherein arithmetic computations predominate, or of the data processing type, wherein data handling operations predominate.

Arithmetic, Fixed Point—(1) A method of calculation in which operations take place in an invariant manner, and in which the computer does not consider the location of the radix point. This is illustrated by desk calculators or slide rules, with which the operator must keep track of the decimal point. Similarly with many automatic computers, in which the location of the radix point is the programmer's responsibility. Contrasted with *arithmetic, floating point.* (2) A type of arithmetic in which the operands and results of all arithmetic operations must be properly scaled so as to have a magnitude between certain fixed values.

Arithmetic, Floating Decimal—see *arithmetic, floating point.*

Arithmetic, Floating Point—A method of calculation which automatically accounts for the location of the radix point. This is usually accomplished by handling the number as a signed mantissa times the radix, raised to an integral exponent; e.g., the decimal number $+88.3$ might be written as $+.883 \times 10^2$; the binary number $-.0011$. as $-.11 \times 2^{-2}$. Synonymous with "floating decimal arithmetic" and contrasted with *arithmetic, fixed point* (1).

Arithmetic, Internal—The computations performed by the arithmetic unit of a computer.

Arithmetic Unit—See *unit, arithmetic.*

Array—A series of items arranged in a meaningful pattern.

Assemble—(1) To integrate subroutines that are supplied, selected, or generated into the main routine by means of preset parameters, by adapting, or changing relative and symbolic addresses to absolute form, or by placing them in storage; (2) to operate or perform the functions of an assembler.

Assembler—A computer program which operates on symbolic input data to produce from such data machine instructions by carrying out such functions as: translation of symbolic operation codes into computer operating instructions; assigning locations in storage for successive instructions; or computation of absolute addresses from symbolic addresses. An assembler generally translates input symbolic codes into machine instructions item for item, and produces as output the same number of instructions or constants which were defined in the input symbolic codes. Synonymous with *assembly routine; assembly program* and related to *compiler*.

Asynchronous—Pertaining to a lack of time coincidence in a set of repeated events. When this term is applied to a computer, it indicates that the execution of one operation is dependent on a signal that the previous operation is completed.

Attendance—Presence of a pupil on days when school is in session. Pupils participating in school-sponsored activities under the guidance and supervision of staff members, either at or away from school, are considered to be in attendance.

Attendance Register—A record containing (a) the names of pupils who have entered or are expected to enter a class or school, (b) identification information about each pupil such as sex, date of birth, and address, and (c) information concerning his entry or re-entry, membership, attendance, absence, tardiness, and withdrawal.

Audit, Trail—A system of providing a means for tracing items of data from processing step to step, particularly from a machine produced report or other machine output back to the original source data.

Auto-Abstract—(1) A collection of words selected from a document and arranged in a meaningful order, commonly by an automatic or machine method; (2) to select an assemblage of key words from a document, commonly by an automatic or machine method.

Automation—(1) The implementation of processes by automatic means; (2) the theory, art, or technique of making a process more automatic; (3) the investigation, design, development, and application of methods of rendering processes automatic, self-moving, or self-controlling.

Automation, Source Data—The many methods of recording information in coded forms on paper tapes, punched cards, or tags that can be used over and over again to produce many other records without rewriting. Synonymous with "SDA."

BIT—(1) An abbreviation of *bi*nary digi*t*. (2) A single character in a binary number.

Band—(1) the gamut or range of frequencies; (2) the frequency spectrum between two defined limits; (3) the frequencies which are within two definite limits and are used for a different purpose; (4) a group of channels. Same as channel (3).

Baud—(1) A unit of signalling speed equal to the number of code elements per second; (2) the unit of signaling speed equal to twice the number of Morse code dots continuously sent per second. Clarified by *rate, bit* and *capacity, channel.*

Binary—A characteristic, property, or condition in which there are but two possible alternatives; e.g., the binary number using 2 as its base and using only the digits zero (0) and one (1). Related to *decimal, binary coded* and clarified by *systems, number.*

Bionics—The application of knowledge gained from the analysis of living systems to the creation of hardware that will perform functions in a manner analogous to the more sophisticated functions of the living system.

Bit, Check—A binary check digit; often a parity bit. Related to *check, parity* and *number, self-checking.*

Bit, Zone—(1) One of the two leftmost bits in a commonly used system in which six bits are used for each character. Related to *overpunch.* (2) Any bit in a group of bit positions that are used to indicate a specific class of items; e.g., numbers, letters, special signs, and commands.

Block—(1) A group of computer words considered as a unit by virtue of their being stored in successive storage locations. (2) The set of locations or tape positions in which a block of words, as defined above, is stored or recorded. (2) A circuit assemblage which functions as a unit; e.g., a circuit building block of standard design, and the logic block in a sequential circuit.

Bootstrap—A technique for loading the first few instructions of a routine into storage; then using these instructions to bring in the rest of the routine. This usually involves either the entering of a few instructions manually or the use of a special key on the console.

Branch—The selection of one or two or more possible paths in the flow of

Branch (Cont'd.)
control based on some criterion. The instructions which mechanize this concept are sometimes called "branch instructions"; however the terms "transfer of control" and "jump" are more widely used. Related to *transfer, conditional.*

Brush—An electrical conductor for reading data from a punch card.

Buffer—(1) An internal portion of a data processing system serving as intermediary storage between two storage or data handling systems with different access times or formats; usually to connect an input or output device with the main or internal high-speed storage. Clarified by *storage, buffer* (4). (2) A logical OR circuit. (3) An isolating component designed to eliminate the reaction of a driven circuit on the circuits driving it; e.g., a buffer amplifier. (4) A diode.

Bug—A mistake in the design of a routine or a computer, or a malfunction.

Calculator—(1) A device that performs primarily arithmetic operations based upon data and instructions inserted manually or contained on punch cards. It is sometimes used interchangeably with *computer.* (2) A computer.

Capacity, Channel—(1) The maximum number of binary digits or elementary digits to other bases which can be handled in a particular channel per unit time. (2) The maximum possible information transmission rate through a channel at a specified error rate. The channel capacity may be measured in bits per second or bauds. Clarified by *rate, bit* and *baud.*

Capacity, Memory—See *capacity, storage.*

Capacity, Storage—The number of elementary pieces of data that can be contained in a storage device. Frequently defined in terms of characters in a particular code or words of a fixed size that can be so contained. Synonymous with *memory capacity* and related to *BIT (4).*

Card, Control—A card which contains input data or parameters for a specific application of a general routine.

Card, Edge Notched—A card of any size provided with a series of holes on one or more edges for use in coding information for a simple mechanical search technique. Each hole position may be coded to represent an item of information by notching away the edge of the card into the hole. Cards containing desired information may then be mechanically selected from a deck by inserting a long needle in a hole position and lifting the deck to allow the notched cards to fall from the needle. Unwanted cards remain in the deck.

Card, Edge Punched—A card of fixed size into which information may be recorded or stored by punching holes along one edge in a pattern similar to that used for punch tape. Hole positions are arranged to form coded patterns in 5, 6, 7, or 8 channels and usually represent data by a binary coded decimal system.

Card, Eighty (80) Column—A punch card with 80 vertical columns representing 80 characters. Each column is divided into two sections, one with character positions labeled zero through nine, and the other labeled eleven (11) and twelve (12). The 11 and 12 positions are also referred to as the X and Y zone punches, respectively. Related to *card, punch* and *card, ninety (90) column.*

Card, Master—A card containing fixed or indicative information for a group of cards. It is usually the first card of that group.

Card, Ninety (90) Column—A punch card with 90 vertical columns representing 90 characters. The columns are divided in half horizontally, such that the vertical columns in the upper half of the card are numbered 1 through 45, and those in the lower half 46 through 90. Six punching positions may be used in each column; these are designated, from top to bottom, to represent the digits 0, 1, 3, 5, 7, and 9 by a single punch. The digits 2, 4, 6, and 8 and other characters may be represented by a combination of two or more punches. Related to *card, punch* and *card, eighty (80) column.*

Card, Programmed—(1) capability of being programmed by punch cards; (2) the capability of performing sequences of calculating operations according to instructions contained in a stack of punch cards.

Card, Punch—A heavy stiff paper of constant size and shape, suitable for punching in a pattern that has meaning, and for being handled mechanically. The punched holes are sensed electrically by wire brushes, mechanically by metal fingers, or photoelectrically by photocells. Related to *card, eighty (80) column* and *card, ninety (90) column.*

Cell—(1) The storage for one unit of information, usually one character or one word. (2) A location specified by whole or part of the address and possessed of the faculty of storage. Specific terms such as column, field, location, and block, are preferable when appropriate.

Cell, Binary—(1) A cell of one binary digit capacity; (2) a one bit register or bit position.

Center, Data Processing—A computer installation providing data processing service for others, sometimes called customers, on a reimbursable or non-reimbursable basis.

Central Processing Unit—See *frame, main (1).*

Chain—(1) Any series of items linked together; (2) pertaining to a routine consisting of segments which are run through the computer in tandem, only one being within the computer at any one time and each using the output from the previous program as its input.

Channel—(1) A path along which information, particularly a series of digits or characters, may flow. (2) One or more parallel tracks treated as a unit. (3) In a circulating storage, a channel is one recirculating path containing a fixed number of words stored serially by word. Synonymous with *band.* (4) A path for electrical communication. (5) A band of frequencies used for communication.

Character—(1) One symbol of a set of elementary symbols such as those corresponding to the keys on a typewriter. The symbols usually include the decimal digits 0 through 9, the letters A through Z, punctuation marks, operation symbols, and any other single symbols which a computer may read, store, or write. (2) The electrical, magnetic, or mechanical profile used to represent a character in a computer, and its various storage and peripheral devices. A character may be represented by a group of other elementary marks, such as bits or pulses.

Character, Binary Coded—One element of a notation system representing alphameric characters such as decimal digits, alphabetic letters, and punctuation marks by a predetermined configuration of consecutive binary digits.

Character, Illegal—A character or combination of bits which is not accepted as a valid representation by the machine design or by a specific routine. Illegal characters are commonly detected and used as an indication of machine malfunction.

Chart, Flow—A graphic representation of the major steps of work in process. The illustrative symbols may represent documents, machines, or actions taken during the process. The area of concentration is on where or who does what rather than how it is to be done. Synonymous with *process chart* and *flow diagram.*

Chart, Logical Flow—A detailed solution of the work order in terms of the logic, or built-in operations and characteristics, of a specific machine. Concise symbolic notation is used to represent the information and describe the input, output, arithmetic, and logical operations involved. The chart indicates types of operations by use of a standard set of block symbols. A coding process normally follows the logical flow chart.

Chart, Process—See *chart, flow.*

Check—A process of partial or complete testing of the correctness of machine operations, the existence of certain prescribed conditions within the computer, or the correctness of the results produced by a program. A check of any of these conditions may be made automatically by the equipment or may be programmed. Related to *check, marginal.*

Check, Automatic—A provision constructed in hardware for verifying the accuracy of information transmitted, manipulated, or stored by any unit or device in a computer.

Check, Automatic (Cont'd.) Synonymous with *built in check; built-in automatic check, hardware check*; and related to *check, program (2).*

Check, Built-in—See *check, automatic.*

Check, Built-in Automatic—See *check, automatic.*

Check, Hardware—Same as *check, automatic.*

Check, Marginal—A preventive maintenance procedure in which certain operating conditions are varied about their normal values in order to detect and locate incipient defective units; e.g., supply voltage or frequency may be varied. Synonymous with *test, marginal,* and *high-low bias test,* and related to *check.*

Check, Parity—A summation check in which the binary digits, in a character or word, are added, modulo 2, and the sum checked against a single, previously computed parity digit; i.e., a check which tests whether the number of ones in a word is odd or even. Synonymous with *odd-even check* and related to *check, redundant* and to *check, forbidden combination.*

Check, Program—(1) A system of determining the correct program and machine functioning either by running a sample problem with similar programming and a known answer, or by using mathematical or logic checks such as comparing A times B with B times A. (2) A check system built into the program of computers that do not have automatic checking. This check system is normally concerned with programs run on computers which are not self-checking internally. Synonymous with *routine check* and related to *check, automatic.*

Check, Routine—See *check, program.*

Circuit—(1) A system of conductors and related electrical elements through which electrical current flows; (2) a communications link between two or more points.

Class—A group of pupils assembled for instruction for a given period of time under one or more teachers in a situation where the teacher(s) and the pupils are in the presence of each other.

Class Period—The portion of the school day set aside for a designated teaching activity.

Clear—To erase the contents of a storage device by replacing the contents with blanks, or zeros. Contrasted with *hold* and clarified by *erase.*

Clock—(1) A master timing device used to provide the basic sequencing pulses for the operation of a synchronous computer; (2) a register which automatically records the progress of real time, or perhaps some approximation to it, records the number of operations performed, and whose contents are available to a computer program.

Clock, Real Time—A clock which indicates the passage of actual time, in contrast to a fictitious time set up by the computer program; such as, elapsed time in the flight of a missile, wherein a 60-second trajectory is computed in 200 actual milliseconds, or a 0.1 second interval is integrated in 100 actual microseconds.

COBOL—*Co*mmon *B*usiness *O*riented *L*anguage. See *language, common business oriented.*

Code—A system of numbers or other symbolic designations used for identifying previously defined items and categories of information.

Code—(1) A system of symbols for meaningful communication. Related to *instruction (1).* (2) A system of symbols for representing data or instructions in a computer or a tabulating machine. (3) To translate the program for the solution of a problem on a given computer into a sequence of machine language or pseudo-instructions and addresses acceptable to that computer. Related to *encode.* (4) A machine language program.

Code, Absolute—A code using absolute addresses and absolute operation codes; i.e., a code which indicates the exact location where the referenced operand is to be found or stored. Synonymous with *one level code* and *specific code* and related to *address, absolute.*

Code, Alphabetic—A system of alphabetic abbreviations used in preparing information for input into a machine; e.g., Boston, New York, Philadelphia, and Washington may in alphabetical coding be reported as BS, NY, PH, WA. Contrasted with *code, numeric.*

Code, Automatic—A code which allows a machine to translate or convert a symbolic language into a machine language for automatic machine or computer operations.

Code, Binary—(1) A coding system in which the encoding of any data is done through the use of bits; i.e., 0 or 1. (2) A code for the ten decimal digits, 0, 1, . . . 9 in which each is represented by its binary, radix 2, equivalent; i.e., straight binary.

Code, Chinese Binary—See *code, column-binary.*

Code, Column-Binary—A code used with punch cards in which successive bits are represented by the presence or absence of punches on contiguous positions in successive columns as opposed to rows. Column-binary code is widely used in connection with 36-bit word computers where each group of 3 columns is used to represent a single word. Synonymous with *Chinese binary code.*

Code, Computer—(1) A system of combinations of binary digits used by a given computer. Synonymous with *machine code.* (2) A repertoire of instructions.

Code, Machine—See *code, computer.*

Code, Machine language—Same as *code, computer* (1) and contrasted with *code, symbolic.*

Code, Numeric—A system of numerical abbreviations used in the preparation of information for input into a machine; i.e., all information is reduced to numerical quantities. Contrasted with *code, alphabetic.*

Code, One Level—See *code, absolute.*

Code, Pseudo—See *code, symbolic.*

Code, Specific—See *code, absolute.*

Code, Symbolic—A code which expresses programs in source language; i.e., by referring to storage locations and machine operations by symbolic names and addresses which are independent of their hardware determined names and addresses. Synonymous with *pseudo-code* and contrasted with *code, machine language.*

Coder—A person who prepares instruction sequences from detailed flow charts and other algorithmic procedures prepared by others. as contrasted with a programmer who prepares the procedures and flow charts.

Coding—The ordered list, in computer code or pseudo-code, of the successive computer instructions representing successive computer operations for solving a specific problem.

Collate—To merge two or more ordered sets of data or ordered cards to produce one or more ordered sets which still reflect the original ordering relations. The collation process is the merging of two sequences of cards, each ordered on some mutual key, into a single sequence ordered on the mutual key.

Collator—A device used to collate or merge sets or decks of cards or other units into a sequence. A typical example of a card collator has two input feeds (so that two ordered sets may enter into the process) and four output stackers (so that four ordered sets can be generated by the process). Three comparison stations are used to route the cards to one stacker or the other on the basis of comparison of criteria as specified by plugboard wiring.

Column—(1) A character or digit position in a positional information format, particularly one in which characters appear in rows and the rows are placed one above another; e.g., the rightmost column in a five-decimal place table, or in a list of data. (2) A character or digit position in a physical device, such as punch card or a register, corresponding to a position in a written table or list; e.g., the rightmost place in a register, or the third column in an eighty column punch card.

Column-Binary—See *code, column-binary.*

Command—(1) An electronic pulse, signal, or set of signals to start, stop or continue some operation. It is incorrect to use command as a synonym for instruction. (2) The portion of an instruction word which specifies the operation to be performed.

Compare—To examine the representation of a quantity to discover its relationship to zero, or to examine two quantities usually for the purposes of discovering identity or relative magnitude.

Compile—To produce a machine language routine from a routine written in source language by selecting appropriate subroutines from a subroutine library, as directed by the instructions or other symbols of the original routine; supplying the linkage which combines the subroutines into a workable routine; and translating the subroutines and linkage into machine language. The compiled routine is then ready to be loaded into storage and run; i.e., the compiler does not usually run the routine it produces.

Compiler—A computer program more powerful than an assembler. In addition to its translating function which is generally the same process as that used in an assembler, it is able to replace certain items of input with series of instructions, usually called subroutines. Thus, where an assembler translates item for item, and produces as output the same number of instructions or constants which were put into it, a compiler will do more than this. The program which results from compiling is a translated and expanded version of the original. Synonymous with *compiling routine* and related to *assembler*.

Computer—A device capable of accepting information, applying prescribed processes to the information, and supplying the results of these processes. It usually consists of input and output devices, storage, arithmetic, and logical units, and a control unit.

Computer, Analog—A computer which represents variables by physical analogies. Thus any computer which solves problems by translating physical conditions such as flow, temperature, pressure, angular position, or voltage into related mechanical or electrical quantities and uses mechanical or electrical equivalent circuits as an analog for the physical phenomenon being investigated. In general, it is a computer which uses an analog for each variable and produces analogs as output. Thus, an analog computer measures continuously whereas a digital computer counts discretely. Related to *machine, data processing*.

Computer, Asynchronous—A computer in which the performance of each operation starts as a result of a signal either that the previous operation has been completed or that the parts of the computer required for the next operation are now available. Contrasted with *computer, synchronous*.

Computer, Buffered—A computing system with a storage device which permits input and output data to be stored temporarily in order to match the slow speed of input-output devices with the higher speeds of the computer. Thus, simultaneous input-output-computer operations are possible. A data transmission trap is essential for effective use of buffering since it obviates frequent testing for the availability of a data channel.

Computer. Digital—A computer which processes information represented by combinations of discrete or discontinuous data as compared with an analog computer for continuous data. More specifically, it is a device for performing sequences of arithmetic and logical operations, not only on data but its own program. Still more specifically it is a stored program digital computer capable of performing sequences of internally stored instructions, as opposed to calculators, such as card programmed calculators, on which the sequence is impressed manually. Related to *machine, data processing*.

Computer, Fixed Program—A computer in which the sequence of instructions is permanently stored or wired in, performs automatically, and are not subject to change either by the computer or the programmer except by rewiring or changing the storage input. Related to *computer, wired program*.

Computer, General Purpose—A computer designed to solve a large variety of problems; e.g., a stored program computer which may be adapted to any of a very large class of applications.

Computer, Parallel—A computer in which the digits or data lines are handled concurrently by separate units of the computer. The units may be interconnected in different ways as determined by the computation to operate in parallel or serially. Mixed serial and parallel machines are frequently called "serial" or "parallel" according to the way arithmetic processes are performed. An example of a parallel computer is one which handles the bits which comprise a digit either serially or in parallel. Contrasted with *computer, serial.*

Computer, Serial—A computer in which digits or data lines are handled sequentially by separate units of the computer. Mixed serial and parallel machines are frequently called "serial" or "parallel" according to the way arithmetic processes are performed. An example of a serial computer is one which handles decimal digits serially although it might handle the bits which comprise a digit either serially or in parallel. Contrasted with *computer, parallel.*

Computer, Solid State—A computer built primarily from solid state electronic circuit elements.

Computer, Special Purpose—A computer designed to solve a specific class or narrow range of problems.

Computer, Stored Program—A computer capable of performing sequences of internally stored instructions and usually capable of modifying those instructions as directed by the instructions.

Computer, Synchronous—A computer in which all operations and events are controlled by equally spaced pulses from a clock. Contrasted with *computer, asynchronous* and clarified by *frequency, clock.*

Computer, Wired Program—A computer in which the instructions that specify the operations to be performed are themselves specified by the placement and interconnection of wires. The wires are usually held by a removable control panel, allowing flexibility of operation, but the term is also applied to permanently wired machines which are then called fixed program computers. Related to *computer, fixed program.*

Configuration—A group of machines which are interconnected and are programmed to operate as a system.

Console—A portion of the computer which may be used to control the machine manually; correct errors; determine the status of machine circuits, registers, and counters; determine the contents of storage; and manually revise the contents of storage.

Control—(1) The part of a digital computer or processor which determines the execution and interpretation of instructions in proper sequence, including the decoding of each instruction and the application of the proper signals to the arithmetic unit and other registers in accordance with the decoded information. (2) Frequently, it is one or more of the components in any mechanism responsible for interpreting and carrying out manually-initiated directions. Sometimes it is called manual control. (3) In some business applications, a mathematical check. (4) In programming, instructions which determine conditional jumps are often referred to as control instructions, and the time sequence of execution of instructions is called the flow of control.

Control, Program—Descriptive of a system in which a computer is used to direct an operation or process and automatically to hold or to make changes in the operation or process on the basis of a prescribed sequence of events.

Conversion—(1) The process of changing information from one form of representation to another; such as, from the language of one type of machine to that of another or from magnetic tape to the printed page. Synonymous with *data conversion.* (2) The process of changing from one data processing method to another, or from one type of equipment to another; e.g., conversion from punch card equipment to magnetic tape equipment.

Conversion, Binary to Decimal—The process of converting a number written to the base of two to the equivalent number written to the base of ten.

Conversion, Data—See *conversion.*

Conversion, Decimal to Binary—The process of converting a number written to the base of ten, or as a decimal, into the equivalent number written to the base of two, or as a binary.

Convert—(1) To change numerical information from one number base to another. (2) To transfer information from one recorded medium to another.

Converter—A device which converts the representation of information, or which permits the changing of the method for data processing, from one form to another; e.g., a unit which accepts information from punch cards and records the information on magnetic tape, possibly including editing facilities.

Copy, Hard—A printed copy of machine output; e.g., printed reports, listings, documents, and summaries.

Counter—A device, register, or location in storage for storing numbers or number representations in a manner which permits these numbers to be increased or decreased by the value of another number, or to be changed or reset to zero or to an arbitrary value.

Course—An organization of subject matter and activities provided for the instruction of pupils on a regular or systematic basis, usually for a predetermined period of time (e.g., a semester, a regular school term, and a two-week workshop). Credit toward graduation or completion of an instructional program generally is given pupils for the successful completion of a course.

Course, Credit—A course for which a pupil receives credit applicable toward graduation or completion of an instructional program.

CPU—*C*entral *P*rocessing *U*nit. See *frame, main (1).*

Credit—The unit of value awarded for the successful completion of certain courses, intended to indicate the quantity of course instruction in relation to the total requirements for a diploma, certificate, or degree. Credits frequently are expressed in terms such as "Carnegie units," "credits," "semester credit hours," and "quarter credit hours."

Cryogenics—The field of technology which uses devices utilizing properties assumed by metals at absolute zero. At these temperatures large current changes can be obtained by relatively small magnetic field changes.

Cybernetics—The field of technology involved in the comparative study of the control and intracommunication of information-handling machines and the nervous systems of animals and man in order to understand and improve communication.

Cycle—(1) See *loop* (*1*). (2) A nonarithmetic shift in which digits dropped off at one end of a word are returned at the other end in circular fashion; e.g., cycle left and cycle right. (3) To repeat a set of operations, indefinitely or until a stated condition is met. The set of operations may be subject to variation on each repetition, as by address changes obtained by programmed computation or by use of devices such as an index register. (4) An occurrence, phenomenon, or interval of space or time that recurs regularly and in the same sequence; e.g., the interval required for completion of one operation in a repetitive sequence of operations.

Data—A general term used to denote any or all facts, numbers, letters and symbols, or facts that refer to or describe an object, idea, condition, situation, or other factors. It connotes basic elements of information which can be processed or produced by a computer. Sometimes data is considered to be expressible only in numerical form, but information is not so limited. Related to *information.*

Data Master—A set of data which is altered infrequently and supplies basic data for processing operations. The data content of a master file. Examples include: names, badge numbers, or pay rates in personnel data; or stock numbers, stock descriptions, or units of measure in stock control data.

Data, Raw—Data which has not been processed. Such data may or may not be in machine-sensible form.

Data-Reduction—The process of transforming masses of raw test or experimentally obtained data, usually gathered by automatic recording equipment, into useful, condensed, or simplified intelligence.

Data, Test—A set of data developed specifically to test the adequacy of a computer run or system. The data may be actual data that has been taken from previous operations, or artificial data created for this purpose.

Datamation—*Data* and auto*mation*. A shortened term for automatic data processing.

Date, Delivery—The date of physical delivery on-site of the components of the computer configuration without regard to whether or not they have been unpacked, placed in final position, or interconnected. Delivery of equipment carries no connotation of operational status.

Date, Installation—The date new equipment is ready for use. The commencement of rental normally begins on the day following the date on which the contractor officially notifies the using organization that the equipment is installed and ready for use, subject to the acceptance and standard of performance provisions of the applicable contract.

Debug—(1) To locate and correct any errors in a computer program. (2) To detect and correct malfunctions in the computer itself. Related to *routine, diagnostic*.

Deck—A collection of cards, commonly a complete set of cards which have been punched for a definite service or purpose.

Decimal, Binary Coded—Describing a decimal notation in which the individual decimal digits are represented by a pattern of ones and zeros; e.g., in the 8-4-2-1 coded decimal notation, the number twelve is represented as 0001—0010 for 1 and 2, respectively, whereas in pure or straight binary notation it is represented as 1100. Related to *binary*.

Decimal, Coded—Describing a form of notation by which each decimal digit separately is expressed in some other number system; e.g., in the 8-4-2-1 coded decimal notation, the number twelve is represented as 0001 0010, for 1 and 2; whereas in pure or straight binary notation it is represented as 1100. Other coded decimal notations used are the 5-4-2-1, the excess three, and the 2-3-2-1 codes.

Decision—The computer operations of determining if a certain relationship exists between words in storage or registers, and taking alternative courses of action. This is effected by conditional jumps or equivalent techniques. Use of this term has given rise to the misnomer "magic brain"; actually the process consists of making comparisons by use of arithmetic to determine the relationship of two terms, whether numeric, alphabetic, or a combination of both; e.g., equal, greater than, or less than.

Decision, Logical—The choice or ability to choose between alternatives. Basically this amounts to an ability to answer "yes" or "no" with respect to certain fundamental questions involving equality and relative magnitude; e.g., in an inventory application, it is necessary to determine whether or not there has been an issue of a given stock item.

Decode—(1) To apply a code so as to reverse some previous encoding; (2) to determine the meaning of individual characters or groups of characters in a message; (3) to determine the meaning of an instruction from the set of pulses which describes the instruction, command, or operation to be performed.

Decoder—(1) A device which determines the meaning of a set of signals and initiates a matrix of switching elements which selects one or more output channels according to the combination of input signals present. Contrasted with *encoder* and clarified by *matrix*.

Definition—(1) The resolution and sharpness of an image, or the extent to which an image is brought into sharp relief; (2) the degree with which a communication system reproduces sound images or messages.

Definition, Problem—The art of compiling logic in the form of general flow charts and logic diagrams which clearly explain and present the problem to the programmer in such a way that all requirements involved in the run are presented.

Delay—(1) The length of time after the close of a reporting period before information pertaining to that period becomes available. Delay may also cover the time to process data and prepare and distribute reports. (2) The retardation of the flow of in-

Delay (*Cont'd.*)
formation in a channel for a finite period of time.

Density, Character—The number of characters that can be stored per unit of length; e.g., on some makes of magnetic tape drives, 200 or 556 bits can be stored serially, linearly, and axially to the inch.

Design, Logical—(1) The planning of a data processing system prior to its detailed engineering design. (2) The synthesizing of a network of logical elements to perform a specified function. (3) The result of (1) and (2), frequently called the logic of a computer or of a data processing system.

Device, Film Optical Sensing—A piece of equipment capable of reading the contents of a film by optical methods; i.e., a system consisting of a light source, lenses, photo-cells and a film moving mechanism. The output of the device is digitized and transferred directly to an electronic computer. An example of such a device is the FOSDIC system developed jointly by the Bureau of Census and the National Bureau of Standards.

Device, Input—The mechanical unit designed to bring data to be processed into a computer; e.g., a card reader, a tape reader, or a keyboard.

Device, Output—The part of a machine which translates the electrical impulses representing data processed by the machine into permanent results such as printed forms, punched cards, and magnetic writing on tape.

Diagram—(1) A schematic representation of a sequence of subroutines designed to solve a problem. (2) A coarser and less symbolic representation than a flow chart, frequently including descriptions in English words. (3) A schematic or logical drawing showing the electrical circuit or logical arrangements within a component.

Diagram, Block—(1) A graphical representation of the hardware in a computer system. The primary purpose of a block diagram is to indicate the paths along which information and/or control flows between the various parts of a computer system. It should not be confused with the term "flow chart." (2) A coarser and less symbolic representation than a flow chart.

Diagram, Flow—See *chart, flow*

Diagram, Logical—A diagram which represents the logical elements of a system and their interconnections without necessarily expressing construction, engineering, or electrical schematic circuit details.

Dictionary—A list of code names used in a routine or system and their intended meaning in that routine or system.

Dictionary, Automatic—The component of a language translating machine which will provide a word for word substitution from one language to another. In automatic searching systems, the automatic dictionary is the component which substitutes codes for words or phrases during the encoding operation. Related to *translation, machine*.

Digit—A sign or symbol used to convey a specific quantity of information either by itself or with other numbers of its set; e.g., 2, 3, 4, and 5 are digits. The base or radix must be specified and each digit's value assigned.

Digit, Binary—A numeral in the binary scale of notation. This digit may be zero (0), or one (1). It may be equivalent to an on or off condition, a yes, or a no. Often abbreviated to *BIT*.

Digital—Pertaining to the utilization of discrete integral numbers in a given base to represent all the quantities that occur in a problem or a calculation. It is possible to express in digital form all information stored, transferred, or processed by a dual state condition; e.g., on-off, open-closed, and true-false.

Diploma, High School—A formal document certifying the successful completion of a secondary school program of studies. In some states or communities, a diploma may be further identified by type such as an academic diploma, a general diploma, or a vocational diploma.

Disk, Magnetic—A storage device on which information is recorded on the magnetizable surface of a rotating disk. A magnetic disk storage system is an array of such devices, with associated reading and writing heads which are mounted on movable arms. Related to *storage, disk.*

Document—(1) A form, voucher, or written evidence of a transaction; (2) to instruct, as by citation of references; (3) to substantiate, as by listing of authorities.

Document, Source—A document from which basic data is extracted.

Documentation—The group of techniques necessary for the orderly presentation, organization, and communication of recorded specialized knowledge, in order to maintain a complete record of reasons for changes in variables. Documentation is necessary not so much for maximum utility as for an unquestionable historical reference record.

Drive, Tape—Synonymous with *unit, tape* and *transport tape,* and clarified by *unit, magnetic tape* and *unit, paper tape.*

Dropout—A pupil who leaves a school, for any reason except death, before graduation or completion of a program of studies and without transferring to another school. The term "dropout" is used most often to designate an elementary or secondary school pupil who has been in membership during the regular school term and who withdraws from membership before graduating from secondary school (grade 12) or before completing an equivalent program of studies. Such an individual is considered a dropout whether his dropping out occurs during or between regular school terms, whether his dropping out occurs before or after he has passed the compulsory school attendance age, and, where applicable, whether or not he has completed a minimum required amount of school work.

Drum, Magnetic—A cylinder having a surface coating of magnetic material which stores binary information by the orientation of magnetic dipoles near or on its surface. Since the drum is rotated at a uniform rate, the information stored is available periodically as a given portion of the surface moves past one or more flux detecting devices called "heads" which are located near the surface of the drum.

Dummy—An artificial address, instruction, or record of information inserted solely to fulfill prescribed conditions, such as to achieve a fixed word length or block length, but without itself affecting machine operations except to permit the machine to perform desired operations.

Dump, A. C.—The removal of all alternating current power intentionally, accidentally, or conditionally from a system or component. An a.c. dump usually results in the removal of all power, since direct current is usually supplied through a rectifier or converter.

Dump, Core—See *dump, storage.*

Dump, Memory—See *dump, storage.*

Dump, Storage—A listing of the contents of a storage device, or selected parts of it. Synonymous with *memory dump, core dump* and *memory print-out.*

EAM—Electrical Accounting Machine. See *machine, electrical accounting.*

EDP—Electronic Data Processing. See *processing, electronic data.*

Edit—To rearrange data or information. Editing may involve the deletion of unwanted data, the selection of pertinent data, the application of format techniques, the insertion of symbols such as page numbers and typewriter characters, the application of standard processes such as zero suppression, and the testing of data for reasonableness and proper range. Editing may sometimes be distinguished between input edit (rearrangement of source data) and output edit (preparation of table formats).

Electronic—Pertaining to that branch of science which deals with the motion, emission, and behavior of currents of free electrons, especially in vacuum, gas or phototubes and special conductors or semi-conductors. This is contrasted with electric which pertains to the flow of large currents in metal conductors.

Element Data—A specific item of information appearing in a set of data; e.g., in the following set of data, each item is a data element: the quantity of a supply item issued, a unit rate, an amount, and the balance of stock items on hand.

Element, Logical—The smallest building block in a computer or data processing system which can be represented by logical operators in an appropriate system of symbolic logic. Typical logical elements are the AND-gate and the OR-gate, which can be represented as operators in a suitable symbolic logic.

Encipher—See *encode*.

Encode—(1) To apply a code, frequently one consisting of binary numbers, to represent individual characters or groups of characters in a message. Synonymous with *encipher*. Inverse of *decode*. (2) To substitute letters, numbers, or characters for other numbers, letters, or characters, usually to intentionally hide the meaning of the message except to certain individuals who know the enciphering scheme.

Encoder—A device capable of translating from one method of expression to another, e.g., translating a message, "add the contents of A to the contents of B." Contrasted with *decoder* and clarified by *matrix*.

Equipment, Automatic Data Processing—(1) A machine, or group of interconnected machines, consisting of input, storage, computing, control, and output devices, which uses electronic circuitry in the main computing element to perform arithmetic and/or logical operations automatically by means of internally stored or externally controlled programmed instructions. Synonymous with *electronic data processing equipment*. (2) The data processing equipment which directly supports or services the central computer operation. Clarified by *equipment peripheral*.

Equipment, Auxiliary—See *equipment, off-line*.

Equipment, Conversion—The equipment that is capable of transposing or transcribing the information from one type of data processing medium to render it acceptable as input to another type of processing medium.

Equipment, Electronic Data Processing—See *equipment, automatic data processing*.

Equipment, Input—(1) The equipment used for transferring data and instructions into an automatic data processing system; (2) the equipment by which an operator transcribes original data and instructions to a medium that may be used in an automatic data processing system.

Equipment, Off-Line—The peripheral equipment or devices not in direct communication with the central processing unit of a computer. Synonymous with *auxiliary equipment*.

Equipment, On-Line—Descriptive of a system and of the peripheral equipment or devices in a system whose operation is under control of the central processing unit, and in which information reflecting current activity is introduced into the data processing system as soon as it occurs. Thus, it is directly in-line with the main flow of transaction processing. Synonymous with *in-line processing*, and *on-line processing*.

Equipment, Output—The equipment used for transferring information out of a computer.

Equipment, Peripheral—The auxiliary machines which may be placed under the control of the central computer. Examples of this are card readers, card punches, magnetic tape feeds and high-speed printers. Peripheral equipment may be used on-line or off-line depending upon computer design, job requirements, and economics. Clarified by *equipment, automatic data processing* and by *equipment, off-line*.

Equipment, Tabulating—The machines and equipment using punch cards. The group of equipment is called tabulating equipment because the main function of installations of punch card machines for some 20 years before the first automatic digital computer was to produce tabulations of information resulting from sorting, listing, selecting, and totaling data on punch cards. This class of equipment is commonly called *PCM* or "tab equipment." Similar to *machine, electrical accounting*, clarified by *tabulator*.

Erase—To replace all the binary digits in a storage device by binary zeroes. In a binary computer, erasing is equivalent to clearing, while in a coded decimal computer where the pulse code for decimal zero may contain binary ones, clearing leaves decimal zero while erasing leaves all-zero pulse codes in all storage locations. Clarified by *clear*.

Error—(1) The general term referring to any deviation of a computed or a measured quantity from the theoretically correct or true value. (2) The part of the error due to a particular identifiable cause; e.g., a truncation error, or a rounding error. In a restricted sense, that deviation due to unrestricted sense, that deviation due to unavoidable random disturbances, or to the use of finite approximations to what is defined by an infinite series. Contrasted with *mistake.* (3) The amount by which the computed or measured quantity differs from the theoretically correct or true value.

Execute—To interpret a machine instruction and perform the indicated operation(s) on the operand(s) specified.

Exempted Child—A child of compulsory school attendance age who is not required to attend school because of a physical or mental condition or for any other reason.

Expulsion—The action, taken by school authorities, compelling a pupil to withdraw from school for reasons such as extreme misbehavior and incorrigibility.

FOSDIC—Film Optical Sensing Device for Input to Computer. See *device, film optical sensing.*

FORTRAN—*For*mula *tran*slator. A programming language designed for problems which can be expressed in algebraic notation, allowing for exponentiation and up to three subscripts. The FORTRAN compiler is a routine for a given machine which accepts a program written in FORTRAN source language and produces a machine language routine object program. FORTRAN II added considerably to the power of the original language by giving it the ability to define and use almost unlimited hierarchies of subroutines, all sharing a common storage region if desired. Later improvements have added the ability to use Boolean expressions, and some capabilities for inserting symbolic machine language sequences within a source program.

Facility, School—A building or site belonging to or used by a school or school system for school purposes.

Feed—(1) To supply the material to be operated upon to a machine. (2) A device capable of feeding material to a machine.

Feed, Card—A mechanism which moves cards serially into a machine.

Feed, Tape—A mechanism which will feed tape to be read or sensed.

Feedback—The part of a closed loop system which automatically brings back information about the condition under control.

Field—An assigned area in a record to be marked with information.

Field, Card—A set of card columns, either fixed in number and position or, if variable, then identifiable by position relative to other fields. Corresponding fields on successive cards are normally used to store similar information.

Field, Control—A constant location where information for control purposes is placed; e.g., in a set of punch cards, if columns 79 and 80 contain various codes which control whether or not certain operations will be performed on any particular card, then columns 79 and 80 constitute a control field.

Field, Fixed—A given field on punch cards or a given number of holes along the edge of an edge punched card, set aside for recording a given type or classification of information.

File—An organized collection of information directed toward some purpose. The records in a file may or may not be sequenced according to a key contained in each record.

File, Detail—A file of information which is relatively transient. This is contrasted with a master file which contains relatively more permanent information; e.g., in the case of weekly payroll for hourly employees, the detail file will contain employee number, regular time, and overtime, the hours such employee has worked in a given week, and other information changing weekly. The master file will contain the employee's name, number, department, rate of pay, deduction specifications, and other information which regularly stays the same from week to week.

File, Master—A file containing relatively permanent information.

Flag—(1) A bit of information attached to a character or word to indicate the boundary of a field. (2) An indicator used frequently to tell some later part of a program that some condition occurred earlier. (3) An indicator used to identify the members of several sets which are intermixed. Synonymous with *sentinel.*

Flow diagram—Same as *chart, flow.*

Format—The predetermined arrangement of characters, fields, lines, page numbers, and punctuation marks, usually on a single sheet or in a file. This refers to input, output, and files.

Frame, Main—(1) The central processor of the computer system. It contains the main storage, arithmetic unit, and special register groups. Synonymous with *CPU* and *central processing unit.* (2) All that portion of a computer exclusive of the input, output, peripheral, and in some instances, storage units.

Frequency, Clock—The master frequency of periodic pulses which schedules the operation of the computer. Clarified by *computer, synchronous.*

Generate—To produce or prepare a specific item in accordance with a specific and defined rule or program over a period of time.

Generator, Program—A program which permits a computer to write other programs automatically. Generators are of two types: (a) the character controlled generator, which operates like a compiler in that it takes entries from a library tape, but unlike a simple compiler in that it examines control characters associated with each entry, and alters instructions found in the library according to the directions contained in the control characters; (b) the pure generator, which is a program that writes another program. When associated with an assembler, a pure generator is usually a section of program which is called into storage by the assembler from a library tape and which then writes one or more entries in another program. Most assemblers are also compilers and generators. In this case, the entire system is usually referred to as an assembly system. Related to *language, problem oriented.*

Generator, Report—A technique for producing complete data processing reports giving only a description of the desired content and format of the output reports and certain information concerning the input file.

Grade—That portion of a school program which represents the work of one regular school term, identified by a designation such as kindergarten, grade 1, or grade 10.

Graduate—An individual who has received formal recognition for the successful completion of a prescribed program of studies.

Guidance Services—Those activities which have as their purpose helping pupils assess and understand their abilities, aptitudes, interests, environmental factors, and educational needs; assisting pupils in increasing their understandings of educational and career opportunities; and aiding pupils in making optimum use of educational and career opportunities through the formulation of realistic goals. These activities include counseling pupils and parents, evaluating the abilities of pupils, assisting pupils to make their own educational and career plans and choices, assisting pupils in personal and social adjustment, and working with other staff members in planning and conducting guidance programs.

HSP—*H*igh *S*peed *P*rinter. See *printer, high-speed.*

HSR—*H*igh *S*peed *R*eader. See *reader, high-speed.*

Hang-Up—A non-programmed stop in a routine. It is usually an unforeseen or unwanted halt in a machine pass. It is most often caused by improper coding of a machine instruction or by the attempted use of a non-existent or improper operation code.

Handling, Data—See *processing, data.*

Hardware—The physical equipment or devices forming a computer and peripheral equipment. Contrasted with *software.*

High Order—Pertaining to the weight or significance assigned to the digits of a number; e.g., in the number 123456, the highest order digit is one; the lowest order digit is six. One may refer to the three high order bits of a binary word as another example. Clarified by *order (3).*

Hold—The function of retaining information in one storage device after also transferring it to another device. Contrasted with *clear.*

Hollerith—A widely used system of encoding alphanumeric information onto cards, hence "Hollerith cards" is synonymous with *punch cards.* Such cards were first used in 1890 for the U. S. Census and were named after Herman Hollerith, their originator.

Hopper—Same as *stacker, card.*

Housekeeping—Pertaining to administrative or overhead operations or functions which are necessary in order to maintain control of a situation; e.g., for a computer program, housekeeping involves the setting up of constants and variables to be used in the program. Synonymous with *red tape.*

IAL—*I*nternational *A*lgebraic *L*anguage. See *language, international algebraic.*

IDP—*I*ntegrated *D*ata *P*rocessing. See *processing, integrated data.*

I/O—See *input-output.*

Image—An exact duplicate array of information or data stored in, or in transit to, a different medium.

Image, Card—A representation in storage of the holes punched in a card, in such a manner that the holes are represented by one binary digit and the unpunched spaces are represented by the other binary digit.

Information—A collection of facts or other data especially as derived from the processing of data. Related to *data.*

Input—(1) Information or data transferred or to be transferred from an external storage medium into the internal storage of the computer. (2) Descriptive of the routines which direct input as defined in (1) or the devices from which such information is available to the computer. (3) The device or collective set of devices necessary for input as defined in (1).

Input-Output—A general term for the equipment used to communicate with a computer and the data involved in the communication. Synonymous with *I/O.*

Input-Output Limited—Pertaining to a system or condition in which the time for input and output operation exceeds other operations.

Inquiry—A technique whereby the interrogation of the contents of a computer's storage may be initiated at a keyboard.

Instruction—The activities dealing directly with the teaching of pupils or with improving the quality of teaching.

Instruction—(1) A set of characters which defines an operation together with one or more addresses, or no address, and which, as a unit, causes the computer to perform the operation on the indicated quantities. The term "instruction" is preferable to the terms *command* and *order*; command is reserved for a specific portion of the instruction word; i.e., the part which specifies the operation which is to be performed and *order* is reserved for the ordering of the characters, implying sequence, or the order of the interpolation, or the order of the differential equation. Related to *code (1).* (2) The operation or command to be executed by a computer, together with associated addresses, tags, and indices.

Instruction, Branch—An instruction to a computer that enables the programmer to instruct the computer to choose between alternative sub-programs depending upon the conditions determined by the computer during the execution of the program. Synonymous with *transfer instruction.*

Instruction, Transfer—See *instruction, branch.*

Intelligence, Artificial—The study of computer and related techniques to supplement the intellectual capabilities of man. As man has invented and used tools to increase his physical powers, he now is beginning to use artificial intelligence to increase his mental powers. In a more restricted sense, the study of techniques for more effective use of digital computers by improved programming techniques.

Interface—A common boundary between

Interface (*Cont'd.*)
automatic data processing systems or parts of a single system.

Interpret—(1) To print on a punch card the information punched in that card; (2) to translate non-machine language into machine language instructions.

Interpreter—(1) A punch card machine which will take a punch card with no printing on it, read the information in the punched holes, and print a translation in characters in specified rows and columns on the card. (2) An executive routine which, as the computation progresses, translates a stored program expressed in some machine-like pseudo-code into machine code, and performs the indicated operations, by means of subroutines, as they are translated. An interpreter is essentially a closed subroutine which operates successively on an indefinitely long sequence of program parameters, the pseudo-instructions and operands. It may usually be entered as a closed subroutine and left by a pseudo-code exit instruction.

Item—(1) A set of one or more fields containing related information; (2) a unit of correlated information relating to a single person or object; (3) the contents of a single message.

Jam, Card—A pile-up of cards in a machine.

Key—(1) A group of characters which identifies or is part of a record or item. Thus, any entry in a record or item can be used as a key for collating or sorting purposes. (2) A marked lever, manually operated for copying a character; e.g., a typewriter, paper tape perforator, card punch, manual keyboard, digitizer, or manual word generator. (3) A lever or switch on a computer console for the purpose of manually altering computer action.

Keypunch—(1) A special device to record information onto cards or tape by punching holes in the cards or tape to represent letters, digits, and special characters; (2) to operate a device for punching holes in cards or tape.

Key Verify—To use the punch card machine known as a verifier, which has a keyboard, to make sure that the information supposed to be punched in a punch card has actually been properly punched. The machine signals when the punched hole and the depressed key disagree.

LPM—*L*ines *P*er *M*inute.

Label—A set of symbols used to identify or describe an item, record, message, or file. Occasionally it may be the same as the address in storage.

Language—A system for representing and communicating information or data between people, or between people and machines. Such a system consists of a carefully defined set of characters, rules for combining them into larger units, such as words or expressions, and rules for word arrangement or usage to achieve specific meanings.

Language, Algorithmic—An arithmetic language by which numerical procedures may be precisely presented to a computer in a standard form. The language is intended not only as a means of directly presenting any numerical procedure to any suitable computer for which a compiler exists, but also as a means of communicating numerical procedures among individuals. The language itself is the result of international cooperation to obtain a standardized algorithmic language. The international Algebraic Language is the forerunner of ALGOL. Synonymous with *ALGOL* and clarified by *language, international algebraic*.

Language, Common Business Oriented—A specific language by which business data processing procedures may be precisely described in a standard form. The language is intended not only as a means for directly presenting any business program to any suitable computer, for which a compiler exists, but also as a means of communicating such procedures among individuals. Synonymous with *COBOL*.

Language, Common Machine—A machine sensible information representation which is common to a related group of data processing machines.

Language, International Algebraic—The

forerunner of *ALGOL*. Synonymous with *IAL* and clarified by *language, algorithmic.*

Language, Machine—See *language, machine oriented.*

Language, Machine Oriented—(1) A language designed for interpretation and use by a machine without translation. (2) A system for expressing information which is intelligible to a specific machine; e.g., a computer or class of computers. Such a language may include instructions which define and direct machine operations and information to be recorded by or acted upon by these machine operations. (3) The set of instructions expressed in the number system basic to a computer, together with symbolic operation codes with absolute addresses, relative addresses, or symbolic addresses. Synonymous with *machine language;* clarified by *language;* related to *language, object;* and contrasted with *language, problem oriented.*

Language, Object—A language which is the output of an automatic coding routine. Uusually object language and machine language are the same, however, a series steps in an automatic coding system may involve the object language of one step serving as a source language for the next step and so forth.

Language, Problem Oriented—(1) a language designed for convenience of program specification in a general problem area rather than for easy conversion to machine instruction code. The components of such a language may bear little resemblance to machine instruction code. (2) A machine independent language where one needs only to state the problem, not the how of solution. Related to *generator, program* and contrasted with *language, machine oriented.*

Language, Program—A language which is used by programmers to write computer routines.

Length, Field—The physical extent of a field. On a punch card it refers to the number of columns. On a tape it refers to bit positions.

Library—(1)A collection of information available to a computer, usually on magnetic tapes; (2) a file of magnetic tapes.

Load—(1) To put data into a register or storage; (2) to put a magnetic tape onto a tape drive or to put cards into a card reader.

Load-and-Go—Refers to an automatic coding procedure which not only compiles the program, creating machine language, but also proceeds to execute the created program. Load-and-go procedures are usually part of a monitor.

Log—A record of everything pertinent to a machine run including: identification of the machine run, record of alteration switch settings, identification of input and output tapes, copy of manual key-ins, identification of all stops, and a record of action taken on all stops.

Logic—(1) The science dealing with the criteria or formal principles of reasoning and thought. (2) The systematic scheme which defines the interactions of signals in the design of an automatic data processing system. (3) The basic principles and application of truth tables and interconnection between logical elements required for arithmetic computation in an automatic data processing system. Related to *logic, symbolic.*

Logic, Symbolic—(1) The study of formal logic and mathematics by means of a special written language which seeks to avoid the ambiguity and inadequacy of ordinary language. (2) The mathematical concepts, techniques and languages as used in (1), whatever their particular application or context. Synonymous with *mathematical logic* and related to *logic.*

Loop—(1) A self-contained series of instructions in which the last instruction can modify and repeat itself until a terminal condition is reached. The productive instructions in the loop generally manipulate the operands, while bookkeeping instructions modify the productive instructions, and keep count of the number of repetitions. A loop may contain any number of conditions for termination. The equivalent of a loop can be achieved by the technique of straight line coding, whereby the repetition of productive and bookkeeping oper-

Loop (*Cont'd.*)
ations is accomplished by explicitly writing the instructions for each repetition. Synonymous with *cycle* (*1*). (2) A communications circuit between a subscriber and the local switching center.

Low-Order—Pertaining to the weight or significance assigned to the digits of a number; e.g., in the number 123456, the low-order digit is six. One may refer to the three low-order bits of a binary word, as another example. Clarified by *order (3)*.

Machine, Accounting—See *tabulator*.

Machine, Data Processing—A general name for a machine which can store and process numeric and alphabetic information. Related to *computer, analog; computer, digital;* and *equipment, automatic data processing*.

Machine, Electrical Accounting—The set of conventional punch card equipment including sorters, collators, and tabulators. Synonymous with *EAM* and clarified by *equipment, tabulating*.

Machine, Electronic Data Processing—See *equipment, automatic data processing*.

Machine, Self-Organizing—A class of machines which may be characterized loosely as containing a variable network in which the elements are organized by the machine itself, without external intervention, to meet criteria of successful operation.

Maintenance, File—The periodic modification of a file to incorporate changes which occurred during a given period.

Maintenance, Preventive—The maintenance of a computer system which attempts to keep equipment in top operating condition and to preclude failures during production runs.

Maintenance, Remedial—The maintenance performed by the contractor following equipment failure, therefore, maintenance performed as required, on an unscheduled basis.

Mark—A rating of achievement or academic progress assigned on the basis of some predetermined scale, e.g., letters (A, B, C, D, F), numbers (4, 3, 2, 1, 0), words or phrases (outstanding, satisfactory, needs improvement), and percentages.

Match—A data processing operation similar to a *merge*, except that instead of producing a sequence of items made up from the input, sequences are matched against each other on the basis of some key.

Matrix—(1) An array of quantities in a prescribed form; in mathematics, usually capable of being subject to a mathematical operation by means of an operator or another matrix according to prescribed rules. (2) An array of coupled circuit elements; e.g., diodes, wires, magnetic cores, and relays, which are capable of performing a specific function, such as, the conversion from one numerical system to another. The elements are usually arranged in rows and columns. Thus a matrix is a particular type of encoder or decoder. Clarified by *encoder* and *decoder*.

Memory—See *storage*.

Memory, External—See *storage, external*.

Memory, Internal—See *storage, internal*.

Memory, Random Access—See *storage, random access*.

Merge—To combine items into one sequenced file from two or more similarly sequenced files without changing the order of the items.

Method, Monte Carlo—A trial and error method of repeated calculations to discover the best solution of a problem. Often used when a great number of variables are present, with interrelationships so extremely complex as to forestall straightforward analytical handling.

Mentally Retarded, Educable—Mentally retarded individuals who are educable in the academic, social, and occupational areas, even though moderate supervision may be necessary. IQ's of these individuals range from about 50 to 75 or 80.

Mentally Retarded, Trainable—Mentally retarded individuals for whom little or no self-support is anticipated, although some improvement in performance is possible, especially in self-care, social and emotional adjustment, and economic usefulness in the home or a sheltered environment. These individuals probably will require a sheltered environment and major supervision throughout their lives. Their IQ's generally range below 50 or 60.

Microsecond—One millionth of a second:

10^{-6} seconds; abbreviated "microsec."

Millimicrosecond—See *nanosecond.*

Millisecond—One thousandth of a second; 10^{-3} seconds; abbreviated "misec." or "ms."

Mistake—A human failing; e.g., faulty arithmetic, use of incorrect formula, or incorrect instructions. Mistakes are sometimes called gross errors to distinguish from rounding and truncation errors. Thus, computers malfunction and humans make mistakes. Computers do not make mistakes and humans do not malfunction, in the strict sense of the word. Contrasted with *error (2).*

Mnemonic—Pertaining to the assisting, or intention of assisting, human memory; thus a mnemonic term is usually an abbreviation that is easy to remember; e.g., mpy for multiply and acc for accumulator.

Mode—(1) A computer system of data representation; e.g., the binary mode. (2) A selected mode of computer operation.

Model, Mathematical—The general characterization of a process, object, or concept, in terms of mathematics, which enables the relatively simple manipulation of variables to be accomplished in order to determine how the process, object, or concept would behave in different situations.

Monitor—To supervise and verify the correct operation of a program during its execution, usually by means of a diagnostic routine used from time to time to answer questions about the program.

Multiplex—The process of transferring data from several storage devices operating at relatively low transfer rates to one storage device operating at a high transfer rate in such a manner that the high-speed device is not obliged to wait for the low-speed devices.

Multiplexing—(1) The transmission of a number of different messages simultaneously over a single circuit. (2) Utilizing a single device for several similar purposes or using several devices for the same purpose; e.g., a duplexed communications channel carrying two messages simultaneously.

Multiprocessor—A machine with multiple arithmetic and logic units for simultaneous use.

Nanosecond—One billionth of a second; one thousandth of a millionth of a second; 10^{-9} seconds. Synonymous with *millimicrosecond.*

Number, Binary—A number, usually consisting of more than one figure, representing a sum, in which the individual quantity represented by each figure is based on a radix of two. The figures used are 0 and 1.

Number, Binary Coded Decimal—A number usually consisting of successive groups of figures, in which each group of four figures is a binary number that represents, but does not necessarily equal arithmetically, a particular figure in an associated decimal number; e.g., if the three rightmost figures of a decimal number are 262, the three right-most figure groups of the binary coded decimal number might be 0010, 0110, and 0010.

Number, Decimal—A number, usually of more than one figure, representing a sum, in which the quantity represented by each figure is based on the radix of ten. The figures used are 0, 1, 2, 3, 4, 5, 6, 7, 8, and 9.

Number, Self Checking—A number with a suffix figure related to the figure(s) of the number, used to check the number after it has been transferred from one medium or device to another. Related to *bit, check; check, modulo N*; and *code error detecting.*

O.R.—Operations Research. See *operations research.*

Off-Line—Descriptive of a system and of the peripheral equipment or devices in a system in which the operation of peripheral equipment is not under the control of the central processing unit. Clarified by *equipment, off-line.*

On-Line—See *equipment, on-line.*

Operation, Computer—The electronic action resulting from an instruction. In general, it is a computer manipulation required to secure results.

Operation, Parallel—The performance of several actions, usually of a similar nature, simultaneously through provision of individual similar or identical devices for each such action. Particularly flow or processing of

Operation, Parallel (*Cont'd.*)
information. Parallel operation is performed to save time over serial operation. Parallel operation usually requires more equipment. Contrasted with *operation, serial.*

Operation, Real Time—The use of the computer as an element of a processing system in which the times of occurrence of data transmission are controlled by other portions of the system, or by physical events outside the system, and cannot be modified for convenience in computer programming. Such an operation either proceeds at the same speed as the events being simulated or at a sufficient speed to analyze or control external events happening concurrently.

Operation, Scheduled—The periods of time during which the user plans to use specified equipment. Such a designation must be made a given number of hours in advance, provided, however, that such scheduled hours of the operation may be modified after that time in the event of an emergency or in the event that equipment failure creates a need for such rescheduling. Usually the foregoing is further modified in that during the performance period, the hours rescheduled as a result of equipment failure usually are not considered as scheduled hours of operation in computing equipment effectiveness.

Operation, Serial—The flow of information through a computer in time sequence using only one digit, word, line, or channel at a time. Contrasted with *operation, parallel.*

Operation, Sequential—The performance of actions one after the other in time. The actions referred to are of a large scale as opposed to the smaller-scale operations referred to by the term *serial operation.* For an example of sequential operation consider $A^x(BxC)$. The two multiplications indicated follow each other sequentially. However, the processing of the individual digits in each multiplication may be either parallel or serial.

Operation, Single Step—A method of operating an automatic computer manually in which a single instruction or part of an instruction is performed in response to a single operation of a manual control. This method is generally used for detecting mistakes.

Operations Research—The use of analytic methods adopted from mathematics for solving operational problems. The objective is to provide management with a more logical basis for making sound predictions and decisions. Among the common scientific techniques used in operations research are the following: linear programming, probability theory, information theory, game theory, monte carlo method, and queuing theory. Synonymous with *O.R.*

Operator—(1) A mathematical symbol which represents a mathematical process to be performed on an associated operand. (2) The portion of an instruction which tells the machine what to do. (3) A machine operator.

Operator, Machine—The person who manipulates the computer controls, places information media into the input devices, removes the output, and performs other related functions.

Order—(1) A defined successive arrangement of elements or events. This term is losing favor as a synonym for *instructions,* due to ambiguity. (2) To sequence or arrange in a series. (3) The weight or significance assigned to a digit position in a number. Clarified by *high order* and *low order.*

Origination, Data—The act of creating a record in a machine sensible form, directly or as a byproduct of a human readable document.

Output—(1) The information transferred from the internal storage of a computer to secondary or external storage, or to any device outside of the computer; (2) the routines which direct (1); (3) the device or collective set of devices necessary for (1); (4) to transfer from internal storage on to external media.

Overpunch—To add holes in a card column that already contains one or more holes. Synonymous with *zone punch* and related to *bits, zone (1).*

PCM—Punch Card Machine. See *machine, electrical accounting* and *equipment, tabulating.*

Panel, Control—(1) An interconnection

device, usually removable, which employs removable wires to control the operation of computing equipment. It is used on punch card machines, to carry out functions which are under control of the user. On computers, it is used primarily to control input and output functions. (2) A device or component of some data processing machines which permits the expression of instructions in a semi-fixed computer program by the insertion of pins, plugs, or wires into sockets, or hubs in the device, in a particular pattern, thus making electrical interconnections which may be sensed by the data processing machine. Synonymous with *plugboard* and related to *pinboard.*

Parallel—(1) To handle simultaneously in separate facilities. (2) To operate on two or more parts of a word or item simultaneously. Contrasted with *serial.*

Parameter—(1) A quantity in a subroutine, whose value specifies or partly specifies the process to be performed. It may be given different values when the subroutine is used in different main routines or in different parts of one main routine, but usually remains unchanged throughout any one such use. Related to *parameter, program.* (2) A quantity used in a generator to specify machine configuration, designate subroutines to be included, or otherwise, to describe the desired routine to be generated. (3) A constant or a variable in mathematics, which remains constant during some calculation. (4) A definable characteristic of an item, device, or system.

Parameter, Program—A parameter incorporated into a subroutine during computation. A program parameter frequently comprises a word stored relative to either the subroutine or the entry point and dealt with by the subroutine during each reference. It may be altered by the routine and/or may vary from one point of entry to another. Related to *parameter (2).*

Pinboard—A type of control panel which uses pins rather than wires to control the operation of a computer. On certain small computers which use pinboards, a program is changed by the operator removing one pinboard and inserting another. Related to *panel, control (2).*

Plugboard—See *panel, control (2).*

Positions, Punching—The specific areas, i.e., row-column intersects, on a punch card where holes may be punched.

Print-Out, Memory—See *dump, storage.*

Printer, High-Speed—A printer which operates at a speed compatible with the speed of computation and data processing so that it may operate *on-line.* At the present time a printer operating at a speed of 250 lines per minute and 100 characters per line is considered high-speed. Synonymous with HSP.

Printer, Line—A device capable of printing 100 or more characters (i.e., one line) simultaneously across a page. Continuous paper advances line by line in one direction past type bars or a type cylinder that contains all characters in all positions.

Printer, Matrix—See *printer, wire.*

Printer, On the Fly—A high-speed line printer using continuously rotating print wheels and fast-acting hammers to print the successive letters contained in one line of text so rapidly that all of the characters in the printed line look as though they were all printed simultaneously.

Printer, Serial—A device capable of printing characters, one at a time across a page. Many variations in serial printers exist: e.g., typewriter; stylus or matrix serial printer; and high-speed, multiple-line stylus or matrix serial printer.

Printer, Wire—A high-speed printer that prints character-like configurations of dots through the proper selection of wire-ends from a matrix of wire-ends, rather than conventional characters through the selection of type faces. Synonymous with *matrix printer.*

Printer, Xerographic—A device for printing an optical image on paper in which dark and light areas of the original are represented by electrostatically charged and uncharged areas on the paper. The paper is dusted with particles of finely powdered dry ink and the particles adhere only to the electrically charged

Printer, Xerographic (*Cont'd.*) areas. The paper with ink particles is then heated, causing the ink to melt and become permanently fixed to the paper.

Procedure—A precise step-by-step method for effecting a solution to a problem.

Process—A general term covering such terms as assemble, compile, generate, interpret, and compute.

Process Chart—Same as *chart, flow*.

Processing, Automatic Data—Data processing performed by a system of electronic or electrical machines so interconnected and interacting as to reduce to a minimum the need for human assistance or intervention. Synonymous with *ADP* and related to *system, automatic data processing*.

Processing, Batch—A technique by which items to be processed must be coded and collected into groups prior to processing.

Processing, Centralized Data—Data processing performed at a single, central location on data obtained from several geographical locations or managerial levels. Decentralized data processing involves processing at various managerial levels or geographical points throughout the organization.

Processing, Data—(1) The preparation of source media which contain data or basic elements of information, and the handling of such data according to precise rules of procedure to accomplish such operations as classifying, sorting, calculating, summarizing, and recording. (2) The production of records and reports. Synonymous with *data handling*.

Processing, Electronic Data—Data processing performed largely by electronic equipment. Synonymous with *EDP* and related to *processing, automatic data*.

Processing, Information—A less restrictive term than data processing, encompassing the totality of scientific and business operations performed by a computer.

Processing, In-Line—See *equipment, on-line*.

Processing, Integrated Data—(1) A system that treats as a whole, all data processing requirements to accomplish a sequence of data processing steps or a number of related processing sequences, and which strives to reduce or eliminate duplicating data entry or processing steps. (2) The processing of data by such a system. Synonymous with *IDP*.

Processing, On-Line—See *equipment, on-line*.

Processing, Parallel—The operations of a computer so that programs for more than one run are stored simultaneously in its storage, and executed concurrently.

Processing, Real Time—The processing of information or data in a sufficiently rapid manner so that the results of the processing are available in time to influence the process being monitored or controlled. Synonymous with *real time system*.

Processor—(1) A generic term which includes assembly, compiling, and generation; (2) a shorter term for "automatic data processor" or *arithmetic unit*.

Program—(1) The complete plan for the solution of a problem, more specifically the complete sequence of machine instructions and routines necessary to solve a problem. (2) To plan the procedures for solving a problem. This may involve among other things the analysis of the problem, preparation of a flow diagram, preparing details, testing, and developing subroutines, allocation of storage locations, specifications of input and output formats, and the incorporation of a computer run into a complete data processing system. Related to *routine*.

Program, Assembly—See *assembler*.

Program, Coded—A program which has been expressed in the code or language of a specific machine or programming system.

Program, General—A program expressed in a computer code designed to solve a class of problems, or specializing on a specific problem when appropriate parametric values are supplied. Synonymous with *general routine*.

Program, Internally Stored—A sequence of instructions stored inside the computer in the same storage facilities as the computer data, as opposed to external storage on punched paper tape and pinboards.

Program, Object—The program which is the output of an automatic coding system. Often the object program is a machine language program ready for execution, but it may well be in an intermediate language. Synonymous with *target program; object routine* and contrasted with *program, source.*

Program, Source—A computer program written in a language (e.g., symbolic or algebraic) designed for ease of expression of a class of problems or procedures, and readable by humans. A generator, assembler translator, or compiler routine is used to perform the mechanics of translating the source program into an object program in machine language. Contrasted with *program, object.*

Programmer—A person who prepares problem-solving procedures and flow charts and who may also write and debug routines.

Programming, Automatic—The method or technique whereby the computer itself is used to transform or translate programming from a language or form that is easy for a human being to produce into a language that is efficient for the computer to carry out. Examples of automatic programming are compiling, assembling, and interpretive routines.

Programming, Linear—A technique of mathematics and operations research for solving certain kinds of problems involving many variables where a best value or set of best values is to be found. This technique is not to be confused with computer programming, although problems using the technique may be programmed on a computer. Linear programming is most likely to be feasible when the quantity to be optimized, sometimes called the objective function, can be stated as a mathematical expression in terms of the various activities within the system, and when this expression is simply proportional to the measure of the activities, i.e., is linear, and when all the restrictions are also linear.

Programming—Minimum access, programming in such a way that minimum waiting time is required to obtain information out of storage. Synonymous with *minimum latency programming* and contrasted with *programming, random access.*

Programming, Multiple—The programming of a computer by allowing two or more arithmetical or logical operations to be executed simultaneously. Contrasted with *programming, serial.*

Programming, Random Access—Programming without regard to the time required for access to the storage positions called for in the program. Contrasted with *programming, minimum access.*

Programming, Serial—The programming of a computer such that only one arithmetical or logical operation can be executed at one time; e.g., a sequential operation. Contrasted with *programming, multiple.*

Punch, X—(1) A punch in the X or 11 row of an 80-column card. (2) A punch in position 11 of a column. The X punch is often used to control or select, or to indicate a negative number as if it were a minus sign. Also called an 11-punch. Synonymous with *eleven (11) punch.*

Punch—(1) To shear a hole by forcing a solid or hollow, sharp edged tool through a material into a die; (2) the hole resulting from (1) above.

Punch Card—A machine which punches holes at designated locations in cards to store data. The data can then be conveyed to other machines or devices which read or sense the holes. Synonymous with *card punch unit.*

Punch, Eleven (11)—See *punch, X.*

Punch, Gang—To punch identical or constant information into all of a group of punch cards.

Punch, Summary—A card punch operating in conjunction with another machine, commonly a tabulator, to punch into cards data which have been summarized or calculated by the other machine.

Punch, Twelve (12)—See *punch, Y (2).*

Punch, Y—(1) A punch in the Y or 12 row of an 80-column card; i.e., the top row of the card. (2) A punch in position 12 of a column. It is often used for additional control or selection, or to indicate a positive number as if it were a plus sign. Synonymous with *twelve (12) punch.*

Punch, Zone—See *overpunch.*

Punching, Multiple—(1) The reference

Punching, Multiple (*Cont'd.*) to punch cards and more specifically to Hollerith cards; (2) the punching of two or more holes in a column.

Pupil—An individual for whom instruction is provided in an educational program under the jurisdiction of a school or school system. No distinction is made between the terms "pupil" and "student"; the term "pupil" is used to include individuals at all instructional levels. The pupil may receive his instruction in a classroom of a school plant or in another location such as his home or a hospital. Instruction may be provided by direct teacher contact or by some other approved means such as television and correspondence.

Pupil Accounting—A system for collecting, computing, and reporting information about pupils.

RAM—*R*andom *A*ccess *M*emory—See *storage, random access.*

Rate, Bit—The rate at which binary digits, or pulses representing them pass a given point on a communications line or channel. Clarified by *baud* and *capacity, channel.*

Rate, Punching—The number of cards, characters, blocks, fields, or words of information placed in the form of holes distributed on cards, or paper tape per unit of time.

Rate, Reading—The numbers of characters, words, fields, blocks, or cards sensed by a sensing device per unit of time.

Read—(1) To sense information contained in some source; (2) the sensing of information contained in some source.

Read, Card—(1) A mechanism that senses information punched into cards. (2) An input device consisting of a mechanical punch card reader and related electronic circuitry which transcribes data from punch cards to working storage or magnetic tape. Synonymous with *card reader unit.*

Read-In—To sense information contained in some source and transmit this information to an internal storage.

Read-Out—To sense information contained in some internal storage and transmit this information to a storage external to the computer.

Reader—See *read, card.*

Reader, Character—A specialized device which can convert data represented in one of the type fonts or scripts read by human beings directly into machine language. Such a reader may operate optically; or if the characters are printed in magnetic ink, the device may operate magnetically or optically.

Reader, High-Speed—A reading device capable of being connected to a computer so as to operate on-line without seriously holding up the computer. A card reader reading more than 250 cards per minute would be called a high-speed reader. A reader which reads punched paper tape at a rate greater than 50 characters per second could also be called a high-speed reader. Synonymous with *HSR.*

Reader, Magnetic Tape—A device capable of sensing information recorded on a magnetic tape in the form of a series of magnetized spots.

Reader, Paper Tape—A device capable of sensing information punched on a paper tape in the form of a series of holes.

Record, Cumulative Pupil—A continuous and current record of significant information regarding the progress and growth of an individual pupil as he goes through school, including information on his personal characteristics, family background, health, school attendance, courses, non-course activities, school progress, honors, interests, aptitudes, out-of-school activities, part-time employment, and plans for the future.

Record, Permanent Pupil—A pupil record considered to have permanent or semipermanent value and which remains in the files of the school or school system.

Record, Pupil—Information about one or more pupils which is kept on file for a period of time in a classroom, school office, system office, or other approved location. A pupil record usually is intended for the use of the person or office which maintains the record.

Recognition, Character—The technology of using a machine to sense and encode into a machine language characters which are written or printed to be read by human beings.

Recognition, Pattern—The recognition of shapes or other patterns by a machine system. Patterns may be, for example, physical shapes or speech patterns.

Record—(1) A group of related facts or fields of information treated as a unit, thus a listing of information, usually in printed or printable form. (2) To put data into a storage device.

Red Tape—See *housekeeping.*

Report—A collection of information which is prepared by a person, unit, or organization for the use of some other person, unit, or organization.

Reporting Period—A period of time for which a report is prepared, e.g., calendar year, school year, regular school term, summer school term, semester, and marking period.

Reproducer, Card—A device that reproduces a punch card by punching another similar card.

Rerun—To repeat all or part of a program on a computer.

Retrieval, Information—The recovering of desired information or data from a collection of documents or other graphic records.

Run—The performance of one program on a computer; thus the performance of one routine, or several routines, linked so that they form an automatic operating unit, during which manual manipulations by the computer operator are zero, or at least minimal.

Routine—A set of coded instructions arranged in proper sequence to direct the computer to perform a desired operation or sequence of operations. A subdivision of a program consisting of two or more instructions that are functionally related; therefore, a program. Clarified by *subroutine* and related to *program.*

Routine, Assembly—See *assembler.*

Routine, Compiling—See *compiler.*

Routine, Diagnostic—A routine used to locate a malfunction in a computer, or to aid in locating mistakes in a computer program. Thus, in general any routine specifically designed to aid in debugging or trouble shooting. Synonymous with *malfunction routine* and related to *debugging* (2).

Routine, General—See *program, general.*

Run, Machine—The execution of one or several machine routines which are linked to form one operating unit.

Running, Parallel—(1) The running of a newly developed system in a data processing area in conjunction with the continued operation of the current system; (2) the final step in the debugging of a system; this step follows a system test.

Scan—To examine every reference or every entry in a file routinely as a part of a retrieval scheme; occasionally, to collate.

Scanner—An instrument which automatically samples or interrogates the state of various processes, files, conditions, or physical states and initiates action in accordance with the information obtained.

School—A division of the school system consisting of a group of pupils composed of one or more grade groups, organized as one unit with one or more teachers to give instruction of a defined type, and housed in a school plant of one or more buildings. More than one school may be housed in one school plant, as is the case when the elementary and secondary schools are housed in the same school plant.

School Census—An enumeration and collection of data, as prescribed by law, to determine the name, age, sex, and post office address of children and youth who reside in a given administrative unit and to secure other information deemed pertinent to education.

School District—A term used synonymously with the term "local basic administrative unit." *See administrative unit, local basic.*

School, Elementary—A school classified as elementary by state and local practice and composed of any span of grades not above grade eight.

School, Junior High—A separately organized and administered secondary school intermediate between the elementary and senior high schools.

School, Junior-Senior High—A secondary school organized on a junior-senior basis and administered under one head as one unit.

School Plant—The site, buildings, and equipment constituting the physical facilities used by a single school or

School Plant (Cont'd.) by two or more schools sharing the use of common facilities.

School, Public—A school operated by publicly elected or appointed school officials in which the program and activities are under the control of these officials and which is supported by public funds.

School, Secondary—A school comprising any span of grades beginning with the next grade following the elementary school and ending with or below grade 12, including the junior high school and other types of high school.

School, Senior High—A secondary school offering the final years of high school work necessary for graduation and invariably preceded by a junior high school.

School System—All the schools and supporting services operated by the board of education of a given administrative unit or by another organization which operates one or more schools.

School Term—A prescribed span of time when school is open and the pupils are under the guidance and direction of teachers.

School Term, Regular—The school term which usually begins in the late summer or the fall and ends in the spring. A regular school term may be interrupted by one or more vacations.

School Term, Summer—The school term taking place in the summer during the period between the end of one regular school term and the beginning of the next regular school term.

School Year—The months that the school is open for students. Usually Sept. through June.

Semester—Half of a regular school term, usually 16 to 18 weeks in duration.

Sense—(1) To examine, particularly relative to a criterion; (2) to determine the present arrangement of some element of hardware, especially a manually-set switch; (3) to read punched holes or other marks.

Sensing, Mark—A technique for detecting special pencil marks entered in special places on a punch card and automatically translating the marks into punched holes.

Sentinel—See *flag.*

Sequencer—See *sorter.*

Serial—(1) The handling of one after the other in a single facility; e.g., to transfer or store in a digit-by-digit time sequence, or to process a sequence of instructions one at a time, i.e., sequentially. (2) The time sequence transmission of, storage of, or logical operations on the parts of a word, with the same facilities for successive parts. Related to *operation, serial* and contrasted with *parallel (2).*

Shop, Closed—The operation of a computer facility where programming service to the user is the responsibility of a group of specialists, thereby effectively separating the phase of task formulation from that of computer implementation. The programmers are not allowed in the computer room to run or oversee the running of their programs. Contrasted with *shop, open.*

Shop, Open—The operation of a computer facility where computer programming, coding, and operating can be performed by any qualified employee of the organization, not necessarily by the personnel of the computing center itself, and where the programmer may assist in or oversee the running of his program on the computer. Contrasted with *shop, closed.*

Signal—The event, phenomenon, or electrical quantity which conveys information from one point to another.

Simulation—(1) The representation of physical systems and phenomena by computers, models, or other equipment; e.g., an imitative type of data processing in which an automatic computer is used as a model of some entity, e.g., a chemical process. Information enters the computer to represent the factors entering the real process; the computer produces information that represents the results of the process; and the processing done by the computer represents the process itself. (2) In computer programming, the technique of setting up a routine for one computer to make it operate as nearly as possible like some other computer.

Simulator—(1) A computer or model which represents a system or phenomenon and which mirrors or maps the effects of various changes in the original, enabling the original to be studied, analyzed, and understood by means of the behavior of the model; (2) a program or routine corresponding to a mathematical model or representing a physical model; (3) a routine which is executed by one computer but which imitates the operations of another computer.

Software—The totality of programs and routines used to extend the capabilities of computers, such as compilers, assemblers, narrators, routines, and subroutines. Contrasted with *hardware.*

Solid State—The electronic components that convey or control electrons within solid materials; e.g., transistors, germanium diodes, and magnetic cores. Thus, vacuum and gas tubes are not included.

Sort—To arrange items of information according to rules dependent upon a key or field contained in the items or records; e.g., to digital sort is to sort first the keys on the least significant digit, and to resort on each higher-order digit until the items are sorted on the most significant digit.

Sort, Block—A sort of one or more of the most significant characters of a key to serve as a means of making workable sized groups from a large volume of records to be sorted.

Sort, Merge—To produce a single sequence of items, ordered according to some rule, from two or more previously unordered sequences, without changing the items in size, structure, or total number; although more than one pass may be required for a complete sort, items are selected during each pass on the basis of the entire key.

Sorter—A machine which puts items of information into a particular order; e.g., it will determine whether A is greater than, equal to, or less than B and sort or order accordingly. Synonymous with *sequencer.*

Space, Working—See *storage, working.*

Stacker, Card—(1) A receptacle that accumulates cards after they have passed through a machine. (2) Synonymous with *hopper.*

Standardized Test—A test composed of a systematic sampling of behavior, having data on reliability and validity, administered and scored according to specific instructions, and capable of being interpreted in terms of adequate norms.

Step, Program—A phase of one instruction or command in a sequence of instructions. Thus, a single operation.

Storage—(1) The term preferred to memory. (2) Pertaining to a device in which data can be stored and from which it can be obtained at a later time. The means of storing data may be chemical, electrical, or mechanical. (3) A device consisting of electronic, electrostatic, or electrical hardware, or other elements into which data may be entered, and from which data may be obtained as desired. (4) The erasable storage in any given computer. Synonymous with *memory.*

Storage, Auxiliary—A storage device in addition to the main storage of a computer; e.g., magnetic tape, disk, or magnetic drum. Auxiliary storage usually holds much larger amounts of information than the main storage, and the information is accessible less rapidly. Contrasted with *storage, main.*

Storage, Buffer—(1) A synchronizing element between two different forms of storage, usually between internal and external. (2) An input device in which information is assembled from external or secondary storage and stored ready for transfer to internal storage. (3) An output device into which information is copied from internal storage and held for transfer to secondary or external storage. Computation continues while transfers between buffer storage and secondary or internal storage or vice versa take place. (4) Any device which stores information temporarily during data transfers. Clarified by *buffer.*

Storage, Core—See *storage, magnetic core.*

Storage, Disk—The storage of data on the surface of magnetic disks. Related to *disk, magnetic* and *storage, magnetic disk.*

Storage, Electrostatic—(1) The storage of data on a dielectric surface, such as the screen of a cathode ray tube,

Storage, Electrostatic (*Cont'd.*) in the form of the presence or absence of spots bearing electrostatic charges, that can persist for a short time after the electrostatic charging force is removed. (2) A storage device so used.

Storage, External—(1) The storage of data on a device which is not an integral part of a computer, but in a form prescribed for use by the computer. (2) A facility or device, not an integral part of a computer, on which data usable by a computer is stored, such as off-line magnetic tape units or punch card devices. Synonymous with *external memory* and contrasted with *storage, internal*.

Storage, Internal—(1) The storage of data on a device which is an integral part of a computer. (2) The storage facilities forming an integral physical part of the computer and directly controlled by the computer. In such facilities all data are automatically accessible to the computer; e.g., magnetic core, and on-line magnetic tape. Synonymous with *internal memory* and contrasted with *storage, external.*

Storage, Magnetic Core—A storage device in which binary data is represented by the direction of magnetization in each unit of an array of magnetic material, usually in the shape of toroidal rings, but also in other forms such as wraps on bobbins. Synonymous with *core storage*.

Storage, Magnetic Disk—A storage device or system consisting of magnetically coated disks, on the surface of which information is stored in the form of magnetic spots arranged in a manner to represent binary data. These data are arranged in circular tracks around the disks and are accessible to reading and writing heads on an arm which can be moved mechanically to the desired disk and then to the desired track on that disk. Data from a given track are read or written sequentially as the disk rotates. Related to *storage, disk*.

Storage, Magnetic Drum—The storage of data on the surface of magnetic drums. Related to *drum, magnetic*.

Storage, Magnetic Tape—A storage device in which data is stored in the form of magnetic spots on metal or coated plastic tape. Binary data are stored as small magnetized spots arranged in column form across the width of the tape. A read-write head is usually associated with each row of magnetized spots so that one column can be read or written at a time as the tape traverses the head.

Storage, Main—Usually the fastest storage device of a computer and the one from which instructions are executed. Contrasted with *storage, auxiliary*.

Storage, Permanent—A method or device used to retain intermediate or final results outside of the machine, usually in the form of punched cards or magnetic tape.

Storage, Program—A portion of the internal storage reserved for the storage of programs, routines, and subroutines. In many systems, protection devices are used to prevent inadvertent alteration of the contents of the program storage. Contrasted with *storage, working*.

Storage, Random Access—A storage technique in which the time required to obtain information is independent of the location of the information most recently obtained. This strict definition must be qualified by the observation that we usually mean relatively random. Thus, magnetic drums are relatively non-random access when compared to magnetic cores for main storage, but are relatively random access when compared to magnetic tapes for file storage. Synonymous with *random access memory* and contrasted with *storage, sequential access*.

Storage, Sequential Access—A storage technique in which the items of information stored become available only in a one after the other sequence, whether or not all the information or only some of it is desired; e.g., magnetic tape storage. Related to *storage, serial* and contrasted with *storage, random access*.

Storage, Temporary—See *storage, working*.

Storage, Working—A portion of the internal storage reserved for the data upon which operations are being performed. Synonymous with *working space* and *temporary storage* and contrasted with *storage, program*.

Student—See *Pupil*.

Subroutine—(1) The set of instructions

necessary to direct the computer to carry out a well-defined mathematical or logical operation. (2) A subunit of a routine. A subroutine is often written in relative or symbolic coding even when the routine to which it belongs is not. (3) A portion of a routine that causes a computer to carry out a well-defined mathematical or logical operation. (4) A routine which is arranged so that control may be transferred to it from a master routine and so that, at the conclusion of the subroutine, control reverts to the master routine. Such a subroutine is usually called a closed subroutine. (5) A single routine may simultaneously be both a subroutine with respect to another routine and a master routine with respect to a third. Usually control is transferred to a single subroutine from more than one place in the master routine and the reason for using the subroutine is to avoid having to repeat the same sequence of instructions in different places in the master routine. Clarified by *routine*.

Suspension—Temporary dismissal of a pupil from school, usually by school personnel having authority granted by the board of education.

System analysis—Synonymous with *analysis, system*.

System, Automatic Data Processing—The term descriptive of an interacting assembly of procedures, processes, methods, personnel, and automatic data processing equipment to perform a complex series of data processing operations.

System, Data Processing Machine—An assembly of data processing machines united by some form of regulated interaction to form an organized whole.

System, Electronic Data Processing—The general term used to define a system for data processing by means of machines utilizing electronic circuitry at electronic speed, as opposed to electromechanical equipment.

System, Exception Principle—An information system or data processing system which reports on situations only when actual results differ from planned results. When results occur within a normal range they are not reported.

System, Information—The network of all communication methods within an organization. Information may be derived from many sources other than a data processing unit, such as by telephone, by contact with other people, or by studying an operation.

System, Information Retrieval—A system for locating and selecting, on demand, certain documents, or other graphic records relevant to a given information requirement from a file of such material. Examples of information retrieval systems are classification, indexing, and machine searching systems.

System, Management Information—A communications process in which data are recorded and processed for operational purposes. The problems are isolated for higher level decision-making and information is fed back to top management to reflect the progress or lack of progress made in achieving major objectives.

System, Number—(1) A systematic method for representing numerical quantities in which any quantity is represented as the sequence of coefficients of the successive powers of a particular base with an appropriate point. Each succeeding coefficient from right to left is associated with and usually multiplies the next higher power of the base. The first coefficient to the left of the point is associated with the zero power of the base. For example in decimal notation 371.426 represents $(3x10^2)$ $+(7 x 10^1)$ $+(1 x 10^0)$ $+(4 x 10^{-1})$ $+(2 x 10^{-2})$ $+(6 x 10^{-3})$. (2) The following are names of the number systems with bases 2 through 20; 2, Binary; 3, Ternary; 4, Quarternary; 5, Quinary; 6, Senary; 7, Septenary; 8, Octal, or octonary; 9, Novenary; 10, Decimal; 11, Undecimal; 12, Duodecimal; 13, Terdenary; 14, Quaterdenary; 15, Quindenary; 16, Sexadecimal, or Hexadecimal; 17, Septendecimal; 18, Octodenary; 19, Novemdenary; 20, Vicenary. Also 32, Duosexadecimal, or duotricinary; and 60, Sexagenary. The Binary, Octal, Decimal, and Sexadecimal systems are widely used in computers. Synonymous with *duodecimal number* and *binary number system;* related to *representation positional;* clarified by *digit, octal and binary*.

System, Real Time—See *processing, real time.*

TLU—Table Look Up. See *table look up.*

Table—A collection of data in a form suitable for ready reference, frequently as stored in sequenced machine locations or written in the form of an array of rows and columns for easy entry and in which an intersection of labeled rows and columns serves to locate a specific piece of data or information.

Table Look Up—To obtain a function value corresponding to an argument, stated or implied from a table of function values stored in the computer. Also, the operation of obtaining a value from a table. Synonymous with *TLU.*

Tabulator—A machine which reads information from one medium, e.g., cards, paper tape, and magnetic tape, and produces lists, tables, and totals on separate forms or continuous paper. Synonymous with *accounting machine,* and clarified by *equipment, tabulating.*

Tag—A unit of information whose composition differs from that of other members of the set so that it can be used as a marker or label.

Tape—A strip of material, which may be punched, coated, or impregnated, with magnetic or optically sensitive substances, and used for data input, storage, or output. The data are stored serially in several channels across the tape transversely to the reading or writing motion.

Tape, Magnetic—A tape or ribbon of any material impregnated or coated with magnetic or other material on which information may be placed in the form of magnetically polarized spots.

Tape, Paper—A strip of paper capable of storing or recording information. Storage may be in the form of punched holes, partially punched holes, carbonization or chemical change of impregnated material, or by imprinting. Some paper tapes, such as punched paper tapes, are capable of being read by the input device of a computer or a transmitting device by sensing the pattern of holes which represent coded information.

Tape, Perforated—See *Tape, punch.*

Tape, Punch—A tape, usually paper, upon which data may be stored in the form of punched holes. Hole locations are arranged in columns across the width of the tape. There are usually 5 to 8 positions, channels, per column, with data represented by a binary coded decimal system. All holes in a column are sensed simultaneously in a manner similar to that for punch cards. Synonymous with *perforated tape.*

Telemetering—The transmission of a measurement over long distances, usually by electromagnetic means.

Theory, Information—The mathematical theory concerned with information rate, channels, channel width, noise, and other factors affecting information transmission. Initially developed for electrical communications, it is now applied to business systems and other phenomena which deal with information units and flow of information in networks.

Theory, Queuing—A form of probability theory useful in studying delays or line-ups at servicing points.

Time, Access—(1) The time it takes a computer to locate data or an instruction word in its storage section and transfer it to its arithmetic unit where the required computations are performed. (2) The time it takes to transfer information which has been operated on from the arithmetic unit to the location in storage where the information is to be stored. Synonymous with *read time* and *real time* and related to *time, write* and *time, word (2).*

Time, Down—The period during which a computer is malfunctioning or not operating correctly due to mechanical or electronic failure, as opposed to available time, idle time, or standby time, during which the computer is functional. Contrasted with *time, up.*

Time, Idle—(1) The period between the end of one programmed computer run and the commencement of a subsequent programmed run; (2) the time normally used to assemble cards, paper, tape reels, and control panels required for the next computer operation; (3) the time between operations when no work is scheduled.

Time, Non-Scheduled Maintenance—The

elapsed time during scheduled working hours between the determination of a machine failure and placement of the equipment back into operation.

Time, Program Testing—The machine time expended for program testing, debugging, and volume and compatibility testing.

Time, Read—See *time, access.*

Time, Set-Up—The portion of the elapsed time between machine operations which is devoted to such tasks as changing reels of tape, and moving cards, tapes, and supplies to and from the equipment.

Time-Sharing—The use of a device for two or more purposes during the same overall time interval, accomplished by interspersing component actions in time.

Time, Up—The time during which equipment is either producing work or is available for productive work. Contrasted with *time, down.*

Transcript—An official record of pupil performance showing all schoolwork completed at a given school and the final mark received in each portion of the instruction. Transcripts often include an explanation of the marking system used by the school.

Transceiver—A device which transmits and receives data from punch card to punch card. It is essentially a conversion device which at the sending end reads the card and transmits the data over the wire. At the receiving end it punches the data into a card.

Transfer, Conditional—An instruction which, if satisfied, is interpreted as an unconditional transfer. If the condition is not satisfied, the instruction causes the computer to proceed in its normal sequence of control. A conditional transfer also includes the testing of the condition. Synonymous with *conditional jump* and *conditional branch* and related to *branch.*

Transform—To derive a new body of data from a given one according to specific procedures, often leaving some feature invariant. Related to *translate.*

Transistor—An electronic device utilizing semiconductor properties to control the flow of currents.

Translate—To change information from one form of representation to another without significantly affecting the meaning. Related to *transform.*

Translation, Machine—The automatic translation from one representation to another representation. The translation may involve codes, languages, or other systems of representation. Related to *dictionary, automatic.*

Translation, Mechanical—A generic term for language translation by computers or similar equipment.

Transmission, Serial—To move data in sequence, one character at a time, as contrasted with parallel transmission.

Transport, Tape—The mechanism which moves magnetic or paper tape past sensing and recording heads and usually associated with data processing equipment. Synonymous with *tape transport, tape drive,* and *feed, tape*; related to *unit, magnetic tape*; and *unit, paper tape.*

Trouble-Shoot—To search for the cause of a malfunction or erroneous program behavior in order to remove the malfunction.

Truancy—The failure of a child to attend school regularly as required by law, without reasonable excuse for his absence.

Tube, Cathode Ray—(1) An electronic vacuum tube containing a screen on which information may be stored by means of a multigrid modulated beam of electrons from the thermionic emitter storage effected by means of charged or uncharged spots; (2) a storage tube; (3) an oscilloscope tube; (4) a picture tube.

Underpunch—A punch in one of the lower rows, 1-9, of an 80-column 12-row punch card.

Unit, Arithmetic—The portion of the hardware of a computer in which arithmetic and logical operations are performed. The arithmetic unit generally consists of an accumulator, some special registers for the storage of operands and results supplemented by shifting and sequencing circuitry for implementing multiplication, division, and other desired operations. Synonymous with *ALU.*

Unit, Card Punch—See *punch card.*

Unit, Central Processing—See *frame, main (1).*

Unit, Control—The portion of a computer which directs the sequence of

Unit, Control (*Cont'd.*)
operations, interprets the coded instructions, and initiates the proper commands to the computer circuits preparatory to execution.

Unit, Magnetic Tape—The mechanism, normally used with a computer, which handles magnetic tape and usually consists of a tape transport, reading or sensing and writing or recording heads, and associated electrical and electronic equipment. Most units may provide for tape to be wound and stored on reels; however, some units provide for the tape to be stored loosely in closed bins. Clarified by *transport, tape* and *unit, paper tape*.

Unit, Paper Tape—The mechanism which handles punched paper tape and usually consists of a paper tape transport, sensing and recording or perforating heads and associated electrical and electronic equipments. Clarified by *transport, tape,* and *magnetic tape*.

Unit, Read Punch—An input-output unit of a computing system which punches computed results into cards, reads input information into the system, and segregates output cards. The read punch unit generally consists of a card feed, a read station, a punch station, another read station, and two output card stackers.

Unit, Tape—A device consisting of a tape transport, controls, a set of reels and a length of tape which is capable of recording and reading information on and from the tape, at the request of the computer under the influence of a program. Clarified by *transport, tape, unit, magnetic tape* and *unit, paper tape*.

Update—(1) To put into a master file, changes required by current information or transactions; (2) to modify an instruction so that the address numbers it contains are increased by a stated amount each time the instruction is performed.

Withdrawal—An individual who has withdrawn from membership in a class, grade, or school by transferring, by completing school work, by dropping out, or because of death.

Word—An ordered set of characters which occupies one storage location and is treated by the computer circuits as a unit and transferred as such. Ordinarily a word is treated by the control unit as an instruction, and by the arithmetic unit as a quantity. Word lengths may be fixed or variable depending on the particular computer.

Word Length, Fixed—Having the property of a machine word which always contains the same number of characters or digits.

Word Length, Variable—Having the property of a machine which may have a variable number of characters. It may be applied either to a single entry whose information content may be changed from time to time, or to a group of functionally similar entries whose corresponding components are of different lengths.

Write—(1) To transfer information, usually from main storage to an output device; (2) to record data in a register, location, or other storage device or medium.

Verifier—A device on which a record can be compared or tested for identity character-by-character with a retranscription or copy as it is being prepared.

Verify—To check a transcribing operation by a compare operation. It usually applies to transcriptions which can be read mechanically or electrically.

Xerography—A dry copying process involving the photoelectric discharge of an electrostatically charged plate. The copy is made by tumbling a resinous powder over the plate, discharging the remaining electrostatic charge, and transferring the resin to paper or an offset printing master.

Zone—(1) A portion of internal storage allocated for a particular function or purpose. (2) The three top positions of 12, 11, and 0 on certain punch cards. In these positions, a second punch can be inserted so that with punches in the remaining positions 1 to 9, alphabetic characters may be represented.

INDEX

Items marked with an asterisk (*) also appear in the Glossary.

Abacus, 10
Accounting machine, 23
Adding machine, 11
Aiken, Howard H., 13-14
American Council on Education, 215
Anderson, G. Ernest, 198
Arnstein, George, 236, 285-86, 289
Association for Educational Data Systems (AEDS), 282
Attendance accounting, 170 *ff.*
  general procedure, 170
  system preparation, 171-75
  types, 170
Attendance accounting system, by products of, 181
  computer based, 180
  punch card, 175
Austin, David B., 186, 188
*Automation, 9 *ff,* 11

Babbage, Charles, 11
Basic Educational Data System (BEDS), 269
Behnk, W., 111, 191
BINAC, 14
Burroughs Corp., 15
Burroughs 280, 31
Bush, Vannevar, 14
Business Equipment Manufacturers Association (BEMA), 15
Business office, applications of data processing, 41-42

Caffrey, John, 284
*Calculating machine, development of, 12
Calculator, 23, (illus.) 26
California Cumulative Record, 215-16
California Educational Data Processing Association (CEDPA), 274, 281
California Guidance Record, 225-27
California State Advisory Committee, 45

Card processors, 25
*Central Processing Unit, 30
Chapin, Ned, 25, 44
CLASS Program (IBM), 198
CLASS instruction system (SDC), 263
*Collator, 23
Collins Radio, 15
*Computer: see Electronic computer
Computer-Based Laboratory for Automated School Systems (CLASS), 263
Computers, programming (wiring) schedule, 98
Conant, James B., 187
Conflict matrix, 188, 198
Control Data Corporation 1604, 31
    Control Data Corporation 3600, 31
    Control Data Corporation 6600, 31, (illus.) 35
Cooperative Plan for Guidance and Admission (CPGA), 218, 265-66
Core storage, 28
*Course, 188
Course tally, 188
*CPU (Central Processing Unit), 30
Cumulative records, basic purpose of, 213
    data recording problems, 216
    recent innovations, 217
    use of, 217
*Cybernation, 3

Data collection, 45 *ff*, 194
Data processing, definition, 17-18
Data processing committee, purpose, 91-92
Data processing installations, delivery schedule, 95
    district size 5000 students, 117
    district size 10,000 students, 118
    district size 15,000 students, 119
    district size 25,000 students, 119
    documentation, 105
    place in school administration, 245-48
    relation to district size, 114-16
    scheduling problems, 107
    school applications, 40-42
    upgrading of equipment, 106
Data processing machines, utilization, 108-10, 111-14
Data processing program, costs of, 111-12, 121, 257-58
Data processing system, regional type, 254-59
Decollator, 25
Design sessions, 60-65
Diebold, John, 3

Digitek 100 test-scoring machine, 157, (illus.) 158, 196, 225
Documents, grid-chart analysis, 55
    classification, 52
    coding, 52
    eliminating, 65
Documents, input, describing, 86
*Documents, source, analysis, 69
*Documentation, need for, 105-06
Docutran (SRA), 159
Dropout data, 181

*EAM, 19
Eccles, W. H., 13
Eckert, J. Presper, 13
Education, goals of, 3-5
*EDP, 19
EDP Analyzer, 59, 60
Educational data processing, definition, 39
    types of installation, 19
Educational data processing publications, 271
Educational Implications of Automation (EIA), 260
Educational Testing Service, 159, 218, 266
"Edumation," 9
Electric Accounting Machines (EAM), 19
Electro-mechanical machines, 19
Electronic computer, 19
    compared to EAM, 19
    functions of, 27
    operations, 30-31
    sizes, 31
    types, 27
Electronic data processing, definition, 17-19
    educators' conception of, 17
    early systems, 13-15
    growth of, 15
    implications for school personnel, 17
    proposals from bidders, 85-90
    selection of equipment, 84-90, 114-15
    selection of site, 94
ENIAC, 14
Evans, Luther, 236
E-Z Sort Cards, 189

FAST test-scoring method, 155
Feasibility study, 42
Files, analysis, 55-56
    description, for bidders, 87

File design, 69
*Flow charts, 49
Forms burster, 25
Fully Automatic Scoring Technique (FAST), 155

GASP (Generalized Academic Simulation Program), 210
General Electric 225, 31
General Precision LGP 21, 31
"Giant brain," 15
Gildersleeve, T. R., 43
Gividen, Noble, 186, 188
Grid chart, 53-55

*Hardware, 30
Hollerith, Herman, 12
Honeywell 200, 31
Honeywell 1800, 31

IBM, 15, 25
- IBM 083, 23, (illus.) 24
- IBM 407, 23, (illus.) 24
- IBM 700-series, 15
- IBM 805 test-scoring machine, 153
- IBM 1230 optical mark scoring reader, 155-57, (illus.) 158, 196, 225
- IBM 1401, 31
- IBM 1401-G, 25
- IBM 7094, 31
- IBM 7030 ("STRETCH"), 31
- IBM 7080, 31
- IBM 9902, 153

Information, shortage of, 234
*Information system, administration, 245-48
- benefits of, 6, 105, 251-53
- capabilities, 8-9
- cost, 8
- definition, 3
- development, 238-40
- director of, 77-79, 244-48, 252
- goal of, 242-44
- justification for, 240
- local or self-contained, 242-54
- need for, 235, 239-40
- organizational pattern, 242-48
- regional center, 254-59

*Input, computer, 18, 27, 30
Input documents, describing, 86
International Business Machines: see IBM.
*Interpreter, 23
Iowa Educational Information Center, 267

Jordan, F. W., 13
Journal of Educational Data Processing, 271

Keysort Cards, 189
*Keypunch, 21
Kornfeld, Leo, 43

Laden, H. N., 43
Lindquist, E. F., 155

Mark I, II, III, IV, 14
Mark reporting, patterns of, 125
Mark reporting system, byproducts of automation, 135-51
    operation, 129-35
    preparation for, 125-26
Master file, 91, Appendix III
Master schedule, 93, 186-88, 203
Mauchly, Dr. John W., 13-14
McKinsey Report, 245-50
*Microsecond, 28
*Millisecond, 28
Minneapolis-Honeywell, 15
Monrobot XI, 31

*Nanosecond, 28
National Cash Register, 15
National Cash Register 315, 31
New England Educational Data Systems (NEEDS), 264-65

Organization chart, 45
*Output, computer, 18, 27, 31
Output documents, describing, 86-87

Palo Alto Project, 270
Pascal, Blaise, 11

Personnel, assignment of, 99
communication problems, 107-10
communication with, 73-75
costs, 112
director of information systems, 77-79
training, 76, 82
manager of data processing, 80-81
staff size, 114-16
Personnel, non-operating, in-service training, 76
Personnel, operating, selection, 77
training, 82
Personnel policies, 72
Personnel requirements, 77-83
Philco 2000, 31
*Plug board, 25
Program Evaluation and Review Technique (PERT), 266
Proposals, bidders', 85-90
Punch card equipment, wiring schedule, 98-99
Punch card, IBM type, 12, 19, (illus.) 20
principle of, 12, 19-21
Remington-Rand type, 19, (illus.) 22
unit record equipment, 21-25
Putnam, John F., 181

Radio Corporation of America (RCA), 15
Radio Corporation of America 301, 31
RCA 601, 31
Reed, Wayne O., 234
Regional center concept, 105, 121, 262
operation, 254
Registration and scheduling, gathering student data, 187
Remington Rand: see Univac
*Reproducer, 21
Reports, interpreting, 107
Research and Development Center in Educational Data Processing, 261-63
Rogers, Dr. Virgil M., 237, 239-40
Royal McBee, 15

Schedules for installation, 93-103
equipment delivery, 95
form and card ordering, 102
wiring or programming, 98
Scheduling, student, 189
computer processing, 194-212
hand processing, 189
punch card processing, 189-91

School applications of data processing, 40-42
Science Research Associates, Inc., 159
Scoring services, 159
Scribe (ETS), 159
Second shift, problems of, 108-10
Section, 188
Services, outside, 110, 159
Slide rule, 11
SOCRATES scheduling system, 196, 210
*Software, 30
*Sorter, 23
Space consideration, 114
Stewart, L. H., 214, 217
*Storage, 27, 28
Stored program machines, 27
Strang, Ruth, 215
"STRETCH" (IBM 7030), 31
Student records, applications of data processing, 40
Student master file, updating of, 180
*Summary punch, 23
Superintendent, role in developing system, 250
*Systems analysis: see Systems study
Systems, conversion of, 99-102
Systems design, 59-71
    finalizing, 98
    implementation, 91-103
System Development Corporation (SDC), 263
Systems study, 39-58

*Tabulator (tab, tabulating machine), 23
Test scoring, guidelines for local operations, 169
    hand scoring, 153
    local machine scoring, 153-58
    procedures, 152
    service agency scoring, 159
Tondow, Murray, 285
Total Information Service (TIS), 268
Traxler, Arthur, 152, 215
"Trigger circuit," 13

Underwood, 15
United States Office of Education (USOE), 269
Unit record equipment, 21-25
    input machines, 21
    manipulating machines, 23
    output machines, 23

Unit record installations (punch card), 19 *ff.*
UNIVAC, 14-15
UNIVAC 120, 23, (illus.) 26
UNIVAC 1004, 25, (illus.) 26
UNIVAC SS 80, 31
UNIVAC SS 90, 31
UNIVAC 1107, 31
UNIVAC LARC, 31

*Verifier, 21
Verifying, need for, 18

Wagner, Dr. Elmer C., 275-78
Wiener, Norbert, 3, 273
Wired control panel machines, 27
Wilkes, Charles, 196, 210
Workman, A. D., 214, 217